TEEN LIFE IN
LATIN AMERICA AND
THE CARIBBEAN

**Recent Titles in
Teen Life around the World**

Teen Life in the Middle East
Ali Akbar Mahdi, editor

Teen Life in Asia
Judith J. Slater, editor

Teen Life in Africa
Toyin Falola, editor

TEEN LIFE IN LATIN AMERICA AND THE CARIBBEAN

Edited by Cynthia Margarita Tompkins and Kristen Sternberg

Foreword by Richard M. Lerner

Teen Life around the World
Jeffrey S. Kaplan, Series Editor

GREENWOOD PRESS
Westport, Connecticut • London

Library of Congress Cataloging-in-Publication Data

Teen life in Latin America and the Caribbean / edited by Cynthia
   Tompkins and Kristen Sternberg ; foreword by Richard M. Lerner.
      p. cm. — (Teen life around the world, ISSN 1540–4897)
   Includes bibliographical references and index.
   ISBN 0–313–31932–4 (alk. paper)
    1. Teenagers—Latin America. 2. Teenagers—Caribbean Area.
   I. Tompkins, Cynthia, 1958– II. Sternberg, Kristen. III. Series.
   HQ799.L28T44 2004
   305235'09729—dc22   2003059644

British Library Cataloguing in Publication Data is available.

Library of Congress Catalog Card Number: 2003059644
ISBN: 0–313–31932–4
ISSN: 1540–4897

First published in 2004

Greenwood Press, 88 Post Road West, Westport, CT 06881
An imprint of Greenwood Publishing Group, Inc.
www.greenwood.com

Printed in the United States of America

The paper used in this book complies with the
Permanent Paper Standard issued by the National
Information Standards Organization (Z39.48–1984).

10 9 8 7 6 5 4 3 2 1

CONTENTS

FOREWORD: TOWARD A WORLD OF POSITIVE YOUTH DEVELOPMENT

In these early years of the twenty-first century a new vision and vocabulary for discussing young people has emerged. Propelled by the increasingly more collaborative contributions of scholars, practitioners, advocates, and policy makers, youth are viewed as resources to be developed. The new vocabulary is legitimated by scholarly efforts at advancing what are termed "developmental systems theories." These models emphasize the plasticity of human development, that is, the potential for systematic change in behavior that exists as a consequence of mutually influential relationships between the developing person and his or her biology, psychological characteristics, family, community, culture, physical and designed ecology, and historical niche.

The plasticity of development legitimizes an optimistic view of potential for promoting positive changes in human life and directs emphasis to the strengths for positive development that are present within all young people. Accordingly, concepts such as developmental assets, positive youth development, moral development, civic engagement, well-being, and thriving have been used increasingly in research and applications associated with adolescents and their world. All concepts are predicated on the ideas that *every* young person has the potential for successful, healthy development and that *all* youth possess the capacity for positive development.

This vision for and vocabulary about youth has evolved over the course of a scientifically arduous path. Complicating this new, positive conceptualization of the character of youth as resources for the healthy development of self, families, and communities was an antithetical theoretical approach to the nature and development of young people. Dating within science to, at least, the publication in 1904 of G. Stanley Hall's two-volume work on adolescence, youth have been characterized by a deficit view, one that conceptualizes their behaviors as deviations from normative development. Understanding such deviations was not seen as being of direct relevance to scholarship aimed at discovering the principles of basic developmental processes. Accordingly, the characteristics of youth were regarded as issues of "only" applied concern—and thus of secondary scientific interest. Not only did this model separate basic science from application but, as well, it disembedded the adolescent from the study of normal or healthy development. It also often separated the young person from among those members of society that could be relied on to produce valued outcomes for family, community, and civic life. In short, the deficit view of youth as problems to be managed split the study of young people from the study of health and positive individual and social development.

The current scholarly and applied work that counters the historical, deficit view of adolescence, and in turn builds upon developmental systems theory to advance the new, positive vocabulary about young people and the growing research evidence for the potential of all youth to develop in positive ways, is both represented and advanced significantly by the *Teen Life around the World* series. More so than any other set of resources currently available to young people, parents, and teachers, the volumes in this series offer rich and engaging depictions about the diverse ways in which young people pursue positive lives in their families, communities, and nations. The volumes provide vivid reflections of the energy, passion, and skills that young people possess—even under challenging ecological or economic conditions—and the impressive ways in which adolescents capitalize on their strengths to pursue positive lives during their teenage years and to prepare themselves to be productive adult members of their families and communities.

Across the volumes in this series a compelling story of the common humanity of all people emerges, one that justifies a great deal of hope that, in today's adolescents, there exist the resources for a humane, peaceful, tolerant, and global civil society. To attain such a world, all people must begin by appreciating the diversity of young people and their cultures and that, through such diversity, the world possesses multiple, potentially productive paths to human well-being and accomplishment. Readers of the *Teen Life around the World* series will be rewarded with just this information.

Ultimately, we must all continue to educate ourselves about the best means available to promote enhanced life chances among all of the world's youth, but especially among those whose potential for positive contributions to civil society is most in danger of being wasted. The books in this series constitute vital assets in pursuit of this knowledge. Given the enormous, indeed historically unprecedented, challenges facing all nations, perhaps especially as they strive to raise healthy and successful young people capable of leading civil society productively, responsibly, and morally across the twenty-first century, there is no time to lose in the development of such assets. The *Teen Life around the World* series is, then, a most timely and markedly important resource.

Richard M. Lerner
Eliot-Pearson Department of Child Development
Tufts University
Medford, MA
September 3, 2002

SERIES FOREWORD

Have you ever imagined what it would be like to live in a different country? What would it be like to speak a different language? Eat different foods? Wear different clothes? Attend a different school? Listen to different music, or maybe, the same music, in a different language? How about practicing new customs? Or, better yet, a different religion? Simply, how different would your life be if you were born and raised in another region of the world? Would you be different? And if so, how?

As we begin the twenty-first century, young people around the world face enormous challenges. Those born to wealth or relative comfort enjoy technological miracles and can click a button or move a mouse and discover a world of opportunity and pleasure. Those born without means struggle just to survive.

Education, though, remains a way out of poverty and for many privileged young people it is the ultimate goal. As more and more jobs, including in the manufacturing and service sectors, require literacy, numeracy, and computer skill, brains are increasingly valued over brawn: In the United States, entry-level wages for people with only a high-school education have fallen by more than 20 percent since the 1970s. Job prospects are bleaker than ever for youths who do not continue their education after high school. And, to be sure, while there are exceptions—like the teenager who starts a basement computer business and becomes a multimillionaire—working a string of low-paying service jobs with no medical insurance is a much more common scenario for those with limited education. And this seems to be true for adolescents in most post-industrialist countries around the world.

Adolescent girls, in particular, are at a disadvantage in many nations, facing sex discrimination as an obstacle to obtaining even basic education and social skills. In the Middle East and South Asia, girls are more likely to be pulled from school at an early age, and are thus less likely to develop critical literacy skills. Across most of the world, girls face more demands for work in the home and restrictions on movement that constrain their opportunities to gain direct experience with diverse social worlds. Similarly, as rates of divorce and abandonment rise worldwide, so do the chances for young women who fail to obtain skills to function independently. And as adults, they are increasingly vulnerable to poverty and exploitation.

ADOLESCENCE AROUND THE GLOBE

Adolescent life is truly plagued by difficulties and determined by context and circumstance. Anthropologist Margaret Mead (1901–1978) may have been the first social scientist to question the universality of the adolescent experience. When Mead contrasted the experience of North American and South Pacific young people in terms of sexuality, she found their experiences and attitudes toward sexuality dramatically different (South Pacific adolescents were more tolerant), and, she contended, adolescence should be seen in the contexts in which people live and dwell. In fact, for Mead and other social scientists, the only definition that can best describe adolescence is at best, restricted to a "period of transition," in which young people are no longer considered children, but not yet considered an adult.

Adolescence is generally understood as the period between the ages of 15–19, with some scholars referring them to up to age 24. The term *young adult* is the most apt term for this age group, and without doubt, the many biological, psychological, and behavioral changes which mark this age, make this a concept that is continually dynamic and fluid in its change. Depending on region of the world, the concept of adolescence or young adult is either emerging, or already well established. Most Western European societies use legal markers to underline the passage to adulthood, commonly set at age 16, 18, or 21. Thus, from country to country, there are minimum legal ages for marriage, for consensual intercourse, and also for access to sexual and reproductive health services without parental consent.

In many developing countries, though, the concept of adolescence has either been non-existent or is relatively new in concept and understanding. Rather than define adulthood by age or biology, children become adults through well-established rites of passage—for example, religious ceremony, or marriage. In India, for example, especially in rural areas, many girls enter into arranged marriages before the onset of their first menstruation cycle, and then, have their first child at around 16 years of age. For these young Indian girls, there is no adolescence, as they shift so quickly from childhood to motherhood Similarly, in traditional Sri Lankan society, young people—once they enter puberty—are expected to get married, or in the case of a male, wear the yellow robe of a monk. To remain single is not held in high esteem because it is considered "neither here nor there."

Yet, the world is changing. Traditional patterns of behavior for young people, and what is expected of them by the adults, are in a state of flux, and in more open societies, adolescence are emerging as a powerful force for influence and growth in Africa, Asia, and Latin America. In these regions, massive economic, institutional and social changes have been brought about by Western colonial expansion and by the move toward a global society and economy. With more young people working in non-agricultural jobs, attending school longer, delaying marriage, adolescents are holding their own ground with adults.

In Indonesia, for example, young boys in urban areas are no longer tied to the farm and have started forming peer groups, as an alternative to exclusive life spent entirely inside the immediacy of their family. Similarly, in the urban areas of India, a many girls attend single-sex schools, thus, spending more time with peer groups, eroding the traditional practice of arranged marriages at an early age. In Nigeria, young people attend school for longer periods of time, thus preparing for jobs in their now modern economy. And in many Latin American countries, where young girls were once also hurried into pre-arranged marriages, now, young girls are staying in school so, they too, can prepare for non-agricultural jobs.

And yet, those without means can only fantasize about what they see of mainstream material culture. As always, money is the societal divide that cruelly demarcates and is unrelenting in its effects on social, cultural, and psychological behavior. Young people living in poverty struggle daily with the pressures of survival in a seemingly indifferent, and often dangerous world. And access to wealth, or the simple conveniences of modern society, makes a considerable difference in the development of the young people. In rural areas in Zimbabwe and Papua New Guinea, for example, simple changes such as building of a road or highway—enabling the bringing in of supplies and expertise—has had profound effects on young people's lifestyles.

When young people must leave their homes—either because of poverty, or increasingly, due to civil war, the result is often unprecedented numbers forced into bonded labor and commercial sex. For example, in the Indian cities of New Delhi, Mumbai, and Calcutta, thousands of young people take on menial jobs such as washing cars, pushing hand carts, collecting edibles from garbage dumps, or simply, begging. In Thailand, still more thousands of young girls earn their living as prostitutes. And in many countries of Eastern Europe, tens of thousands of young people are believed to be not attending school or formally employed, but instead, engaging in drug trafficking. Worldwide, the streets and temporary shelters are home to between 100 and 200 million children and adolescents, who are cut off from their parents and extended families (World Health Organization, 2000). What is it like to be them? What is it like to be young, scared, and poor?

Since the 1980s political and civil rights have improved substantially throughout the world, and 81 countries have taken significant steps in democratization, with 33 military regimes replaced by civilian governments. But of these fledgling democracies, only 47 are considered full democracies today. Only 82 countries, representing 57 percent of the world's population, are fully democratic.

Economically speaking, the proportion of the world's extremely poor fell from 29 percent in 1990 to 23 percent in 1999. Still, in 1999, 2.8 billion people lived on less than $2 a day, with 1.2 billion of them surviving on the margins of subsistence with less than $1 a day. In 2000, 1.1 billion people lacked access to safe water, and 2.4 billion did not have access to any form of improved sanitation services.

And armed conflict continue to blight the lives of millions: since 1990, 3.6 million people have died as a result of civil wars and ethnic violence, more than 16 times the number killed in wars between states. Civilians have accounted for more than 90 percent of the casualties—either injured or killed—in post–cold war conflicts. Ninety countries are affected by landmines and live explosives, with rough estimates of 15,000 to 20,000 mine victims each year.

TEEN LIFE AROUND THE WORLD—THE SERIES

The Greenwood series *Teen Life around the World* examines what life is like for teens in different regions of the world. These volumes describe in detail the lives of young people in places both familiar and unfamiliar. How do teens spend their days? What makes their lives special? What difficulties and special burdens do they bear? And what will be their future as they make their way in their world?

Each volume is devoted to a region or regions of the world. For the purpose of this series, the volumes are divided as follows:

- Teen Life in Africa
- Teen Life in the Middle East
- Teen Life in Europe
- Teen Life in Central and South America and the Caribbean
- Teen Life in Asia

Readers can see similarities and differences in areas of the world that are relatively close in proximity, customs, and practices. Comparisons can be made between various countries in a region and across regions. American teens will perhaps be struck by the influence of American pop culture—music, fashion, food—around the world.

All volumes follow the same general format. The standardized format highlights information that all young people would most like to know. Each volume has up to fifteen chapters that describe teen life in a specific country in that region of the world. The countries chosen generally are representative of that region, and attempts were made to write about countries that young people would be most curious to learn more about.

Each chapter begins with a profile of the particular country. Basic political, economic, social, and cultural issues are discussed and a brief history of the country is provided. After this brief introduction to the specific country, an overview of teen life in that country is given, with a discussion of a teenager's typical day, family life, traditional and non-traditional foods, schooling, social life, recreation, entertainment, and religious practices and cultural practices. Finally, each chapter concludes with a list of resources that will help readers learn more about this country. These resources include nonfiction and fiction, web sites, other sources to find information on the country, such as embassies, and pen pal addresses.

Although these chapters cannot tell the complete story of what it means to be a teenager in that region of the world and recognizing that perhaps there is no one typical lifestyle in any country, they provide a good starting point for insight into others' lives.

The contributors to this series present an informative and engaging look at the life of young people around the world and write in a straightforward manner. The volumes are edited by noted experts. They have an intimate understanding of their chosen region of the world—having either lived there, and/or they have devoted their professional lives to studying, teaching about, and researching the place. Also, an attempt was made to have each chapter written by an expert on teen life in that country. Above all, what these authors reveal is that young people everywhere—no matter where they live—have much in common. Although they might observe different social customs, rituals, and habits, they still long for the same basic things—security, respect, and love. They still live in that state where they half child/half adult, as they wait anxiously to become a fully functioning members of their society.

As series editor, it is my hope that these volumes, which are unique in publishing in both content and style, will increase your knowledge of teen life around the world.

Jeffrey S. Kaplan
Series Editor

REFERENCES

Baru, R. "The Social Milieu of the Adolescent Girl." In *Adolescent Girl in India: An Indian Perspective*, ed. S. Mehra. Saket, New Delhi: MAMTA, Health Institute for Mother and Child, 1995.

Caldwell, J.C., P. Caldwell, and B. K. Caldwell. "The Construction of Adolescence in a Changing World: Implications for Sexuality, Reproduction, and Marriage." *Studies in Family Planning* 29, no. 2 (1998): 137–53.

Dehne, K.L., and G. Reidner. "Adolescence: A Dynamic Concept." *Reproductive Health Matters* 9, no. 17 (2001): 11–16.

Deutsche Gesellschaft fur Technische Zusammenarbeit. *Youth in Development Cooperation: Approaches and Prospects in the Multisectoral Planning Group "Youth."* Eschborn: GTZ, 1997.

Disanyake, J.B. *Understanding the Sinhalese*. Columbo, Sri Lanka: Chatura Printers, 1998.

Goswami, P.K. "Adolescent Girl and MCH Programme in India." In *Adolescent Girl in India: An Indian Perspective*, ed. S. Mehra. Saket, New Delhi: MAMTA, Health Institute for Mother and Child, 1995.

Larson, Reed. "The Future of Adolescence: Lengthening the Ladders to Adulthood." *The Futurist* 36, no. 6 (2002): 16–21.

McCauley, A.P., and C. Salter. "Meeting the Needs of Young Adults." *Population Report*, Series J, no. 41 (1995): 1–39.

UNAIDS. *Sex and Youth: Contextual Factors Affecting Risk for HIV/AIDS*. Geneva: UNAIDS, 1999.

UN Development Report. 2002.

World Health Organization. 2000.

INTRODUCTION

Cynthia Margarita Tompkins and Kristen Sternberg

Geographically, Latin America extends from the border of the United States to Cape Horn; however, the territory of the southernmost countries, Argentina and Chile, flows into Antarctica. Though Latin America technically includes the Caribbean Islands, it is usually considered to be the 20 republics that emerged from the territories once colonized by the Spanish, Portuguese, and French. In this volume, "Caribbean" refers to the region also known as the West Indies, which includes all of the islands on the Caribbean Sea from the tip of the Florida Peninsula to the northern coast of South America. Spain, Portugal, France, and The Netherlands also colonized these islands. At present, they include 23 political entities.

The rich legacy of Latin America and the Caribbean is compounded by another term, "post–Latin American," that refers to the questioning and redefinition of geographical borders and notions of identity. In Latin America, uneven and unequal modernization has led to a collage of temporalities within individual nations. Indigenous cultural customs, rituals, and traditions remain juxtaposed with postmodern Western trends. It seems that only extreme contrasts are constant in Latin America and the Caribbean.

HISTORICAL BACKGROUND

Although language variations of native populations in the New World include over one hundred linguistic families and hundreds of dialects, at present, most Latin Americans speak Spanish, Portuguese, or French.

Some speak English or Dutch. Some, especially in Brazil and the Caribbean, speak remnants of African languages. However, indigenous languages such as Nahuatl, Quechua, or Guarani remain the native tongues for millions.

European conquest and colonization influenced language, religious practices, and the law. As a result, there are more Spanish and Portuguese speakers in the Americas than in the Iberian Peninsula and most of the world's Roman Catholics live in Latin America. The Spaniards and the Portuguese arrived at a continent inhabited by 50 million people, almost as many as there were in Europe at that time. In the New World, indigenous tribes had developed highly sophisticated civilizations. Astronomy, architecture, painting and other arts, bridge building, and theater are only a few of the many areas in which they excelled.

When the Europeans arrived, biological warfare was unleashed in the Americas. Due to their long isolation, native peoples lacked adequate defenses. The exploitation of the labor of indigenous peoples also contributed to their genocide. Once the Arawak (Indians who, at the time of Columbus, inhabited the Greater Antilles and Puerto Rico) were virtually wiped out, colonizers turned to African labor. At least 10 million Africans were brought across the Atlantic before the institution of slavery ended around the mid-nineteenth century.

Over the years, the natives continued to resist the colonizers. In Guatemala, the Maya withdrew into the jungle, where they maintained an independent kingdom for more than two centuries. In Brazil, runaway slaves created a kingdom named Palmares. In Peru, constant Indian rebellions led to the Tupac Amaru revolt of 1780, which took 100,000 lives and five years to control. Indigenous commitment to the community rather than to the individual, manifested in terms of reciprocity and ceremonial squander, was a form of resistance that impoverished them economically but strengthened them politically.

At present, in many Latin American countries, indigenous groups span national borders. For instance, the Aymara live in Peru, Bolivia, Chile, and Argentina. There are Quechuas in Bolivia, Ecuador, and Peru. Transnational Native American ethnic groups have come to the limelight for their commitment to ecological issues and human rights. Rigoberta Menchú Tum, a Mayan indigenous woman from Guatemala, received the Nobel Peace Prize in 1982. Her struggle against oppression began when she was a teen.

Europeans mixed with African cultures in many nations—notably Brazil, Cuba, and the Dominican Republic—and Spaniards mixed freely with native women, giving birth to a mestizo race. The Spanish and the

Portuguese attempted to implant their culture in the New World but they had to adapt to the land and new conditions of life. Furthermore, though the conquest attempted to deprive native cultures of their religion, art, science, and writing (in the case of the Aztecs and the Mayans), far from being obliterated, they deeply influenced the culture of the New World, especially in regards to daily and domestic life.

While the American and French revolutions sparked the independence movements of the early nineteenth century, they did not end European influence. To the contrary, with the advent of the Industrial Revolution, Latin America and the Caribbean were relegated to the role of exporters of raw materials and importers of manufactured goods. Relations between Latin America and the United States were tainted with hostility in the nineteenth century. In the twentieth century, U.S. intervention in quashing socialist revolutionary reforms in Guatemala, Chile, Nicaragua, and Cuba led to flares of animosity from the mid-1950s through the 1980s. In the late 1980s and 1990s, Latin American democracy superseded military dictatorships (such as those of Argentina and Chile); however, the apparent, initial success of neoliberal models led to catastrophic results. At present, living standards have slipped. The number of Latin Americans has more than doubled that of 30 years ago but the poor are much worse off than they were 20 years ago. According to the Economic Commission for Latin America (CEPAL), by the end of 2002, 190 million Latin Americans, or 44 percent of the population, will live below the poverty line.

In general terms, modern influences mingle with traditions, customs, foods, and religions that have been influenced by indigenous populations as well as the slave trade. African belief systems permeate religious practices in Brazil and the Caribbean. Recent decades, however, have marked the acceleration of transformations, and the ecological and sociological impact on the environment has been intensified by the advance of technology, the stress of economic growth, and a population explosion.

SOCIAL CONDITIONS

Geography and historical conditions impacted the infusion of European, native, and African cultures. Each colonizing culture left its imprint on Latin America and the Caribbean. For instance, the Spanish colonization, purportedly undertaken in the name of that country's crown to convert natives to Catholicism, united the spheres of state and church, a link that remained strong until the twentieth century. Furthermore, the Catholic stress on the afterlife was useful to the state because it diverted attention from current social conditions. Other values derived from

Catholicism such as the design of divine providence, paternalism, sin, sacrifice, and repentance diminished personal responsibility since the solution was in God's hands. The link between state and church had other repercussions. Forced conversions led to internal resistance, therefore Indians were apparently faithful to the Christian creed but inwardly loyal to their own convictions. A double standard arose regarding political convictions given that legitimacy was derived from the relations between state and church. It also appeared regarding behavioral patterns of compliance, since people adhered to the following rationalization: I comply but I lie. In addition to having a rebellious attitude toward authority that is typical of teens, a double standard arises in their relation to the church. Typically, Catholic teens have already taken their first Communion. Since confirmation is a required sacrament for marriage, teens comply, but it does not mean they will be active churchgoers. Nor does it mean they will be concerned with church activities.

During the 1970s and 1980s, part of the Catholic Church became committed to the cause of the poor. Accordingly, the task of a good Christian was to build the Kingdom of God on earth. For the most part, society was conceived of in socialist terms. Liberation theology gained popularity and attracted a broad base of youth throughout Latin America. In general, military repression, which took different forms according to the country, put an end to the movement. Today, an increasing number of youth are converting to Evangelical, Pentecostal, and Protestant sects.

Paradoxically, remnants of sixteenth- and seventeenth-century Spanish and Portuguese culture are still evident in patterns of behavior throughout Latin America and the Caribbean. These influences include the central position of the family; the *compadrazgo* system of ceremonial kinship; double standards regarding sexual morals; an emphasis upon social class, which includes a disdain for manual labor and a high regard for etiquette; a continued veneration of saints; and a love of religious processions and festivals. For the most part these values continue to be instilled in Latin American teens.

In the last few decades Latin America has been transformed from a number of primarily agricultural, peasant economies, into highly urban societies. The process has led to mass unemployment, homelessness, and starvation. Rural exodus and the concentration into megalopolises (gigantic cities), such as Mexico City, São Paulo, and Buenos Aires, resulted in pollution and the rise of environmental diseases. An increase in urban violence resulted in the criminalization of entire sectors of the population. The fear of urban violence unleashed an increase of repressive surveillance. The elite locks itself up in gated communities. The poor can no longer depend on the old-style system of favors from local caciques (political bosses). Neither are they integrated into the consumer society offered by the media.

The conspicuous consumption of imported goods has become an important characteristic of the upper and middle classes in Latin America. Ironically, the media also persuades the poor to acquire goods they can ill afford. The globalized media has persuaded them that they have to adopt the standards of consumption and styles of dress, entertainment, housing, and so on of their counterparts in North America and western Europe. In the process, national values are superseded by global standards. However, though transnational corporations and international financial agencies have begun to undermine national structures, globalization also has the opposite effect, giving rise to the resurgence of traditional identities and values.

The widely touted economic miracles produced by military regimes during the 1970s transformed Latin America into an area beset by informal economies and debt. However, popular resistance still flares up. For instance, on December 19, 2002, Argentineans expressed their discontent by banging on pots and pans. That *cacerolazo* toppled Fernando de la Rúa's administration.

TEENS

With the exception of English-speaking countries in the Caribbean, the term "teen" is meaningless in the region. Most publications follow the categorization set by Article 1 of the United Nations (UN) Convention on the Rights of the Child: "A child means every human being below the age of 18 years unless, under the law applicable to the child, majority is attained earlier" (Green 1998, 212). The UN declared 1985 International Youth Year. "Youth" was defined as the period between 15 and 24 years old. The event resulted in a number of studies on the predicament of youth in Latin America and the Caribbean, aimed at changing current policies. According to the United Nations Economic, Scientific, and Cultural Organization (UNESCO), in rural areas an 11- or 12-year-old child is already struggling to find work or merely to survive, and therefore he or she is no longer a child. Similarly, the Food and Agriculture Organization (FAO) considers all those between the ages of 10 and 24 to be youth.

"Youth" is defined by a number of factors. Biologically, youth is defined as the onset of reproductive capacity (puberty). Socially, it ends when the subject can be economically independent and begin his or her own family. A traditional Latin American rite of passage was the *quinceañera*, a party held when girls turned 15, marking her entrance into the adult world. Though many well-to-do girls get a nose job or take a trip instead, the custom still survives. For males, adulthood began when they were drafted, at age 18. However, at present, compulsory draft is no longer prevalent in the region.

In general, the challenge upper- and middle-class youth face is how to negotiate the transition between the closed and protected family unit and the enigma of social expectations. Youths have to negotiate their personal independence vis-à-vis the requirements of an increasingly technological society.

The number of children on the streets often strikes visitors to Latin America and the Caribbean. This is not surprising given that 37 percent of the population is under 16, compared to 21 percent in the industrialized world. While well-to-do children tend to live secluded lives, the poor work for a living and can often be seen on the streets. The International Labor Organization estimated that 15 percent of children between the ages of 10 and 14, i.e., 7.6 million, worked (Alarcón 2000, 1). According to UN figures, 1 in 5 10- to 14-year-olds work in Brazil, Honduras, and Haiti, and more than 1 in 10 in most Latin American and Caribbean countries. The higher proportion of boys counted underlines the invisibility of the work girls perform at home. Additionally, many 12- and 13-year-old girls work as maids. In fact, 90 percent of domestics are girls and female youth (Alarcón 2000, 19). Rigoberta Menchú Tum's testimony records the subhuman treatment Indian girls often experience as maids. Many other female teens are subjected to sweatshop conditions in textile *maquiladoras* throughout Central America. In Guatemala, Mayan families seasonally migrate to find work harvesting coffee, cotton, and sugarcane. Harvesting involves the labor of children and teens. Likewise, in Honduras, minors harvesting melons and watermelons are paid per unit. Nicaraguan youth also harvest coffee, cotton, sugarcane, and bananas. Finally, Chilean minors are employed in modern agrarian enterprises, where they select seeds, harvest, and select and pack produce.

Working children and adolescents compete from a disadvantaged position in the job market; furthermore, they perpetuate the transmission of poverty from generation to generation. The Latin America and the Caribbean region is one of the main areas of child exploitation and the violation of human rights. While child labor is nominally illegal, 8 out of 10 Latin American families enduring extreme poverty depend on the work of children and adolescents for 10 to 25 percent of their total income. However, these figures do not include the work of those who are not remunerated for the work they do at home. Given that youth comprise about half of the economically active population, their work nets about 50 percent of the income, goods, and services a family requires. Therefore, the effort of international organizations such as the United Nations Children's Fund (UNICEF) to end child labor is unrealistic unless poverty can be eradicated. A relatively new phenomenon in the area is the recent organizing of child/adolescent workers in Peru, Brazil, and Nicaragua.

Once on the street, youths are exposed to violence, drugs, prostitution, and gangs. The reaction of the state varies between efforts at social cleansing, police brutality, a legal system that criminalizes them, and ineffective reformatories. In Latin America and the Caribbean, 75 percent of minors going through the legal system are male. They are often more than four years behind at school. They reside in marginal areas such as shantytowns. Their subsistence is based on unskilled labor or illicit activities. They help to support a family structure of sorts, either a nuclear family or another group that gives them protection. Their father is typically an unskilled, out-of-work laborer. Their mother may perform domestic work (as a maid), sell small items on the streets, or engage in prostitution. Like the father, she is usually unemployed or works only part-time. More often than not, the father is missing from the family structure. Eighty-nine percent of prosecuted youth live in conditions of extreme poverty, a condition shared by 40 to 60 percent of the population. The high rate of unemployment, which reaches 60 percent among youth in Latin America and the Caribbean, is certainly a factor prompting them to illegal activities.

Secondary education is far less available than is primary education in the region. Moreover, dropping out of school and grade repetition become more problematic. Dropping out of secondary school in rural areas is common due to the family's need for laborers and the fact that schools have not adapted to the realities of rural life.

Family life is of primary importance. In addition to a nuclear family, the lives of most teens in Latin America and the Caribbean revolve around an extended family that includes blood relatives (grandparents, uncles, aunts, cousins, etc.) as well as social links (i.e., compadres, or godparents). In general, teens live with their families until they become independent, that is, until they marry. Depending on the career chosen, and their socioeconomic status, Latin American youths may or may not leave home to go to college. Most, however, do not. While middle- and upper-class parents in Latin America and the Caribbean try to dissuade youths from working so they can concentrate on their studies, for lower-class teens, work is not a choice. Dating rituals vary. Premarital sex is occurring with increasing frequency; correspondingly, the age at which youths become sexually active tends to decrease. Rural teens of lower socioeconomic status tend to marry earlier than do their urban counterparts: In urban areas, marriages are routinely postponed until teens graduate from college. Still, as time passes the incidences of divorce and separation are growing. The growing number of broken families is reflected in the increase of teen pregnancies and drug abuse.

Globalization is an ongoing process in Latin America and the Caribbean and teens consume the goods it offers. A number of fast-food chains have followed McDonald's footsteps but many teens still prefer their native cuisine. In other cases, McDonald's and its clones have adapted to national customs by adding typical ingredients, such as peppers, to the fare. Hegemonic cultural influence is exerted through music (rock, rap, jazz, etc.), Hollywood movies, and TV. Though they tend to be attuned to the latest hits by Britney Spears, NSync, the Barenaked Ladies, and so on, Latin American and Caribbean teens adapt U.S. cultural production to their needs, giving rise to their own varieties of rock, punk, and rap.

In Latin America and the Caribbean all aspects of teen life, such as standard of living, family life, and access to education, recreation, and entertainment, hinge upon social class. The social paths of the elite and the indigent rarely cross. In addition to the overriding effect of socioeconomic status, especially in countries with either high percentages of indigenous population or *mestizaje* (miscegenation, with indigenous peoples or those of African descent) the impact of ethnicity is significant. Region also plays a major role insofar as rural youths tend to be more traditional. Underprivileged youth are criminalized. Brazilian death squads mow down street children with impunity. Though factors such as the following affect all sectors of the population, youths are particularly hard hit. Drug trafficking is on the rise. Guerrilla unrest continues to affect Colombian youth. The plight of indigenous peoples, in Guatemala and throughout Latin America, continues to be dire.

Paradigms have shifted. The parents of today's teens came of age in the '60s. They were exposed to alternative lifestyles (such as being hippies) as well as the socialist and the sexual revolution. However, they have also survived the brutal state repression unleashed by military dictatorships, such as those of the southern cone and Brazil. The (military) imposition of capitalist ideology through neoliberal economic models deeply affected Latin Americans. Thus, in general, if past generations were anti-American, anticapitalist, socialist, and committed to solidarity, more recent generations are defined by pro-Americanism, capitalism, efficiency, individualism, and personal success (see Geirola and Pierini, "Argentina," this volume).

As may be inferred from the following chapters, in Latin America, child rearing and household chores typically fall to females whether or not they work outside the home. Family decisions tend to be made by the male head of household but decision making is shared when both parents work outside the home. In most countries, however, economic factors undermine family structure. For example, it's harder for family members to share a meal when both parents work. In other cases, economic need forces parents to migrate and grandparents end up raising children and teens. In more extreme cases, migration becomes the best—and sometimes the only—option for all family members.

Over the last five centuries, Latin American teens, children, and youth have largely been omitted from history books. Additionally, most of them left no accounts of their lives. At present, nongovernmental organizations throughout Latin America and the Caribbean are recording and publishing the autobiographical narratives of adolescents at risk or on the streets.

ABOUT THIS VOLUME

Though each of the nations within Latin America and the Caribbean laid a strong claim for inclusion in this volume, space restrictions necessitated editorial choices. *Teen Life in Latin America and the Caribbean* addresses the following 15 countries: Argentina, Brazil, Chile, Colombia, Cuba, the Dominican Republic, Ecuador, El Salvador, Guatemala, Haiti, Jamaica, Mexico, Peru, Puerto Rico, and Venezuela. With their selections, the editors strove to include a variety of colonial experiences; for example, Spain, Portugal, France, England, and The Netherlands all once colonized parts of Latin America. Cultural variety was perceived to be of special interest or relevance to teens; however, there were more resources for some countries than others. El Salvador is one example. Its current economic crisis, which exerts a significant effect on education, was compounded with other disasters, such as the earthquakes that devastated that nation in the year 2000. In addition to losses in infrastructure, access to printed material became even more difficult than it had been previously.

"Teen" is a term used in the English-speaking world for which there is no equivalent in Spanish, Portuguese, or French. The teens referred to here are from middle school to early college age. Each chapter in *Teen Life in Latin America and the Caribbean* follows a series format. The variety of approaches to the format attests to the uniqueness of each contributor. All contributors are from the country they write about or have visited there. Many of the chapters, for example, the Chile, Mexico, Puerto Rico, and Peru chapters are enhanced by interviews, either with family members or with teens of the respective countries.

Finally, teens are not a hot topic in the social sciences research of most Latin American countries; therefore, this volume fills a dire need. Rossana Reguillo Cruz, a Mexican researcher, is one of a very few who shows a focused and continued publication agenda on youth culture. Therefore, we have invited her to address the issue in the following section.

RESOURCE GUIDE

Alarcón Glasinovich, Walter. "El trabajo de niños y adolescentes en América Latina y el Caribe: Situación, políticas y retos en los años noventa." In *Trabajo Infantil Doméstico: ¿Y quien la mandó a ser niña?*, eds. Gladys Acosta Vargas, Emilio García Méndez, and Soraya Hoyos. Santafé de Bogotá, Colombia: Unicef. fondo de las Naciones Unidas para la infancia, Tercer mundo editores, 2000.

Beltrán, José Miguel Nacimiento, et al. *A la franca . . . Buscando un nuevo paradigma sobre Niños y Adolescentes en la Calle*. Lima: Asociación Católica Educativa Hogar de Cristo and Centro de Estudios y Solidaridad con América Latina, 1998.

Boudewijnse, Barbara, André Droogers, and Frans Kamsteeg, eds. *Algo más que opio: una lectura antropológica del pentecostalismo latinoamericano y caribeño*. San José, Costa Rica: Editorial Dei, 1991.

Casimir, Jean. *The Caribbean: One and Divisible*. Santiago: United Nations Economic Commission for Latin America and the Caribbean, 1992.

Crosby, Alfred W. "The Disastrous Effects of Disease." In *The Colonial Experience*. Edited by Lewis Hanke. Vol. 1 of *History of Latin American Civilization*. 2d ed. Boston: Little, Brown and Company, 1973.

Economic Commission for Latin America, et al. (CEPAL). *Children and Youth in National Development in Latin America. Report of Conference*. Santiago: United Nations Children's Fund, 1965.

———. *La juventud en América Latina y el Caribe: Plan de Acción Regional en relación con el Año Internacional de la Juventud*. Santiago: United Nations, 1985.

García Mendez, Emilio, and Elías Carranza, eds. *Del revés al derecho: La condición jurídica de la infancia en América Latina*. Buenos Aires: Editorial Galerna, 1992.

Green, Duncan. "Appendix: The UN Convention on the Rights of the Child." In *Hidden Lives: Voices of Children in Latin America and the Caribbean*. London: Cassell, 1998.

Harris, Richard L. "The Global Context of Contemporary Latin American Affairs." In *Capital, Power, and Inequality in Latin America*, eds. Sandor Halebsky and Richard L. Harris. Boulder: Westview Press, 1995.

Henríquez-Uureña, Pedro. *Historia de la cultura en la América Hispánica*. Translated and with a supplementary chapter by Gilbert Chase. New York: Praeger, 1966.

Hetch, Tobias. *Minor Omissions: Children in Latin American History and Society*. Madison: University of Wisconsin Press, 2002.

Jain, Ajit. *Caribbean Youth and the International Year: A Study of Youth in the Caribbean Countries with Particular Reference to Jamaica and Guyana*. Kingston, Jamaica: Bustamante Institute of Public and International Affairs, 1986.

Kearney, Michael, and Stefano Varese. "Latin America's Indigenous Peoples: Changing Identities and Forms of Resistance." In *Capital, Power, and Inequality in Latin America*, eds. Sandor Halebsky and Richard L. Harris. Boulder: Westview Press, 1995.

Keen, Benjamin, ed. *Latin American Civilization: History and Society, 1492 to the Present*. Boulder: Westview Press, 1986.

Lehmann, David. *Democracy and Development in Latin America: Economics, Politics, and Religion in the Post-War Period*. Cambridge, U.K.: Polity Press, 1990.

Liebel, Manfred. *Protagonismo infantil: movimientos de niños trabajadores en América Latina*. Nicaragua: Editorial Nueva Nicaragua, 1994.

"Para la Cepal, América Latina tiene más pobres." November 8, 2002. http:///www.lanacion.com.ar/02/11/08dg_44822.asp.

Pendle, George. *A History of Latin America*. Harmondsworth, Great Britain: Penguin Books Ltd., 1963.

Post, David. *Children's Work, Schooling, and Welfare in Latin America*. Boulder: Westview Press, 2001.

Rigoberta Menchú, Tum. *I, Rigoberta Menchú: An Indian Woman in Guatemala*. Translated by Ann Wright. London: Verso, 1984.

Rodríguez-Monegal, Emir. "The Integration of Latin American Cultures." In *Contemporary Latin American Culture: Unity and Diversity*, ed. C. Gail Guntermann. Tempe, Ariz.: Center for Latin American Studies, 1984.

Salazar, María Cristina. "Child Work and Education in Latin America." In *The Child in Latin America: Health, Development, and Rights*, eds. Ernst J. Bartell and Alejandro O'Donnell. Notre Dame, Ind.: University of Notre Dame Press, 2001.

Salcedo, G., José Joaquín, Hernando Bernal Alarcón, and Nohora Inés Gutiérrez S. *Latin America: An Agonizing Dilemma*. Translated by Luis Zalamea. Miami: Publicaciones Violeta, 1991.

Wagley, Charles. *The Latin American Tradition: Essays on the Unity and the Diversity of Latin American Culture*. New York: Columbia University Press, 1968.

Winn, Peter. *Americas: The Changing Face of Latin America and the Caribbean*. Updated ed. Berkeley: University of California Press, 1999.

Yúdice, George, Jean Franco, and Juan Flores, eds. "Introduction." In *On Edge: The Crisis of Contemporary Latin American Culture*. Minneapolis: University of Minnesota Press, 1992.

TEENS AT THE BORDER: FOR A POLITICS OF REPRESENTATION

Rossana Reguillo Cruz

Translated by Cynthia Margarita Tompkins

Latin American youths are in a crisis. They are an extremely vulnerable group in a collective society that is confronting dire poverty in the face of raging globalism. As the state withdraws from its role as provider of basic needs and as its power to ensure human rights decreases, the youths it abandons, especially those who do not fit the role of consumer-citizen (García Canclini) are stigmatized. As the condition of poverty is transformed into an identity, deprived youths become synonymous with danger. In addition to the mass media, the process of demonization involves an educational system unable to provide real alternatives, a legislative effort aimed at reducing the penal age to create the figure of the juvenile delinquent, and the fear underlying the punitive actions of city governments.

The profound differences among countries in Latin America and the Caribbean are rooted in economic and historical factors. The latter include the legacies of conquest and colonization, the impact of the Catholic church, the different models taken to build and modernize each nation, and the weakness of the democracies that resulted in the twentieth-century diaspora. These key factors must be taken into consideration to understand the predicament of youths today.

By linking data on young immigrants of Latin American and Caribbean origin to institutional failure, to different populations' lack of faith in their respective countries' politics, it may be inferred that in addition to being a sign of the times, migration is also a result of a growing feeling of exclusion experienced by millions of youths. Nowadays, however, rather than an indicator of better living conditions, migration is a sign of a prolonged crisis that may be attributed to the interrelation of the state's failure to meet the requirements of social responsibility (health care, schooling, etc.), the strengthening of capitalism, and the exacerbation of the socioeconomic crisis for the generations born after the 1980s.

Though these processes are global rather than strictly Latin American, their interrelationship affords an understanding of the increase in migratory flux and the disenchantment and uncertainty of the young. The impact of economic factors on everyday life is evidenced in the fact that Latin America and the Caribbean, with a population of 494 million, of which just over 32 percent are not yet 15 years old, allocate most of their resources to servicing (but not paying) their foreign debt.

The Argentine collapse illustrates the danger of subordinating the welfare of the population to the design of a global market that bulldozes vulnerable economies. Data on the growing disparity between rich and poor countries as a result of a capitalist, free-market economy are abundant. For instance, according to the Index of Human Development of the United Nations, in 1999 the combined income of the richest 10 percent in the United States (25 million people) surpassed that of the 43 percent poorest (2 billion) in the world.

Latin American teens share a deep distrust of politics. They are disenchanted with most forms of institutionalized participation and electoral options. Nevertheless, that they group around issues and that they continue to construct cultural identities shows that their attitudes and actions are imbued with profound political meaning.

Paradoxically, "the young practice a highly political rejection of politics" (Beck 1999, 11). Considering that political parties (and governing officials) lack projects for the young, that youths are addressed only perfunctorily because they are considered electoral booty, and that corruption and abuse of power have become daily spectacles, teens' lack of faith in politics should not be surprising. Lacking a referent, politics becomes an absurd tool that results in even more poverty, unemployment, and corruption.

In urban Brazil there are over four million youths between 15 and 19 years of age who live in poverty. In Mexico, there are almost three million, and in Colombia more than a million. Over 70 percent of urban youths live in poverty in Honduras, 58 percent in Ecuador, and 53 percent in Bolivia.

Youths are subject to police brutality and to the stigma of their teachers, who feel overwhelmed by the transformation of disenchantment into a silent demand for which they have no answers. Youths also feel cornered by daily evidence of a lack of possibilities and the enormous difficulty posed by integration, or in other words, to fit and be included in society. So, the inevitable question is how the vacuum left by the state and other modern institutions such as the family, school, and church—which also face crises of legitimacy—will be filled.

Three powerful actors appear in the sterile landscape: drug trafficking, new religious movements, and the market. Within that landscape, the culture is ripe for illegality, individualism, and hedonism.

ESCAPING POVERTY

The relationship between youth identities and the culture of illegality cannot be understood from a standpoint of prejudice or moral condemnation. Thus, drug trafficking becomes a viable option for excluded youths. Ballads about drug kingpins have had a powerful effect on youth culture in Mexico and Colombia. Similarly, Argentina's shantytown's *cumbia* (popular music in which lyrics often depict the reality of impoverished youth with strong doses of machismo while glorifying the transgressive abilities of young shantytown dwellers) offers an alternative way of searching for social inclusion and of understanding the world.

According to indicators of human development in Latin America and the Caribbean (PNUD) 10 years of schooling are required for individuals to have a 90 percent chance of overcoming poverty. But empirical research, along with a great number of annual reports, indicate that the number of registered students is decreasing (in Bolivia, Ecuador, Haiti, Honduras, Trinidad and Tobago, Colombia, and Panama, among others), which means that a significant number—between 48 and 64 percent—of youths' opportunities are being restricted. Considering that approximately two million, or 5 percent, of youths neither work nor study, it is not surprising that drug trafficking has become an alternative to overcoming poverty (CEPAL).

OVERCOMING CONFUSION

The explosion of religious offerings shows an intense need to endow reality with transcendental meaning, especially since recent political institutions have failed to do so.

Though not well documented, research suggests the growing importance of belief in the construction of youth identities and movements. For instance, Mexican *Raztecas*—youths who have combined reggae music and its style with traditional indigenous Mexican culture—and Puerto Rican *rastainos* (Puerto Rican equivalent of *Raztecas*) have borrowed not only from Rastafarian[1] aesthetics but also from Aztec and Taino indigenous traditions to create a new movement, anchored in music,[2] that attempts not only to recover traditional knowledge but also to apply it to the contemporary world.

Despite being denied by the official stories of the region, the return to origins and the exploration of Négritude (as a way to reassess African culture and to protest against French colonialism and assimilation) are significant in the worldview of indigenous peoples. Many Rastafarian youths abandon their given names as they are baptized once again. They choose to die symbolically in Western life and to be reborn into a lifestyle that appears more responsive to their search for roots.

However, this inherently human quest for meaning is also an expression of disenchantment resulting from the current malaise regarding Westernization, capitalism, and globalization. Moreover, several religious groups are capitalizing on this uneasiness by promising meaning and a better future. Although these sects have found numerous new converts in Latin America and the Caribbean, what is at issue is not loss of control by traditional churches but the expansion of an individualistic worldview that undermines social commitment.

Conversely, the mushrooming of groups focused on death is equally important. The so-called gothics or darkies organize around cults of vampires and wolves and the tantalizing vertigo that results from facing death. The *poètes maudits* such as nineteenth-century French poet Baudelaire's *The Flowers of Evil* are classics among these youth. Dark aesthetics and deep depression mark gothics from Buenos Aires (Argentina) to Los Angeles, passing through Santiago (Chile), Guadalajara, and Tijuana (Mexico).

Death becomes highly significant among certain groups. Data from the Universidad Nacional Autónoma de México shows a 200 percent increase in suicides in the last 30 years. Suicide is the second leading cause of death among 15- to 19-year-old Mexican youths.

TO BE, TO BELONG

Cultural goods such as clothing have become the foundation of individual and group identity. As styles, punk, surf, sport, Rastafarian, neo-hippie, rap, and heavy metal aesthetics not only allow youths to recognize their peers but also provide a feeling of belonging.

The profitable and expanding sneaker industry is one of the best examples of the brand-name phenomenon. For instance, with slightly over 43,000 employees worldwide, Nike's reported sales for 1997 were $9.2 billion, which represented a 42 percent increase over the amount reported in

1995. The popularity of sneakers, however, goes beyond the sports world. Sneakers are considered a mark of distinction and even represent power among the have-nots.[3] The most dramatic manifestation of this phenomenon has been taking place for years in Venezuela: "Fetishism developing in the neighborhoods regarding certain brands of sneakers is such that most of the youths discovered dead during the last two years were found barefoot.... We have come across youngsters living in huts, which didn't even have a cot; however, they would keep their Nikes under lock and key."[4]

It would be simplistic to infer a cause-and-effect relationship between global industry marketing strategies and youth violence. But an analysis of youth identity must include the politics of consumerism, which involves capitalism as much as an understanding of cultural values.

The growing gap between those who are connected and those who are not must be addressed. Unequal access to new information technologies, such as the Internet, may be comparable, without exaggeration, to a new literacy. Despite the growth of new networks and technological infrastructures, the armies of the illiterate vastly outnumber the privileged youths who are able to connect themselves to the world of information by means of these devices.

According to data gathered by the National Youth Poll in Mexico,[5] while 77 percent of households where youths live have a TV (with an open signal), only 6 percent have access to the Internet.

BETWEEN STIGMATIZATION AND DEMONIZATION

Government officials, the school system, and the media tend to resort to stigmatization and demonization to confront the problems of youths. Demonization increases as the region's capacity to govern decreases. For instance, after just eight days on the job (in May 2001), Amadeo D'Angelo, the Chief of Police in Buenos Aires, declared that "we will surround the shantytowns to prevent delinquents from coming out." He added, with complete composure, "groups of youths are synonymous with crime." In El Salvador, youth gangs known as *maras* have come to be considered the most serious criminal problem. Two main *maras* fight inch by inch for territory. As their practices become increasingly violent, their influence extends rapidly toward Guatemala.

In Caracas, Venezuela, between 1994 and 1996, minors comprised 40.3 percent of the total arrests or detentions. Of 43,146 minors detained, 32.6 percent were arrested for suspicion, lack of documentation, or background checks (Briceño and Pérez 1999), which leads us, once again, to stigmatization.

These constructs speak of the failure of the adult world and of its institutions to face an issue that should not be interpreted from the standpoint of warriors and victims. On the contrary, it demands that the world focus urgently on the predicament of the young and that citizens bear in mind that self-representation in the public space is a fundamental right.

NOTES

[Editor's note]. Adapted from Rossana Reguillo's "Jóvenes en el borde: Por una política de la representación," which was translated by Cynthia Margarita Tompkins.

1. Jamaican religious and political movement based on a return to Africa and its roots (Ethiopia), which will come to pass when the god Jah sends a sign that will end the exodus of the black population.

2. Nowadays music is fundamental in the construction of ascription and difference in youth identity. Punks, ravers, Rastafarians, and heavy metal followers derive more than style from musical expression; music becomes the main point of reference in constructing themselves as differentiated social actors. See Reguillo's "El lugar desde los márgenes Músicas e identidades juveniles." *Nómadas*, no. 13 (2000b).

3. In 1997, during her stay as an exchange professor in Puerto Rico, Reguillo Cruz was able to confirm that gold and sneakers valued in excess of $400 identified drug trafficking youth. At the shops selling brand-name clothing and shoes in the Plaza Las Américas—the mecca of Latin America's consumerism—one sees many youths with rolls of dollars spending $250, equivalent to the per capita income of a Haitian family, on a pair of sneakers.

4. Words of Inspector Carlos Prieto of the Homicide Division, reported by José Roberto Duque and Boris Muñoz, *La ley de la calle. Testimonios de jóvenes protagonistas de la violencia en Caracas* (Caracas, Venezuela: FUNDARTE, 1995): 163.

5. Reguillo Cruz took part in the conceptual and methodological design of the section on Political Culture, Organization, and Juvenile Participation in the poll. One of the main hypotheses that she worked with was access to cultural goods as fundamental mediation in the construction of political identities. See Reguillo Cruz, *Cartografía de la cultura política de los Jóvenes Mexicanos. I Encuesta Nacional de Juventud.* CD-ROM. (Mexico City: Instituto Mexicano de la Juventud, 2001). See also Reguillo Cruz, "Los movimientos sociales, notas para una discusión desde Latinoamérica," *Documentación Social. Revista de Estudios Sociales y de Sociología Aplicada*, no. 90 (1993); "Un malestar invisible. Derechos humanos y comunicación," *Chasqui*, no. 64 (1998); and "Estrategias del desencanto. Emergencia de culturas juveniles," in *Enciclopedia Latinoamericana de Sociocultura y Comunicación* (Buenos Aires: Norma, 2000).

RESOURCE GUIDE

Beck, Ulrich, ed. *Los hijos de la libertad. Contra las lamentaciones por el derrumbe de los valores*. Buenos Aires: Fondo de Cultura Económica, 1999.

Briceño, Roberto, and Rogelio Pérez, eds. "La violencia en Venezuela: dimensionamiento y políticas de control." Banco Interamericano de Desarrollo (BID), Documento de Trabajo, no. 373. Washington, D.C.: 1999.

Calvo Buezas, Tomás. *Racismo y solidaridad de españoles, portugueses y latinoamericanos: los jóvenes ante otros pueblos y culturas.* Madrid: Ediciones Libertarias, 1997.

CEPAL. *Adolescencia y juventud en América Latina y el Caribe: problemas, oportunidades y desafíos en el comienzo de un nuevo siglo.* Serie Población y Desarrollo, no. 9. Santiago: CEPAL/CELADE/OIJ, 2000.

Davenport, William. "Dos tipos de valor en la porción oriental de las islas Salomón." In *La vida cultural de las cosas. Perspectiva cultural de las mercancías. Colección Los noventa,* ed. Arjun Appadurai. Mexico City: CNCA/Grijalbo, 1991.

Duque, José Roberto, and Boris Muñoz. *La ley de la calle. Testimonios de jóvenes protagonistas de la violencia en Caracas.* Caracas, Venezuela: FUNDARTE, 1995.

García Canclini, Néstor. *Consumidores y ciudadanos. Conflictos Multiculturales de la Globalización.* Mexico City: Grijalbo. 1995.

Hobsbawn, Eric. *Bandits.* New York: The New Press, 2000.

Instituto Mexicano de la Juventud. *Jóvenes mexicanos del siglo XXI: Primera Encuesta Nacional de Juventud.* Mexico City: Instituto Mexicano de la Juventud, 2000.

Martínez Pizarro, Jorge. *Migración Internacional de jóvenes latinoamericanos y caribeños. Protagonismo y vulnerabilidad.* Serie Población y Desarrollo, no. 3. Santiago: CEPAL, 2000.

Organización Panamericana de la Salud (OPS). "Proyecto ACTIVA. Actitudes y normas culturales frente a la violencia en ciudades seleccionadas de América Latina y España." 1999. http://www.paho.org/Spanish/HCP/HCN/VIO/activa-project.htm.

PNUD. *Informe sobre Desarrollo Humano 2001.* New York: Programa de las Naciones Unidas para el Desarrollo, 2001.

Reguillo, Rossana. *Cartografía de la cultura política de los Jóvenes Mexicanos. I Encuesta Nacional de Juventud.* CD-ROM. Mexico City: Instituto Mexicano de la Juventud, 2001.

———. "Estrategias del desencanto. Emergencia de culturas juveniles." In *Enciclopedia Latinoamericana de Sociocultura y Comunicación.* Buenos Aires: Norma, 2000.

———. "El lugar desde los márgenes. Músicas e identidades juveniles." *Nómadas,* no. 13 (2000b): 40–53.

———. "Un malestar invisible. Derechos humanos y comunicación." In *Chasqui,* no. 64 (1998).

———. "Los movimientos sociales, notas para una discusión desde Latinoamérica." In *Documentación Social. Revista de Estudios Sociales y de Sociología Aplicada,* no. 90 (1993).

Salazar, Alonso. *No nacimos pa'semilla.* Bogotá: CINEP, 1990.

Vallejo, Fernando. *La Virgen de los Sicarios.* Madrid: Alfaguara, 2001.

Chapter 1

ARGENTINA

Gustavo Geirola and Aída Pierini

INTRODUCTION

Argentina, with nearly 3,800,000 square km, is the second largest country in South America. Although most of its coastline lies on the Atlantic Ocean, it shares international borders with Chile, Brazil, Uruguay, Bolivia, and Paraguay. From the Andes to the Atlantic, from the tropic to Patagonia, Argentina displays different physical areas that geographers typically recognize as the North, Andes, Mesopotamia, Pampas, and Patagonia. The climate ranges from subtropical in the north to very cold in Tierra del Fuego, but it is temperate and quite healthy in the densely populated central zone, where a general population of 37 million people tends to concentrate. Historically, Argentina has welcomed immigrants from many countries and different languages and ethnicities. However, Spanish is the official language of the country and, in general, people of the second generation of immigrants' descendants adopt Spanish as their basic language.

At the end of the nineteenth century and during and after World Wars I and II, immigrants from Italy, Spain, France, Germany, the United Kingdom, Eastern Europe, and the Middle East brought their traditions and languages and incorporated Western culture into the country. Eighty-five percent of the population is of European origin. However, many indigenous peoples (the Coya, Toba, Mapuche, Guaraní, etc.) remain in marginalized areas of the country. Recently, immigrants from Asia (notably Korea, China, and Japan) arrived in Buenos Aires, the capital city of Argentina where the federal government is located. Recent emigrants from

Asia have their own neighborhoods and schools and tend not to mix with the whole population.

Although many religions are venerated, Roman Catholicism is the official cult (90 percent of the population is nominally Catholic, but only 10 percent actively practices). Only 2 percent of the population are Jewish and 2 percent are Protestant.

The Argentine Constitution endorses civil, social, and political rights for children and adolescents under 18. In this respect, youths are free to express their opinions and perspectives and they have the right to be taken into account in the public sphere. Argentina is a country where, during the twentieth century, formal democracy was regularly interrupted by military coups. From very early in the last century, Argentina wanted to be a modern country but modernization was a painful process, especially because of the economic, social, and political consequences that it brought to the lower class. However, the country was able to consolidate a large middle class, concentrated mainly in Buenos Aires and in the principal cities of some provinces. Like workers, young people have been expressing themselves since the Perón era began in 1945. However, dissidents of the regime were also persecuted during Perón's 10 years in power. In the 1960s and '70s, especially after the Cuban Revolution in 1959, Latin America in general and Argentina in particular were enthralled by Marxist theories, whether in a reformist or a revolutionary way. That political agenda based its power on the younger generation, the same one that would be brutally persecuted, annihilated, or expelled into exile. During the last dictatorship, from 1976 to 1983, the state and its institutions, in particular the military and police, systematically terrorized the population. It had also a cultural apparatus that imposed the ideological agenda of the government and affected (or tried to affect) all sectors of the nation. However, many people resisted. What we consider today to be characteristic of young people is very different from the characteristics of the generations that lived during and after dictatorship. If past generations were anti-American, anticapitalist, socialist in diverse degrees, and committed to solidarity and collectivism, more recent generations are defined by pro-Americanism, capitalism, efficiency, individualism, and personal success. Youths' behavior today has to be understood from this historical point of view.

Since 1983 Argentina has had a democratic system, but the country has experienced difficulties due to the almost complete destruction of democratic values and institutions during the last dictatorship. In the last 10 years, and after the end of the cold war, the country has experimented with neoliberal economic programs mostly supported and imposed by the

United States. If, on the one hand, democratic institutions were rehabili-
tated, on the other hand citizens saw their lives progressively coerced and
transformed by economic pressures. Young people today deal with difficult
problems, such as poverty, political corruption, learning disabilities, unemployment, mass media's appalling influence, and social violence.

Since 1983, many efforts have been developed by social researchers and
democratic institutions in the country in attempts to heal the cultural and
social spheres devastated by the dictatorship. Specifically, many research
projects have focused on youngsters and their culture: how they live,
speak, dress, and entertain themselves and the ways they deal with the
labor market and their education. According to published essays, young
people are one of the main topics of concern for the general population,
which is reasonable because the future of the nation depends on them.
Since youth is a social and a cultural construction, it was necessary for researchers to define concrete parameters identifying what it is to be young
in general and what it is to be young in Argentina. It is understood that
young people try to differentiate themselves from their parents and the
previous generation. Teens are considered neither children nor adults:
rather, they are regarded as children in certain activities and as adults in
others. Bearing in mind the complex economic structure and social diversity of the country, the focus of this chapter is middle-class teenagers who
live in the city of Buenos Aires or its suburbs.

TYPICAL DAY

Argentinean teens do not like to get up early in the morning. They only
do it when they have to, that is, when they have morning classes. The
morning meal is not formal and many youngsters do not even take time to
eat breakfast. When they do, they prefer a continental breakfast, that is,
with tea or Argentinean coffee. Some have milk or yogurt. They eat toast
with butter and preserves, or cookies. Few have incorporated cereal into
their diet, and those who do try it are usually female because of their obsession with their health and body image.

Lunch in Buenos Aires is eaten between 12:30 and 1:30 P.M. When
both parents work outside of the house it is unusual for them to come
home for lunch. Consequently, adolescents have lunch by themselves, before school (if they attend afternoon shift) or after (if they go to school in
the morning). In both cases, lunch is usually frugal; they prefer foods that
require little preparation other than heating in a microwave. Known as
chatarra foods, their popularity is rising. The Americanization of Argentinean youth is well evidenced by their growing consumption of conve-

nience foods. Dinner is usually served between 9:00 and 10:00 P.M. and tends to be a time for the family to be together. Schedules for lunch and dinner are not very strict and they vary depending on a family's habits. In daily life, it is common for teens, especially those between 13 and 17, not to be overly concerned about personal cleanliness. They are also informal about their dress. Depending on their parents' economic status, youngsters advocate consumerism at various levels. They love to exhibit clothes by designer brands. These teens are called *marquistas* because they buy only those products promoted by TV ads, newspapers, and teen magazines.

FAMILY LIFE

A typical family in Buenos Aires is composed of two parents and one or two children, and in rare occasions by more than two. Usually both parents work; however, the responsibility for the home still falls upon the shoulders of the mother. It is important to emphasize that males are gradually taking responsibility for what have traditionally been considered female chores. In general, teens live with their families. However, the number of divorces resulting in single-parent households in Argentina is growing. In most of those cases children live with their mother, while the father is obliged to provide child support until his children reach the age of 18. That compromise is not fulfilled spontaneously, which is the cause for a large number of lawsuits. Beyond the economic instability, teens have to deal with many hours alone at home or look for jobs to help their mother. Sometimes it becomes problematic, because persons under the age of 18 cannot obtain driving licenses. Nonetheless, after that age, even if they obtain licenses it is not common for youths to own their own cars. While there is a huge difference depending on social class, few middle-class families can afford more than one car.

Generally, parents have no participation in their teens' schools. Sometimes they are invited by teachers to discuss specific problems—mostly those linked to disciplinary regulations or learning disabilities. Parents are seldom invited to attend special meetings addressed to them; if invited, few participate.

TRADITIONAL AND NONTRADITIONAL FOOD DISHES

The main staple in Argentina is meat. It is eaten regularly, in simple or in more sophisticated dishes depending on tradition, economics, and time available for mothers to cook. Shopping is done on a weekly basis in supermarkets or neighborhood grocery stores. Traditional farmers' markets are preferred by many families, not only because they can get fresh food for daily consumption but also because their personal relationships with the owners allow them to have special financial arrangements in times of economic difficulty.

Generally, women prepare the food though more and more men are sharing the cooking responsibilities. Barbecued meat (*asado*) is tradition-ally prepared by men. As that is a meal that requires much preparation and cooking time, it is generally made on weekends. Pasta is consumed as well: It is a heritage of Italian culture in Argentina. Since pasta is inex-pensive and defeats hunger well it is becoming indispensable for poorer families. Popular dishes with teens are *Milanesa con papas fritas* (veal parmigiana with French fries), pizza, and hamburgers. Teens' preferences sometimes differ from their parents'. However, parents usually give in to children's taste to avoid family conflicts over food.

In recent years, ethnic and vegetarian restaurants have been frequently visited by Argentineans. However, teens prefer to meet and eat in American-style fast-food restaurants, which are more affordable. Lately, these restaurants have had to adapt to the Argentinean lifestyle. For ex-ample, some McDonalds have transformed themselves into cafeterias or become more flexible regarding the amount of time teens may linger.

SCHOOLING

Education has historically been highly valued in Argentine society, and it is still important for the new generation of teens. Since at least 1916, families and youngsters have based their hopes for a successful life upon education. Although this attitude is threatened by the current neoliberal economic program, recent research shows that 59 percent of youngsters see education as a necessary step to getting a safe and stable job and se-curing their future (Sidicaro and Tenti Fanfani, 34).

Mandatory education begins at age 6 and ends at 14. The Argentine Constitution guarantees a free lay education for all who live in the coun-try. High schools—also called secondary schools—are free, although there are many private schools (primary and high schools, and schools for chil-dren with special needs) sponsored by churches or by ethnic or religious communities. In Buenos Aires, the two major public secondary schools belong to the University of Buenos Aires (National School of Buenos Aires and Superior School of Commerce Carlos Pellegrini). They are highly coveted by students as the academic preparation there is complete and prestigious. Acceptance at these schools is restricted. Candidates

Uniformed schoolgirls, Buenos Aires, Argentina. © A. Tovy/TRIP.

have to endure a demanding exam for which they prepare for an entire year. Students who graduate from these schools tend to have a better chance of being accepted at the university later on. In fact, they can take one additional year of high school and enroll directly in any academic program at the University of Buenos Aires.

Schools differ in their physical infrastructure depending on whether they are public or private. The differences are obvious. The curricula also differ substantially, especially concerning the lowest passing grade. The two schools administrated by the University of Buenos Aires—already mentioned above—are rigorous and students have to study a lot and in a timely manner in order to keep pace. Other public schools are less demanding. Among private schools there is also a significant difference between levels of study required from students. Each school—private or public—imposes a different study level on its student body. The most demanding require students to study at home, conduct research in libraries, and meet in small groups to complete specific assignments.

Promotion from one grade to the next is guaranteed when a certain level of proficiency is obtained in all subjects taught. Classes start in March and end in December each year. Grades are computed every trimester.

The typical school schedule is Monday to Friday, in the morning (8:00 A.M. to 1:00 P.M.) or afternoon (1:00 P.M. to 6:00 P.M.). There are also high schools with evening shifts (7:00 P.M. to 11:00 P.M.), attended especially by students who work during the day. Students who do not obtain the average grade required by the school have to take an exam in order to pass to the next level.

Due to the neoliberal economic agenda applied to Argentina over the last 10 years, retention has become a progressively difficult issue for educational authorities. Unquestionably, absenteeism has increased in the last few years, especially among lower-class students. In fact, lower-class families cannot afford the cost of books and school supplies. Consequently, instead of being able to support teens at school, they need the adolescents to work and help their families economically. Expenditures related to school, even free public schools, have become too high for working-class families. Of course, absenteeism is even higher in the outskirts and provinces.

Teens' misconduct at school has many causes. One is related to a perceived imbalance between the encyclopedic knowledge presented by the curriculum and the concrete demands and skills required to compete in the labor market. Most students complain, for example, that the school does not address important subjects such as sex education, AIDS, drugs, globalization, political events, and unemployment.

The structural unemployment that affects the country promotes different social problems. For example, many students who graduate from secondary school cannot find jobs and, in general, those who finally get them are overeducated. Many who do not complete secondary school experience difficulties in getting decent jobs in the labor market. Normally, they do not work while in high school. Students from middle-class families with higher incomes are usually the ones who go to private schools. Among private schools, some are more accessible (they are usually parochial, as they receive subsidies from the state and thus are less expensive), while others have higher rates. The latter are schools with double shifts and bilingual education: in most cases the languages taught are Spanish and English, except for schools of various ethnic communities (for example, Italian or German) that teach Spanish and the language spoken in the community.

The National University is still tuition-free but private universities, although costly, are also available for upper-class students. The University of Buenos Aires, with more than 140,000 students, is the largest in South America and is recognized internationally. In recent years, due to financial difficulties, authorities have tried to impose tuition and, for this reason, political discussion among students and between students and university authorities has become permanent.

According to social research, 98 percent of children have completed primary school, but only 45 percent have completed the secondary level. Only 20 percent finally graduate from universities (Sidicaro and Tenti Fanfani 1998, 37–38). Recently, due to economic pressures, many university graduates are looking for jobs abroad and, consequently, the country's best-educated people are going into exile. Doubtless, this phenomenon will promote new social problems in the future.

SOCIAL LIFE

The social life of young people in Argentina differs depending on social class and place of residence. It is worth emphasizing that teens' cultural habits seem to be rapidly transforming, in a country that traditionally had a large middle class that is being affected by new economic policies and progressively becoming marginalized and impoverished. Another important aspect is that teens born since 1983 have grown up entirely (and for the first time in Argentina) under democracy. According to social researchers, the fashion and other mass industries target this generation especially. Teens are constantly bombarded with advertising.

Unlike teens of previous generations, today's teens assimilate consumerism and individualism, and display a remarkable apathy toward politicians and partisanship: 94 percent of 18 year olds are not affiliated with any political party (Sidicaro and Tenti Fanfani 1998, 39). They do not feel represented by politicians and also reject politics because they perceive it as corrupt, bureaucratic, and stagnant. Still, unlike their parents, they seem to be interested in the country, its economic transformation, and the future of the nation. While many have no access to the Internet and other technologies, they are strongly impacted by the information revolution and an increasing lack of economic and cultural resources.

If teens can obtain jobs, they work; if they cannot, they steal. For them, it seems that there are no frontiers between what is legal and what is not. The increase in delinquency among young people shows that delinquents no longer come primarily from the marginalized sectors of the population.

On the contrary, young delinquents are educated, and vandalism and robbery are defined not as a countercultural experience, as in the United
States, but as a viable alternative during the economic crisis.

Many teens invent their own jobs. They are known as *trabajadores de fin
de semana* (weekend workers). Plazas and streets in Buenos Aires become
crowded with these craftsmen, clowns, diviners, living statues, mimes,
and jugglers. Others wash cars or walk dogs during the week. Some organize and appear in public events, especially during holidays. Buenos Aires
has an intense cultural life. Puppeteers, actors, and musicians populate
public spaces. Teens concentrate in the Teatro Municipal General San
Martin, in traditional neighborhoods (*barrios*), such as Recoleta, and in
suburban plazas, where high-quality shows of all kinds, mostly sponsored
by local governments and cultural institutions, are offered. The famous
Barrio de la Boca and other neighborhoods have their own theater
troupes and amusing parades comprising dancers, musicians, and sometimes, especially for carnival, floats that depict in allegorical terms scenes
that refer to political events. Most of these youths initiate their artistic careers by participating in these spectacles. For others, cultural activities
allow them to earn extra money on weekends.

In Buenos Aires, class differences can be felt even among teenagers.
They frequent places depending on where they live (which in turn is dependent on the social class they belong to). Middle-class teens make
friends with classmates and through sports clubs.

High schools in Argentina's capital are within a half-hour's travel from
students' homes. Students go to school by foot, bus, or subway. When not
at school, they usually spend a good part of their day at home doing homework, studying, watching TV, or chatting on the Internet. The most-
watched TV programs without any distinction of gender or age are music
videos. Depending on the rules of the high schools they attend—there is
a significant variation among the levels of the different high schools—
very often teenagers have to get together in groups of three or four to engage in research projects. In such cases, they prefer to work in libraries or
even in bars (McDonald's, for example).

Bulimia, anorexia, and other eating disorders are common among
teenagers, especially girls. According to a recent public poll organized by
ALUBA (Association for the Struggle against Bulimia and Anorexia), 26
percent of girls manifest eating disorders. Men are victims as well, although in smaller numbers. Being slim is imposed by the media as a fashion and as a mark of beauty, especially for women, to the point that the
government sanctioned a law that coerces clothing manufacturers to offer
a range of sizes and that requires stores to display them (Faiola 1997).

The latest generation is very homogeneous in its dress. Adolescents choose clothes based upon comfort and functionality. There is an interesting opposition between individualism and conformity. On the one hand, teens love to explore stores in which secondhand clothes are exhibited. They are fascinated with managing their look, by mixing and matching pieces taken from old clothes without a thought for gender or style. They try to be original, singular, and informal and, for that reason, spend their free time walking streets in search of exotic stores where something that is old might be recycled or restored.

On the other hand, teens want to belong to a group or, rather, to a tribe. The tribe is a cultural minority, a group that identifies its members by means of clothing, music, and gathering places (bars, discos, and pubs, for instance). If there is a degree of homogenization, it is not massive. The trend to be visible, special, and unique clashes with a need to be global and invisible. The amount of thought given to clothing—at least for upper-class teens—contrasts with an analogous tendency to unveil their bodies, sometimes simply as a way to erotically exhibit their skin. Teens are entranced with body painting, body piercing, and tattoos.

Unlike older upper-class teens, who select clothes according to the current fashion and who are obsessed with their looks, the latest generation rejects the dictatorship of fashion and is instead attracted by lower-class preferences in clothes and music. In general, middle-class youngsters wear leather jackets and comfortable shoes. Furthermore, they do not often attend gyms and have no prejudices about gender performance. Many males, for example, wear long hair and earrings, while females may sport masculine clothes and short hair. This is not seen as a sign of rebellion as was the case with previous generations. The new generation does not pretend to be guided by either efficiency or transgression.

With the exception of teens who receive a repressive religious education from their families, most adolescents start their sexual life during their teenage years. The average sexual initiation age—for both men and women—is considered to be between 15 and 17. According to interviews conducted in 1995, 67 percent of the teens confessed that they were not afraid of AIDS, and one can speculate that it is not due to unprotected sex but, on the contrary, to the fact that they know how to protect themselves. Parents have little or no control over that aspect of their children's lives (Sidicaro and Tenti Fanfani 1998, 46).

Parents are interfering less and less with the decisions of adolescents. Paradoxically, teens (especially middle-class ones) are becoming, on the one hand, increasingly dependent from an economic point of view and, on the other hand, more and more independent in their social lives and

choice of friends. The rising unemployment rate has produced a new social phenomenon: Whether one or both parents stay at home without
jobs, new family conflicts develop between parents and among parents
and children. In those cases, domestic violence is not unusual, with the
typical consequence that teens may run away from home or become involved in drugs and delinquency.

According to a poll organized in 1995 by UNICEF-Argentina, many
young people felt that they had been objects of social aggression. Forty
percent declared that they were not respected by society and 24 percent
did not feel respected by their teachers. Twenty-two percent had been
physically attacked in public places and 62 percent of youngsters who had
been arrested claimed to have been maltreated by the police (Sidicaro
and Tenti Fanfani 1998, 51).

Despite the well-known machismo of Argentinean culture in general,
and Buenos Aires in particular, many male teens—as happens in countries all over Latin America—are bisexual or, at least, have a homosexual
experience in their early youth. It is not unusual for males to go first to
straight discos with their girlfriends, and later to visit gay ones. Only ef-
feminate males are stigmatized as homosexuals. Lesbianism may be more
difficult to identify because body contact is common among girls and is acceptable. Argentinean men, as soon as they become friends, tend to kiss
each other only when they shake hands.

RECREATION

Sports are gender oriented: In Argentina, soccer is exclusively a male
sport. The national sports hero is internationally acclaimed soccer player
Diego Armando Maradona. Women do not overwhelmingly favor a specific sport. At school, girls routinely play hockey or volleyball. Although
some teenagers participate in sports such as tennis, swimming, gymnastics, and rowing, most are not keen on sports, especially when hard training is required. Only a few activities (like tennis and swimming) are
practiced by both males and females during adolescence.

ENTERTAINMENT

Among teenagers, the most common places for entertainment are discotheques. In general, most discos are for straight boys and girls. However,
in the last 10 years, gay bars and discos have proliferated and are well attended. Whether in gay or straight discos, teens are attracted by rock,
techno, hip-hop, drum and bass, progressive, trance, and jungle musical

styles. They also listen to pop music, along with Argentinean rock and Latino rhythms. They are attracted also to *cumbias villeras, cuartetazos,* and *bailantas* (cultural phenomena that, for the first time in the history of Argentina, come from the provinces and the lower class).

Most teens reject crowded clubs and mass tastes, with the exception of massive recitals at stadiums; yet, paradoxically, some tribes have their own discos. Tribes also have unique places and enjoy a variety of social scenes. These places—especially those attended by upper-class teens—are characterized by darkened rooms and a common costume and language. They dance alone or close to someone, but with their bodies separate. A dance partner's gender is not important: The main goal is to enjoy dancing. Dance seems to be a monologue without style. Teens are free to dance as they like, with no rules. To some degree, these discos are part of the global culture.

Some youths continue the revival of tango. Many tango regularly in public spaces (pubs, plazas, and homes, all of them known as *bailongos*). Unlike rock and *cumbias,* the tango is a very sophisticated dance, with strict rules to follow. It is a dialogue between two partners, who merge into one through a controlled choreography that requires many hours of learning and training.

On weekends, disco-goers usually go to bed late at night (or, more accurately, early in the morning, since discos stay open until 6:30 A.M.) and then sleep until early afternoon. A distinctive characteristic of teenage culture in Buenos Aires is that many discos open after midnight. Although laws prohibit minors (those under 18 years of age) in such clubs, control is in fact not very strict. This is an issue for parents and often leads to conflicts as they try to control what their children do during these night retreats. Some parents are more rigorous and others are more relaxed. It depends on family tradition, the parents' character, the children's personalities, and how well the parents know their children's friends. The nightclub schedule is typical for the 18-and-over clubs. Adolescents between 13 and 18 attend clubs with a matinee schedule that close at midnight. Once again, control is not very strict, especially for females. After the age of 15 or 16, girls can easily access clubs that are technically for adults only.

Although in those places a considerable amount of alcohol is consumed, a main reason for going late is economic. In fact, teens usually meet at 11:00 P.M. around liquor stores (known as *maxi-kioskos* or drugstores [some use the English term]). In those places teens may buy beer and drink as much as they want because a large bottle of beer (US$1) is relatively inexpensive. It is cheaper than at the disco, where beer is typically sold at $5 per glass. Thus, they drink before going to dance and for this reason they go to discos late. Another reason for going so late has to do with transportation. In general, although Buenos Aires is a city where public transportation operates 24 hours a day, it is safer to use the system after 7:00 A.M. Buses, metros, and trains expand their daily schedule early in the morning and teens take advantage of this service.

Many teenagers smoke cigarettes and some smoke marijuana. In dance clubs, consumption of alcohol and drugs is high and is progressively increasing, but is not yet as common as it is in the United States. There are sometimes fights among rival groups, and club bouncers, who determine who may or may not enter, might use violence in their discrimination.

Generally speaking, teens do not read books and do not like newspapers and news in general. They repeat what they hear about what is going on in the world. The latest generation is convinced that real power is beyond the national borders and that the country is manipulated from outside. For these reasons, they prefer their already-known, private worlds and only admit what is entertaining. Thus, they generally only read popular magazines.

Some pubs in Buenos Aires are revitalizing the tradition of literary salons (salones literarios), a tradition that was practiced during the nineteenth century and has survived in some provinces. In the pubs, young people might introduce their poems and music to a select audience of peers. They drink while they listen and there are sometimes books around to be read. Some pubs have also incorporated computers that allow teens to chat on the Internet while they are drinking and listening to music. In general, reading may occur if it is brought into a performance experience. Computers sit side by side with candles, and microphones and erotic poetry merge in a scented atmosphere.

At the cinema, teens prefer American movies. Sporadically they select Argentinean, European, or Latin American films only when those movies have been emphatically promoted. They rarely go to the theater. Entertainment is restricted to video games, sports, or rock concerts. Unlike what happens with movies, they tend to support national bands because they can identify with the songs' rebellious messages that, paradoxically, are supported by the music industry.

Many teens, especially those who have grown up under democracy, are very supportive of human rights and consequently participate in many nongovernmental organizations (NGOs). Many teens are involved in solidarity deeds and volunteer with civic organizations that help people with disabilities, poor children, or retired adults, for instance. The Grupo de Arte Callejero (Street Art Group) deserves special mention. It is composed of young people working for HIJOS, an organization dedicated to identifying children whose parents were made to disappear by the military during the dictatorship, and who were subsequently given in fraudulent adoption to new parents, selected primarily from among military families.

RELIGIOUS PRACTICES AND CULTURAL CEREMONIES

The cultural heterodoxy of cosmopolitan cities, such as Buenos Aires, does not allow the existence of a traditional folk or religious holiday in which teenagers participate on a massive scale. There are various religions practiced. Christianity and Judaism together constitute the vast majority. However, there is not a single religious celebration that might be identified as an expression of collective participation. With Catholicism, however, as the official religion of the nation, holidays (like Christmas) are regularly observed by most. In general, religious holidays are celebrated at home or in temples. Usually, during those days, teens share only lunch or dinner with their families and later meet friends in bars and discos. Teens' participation in religious observance is decreasing. Other traditional celebrations, like the *quinceañeras*, a 15th birthday celebration for girls, are also disappearing.

CONCLUSION

The unprecedented political events during the last weeks of December 2002, when middle-class youth—for the first time in many years—massively and peacefully protested against the president and other government officials at the National Congress, require serious discussion. Teens' relationship with politics is a very controversial issue. Historically, the most recent generations grew up during and/or after the last and cruelest dictatorship (1976–1983), which demonized political participation and originated massive exiles and the disappearance of more than 30,000 people. Activism among students was strongly affected by state terrorism. As a result, teens show a conspicuous skepticism about social transformation and revolutionary action. They trust no institution. Despite a trend toward the political left, more than 40 percent are undecided between it and the opposing right. They do not openly manifest political or partisan preferences. However, after several years of formal democracy, student organizations have slowly started to discuss political issues and to organize student councils of representation within the education system. Most of these organizations have become active in supporting workers on strike, unions, and diverse resistance movements, such as Madres de Plaza de Mayo.

In general, researchers agree on identifying two groups: On the one hand, there is a sector that points to neoconservatism. These teens work hard and look for professional success. They also believe that a good project, one with a controlled schedule, is feasible even in a country where economic and social instability is the norm. On the other hand, there is another sector that is far from believing in the laws of the market. They are inclined to creative alternatives, especially those related to art. What seems to unify both sectors (as is very well documented in the latest Argentinean movies with teens as central characters and as manifested in teens' participation during the protests in December 2002), is their rejection of authoritarianism and political corruption and their subordination to technological domination.

Beyond this ideological differentiation, there is a sector of teens brutally marginalized by the economic neoliberal agenda imposed upon the country. They belong to the other nation, the no-longer-invisible Argentina. They comprise a desperate tribe known as *chicos de la calle* (street children). They can be seen everywhere in Buenos Aires and surrounding cities. Like their upper- and middle-class peers (although for different reasons), they do not belong to specific neighborhoods and do not seem to be worried about their national identity but rather about surviving. They sleep in plazas, under freeways, and in subways. They have no choice of clothes: They put on what they can get from garbage cans. They do not send e-mails nor are they admitted into decorated discos. They sell what they can, wash cars, prostitute themselves, or simply beg and live on charity. They live and die anonymously.

Filmmakers and novelists are increasingly portraying youths in very different ways than does TV. On television, teens always appear dancing, as if that were their exclusive preoccupation. Their idols become fetishes that are easily replaced and endlessly repeated. Reality shows promote an ideology of exclusion, punishment, and a suspicious justice based not on laws but on sentimental opinion and identification. More sophisticated programs are a symptom of the kind of knowledge that is required by the postmodern society: superficial, encyclopedic data mixed with frivolous updated information deliberately promoted by television itself, with puzzlers like the name of the latest girlfriend of a publicized singer. In *telenovelas* (soap operas), teens deal with love as a cliché that has nothing to do with the way young people experience love in their real lives. On the contrary, novelists and filmmakers are more interested in reporting the economic, social, or cultural misery and defenselessness in which youngsters live in Argentina. Early novels by Enrique Medina, such as *Las tumbas* (*The Tombs*, 1971)—filmed by Javier Torre in 1991—and *Perros de la noche* (*Dogs of the Night*, 1978)—filmed by Teo Kofman in 1986—explore the economic, social, cultural, and institutional violence exercised on young people. Award-winning, recent films such as *Martin H*, directed by Adolfo Aristarain in 1997; *Pizza, birra, faso* (*Pizza, Beer, Cigarettes*, 1997), directed by Bruno Stagnaro and Adrian Caetano; *Mundo grúa* (*Crane World*, 1999), directed by Pablo Trapero; and *La ciénaga* (*The Swamp*, 2000), directed by Lucrecia Martel, show a desolate country in which youngsters confront their last resistances and their lack of a future. Finally, award-winning novels by Diego Pazskowsky (*Tesis sobre un homicidio* [*Thesis on a Homicide*], 1999); Pablo Toledo (*Se esconde tras los ojos* [*Hidden behind the Eyes*] 2000); and Patricia Sagastiazábal (*Un secreto para Julia* [*A Secret for Julia*], 2000) focus respectively on how young people debate their identities in a hopeless challenge to the law; the corrupted, mass-media system infiltrating personal and social relationships; and the impact of hidden secrets of the past upon a new generation.

Intellectuals have recently explored how social behavior, especially teens' behavior, must be understood as it relates to technology and mass media. Some scholars have pointed out how audiovisual experiences may change the way people perceive or construct reality. While formal education is still based on printed books and the acquisition of writing and reading skills, technology promotes the idea that by operating computers people can successfully achieve great goals, especially in the labor market. This utopian assumption devaluates traditional education and creates conflicts among schools and students. TV and video games also promote an artificial sense of time and history. On the one hand, technology is characterized by its speed. Fast food, fast communication, and fast contacts define fast culture. Thus, history is easily reduced to a permanent present. Although the idea of a fast culture appears as a democratizing force—in the sense that everyone has the same opportunities to access technology—it is not difficult to demonstrate that only a small sector of the population has access to technology and its power. Poor people, especially poor teens, are progressively marginalized from technology. However, technology's impact on culture, even though access to it is not democratic, has become strong and definitive in all of Argentinean culture during the last two decades. On the one hand, technology allows youths access to music and fashions from around the world. On the other hand, technology connects them to peers spread all over the world and defines local communities (whether virtual or not). It has not yet been researched enough how communication technology has simultaneously imposed the paradoxical enlargement of the imagined nation and a strong sense of local belonging, which, lately, has turned into a desperate feeling of imprisonment and a desire to emigrate. In any case, a perception of centrality and a definite nationality, as it happened at least until the '70s, is no longer available.

Thus, at least two consequences can be detected in youth culture. First, teens' fascination with what has been called retro. The past is recycled without its former critical revolutionary potential. Fashion, for example, will look back to the '60s or '70s for inspiration, but put aside the insurgent, insubordinate, and even anarchistic meaning it had for those former generations. Pubs and discos in Buenos Aires—especially those attended by upper- and middle-class teens—are decorated according to retro-techno-medieval-gothic scenographies derived from video games, comics, and films. The revolutionary Che Guevara became an icon easily commodified by mass media on T-shirts and other products without any sense of political threat, a nostalgic recuperation of the past without the history. The future is envisioned as a predictable serial repetition. Secondly, there is a new familiarity that is no longer attached to parenthood. Teens choose to belong to tribes by recognizing traits that identify them with a group, giving them a sense of belonging while at the same time differentiating them from each other.

RESOURCE GUIDE

Abiad, Pablo. "Casi la mitad de los condenados tiene 25 años o menos y son primerizos." *Clarín*, April 7, 2002. http://www.clarin.com/diario/hoy/s-04015.htm.

Appadurai, Arjun. *Modernity at Large. Cultural Dimensions of Globalization.* Minneapolis: University of Minnesota Press, 1998.

Belloc, Bárbara. *Tribus Porteñas. Conejillos de Indias y Blancos Ratones: Un breviario de Zoología Urbana.* Buenos Aires: Perfil Libros, 1998.

Bergero, Adriana J., and Fernando Reati, eds. *Memoria colectiva y políticas de olvido. Argentina y Uruguay, 1970–1990.* Rosario, Argentina: Beatriz Viterbo Editora, 1997.

"Clase 83: Radiografía de una generación nacida y criada en democracia." *Clarín*, August 12, 2001. http://www.clarin.com/diario/hoy/p-292017.htm.

Daneri, Alberto. "Solos frente al espejo." *Viva*, 13 January 2002, 14.

"Entre el temor, el desencanto y la esperanza." *Clarín*, August 12, 2001. http://www.clarin.com/diario/hoy/p-292020.htm.

Faiola, Anthony. "Argentina: Una de cada 10 jóvenes padece bulimia y anorexia." *Clarín*, July 5, 1997. http://www.geocities.com/mercurioinforma/artic argentina.htm.

Foster, David W. *Contemporary Argentine Cinema.* Columbia: University of Missouri Press, 1992.

———. *Violence in Argentine Literature. Cultural Responses to Tyranny.* Columbia: University of Missouri Press, 1995.

Gentile, Laura. "Asociaciones de amigos: los que todavía trabajan por amor al arte." *Clarín Cultura*, 13 January 2002, 42.

Giberti, Eva, et al. *Hijos del rock: Una mirada psicoanalítica sobre los adolescentes y el rock.* Buenos Aires: Editorial Losada, 1996.

Giberti, Eva, and Ana María Fernández, eds. *La mujer y la violencia invisible.* Buenos Aires: Editorial Sudamericana, 1989.

"Historias solidarias de chicos que ven la realidad." *Clarín*, August 12, 2001. http://www.clarin.com/diario/hoy/s-04401.htm.

Kolesnikov, Patricia. "Claves para comprender el lenguaje de los más jóvenes." *Clarín* 23 December 2001, 46–47.

"Los jóvenes dicen todo lo que piensan." *Clarín*, August 17, 2001. http://www.clarin.com/diario/hoy/s-03901.htm.

Poderti, Alicia. *Interpelaciones. Cultura Tecnológica, Re-ingeniería Educativa y Empoderamiento Regional.* Salta, Argentina: Consejo de Investigación de la Universidad Nacional de Salta, 2001.

Rodriguez, Carlos E. "Muerte en la cuna: La fórmula para estar seguro." *El País,* May 1999. http://www.madres.org/periodico/may99/seguridad/seguri1.htm.

Sarlo, Beatriz. *Escenas de la vida postmoderna. Intelectuales, arte y videocultura en la Argentina.* Buenos Aires: Ariel, 1994.

———. *Instantáneas. Medios, ciudad y costumbres en el fin de siglo.* Buenos Aires: Ariel, 1996.

———. *Tiempo presente. Notas sobre el cambio de una cultura.* Buenos Aires: Siglo XXI Editores Argentina, 2001.

Sidicaro, Ricardo, and Emilio Tenti Fanfani, eds. *La Argentina de los jóvenes. Entre la indiferencia y la indignación.* Buenos Aires: UNICEF/Losada, 1998.

Nonfiction

Foster, David William, Melissa Fitch Lockhart, and Darrel B. Lockhart. *Culture and Customs of Argentina.* Westport, Conn.: Greenwood Press, 1998.

Lewis, Daniel K. *The History of Argentina.* Westport, Conn.: Greenwood Press, 2001.

Web Sites

http://csf.colorado.edu/argentina/authors/indexsp.html
Autores Jóvenes de Argentina (Young Argentine Writers' Page).

http://www.geocities.com/jovenes_catolicos/argentina.html
Grupos juveniles de Hispanoamerica y el mundo.

http://www.hispaniconline.com/links/
Hispanic Online: Links and Contacts.

http://www.haruth.com/JewsArgentina.html
Jewish Argentina.

http://www.monografias.com/trabajos/jovenesdictadura/jovenesdictadura.shtml
Los jóvenes durante la última dictadura argentina.

http://dir.yahoo.com/Regional/Countries/Argentina/
Places in Argentina.

Pen Pal Information

http://ar.gay.com/
Gay.com Interactive Services in Spanish.

http://www.kidlink.org/cgi-bin/htsearch
Kidlink: Empowers children to build global social and knowledge networks.

http://170.224.13.168/asp/quickstart.asp
Pen Pal Argentina.

http://www.terra.com.ar/
Terra: Canales y Servicios en español.

Chapter 2

BRAZIL

Lizbeth Souza-Fuertes

INTRODUCTION

Brazil lies in eastern South America, bordering the Atlantic Ocean. It shares borders with Uruguay, Argentina, Paraguay, Bolivia, Peru, Colombia, Venezuela, Guayana, Surinam, and French Guayana. Brazil was discovered by Portuguese explorer Pedro Álvares Cabral (and Portuguese has been the official language of Brazil to this day). In 1822, Dom Pedro I became Brazil's first emperor. After his abdication, his successor (Dom Pedro II) reigned until 1889, at which time Brazil became a republic.

Since then, Brazil has suffered several military interventions as well as periods of democracy. Currently its president is Luiz Inácio Lula da Silva, who began his term on the first of January of 2003. He is a member of the workers' party (Partido Trabalhista) and a unionist. One of his goals is to combat hunger through the Zero Hunger program, which became effective at the end of January 2003. He hopes industrialized countries will take on this task as well. Fernando Henrique Cardoso, the past president, is a recognized researcher and long-time university professor. He became minister of finance during a period of rampant inflation in the 1980s and '90s and subsequently created the Real Plan, which brought inflation down to single-digit numbers. In 1987, inflation was out of control at 337.9 percent; in 1997 it had gone down to 4.1 percent. Consequently, the consumer price index decreased to 5.5 that same year (CEPAL 2000b, 214).

Brazil's currency is the real. Its economy is based mostly on the export of coffee, minerals, fruit, petroleum, and manufactured products. Brazil's industry has developed intensively since the 1960s. Another means of expansion has been tourism, especially in Rio de Janeiro, Salvador in the northeast, and in colonial cities, such as Ouro Preto, as well as in Iguassu Falls.

The estimated birth rate for 2001 was close to 18.5 percent, while the death rate was only one half of that, at approximately 9.3 percent. The average life expectancy at birth for the year 2000 was 62.9 years (World Fact Book, 3) and the average infant mortality rate was 38.1 (per 1,000 live births) (CEPAL 2000, 51). In the year 2000, the economically active population was approximately 80 million (72). Brazil's urban population is one of the highest in Latin America. Although a few important cities, such as São Paulo and Brasília, are located in the interior, the majority lie near the coast.

Brazil is a mixture of many diverse ethnic groups, mainly of Portuguese, African, and Indian origin. One can also add other important groups, such as the Japanese, Italians, Arabs, and Germans, who came mostly at the end of the nineteenth century or during the first half of the twentieth, as a result of numerous emigrations.

Understanding Brazil's ethnic makeup and distribution is key to understanding that country. The northeast consists primarily of mixed Indian and Europeans (*mestizo*) and African peoples. The central and southern coasts, where most European immigrants live, are highly developed socially, economically, and culturally. Brazil is the most unequal country in the world in terms of human development.

While a small upper class controls the major businesses and owns most of the land, in general Brazilian teens are not aware of the problems their country faces on a daily basis. Many live and study abroad. The Brazilian middle class has been downsized, causing its role in the economy to diminish, and youths have seen their educational and employment opportunities diminish. Living in a world of poverty, the working class suffers. Nevertheless, the percentage of poor and indigent families by rural and urban areas has decreased. Poverty has seriously affected the lives of youths in general, especially those in rural areas. In 1996, the poverty level among rural children and teenagers was as follows: 0–5 years: 72 percent; 6–12 years: 71 percent; 13–19 years: 60 percent; while of the total population, rural poverty levels were at 56 percent (CEPAL 2000b, 179).

Brazil has a young population. In 2000, 28.8 percent were in the 0–14 years bracket and 36.5 percent in the 15–34 years bracket. These high percentages have been taken into consideration by the Catholic and Protestant churches and they have become an anchor for the young, guiding them in moral issues and defending family structure and values as well as voicing their concerns about social injustices.

Approximately 80 percent of Brazilians declare themselves to be Catholic. A characteristic of the Catholic Church during recent decades is its stance in favor of the poor and marginalized, in relation to the young and to women in general.

Both the Catholic and Protestant churches have played a role in the institutionalized violence that has taken place in Brazil as a consequence of the enormous social inequalities as well as political corruption that, in turn, has generated social violence, so intense as to be almost of epidemic proportion. The church has been immersed in the corruption and political instability that have dominated Brazil during the last three decades. Violence and the high degree of delinquency that dominates Brazilian society reflect the general situation today. Another problem is drugs. Although not a drug-producing country, Brazil is a consumer and, of more concern, it serves as a link for incoming and outgoing Colombian and Bolivian drugs.

Unemployment also plays a direct role in the lives of teens. In 1999, the six largest metropolitan areas, including São Paulo, Rio de Janeiro, and Porto Alegre, had an unemployment rate of 7.6 percent, while the rate for 15–24 year olds was 17.3 percent, with women having fewer jobs than men. The labor system in Brazil, as in many Latin American countries, is quite different from that in the United States. In Brazil there are few part-time jobs. While, in the United States, an average teenager might work at a local grocery store, a department store, or a McDonald's for a few hours a week after school, in Brazil such a thing is unheard of. Part-time jobs are rare, not only for teenagers but for all ages. Hiring full-time workers means an employer must provide full benefits, 30 days of vacation, and up to four months of paid maternity leave. While labor laws protect workers to a larger extent than in the United States, there are fewer jobs to come by because of the system.

TYPICAL DAY

A typical day in the life of a teenager begins with breakfast, which routinely consists of hot milk with coffee (*café com leite*), fresh bread, fruit, and yogurt. When it's time for school, students usually take public transportation, either a bus or a minibus (in-between a taxi and bus in size). Many times parents will drive their teens to school, which is generally located from 10 to 20 minutes from home. On weekends, teenagers can sleep in. At the elementary and middle school levels, two schedules are offered: morning and afternoon. At most high schools and universities, three schedules may be offered: one from 7:30 a.m. until 12:45 P.M., a second from 1:30 to 6:45 P.M., and a third from 7:00 to 11:45 P.M.

Students in middle school usually take courses such as Portuguese, mathematics, science, history, geography, physical education, art, and English or Spanish (as foreign languages). In high school they study Portuguese, Brazilian literature, mathematics, physics, chemistry, biology, history, geography, foreign languages (mostly English, but in the last five years Spanish has also become a popular language of study), and physical education. At many private (religious) schools, students also take classes in religion, philosophy, art, music, and political science.

After returning home from school, students have lunch with their families. Lunch is the main meal of the day and most people have two hours off for it. A typical lunch includes rice and beans, meat or fish, salad, vegetables, and sometimes pasta. Dessert is fruit or one of the many Brazilian desserts typical in that country, such as *pavê* (a kind of ice cream layered with cookies), *pudim* (flan, a thick custard), and *brigadeiros* (small, round sweets made of chocolate and condensed milk), to name a few. After lunch, students do homework, play sports, or go to private lessons (such as English, swimming, ballet, music, computers, or sports). In the afternoons, many teenagers use computers to surf the Internet, read e-mail, and spend time in chat rooms. They may visit with friends at a local mall or in each other's homes. In the early evening they have dinner with their families and watch television. Bedtime is around 11 P.M. On weekends, teenagers go shopping, to the movies, on trips with their friends and/or families, and to local cafés.

In the upper class, activities and schedules tend to be similar but those teens usually attend private schools. At the high school and university levels many are sent abroad, especially to the United States, for their studies. In the working class, many teenagers drop out of school in order to work and help support their family. A few drop out only to spend time with friends or play sports. There are also many teenagers in the *favelas* (slums) and others who simply live on the streets. They lack adequate nutrition and if they attend school, it is usually not for very long. They have trouble integrating into society and in large part will constitute the future generations of marginalized people who often live on the verge of criminal activities.

FAMILY LIFE

Brazilians follow the Iberian cultural tradition of gathering as a family for lunch and dinner whenever possible. During the week, different schedules might not allow all family members to be together daily for lunch, which is the main meal, but most gather for dinner. It is common to have extended family members over for a meal. Lunch usually takes place between 12:00 and 2:00 P.M., when most people have a lunch break. Dinner is around 7:00 P.M., as the workday ends at 6:00. Women generally prepare the meals. Food is usually prepared from scratch, by either the mother or a maid (called an *empregada* or *faxineira*. *Empregadas* are full-time employees while *faxineiras* come in for one or more days a week to work for several hours). Family members converse during meals. There is freedom for all to ask questions and give opinions. It is also common for the family to watch television after dinner.

As with most Latin American societies, the Brazilian family is patriarchal. In many families, only the father works, although the percentage of middle-class families in which both parents work is high.

The father's role is a dominant one: He makes or approves all important decisions. Nevertheless, mothers (and women in general) have gained more recognition and prestige in society, not only through their traditional role as homemaker but also in the professional world. Decisions related to the future of the children are usually made by both parents. Much depends upon the cultural and social class of the parents.

It is always difficult to make generalizations about Brazilians because not only are economic levels and geographic location determinants of one's social and cultural class, they also establish the kinds of relationships that take place among family members. Coastal cities in central and southern Brazil are almost European in nature due to their economic development as well as their social and cultural levels. In those areas, dialogue among parents and children is no different from that among European families. That is, the communication lines are clearly open.

In rural areas, which are traditionally more conservative, the relationship between parents and children may be more limited. There is a tendency for both parents to work outside the home in urban areas, as is the trend in other countries. This directly affects the upbringing of children, as control and communication take on different aspects. Rural areas have not been as affected by this, because often both parents work on the farm or the mother is a homemaker while the children help out as needed.

To be of legal drinking age, one has to be 18 years old in Brazil. However, this is simply a theoretical restriction. It is not something people are concerned about, nor is it rigidly applied. Teenagers are allowed to drink at a younger age, but at the same time they are not encouraged to do so. They might have wine with a meal, if the family does. Nevertheless, since there is not a strict restriction on drinking, in general teenagers do not overdo it.

The legal driving age is 18, but the percentage of teenagers who own cars is extremely low. Usually upper-class teenagers are the few who might actually be driving their own cars at 18. It is rare to find families that own more than one car, as there is a vast public transportation system in most cities and there is no real need to own many cars, even when the family can afford more than one. Therefore, not many teenagers drive.

TRADITIONAL AND NONTRADITIONAL FOOD DISHES

Even though American fast foods entered the Brazilian market during the last decade, what teenagers usually eat are traditional Brazilian foods, which are nutritious and varied. These include a variety of dishes and basic products; some (such as rice and beans) are popular throughout the country while others are regional. On the coast it is common to eat fresh fish prepared in a variety of ways. The immense varieties of fruit, vegetables, and seasonings in Brazil are sold at open markets, usually on a specific day of the week, where everybody goes to buy the freshest produce possible. Grocery stores are where people buy food on a daily basis.

For Christmas and other festivities special meals are prepared. Brazilian food is based largely upon Portuguese and African culinary traditions, although there is a small degree of indigenous influence. From the Portuguese, Brazil inherited methods for preparing fish and stew. From the Africans they inherited the use and combinations of different seasonings as well as a special technique for frying food. Some foods of African origin are *farofa de dendê*, made of yucca and dendê oil; fried bananas, *sarapatel*, made of pork gizzards; and *arroz de hauca*, which consists of rice, dried meat, and vegetables. African culinary influences occur mostly in the northeastern region.

Brazil's most typical dish is *feijoada*, a combination of Portuguese and African culinary traditions. Its main ingredients are black beans, several different cuts of pork (such as sausage and bacon), onions, and garlic. *Feijoada* is cooked for several hours and then served with rice, yucca flour, sautéed collard greens, and oranges. In southern Brazil, more specifically in the state of Rio Grande do Sul, the typical dish is *churrasco*, a barbecue of meat grilled on very large skewers. It shares similarities with the *churrasco* prepared in Argentina and Uruguay. In the state of Bahia, where one sees a very clear influence of African cuisine, some of the dishes are *peixe na folha da bananeira* (fish rolled in a banana leaf), *casquinha de caranguejo* (fried crab with eggs), and *carne de sol com purê de aipim* (a meat dish prepared with yucca puree). Dishes that have a clear Portuguese influence include onion and cheese soup; *caldeirada de peixe*, a dish prepared with shellfish, fish, and tomatoes, along with potatoes and other vegetables; *bacalhau assado na brasa* (grilled cod); and *arroz-de-carreteiro*, rice made with meat and vegetables. Strange as it might seem, teenagers in general love these dishes. What they also like very much are the rich and varied Brazilian desserts, such as *bolo-rei* (king cake), made with wheat flour, butter, and fruit; *fios de ovos* (egg threads), made with eggs and sugar; *canjica* (white hominy), made with white corn, sugar, and cinnamon; *compota de mamão verde e abacaxi* (a sweet made with unripe fruit and sugar); *doce de abóbora*, a pumpkin jam; *suspiros*, meringue, made of egg whites and sugar; *baba de moça*, a dessert made with coconut and oil; *trocinhos do céu* (bits of heaven), made of sugar, butter, eggs, chopped cashews, and wheat flour; and *doce de leite*, a thick mixture of cooked milk, sugar, and cinnamon. All meals in Brazil end with a *cafezinho*, strong Brazilian coffee served in a demitasse cup with one or two teaspoons of sugar added.

For holidays and festivities, special meals are prepared. At Christmas, baked pork tenderloin; turkey; *camarões recheados* (fried stuffed shrimp with vegetables); and *bacalhau ao forno* (baked cod with potatoes, olive oil, and vegetables) might be served.

SCHOOLING

Elementary and middle school education are obligatory and no doubt the number of students has increased significantly during the last two decades, but it should be more, according to Brazil's economic level. The literacy rate for the population aged 15 and over was 83.3 percent in the year 2001 (World Fact Book 2001, 4). Enrollment rates decline in middle and high school. There are many dropouts at both levels and, consequently, not many Brazilians continue their studies at the university level.

Gender discrimination or even discrimination among ethnic groups rarely exists in the educational domain. What one does find is a marked difference between public and private education at the high school level. Private education at this level is expensive and elitist and most private schools are church-related (largely Catholic or sometimes Protestant). For the most part, teachers are well prepared and competent, although many lack motivation in their work due to low salaries and a lack of educational resources. In high school, classes maintain a balance between the sciences and humanities. Many core courses taken by freshmen and sophomores at the American university level are studied at the high school level in Brazil. Requirements to pass each year are rigorous. At the university level, after taking the entrance exam (*vestibular*), which consists of a five-day test of all subjects covered in high school, the student begins to take classes in his or her major in the first year of study. The student

Brazilian girls hang out outside school. Courtesy of Lizbeth Souza-Fuertes.

spends all four or five years of university study focusing on his or her cho-sen major.

The educational system is often unequal and inefficient; it is a system in which one will find excellent schools contrasting with some in very poor conditions. In rural areas, for example, school facilities tend to be basic. One consequence is that during the last two decades enrollment in pri-vate schools has been much higher than in public schools. This is because public schools have deteriorated and those families who can afford to do so send their children to private schools.

Students from private schools are better prepared to take the entrance examination (*vestibular*) required of all students entering a university. It is a highly competitive exam and students are classified according to their choice of major. For example, if a student's first choice of major is com-puter science, he or she will compete with all the other students who have computer science as their first choice (and not against all students taking the *vestibular*). Students with less competitive majors have anywhere from 20 or more candidates seeking one opening, while some students trying to pass the exam in a specific major compete with over 100 candidates.

One aspect that Brazil has developed at the university level is schedul-ing flexibility. Most universities offer evening courses as many students work during the day and go to school at night.

SOCIAL LIFE

A characteristic of Brazilian teenagers in general is that they tend to have an excellent rapport with their peers and families. Some private institutions have separate schools for males and females. This tradition was common until the 1970s, but nowadays it is more rare. Teenagers are constantly together, attending school, studying together, or playing sports. They also meet at dance clubs, cafés, sports clubs, on the beach, and at the mall.

Parents usually do not interfere with their children's friendships or relationships. In the upper class there is concern, however, about whom their children interact with, as parents want to maintain the social status of the family by having their children marry into the same class. On the other hand, although there is no strict social structure that would prevent communication among social classes, the fact is that teenagers from the middle and upper classes rarely socialize with those of the lower class.

Dance clubs are some of the many places where teens meet. In the past, Brazilian and Latin American popular dances were offered at dance clubs. Nowadays, popular music is influenced mostly by American music, although national dances such as the samba, *frevo*, and maxixe are commonly danced. A few years ago the *lambada*, a dance born in northern Brazil, became an international craze.

Teenagers (and adults) follow European fashion. Both young men and women wear blue jeans and T-shirts. Females also wear blouses and skirts or dresses. It is more common to see Brazilian women in dresses and skirts than among their American counterparts. It is not socially acceptable to wear shorts on the streets unless one lives in a beach city. Otherwise khakis, jeans, dresses, and skirts are the norm. Private (and some public) schools at the elementary level usually require uniforms. At the high school level that custom has slowly been eliminated, with few schools requiring uniforms, although they do have dress codes.

Parents are generally open-minded about what their children wear and, again, the city in which they live dictates the code. Beach cities, such as Rio, Recife, and Fortaleza, tend to be more liberal about what clothing is acceptable. Also, from Rio up to the north of the country, temperatures are usually above 60 degrees all year round, which calls for summer clothing most of the time.

From a young age Brazilians learn to follow current fashion in clothing and there has always been a concern about having a perfect figure, due mostly to the fact that so many people live on the coast and wear swimming suits frequently. Young Brazilians are fascinated by the prospect of becoming fashion models, like Gisele Bündchen. Recently, for example, there were 128 candidates registered to take the entrance exam for each opening available at the Medical School at the University of São Paulo (one of the most prestigious schools in the country). However, at the auditions to become a top model at the Ford modeling agency, there were 2,600 candidates for every opening. The Elite modeling agency experienced the same thing. All candidates were between 13 and 19 years old. Not only are teens fascinated by the possibility of a modeling career, but a criterion has also been established for the ideal model: tall (over 5'7"), very thin, elegant, and white. What is most interesting is that people with these characteristics are not the norm in Brazil, except in the southern region. Brazilian females view models as icons of glamour and wealth and, perhaps, being one as an easy way of climbing to the top of the social ladder.

Premarital sex occurs on a regular basis among teenagers, even though families teach their children the traditional value of abstinence whenever possible. There is a large amount of information available to teenagers about sexual activity and its possible consequences. Abortion does not appear to be a common practice, but since it is illegal there are not enough trustworthy data to confirm the numbers of abortions that may actually take place.

RECREATION

Sports are engaged in on a regular basis, in cities and rural areas alike. Without a doubt, the most popular sport in Brazil is soccer. In Brazil, the only country to have won five World Cups, boys learn to play soccer as soon as they are able to run. More women have begun participating in recent decades.

Teens also play other sports, such as tennis, basketball, and swimming. In coastal areas, most sports relate to the beach and sea: Swimming, sailing, beach soccer, and beach volleyball are examples. The fact that schools are not, in general, equipped with sophisticated sports equipment does not prevent students from playing sports. It is important to keep in mind that sports play a different role in schools in Brazil than they do in the United States. In Brazil, physical education and sports are part of the school curriculum. However, they do not create teams to compete against other schools, nor are professional sports developed through the school system. Anybody seriously interested in playing a specific sport will look for the equivalent club to take lessons and play after school.

Since soccer is Brazil's main sport, soccer players are usually the most popular sports heroes. A classic example is Pelé, widely considered the best soccer player of all time. Another sports hero is tennis player Gustavo Kuerten. He became the number one tennis player on the ATP (Brazilian Tennis Association) list. Excelling at sports is a quick and easy way to rise in social class.

Female role models include Hortensia, an outstanding volleyball player.

ENTERTAINMENT

The average Brazilian teenager has many entertainment options. As mentioned, some of the most common activities include meeting at cafés, malls, dance clubs, or city and neighborhood sports clubs.

Television programs of interest to teens consist mainly of Brazilian soap operas, sitcoms (from both Brazil and the United States), and comedies, but specific shows for teenagers are more difficult to come by. The most popular children's program, known even at the international level, is *Xuxa*, performed by Maria de Graça Meneghel.

Teens can watch all of the national television channels only with an antenna. Many American movies, dubbed into Portuguese, are shown on TV. The main Brazilian television channel is TV Globo, which offers a gamut of programming. It is the fourth-largest channel in the world and it exports 85 percent of Brazilian soap operas to many other countries. Soap operas, with their reenactments of novels, folk stories, and other traditions, are an important aspect of Brazilian television. They are on during prime time, from 6:00 to 9:00 P.M. every weekday. Cable is also readily available, with many international channels.

Traditional and modern Brazilian, classical, Latin American, rock, and American pop music provide all kinds of entertainment for teens. Some Brazilians try to maintain folklore and cultural traditions, although that movement is stronger in the northeast. In general teenagers like to go to dance clubs or to parties at friends' houses, where they also dance. Some popular dances are the samba, *frevo*, *axé*, *maracatu*, *pastorinhas*, and *coco de roda*.

In Brazil there is a strong interest in literature for adolescents. Some well-known books are *Depois daquela viagem* (*After that Trip*), by Valeria Piassa Polizzi, which is a diary of a young man with AIDS; *Para gostar de ler* (*To Like to Read*), by Carlos Drummond de Andrade, Fernando Tavares Sabino, and Paulo Mendes Campos; *Coisas que toda garota deve saber* (*Things All Young Women Should Know*), by Carlos Vilela; and *Cochilos e Sussurros* (*Naps and Whispers*), by Elson Gabriel Garcia.

There is also a specific interest in literature by Afro-Brazilians, developed by literary groups such as *Quilombhoje*, which consists of writers such as Luiz Silva "Cuti," Oswaldo Camargo, Paulo Colina, Conceição Evaristo, Esmeralda Ribeiro, Roseli Nascimento, and Abelardo Rodrigues.

RELIGIOUS PRACTICES AND CULTURAL CEREMONIES

The major religion in Brazil is catholicism and although most teenagers do not attend the Catholic church on a regular basis, there has been a strong charismatic movement which has attracted a number of youth during the last decades. On the other hand, the Pentecostal church is one of the fastest growing religions and it too has attracted many teenagers. They participate in meetings where they sing modern Christian music, including many songs composed by themselves. On the other hand, African religions play an active role in Brazil, such as umbanda, macumba, or candomblé, and there are a number of youth who attend as well.

Carnaval is a five-day national holiday in Brazil that takes place immediately before Lent, usually at the end of February or beginning of March. People take to the streets and neighborhood dance clubs to dance the nights away. The largest celebration takes place in Rio, where the schools of samba perform in the *sambódromo*, a type of open stadium built specifically to host *Carnaval*. In Salvador and Recife other major celebrations take place. The whole country celebrates, dances, drinks, and has fun. People of all ages participate.

Other forms of entertainment in the southern region include the largest annual livestock fair in South America, which takes place in September, and the *festa da uva* (grape festival), which occurs every four years. It celebrates the production of grapes and wine. These festivities share some common characteristics with Argentina and Uruguay.

In the northeast, predominating festivities are those with a strong religious component of syncretic characteristics with African influence. Others are *capoeira*, a martial arts/dance with centenary African traditions, the festivity of *bumba-meu-boi*, and *São João*, at which celebrants usually dance *forró*, dressed in folklore costumes.

Other festivities relate to family traditions. For example, birthdays are celebrated among family and friends. When a young woman turns 15, there is usually a large party in honor of her perceived passage into adulthood (*quinceañera*). In some upper-class social circles, these parties take place at a country club or other social club. This custom is less important in Brazil than in some other Latin American countries, such as Mexico, where the *quinceañera* is a major event.

Many of the more traditional festivities take place in rural areas. These popular celebrations present not only Brazil's cultural and traditional wealth, but have also contributed to the creation and performance of a wide variety of music. Brazilians love music and each region has its own musical characteristics and flavors.

Some of the more traditional and important festivities are of a religious nature, such as Christmas. Other festivities include the religious celebration of *Nossa Senhora de Aparecida* (Our Lady of Aparecida) and *Navegantes* (Seafarer). All reflect the blended nature of Brazilian culture as a result of the miscegenation of Portuguese, Africans, and Indians, all of whom have combined to create a new culture. This new culture maintains the stronger Portuguese traditions but at the same time it is transformed and enriched by the different ethnicities of this enormous nation.

CONCLUSION

The problems that Brazilian teenagers face are varied. In some countries, conflict between generations is a major issue, while in Brazil it is not so much, due in part to the open relationships children generally have with their parents, but also to the daily realities they face, which often include violence or, in the case of the lower class, marginalization. Since jobs are harder to come by in the smaller cities and in rural areas, many teens move to larger, urban centers in hope of finding better jobs and educational opportunities. This causes an imbalance. Teenagers whose families can afford it are sent to study abroad in Europe and the United States.

Another issue is the reality of Brazil's many street kids. Due to abject poverty, many adolescents, mostly those in large cities, live or at least spend a good portion of the day on the streets. Many times they are used by drug dealers to distribute drugs. Young women may be forced to enter into prostitution, and violence (inflicting and/or becoming a victim of) is common. Nevertheless, there are several institutions that support and try to better these teenagers' lives. In Brasília, the nation's capital, there are centers such as Adolescentro, where teenagers can study, use computers, and receive guidance and Projeto Praia (Beach Project), at which teenagers at risk, for example those who have been abandoned or sexually abused, can receive help. Other centers throughout the country include Conselhos Tutelares (Guardian Counseling Centers), which are in charge of both children and adolescents and offer counseling, intervention, and a general support system. The project RIR takes care of adolescents with drug problems, ones who are pregnant, and ones who have been sexually abused.

Brazilian teenagers are generally very friendly and outgoing. They love spending time with family and friends, music, dancing, and entertainment in all forms. However, Brazil is a country with enormous social differences. In Rio de Janeiro and São Paulo, the upper and lower classes live side by side; while some teenagers have access to excellent education and jobs, others have few opportunities for improvement.

RESOURCE GUIDE

Birdsall, Nancy. *Opportunity Foregone: Education in Brazil.* Washington, D.C.: Inter-American Development Bank, 1996.

CEPAL (Comisión Económica para América Latina e el Caribe). *Desarrollo y bienestar.* Santiago: Naciones Unidas, 2000.

CEPAL. *Panorama social de América Latina, 1999–2000.* Santiago: Naciones Unidas, 2000b.

Dabéne, Olivier. *América Latina en el siglo XX.* Madrid: Editorial Síntesis, 1999.

Dimenstein, Gilberto. *Brazil: War on Children.* New York: Latin America Bureau, Distribution in North America by Monthly Review Press, 1991.

Drummond de Andrade, Carlos, et al. *Para Gostar de Ler.* São Paulo: Editora Ática, 1977.

Meireles, Cecilia. *Janela Mágica.* São Paulo: Editora Moderna, 1988.

Veríssimo, Érico. *Gato Preto em Campo de Neve.* Porto Alegre, Brazil: Editora Globo, 1947.

———.*O Tempo e o Vento: o Continente, o Retrato, o Arquipélago.* Porto Alegre, Brazil: Editora Globo, 1950.

World Fact Book. "Brazil." 2001. http://www.cia.gov/cia/publications/factbook/geos/br.html.

http://www.lib.ohio-state.edu/latweb/Ted%20Art%20Brazil.htm

http://www.brazilcham.com/reuters/articles/Brazil.html

http://www.brazilcouncil.org/links/links_brazilnews.asp

http://dailynews.yahoo.com/full_coverage/world/brazil/

http://wwics.si.edu/brazil/

http://www.magportal.com/c/soc/reg/am/bra/

Elections. http://www.americas-society.org/coa/publications/BrazilPage.html

Travel. http://gosouthamerica.about.com/cs/brazil/

http://www.travelnotes.org/LatinAmerica/Brazil/

Nonfiction

Anthony, Patricia. *Cradle of Splendor.* New York: Ace Books, 1996.

Eakin, Marshall C. *Brazil: The Once and Future Country.* New York: St. Martin's Press, 1997.

Haverstock, Nathan, and E. W. Egan. *Brazil—In Pictures.* Minneapolis: Lerner Publications Co., 1987

Hudson, Rex. *Brazil: A Country Study.* Washington, D.C.: G.P.O., 1998.

Krich, John. *Why Is This Country Dancing? One-Man Samba to the Beat of Brazil.* New York: Simon and Schuster, 1993.

Léry, Jean de. *History of a Voyage to the Land of Brazil, Otherwise Called America.* Berkeley: University of California Press, 1990.

Levine, Robert M. *The History of Brazil.* Westport, Conn.: Greenwood Press, 1999.

Morrison, Marion. *Brazil.* Austin: Raintree Steck-Vaughn, 1994.

Rebhun, Linda-Anne. *The Heart Is Unknown Country: Love in the Changing Economy of Northeast Brazil.* Stanford, Calif.: Stanford University Press, 1999.

Richard, Christopher, and Leslie Jermyn. *Brazil.* New York: Benchmark Books/Marshall Cavendish, 2002.

Vincent, Jon. *Culture and Customs of Brazil.* Westport, Conn.: Greenwood Press, 2003.

Web Sites

http://memory.loc.gov/frd/cs/brtoc.html
Brazil—A Country Study.

http://www.brazilinfo.net/sky3/usbrazi2/public_html/
Brazil Infonet.

http://www.brol.com/
BR Online Travel (BROL).

http://www.brazilcouncil.org/
Brazil–U.S. Business Council.

http://www.cia.gov/cia/publications/factbook/geos/br.html
CIA: The World Factbook.

http://www.brasilemb.org/
Embassy of Brazil.

http://www.greenpeace.org.br/
Greenpeace Brasil.

http://jbonline.terra.com.br/
Jornal do Brasil Online.

http://www.uoregon.edu/~sergiok/brasil.html
Meu Brasil by Sergio Koreisha.

http://research.sun.com/brazil/
Project Brazil Overview.

http://www.brasil.gov.br/
República Federativa do Brasil.

http://www.soccerage.com/en/25/00002.html
SoccerAge.com.

http://pasture.ecn.purdue.edu/~agenhtml/agenmc/brazil/recipes.html
A Taste of Brazil.

http://www.terra.com.br/
Terra.

Pen Pal Information

http://www.parlo.com/
Parlo Inc.

http://www.geocities.com/paulina_a_m/links.html
Penpals for You.

http://www.pen-pals.net/
Pen-Pals.net—The World's Largest Pen Pal Site.

Chapter 3

CHILE

Regina Akel

INTRODUCTION

Chile is a unique country in many respects, not the least of which is its unusual geography. Located on the Pacific coast of South America, lying south of Peru and Bolivia, its coastline is over 4,000 miles long and at the narrowest point it is only 61 miles wide (Angostura de Paine).

The Cordillera de los Andes mountain range serves as a natural border that separates Chile from its neighbor to the east, Argentina. There is another, lower, mountain chain that runs parallel to the coast, called Cordillera de la Costa. Between these two ranges there are fertile valleys, especially in central Chile, where grapes, apples, pears, kiwis, peaches, avocados, custard apples, papayas, and cherries, besides wheat, corn, and root vegetables are produced.

There are desertlike areas in the north; a Mediterranean climate and fertile valleys in the center; and forests, lakes, and glaciers in the south, where the weather is colder and rainier.

There are many places of interest in Chile. Among them are the Atacama Desert, a vast expanse of dry, dusty, and windy land where some of the principal copper mines are located, and also the town of San Pedro de Atacama with its famous museum. The museum has well-preserved mummies and samples of pottery and textiles, some of which date from 9,000 B.C. Another exciting place is Easter Island, some 2,300 miles off the mainland; this island is characterized by the Moai, large, mysterious, humanlike figures made of volcanic rock that are found all over the island, usually looking away from the sea. In the south is the island of Chiloé, very green and rainy, with its own distinctive culture and traditions; the laguna San Rafael with its remarkable glaciers; and Torres del Paine, a breathtaking mountain range that borders lakes, lagoons, and waterfalls, as yet untouched by human hands. The country begins to break down into islands after the city of Puerto Montt; these places are hard to reach except by air, and even harder to reach in the winter months (July to September).

Chile is divided into 12 regions, with Santiago, the capital, as the 13th. The head of government is the president of the republic, who is elected by direct vote every six years and cannot be reelected for the following period. The president and the secretaries of state, called *ministros*, make up the executive branch. Congress, the legislative branch, is divided into two chambers: the Senate (46 members) and the Chamber of Deputies (120 members). The judiciary system follows the Napoleonic Code, that is, judges are accusers and investigators at the same time. This system has proven slow and not always fair, so it is being reformed and will eventually have a structure similar to the trial-by-jury one in the United States.

Chile's main exports are copper and other minerals, fruit, fish, and fish byproducts; tourism is a big industry. Another valuable and intangible asset that most Chileans recognize and take pride in is its stability, both political and economic. Nowadays, there is discontent because of high unemployment (9.8 percent) and little government support for the unemployed but, on the other hand, the country pays its debts and keeps inflation under control. Citizens are aware that they must fulfill their duties regarding taxation, but at the same time they know very well that they have a say in the way their money is spent. As there is free speech, they can complain if the government's policies are not satisfactory and they can also express their discontent through their votes.

Chilean teenagers today have known only democracy as a system of government and tend to disassociate themselves from the authoritarian regime that ended in 1990. Nor are they much interested in politics, politicians, voting, participating in rallies, or listening to political speeches because they don't have much faith in them, as they say repeatedly. During Salvador Allende's regime (1970–73) they participated much more in the events of the day, either on one side or the other, but that may have been a reflection of the growing feeling of power and responsibility the young had begun to experience in Europe and the United States since 1968.

Like most other Latin American countries, Chile was first a Spanish colony. The region was first visited by Diego de Almagro in 1536 and shortly thereafter (in 1541) by Pedro de Valdivia, who founded cities and brought the first settlers. At the beginning of the seventeenth century, ongoing fighting forced Spanish conquerors to create a frontier between their position in central Chile and the Araucanians in the south. The region where the southern city of Temuco is located is still called La Frontera. The Catholic missionaries that accompanied the Spanish troops crossed the frontier toward Araucanian territory. They founded missions in their attempts to convert the natives to Christianity and also to provide a basic, formal education. In some places the Araucanians accepted the presence of the priests, but in most cases they continued their old religious practices and beliefs.

During the colonial years (1541–1810) Chile was part of the viceroyalty of Peru. In 1808 Napoleon invaded Spain and the Chilean citizens decided in 1810 to form a kind of provisional government (Junta de Gobierno) that would rule the colony in the name of the king of Spain. On July 4, 1811, the first National Congress was inaugurated; one of the most important measures taken by that institution was to abolish slavery. Chile was the third country in the world to do so.

In 1814, coinciding with the decline of Napoleon, Spanish rule was reinstated in Chile. However, generals José de San Martín and Bernardo O'Higgins (*Ejército Libertador*), with a combined Chilean and Argentine army, drove out the Spanish and restored Chilean rule. For a short time, Bernardo O'Higgins was head of the new government.

During the years remaining in the nineteenth century there was war with Peru and Bolivia (1879), along with the revolution of 1891, which pitted President José Balmaceda against Congress. The president's army was defeated and in the following years a parliament of several parties ruled. But this system of government failed as well, when it became unable to solve the country's serious social and economic problems.

Another significant event took place in the second half of the nineteenth century, when the government invited a great number of German families to settle in the south of Chile, in what is known as the Lake District. Vicente Pérez Rosales organized the new settlers and distributed land among them. Within a few years, the German settlers turned the wild, hilly, and rocky forests into arable land. The best cattle farms in the country were also started there at that time. Toward the end of the century came people from other European countries, like England, France, Italy, Greece, and Croatia. Also, a great number of Chinese people settled in the north to work on the railways. Around that time migration from the Middle East began as well and continued until the twentieth century; immigrants came from Lebanon and Syria, but mostly from Palestine. All of these groups came to join and mingle with the original main body of Spanish descendants and Spanish/indigenous descendants.

In 1924 there was a short period of military rule but the elected president, Arturo Alessandri, was reinstated the following year. Also in 1925 a new constitution came into force. Left-wing parties gained much influence from 1930 onward and played important roles in the elections of presidents. However, the right-wing parties remained in actual control. But the most significant fact of this period in Chile has to do with women and voting. As early as 1935 they were allowed to vote in municipal elections; in 1951 they took part for the first time in parliamentary elections and the next year they voted in the presidential elections.

In September of 1970, the presidential candidate of the left-wing parties (Unidad Popular), Salvador Allende, won the election by a narrow margin. Three years later he was deposed during a military coup and thereafter followed 17 years of military dictatorship under General Augusto Pinochet. Democracy was restored in 1990 when Patricio Aylwin was elected president.

According to the latest census (2002), 9.6 percent of the population consider themselves as belonging to a native Chilean group. Of these, around 1,300,000 are Mapuche. A third of them live in communities in the south, where they practice their own language, culture, religion, and traditional way of life. The rest of the Mapuche population lives in cities, mostly in Santiago, where they tend to concentrate in the poorer sections.

The Mapuches are the largest Chilean ethnic group. Aimaras and the Atacameños live in small communities in the north, mostly near the Andean region and in cities like Arica, Iquique, and Antofagasta. In the south, in even smaller groups, live descendants of Alacalufes and Yaganes and on Easter Island there are about 3,000 descendants of the original Polynesian inhabitants.

In 1993 a law favoring the native Chileans (*Ley indígena*) was sanctioned in Parliament, which accords legal status to the different Mapuche communities, protects their right to own their land, and promotes the preservation of Mapuche culture, among other things. In general, native Chileans find that this bill is a step forward in the recognition of their rights but that it is not nearly enough, that much more should be done (Villalobos 2002, 124).

Since the 1970s, but mostly during the 1990s, the population in general has become more aware, more considerate, and more caring in relation to the original inhabitants of the country. The great majority of Chileans nowadays (71 percent) admit that they feel close to the cultural heritage of native inhabitants of which the Mapuches are the largest group (Villalobos 2002, 123).

How do present-day Mapuches feel? One of the most important issues among Mapuches and Pehuenches is the restitution of their land; another is their strong opposition to the installation of a hydroelectrical plant in the south. To bring attention to these issues, the national leaders marched on the city of Concepción on October 12, with their people dressed in traditional costumes, accompanied by members of political parties and watched by a supportive crowd.

CONADI, a government office in charge of the recognized ethnic groups, gives figures that are slightly different from those of the United Nations Program for Human Development (PNUD). CONADI states that a million descendants of the original native groups live in Chile, and that half of them live in the capital. The rest, distributed from north to farthest south, are the Aimaras, Atacameños, Rapa-Nui, Coyas, Mapuches, Alacalufes, and Yaganes. What is clear in both reports is that, in number, the Mapuches surpass by far all other groups. Apart from the injustices their ancestors had to suffer, from the middle of the nineteenth century onward when they began to be dispossessed of their land, they have also had to endure, through many decades, the contempt of their fellow nationals. For a long time they were considered different, ignorant, and awkward.

These two situations are being modified. More than 740,000 acres have been returned to the Mapuches since the passing of the *Ley indígena* in 1993. Apart from this, CONADI's goal is to create instances where the Mapuches can participate in the culture and the economy of the country so that they feel as if they are a part of it (Downey 2002, C5).

TYPICAL DAY

As in most other parts of the world, in Chile a teenager's life is centered on school. Schools have both morning and afternoon shifts, so that each establishment can double its capacity and every student can be guaranteed a place. This situation has started to improve slowly: it is obvious that it does not benefit the students to have all their mornings or all their afternoons free, because both parents are usually away at their places of work during the day. Left alone, youngsters of all ages very seldom study or do their homework and, most of all, their need for affection or even attention is not satisfied.

The typical day varies if the teenager lives in a rural area or in a town or city. In the country, students have to rise very early, around 5:00 or 6:00 in the morning, in order to walk to school or to the nearest bus stop. In some regions it may take them up to two hours to reach their destination. Once there, the school provides their breakfast and lunch, and they usually start their way back home around 2:00. On their return they help their parents on the farm, do their homework, perhaps listen to music, and have supper before going to sleep. In some areas, particularly in the south, municipalities have founded free boarding schools for boys and girls who live too far from the villages. These students live in special school buildings from Monday through Friday and spend only weekends at home.

As houses are very isolated from each other, teenagers who live in the countryside do not have much of a social life except on weekends, when they go to the nearest village to do their shopping, attend church ceremonies, meet other young people, and, if their parents allow it, go to a disco on Saturday night. Rural youngsters envy the freedom their peers in larger cities enjoy.

Life is certainly easier for teenagers who live in cities. If they have classes in the morning they get up around 6:30 or 7:00. Students of higher socioeconomic status are driven to school by their parents and picked up in the afternoon; there are also carpools or special school vans that transport them. Once they arrive home they have lunch, talk on the phone with friends for hours (mostly, but not always the girls), listen to music, visit friends or classmates who live nearby, watch television or videos, sit in parks with other teens, and, sometimes, study.

Invariably, all the young people who live in cities visit malls two, three, or even more times a week. In those places they meet friends, walk around, talk, and window-shop; if they happen to have money to spare they will have something to eat. Their favorite foods are French fries, hamburgers, hot dogs, and Cokes, and they find plenty of those treats in the malls.

Chilean teenagers normally do not work, except in rural areas where they help their families in the farm chores; those in the cities sometimes help their parents when they have a small family business or shop. It is illegal in Chile to hire a worker under 18; teenagers who are 15 or older may work only part-time, and for that they must have written permission from their parents. A few deliver pizzas or videos, but as they must be at least 18 to ride a motorbike, parents find this kind of work dangerous. The most common and accepted legal occupation for teenagers of low-income families in Chile is that of packer in a supermarket.

Natalie is 17 years old, the second of eight children; her stepfather is a construction worker and her mother is in poor health and cannot do very much except take care of the smaller children (interview by author, Santiago, November 12, 2002). Natalie feels lucky to have been accepted as a packer in a supermarket 16 miles from her house, as this allows her to

Natalie, 17, and Javier, 16, work every afternoon packing grocery bags in a supermarket, Santiago, Chile. Courtesy of Regina Akel.

contribute to household expenses and to have some pocket money. She has to attend school only in the afternoons, so she starts work at 8:00 A.M., packs customers' bags until 1:00 P.M., has something to eat (the supermarkets do not provide meals), and then sets off for school. On weekends Natalie must be on duty all day, but the effort is greatly compensated as on those days she makes more money. When the government tried to regulate the packers' contracts, there was strong opposition from the packers themselves.

On slow days during the week Natalie makes as little as US$2 in tips, but on weekends she can make five or six times that amount. With those earnings (about US$100 a month) Natalie buys food, notebooks, and other materials for school; pays her bus fare (although rates are reduced for students); and sometimes has a little left over to buy herself something pretty. In tuition-free schools, the state provides breakfast, lunch, and textbooks for all students but Natalie says that there are always other expenses that have to be covered by the student or the family. When she finishes secondary school Natalie plans to study to become an accountant; however, she is not certain at present whether she will be able to achieve her goal.

Not all low-income teenagers' lives are like Natalie's. Many of them don't do any work, in some cases because their parents don't want them to, but in others because it is their personal choice. Middle- and upper-class teens don't work at all for two reasons: first because it has never been the custom that they should and, second, because there are no openings for student workers, even if they wished to combine work with their studies. However, there is one similarity shared by young people of all social classes: Very few find either of their parents in the house when they arrive home from school and they have to rely on friends, rather than family, for companionship and support.

There are a number of very poor families, especially in the larger cities, who live in bad conditions. These conditions are sometimes the result of (1) migration from the country into an urban area, a trend seen in many other parts of the world; (2) alcoholism, which prevents many people from getting and keeping a job; and (3) disregard of the essential role of education and personal improvement, among other reasons. Certainly it is the children who suffer the most in these poor living conditions; it is hard to imagine someone not having running water nowadays, or sleeping five to a bed, but those are some of the hardships they have to endure. In the winter months cold and rainy weather make life even harder for every member of the family. Among extremely poor Chilean teens, all of them attend primary school, and most try to complete the four years of high school in order to find better jobs, either to help their families or to be able to start a family themselves. Government and the United Nations Children's Fund (UNICEF) studies show that extreme poverty has decreased in Chile by at least 10 percent in the past 10 years, but there is still much to be done. A smaller but significant group of youngsters in this situation don't attend school at all. Many leave their houses to live in communities under bridges, while others are led to prostitution or drug peddling. Whenever government or church institutions try to rescue young people from these conditions by interning them in special or foster homes, they usually run away and return to their communities or more lucrative activities. When some of them were interviewed by the press after their escape, they explained that they cherish their freedom above everything else.

FAMILY LIFE

According to a 1999 study done for UNICEF, 72 percent of Chilean children live with both parents, 23 percent live with only the mother, and 3 percent with just the father. The statistics published by UNICEF also show that the children and teenagers chosen for this research were between 7 and 18 years old and belonged to low-, middle- and high-income families. Over 80 percent of these children declared that their relationship with their parents was good or very good. Yet two years later, research undertaken for PNUD found that 31 percent of Chileans believe that the family as an institution is in critical condition, 28 percent feel that it is a source of tensions and conflicts, and, paradoxically, only 28 percent consider the family a shelter from society (Desarrollo Humano, 206).

It is undeniable that in Chile, as in many other parts of the world, the concept of family has changed greatly. One reason is that the family circle has become smaller and now it usually consists only of parents and children, while 30 years ago the extended family was the norm and the larger group lived together in large homes. Nowadays houses have become smaller. Low-income urban families, especially in Santiago, can afford nothing better than a 90 square feet walk-up apartment in the outskirts of the city. Living conditions are improved, of course, in higher income families, but most teenagers complain that they have little space and no privacy.

Another important change in Chilean families has taken place in the nature of the bonds between its members (Villalobos 2002, 205). The traditional sequence of getting married, of having children afterward, and of those children leaving the family home when they themselves marry, has been altered. Marriages break up, and so do families. Also, young people don't wait anymore to be married before having children. As recently as 1992, 58.2 percent of 15- to 19-year-old girls who gave birth were not married, while in 1970 the percentage was only about half as much (De la Lastra 1992, 18). These situations reveal that the traditional forms of family structuring are changing rapidly. The Chilean family is nowadays a "social construction undergoing changes" (Villalobos 2002, 206).

The most fundamental change in Chilean families of all levels lies in the modification of traditional roles, says the PNUD report. As children now have more direct access to information, they have less need of their parents as mediators between them and the outside world. Moreover, in many cases, it is children themselves who teach their parents skills that may allow them to interact with a society that is evolving at a breathtaking speed. Computers, the Internet, and the prevalence of images over language are aspects that validate this perception (Villalobos 2002, 207).

It has become more and more common for both parents to work outside the home, in Chilean families of all income levels. This, and the fact that some children have classes in the mornings and others in the afternoons, makes it very hard for all family members to be together at mealtimes during the week. Since teenagers usually go out on Friday and Saturday nights and sleep late the following mornings, there are some families that are hardly ever together. This last situation changes in the more traditional middle- and high-income families, who make it a rule to meet at least at mealtimes on weekends, family gatherings, or church ceremonies.

The distribution of household chores falls more heavily on the mother. Teenagers help, but not always willingly. PNUD quotes statistics compiled by a government department that shows that in Chilean homes, 77 percent of women do the cleaning, as opposed to only 25 percent of men. Eighty-eight percent of women do the cooking. Caring for children is also their responsibility: 75 percent of women versus 34 percent of men. In other chores like shopping, driving, and household repairs, the differences are not as great (Villalobos 2002, 217).

The legal age for drinking alcohol and also for driving in Chile is 18 but, in recent years, drinking has become a real problem among teenagers of all social levels. It is, of course, forbidden to sell alcohol to minors, and the government and the municipalities are forever trying to enforce different sorts of restrictions, like limiting the opening and closing hours of liquor stores, pubs, and discos. Andrés is a typical Chilean teenager. At present he is 18, has just finished secondary school, and is now attending a technical training school. He and his girlfriend already have a baby, but each of them lives with his or her parents and are in no hurry to get married; nor is there pressure from society or their families to do so, as there would have been 30 years ago. Andrés described his life as follows: "Whenever I wanted a drink, I only had to ask an older person to buy it for me in exchange for a fee." As for the closing hours of pubs and discos, he added that the authorities should know that those that appear to close their doors at 4:00 or 5:00 in the morning actually carry on their activities in soundproof basements until well into the morning. "I spend all week longing for the weekends when I'll have a chance to visit one of these places and have fun," he confessed. Needless to say, Andrés's girlfriend doesn't accompany him on these sprees, as she has to take care of their baby.

There has been an alarming increase in alcohol consumption among teens since 1994; some studies report that 70 percent of the 12–17 age group drink regularly, and that the starting age of their habit is around 13 (Atica 1999, 1). Beer is the most popular beverage and researchers have found that girls drink it as much as boys, although not for the same reasons. Male drinkers use alcohol as a means of escaping reality, as a rite of passage from childhood to adolescence, or to bolster their courage if they feel shy in everyday life. Female teenagers say they drink to be sociable, and prefer not to become totally drunk as that might make them lose control (2).

There is a great deal being done about this problem, especially by churches and related institutions, in the first case to keep teenagers away from drinking, and secondly to rehabilitate them. The most important of these institutions is the Hogar de Cristo (House of Christ), which has centers in almost every city in Chile; in them, young people are housed, fed, and counseled by other teens who have overcome the habit; new-comers are guided into discovering their potential and encouraged to find positive ways to express themselves. Another remarkable aspect of this in-stitution is that its doors are always open and patients are free to leave whenever they wish.

TRADITIONAL AND NONTRADITIONAL FOOD DISHES

As Chile is a country with a long coastline, there are several traditional dishes that have seafood as the main ingredient. The most popular is *caldillo de congrio*, a soup in which pieces of fish (a kind of eel) are cooked slowly in fish stock and white wine along with sliced onions, potatoes, and carrots. Another traditional dish is the *empanada*, which is essentially a meat pie. Chileans consider it *the* typical Chilean food. The *empanada* consists of juicy small pieces of meat cooked in oil, chopped onions, pa-prika, and cumin. This filling is put into a dough made with flour, eggs, butter, and warm, salted water; the dough is then sealed carefully and baked for 20 to 30 minutes.

There are many other traditional dishes made with chopped or mashed corn, along with potato pancakes; *curanto* (a sort of clambake with many ingredients), for which Chile is famous; and *sopaipillas*, fried-dough discs made with flour and mashed pumpkin, which are mandatory when there is a heavy rain. The origin of this custom is unknown.

These dishes take rather long to prepare, so most families buy them ready-made at supermarkets. When people cook during the week they prefer pasta or rice with meat, eggs, or fish. There is usually a salad to go with these preparations, the most common being made up of lettuce, tomato, celery, and root vegetables. Teenagers enjoy most of these foods, but certainly they prefer—above everything else—hamburgers, French fries, hot dogs, and Cokes.

There are no major conflicts between parents and adolescents over food. The only concern parents, teachers, and counselors have about teens and food is the increasing number of adolescents with eating disorders; a great percentage are overweight and there is also an alarming spread in anorexia, mainly among female teenagers of higher socioeconomic levels. As these two extremes are threatening the future lives of young people, parents' associations as well as schools and the government are trying to devise programs for prevention, rehabilitation, and information on the many aspects of food consumption.

SCHOOLING

According to the latest census (2002), 98 percent of the Chilean population is literate. In this country there are tuition-free private schools subsidized by the state, tuition-free public schools managed by the municipal governments, and private schools for which a fee is required. Four years of high school can be oriented either to the sciences and the humanities or to technical studies. The latter combines general studies with basic training in technical skills, for example, those demonstrated by mechanics, electricians, and plumbers.

The government, through the Ministry of Education, provides the main guidelines for school programs, but each institution has a certain amount of freedom to design its priorities. A typical school day begins at 8:00 in the morning and each class period lasts 45 minutes (some subjects last two periods in a row), with breaks in-between. During breaks students are encouraged to participate in sports like basketball or ping-pong. There are gym classes at least once a week, and also yearlong preparations for athletic interschool competitions that take place in November, at the end of the school year.

There are schools for people with special needs, for example, the blind and the mentally disabled, in most major cities. Moreover, schools must accept and attend to the needs of any student with a physical disability; if they should fail to do so, they might lose the government's subsidy. Yet, the most unusual of all the special schools is the one founded several years ago by a former mayor of one of the most affluent municipalities in Santiago. It is called La Puerta (The Door) and it accepts absolutely all students rejected or expelled from other schools in the city because of bad behavior, poor grades, or even worse problems.

The curricula are basically the same in all schools; they include the usual subjects at both the primary and secondary levels: mathematics, physics, chemistry, Spanish, and English, with the addition of the Study and Understanding of Society in primary school. This subject deals with themes like human rights, the environment, equality, and respect for cultural diversity. This same subject is called History and Social Sciences in high school, and its contents include political institutions of the nation, the rights and duties of citizens, democracy and its component institutions, national identity, labor laws, and human rights, among others. One very important content of this course is language and communication, formerly included in the Spanish course program: it focuses on the coding and decoding of messages and the analysis of journalistic and advertising texts (Villalobos 2002, 133).

Learning is assessed through test scores and every student must pass an examination in order to proceed to the next level. Scores earned throughout the year count toward the final grade. In classes there is less lecturing and book work than there was 20 years ago. Teamwork is encouraged and students have to find facts for themselves or in groups. They have to go to libraries, interview people, read and study newspapers, and even write and act in plays. In secondary schools they also have to read a great deal, mostly novels: classical, Chilean, Latin American, Spanish, and French and English in translation. Unfortunately, teenagers nowadays do not like reading very much, and they see reading assignments as one of the hardest.

After they finish secondary school students can pursue technical training at a two-year college or attend university. For the latter they must take a national aptitude test, which is being reformed at present. In general, teenagers in Chile view schooling as a preparation for life, for work, or for the university. According to a study by Time Research for UNICEF in 1999, 68 percent of Chilean teenagers want to attend university, 18 percent prefer to follow a technical career, 12 percent would like to start working immediately, and only 5 percent intend to devote themselves to the arts or to sports. Desertion is high in secondary schools, but hopefully this will be remedied when attendance in high school becomes mandatory for teenagers under 18.

SOCIAL LIFE

Teens in Chile have an intense and varied social life, with differences according to economic status, religious orientation, and the section of the country they live in. For example, teenagers in Punta Arenas, which is the southernmost city in the world, meet at each other's homes for formal or informal gatherings, as the cold, snow, and strong Arctic winds, present most of the year, leave little opportunity for other kinds of social activities. On the other hand, in northern Chile, the climate of the coast is very mild throughout the year, so teens spend a great deal of their leisure time outdoors, bathing on the beach during the day and listening to the radio, dancing, or playing the guitar and singing in the evenings. In general, teenagers have many opportunities to meet each other, through the neighborhoods in which they live, their schools (mostly coeducational), their brothers' or sisters' friends, friends of other friends, and their churches, among many others.

Most churches offer opportunities for young people to meet; they can participate in choir practice and church ceremonies; organize social gatherings, sports meetings, and drama groups; visit the sick; and help the needy. Another important place where young people meet in Santiago and the major cities are the social and sports centers founded by descendants of the many European and Middle Eastern groups that have lived in the country for generations. There teens hold dances, parties, and wedding celebrations, and practice sports like tennis, hockey, basketball, or swimming, either for pleasure or for competition. There are, for example, the Estadio Francés (French Club), the Estadio Español (Spanish Club), The Prince of Wales Country Club (U.K.), The Club Manquehue (German), the Lebanese Club, the Palestinian, the Israeli, and so on. Normally, a person does not have to be a direct descendant of a certain group in order to enroll in one of these clubs and young people visit them at least once a week in winter and every day during the summer months.

Some schools in this country have social gatherings, but usually they are held only once a year, around November; they are not a common practice. As for norms of behavior, they are similar to those of teenagers in the United States. In the larger cities, especially Santiago, young people tend to have more freedom; they usually go out when they want to and they don't have curfews. In smaller towns, or among members of certain church groups or of more traditional families, outings of teenagers are more regulated: they take place only on weekends, their destination is known, and their parents drop them off and pick them up at prearranged times.

Clothing is also similar to that worn by teens in most of the world: blue jeans, sneakers, and T-shirts. Males may complement this outfit with baseball caps turned backward.

Most studies agree that nearly 75 percent of teenagers have had sexual experiences from the age of 14 onward. The exceptions are those who belong to traditionally strict religious groups or movements like the Opus Dei in the Catholic Church, or the Mormon Church. Needless to say, there are teenagers who don't belong to any religious group and abstain from sex for other reasons. In general, young people in Chile are very well informed about the risks and responsibilities involved in premarital sex; yet, "at least with regard to pregnancy, half the children born of adolescent mothers are the result of that practice" (De la Lastra 1992).

RECREATION AND ENTERTAINMENT

According to a study made by UNICEF in 1999 (UNICEF Chile), 63 percent of Chilean teenagers of all social groups stated that their principal form of entertainment was watching television. Forty percent preferred to be with their friends and 33 percent chose listening to music above all other activities. Only 18 percent favored sports; reading was last on the list with only 12 percent. Video games and the Internet are two of the main ways teenagers spend their free time. Most teens and young people in their twenties find that open-air music recitals cannot be missed. There are six or seven main events of this kind every year and according to the weekly teen newsmagazine *Zona de Contacto*, there are smaller recitals of rock music, electronic music, and electro pop every week, along with musical sessions conducted by favorite national and international DJs on Friday and Saturday evenings ("Zona de Contacto").

There is also an international music recital, the Festival de Viña del Mar, which takes place once a year in February (at the end of summer). This event is well known, at least in Latin America, mainly because the audience, which consists mostly of teenagers of both sexes, can make or forever destroy a singer, a comedian, or musical group. This has been going on for almost 40 years, and even though there have been countless generations of teenagers through the years, they are always called "The Monster" and are spoken of in the present tense, because of their power and the cruel way in which they occasionally exercise it.

The sport that everyone follows is soccer. Teens and adults alike, mostly men, can be passionate and sometimes violent about it. If their team wins, they become deliriously happy; they experience the opposite when their team loses. The different neighborhoods of the cities and towns nearly always have a soccer field, and there teenagers and adults play or watch others play most weekends. There is not much boating or sailing in Chile, except in the higher-income groups; the same can be said about skiing. Tennis became popular among young people of both sexes, particularly when the Chilean champion Marcelo Ríos was ranked first in the world for a time. The YMCA offers a variety of sports in its centers in Santiago and the larger cities to young people of both sexes, from ages 15 to 21.

YMCA centers offer volleyball, basketball, karate, and swimming. The fee is at present US$23 per month, and though it is not high, many families find it expensive in this time of high unemployment.

Hunting as a sport is not a widespread practice in this country, especially among teenagers who are conscious of the environment, conservation, and endangered animal species. For nearly 15 years the government has forbidden the hunting of foxes, pumas, and seals. It is unusual to see a woman wearing a fur coat these days, and the few who do are over 50—never teenagers.

RELIGIOUS PRACTICES AND CULTURAL CEREMONIES

As in the other Latin American countries that began as Spanish colonies, Catholicism is the main religion in Chile. Research done in 2001 showed that 73 percent of the population declared themselves to be Catholic, 17 percent Evangelical (Methodist, Pentecostal), and 1 percent Mormons, while 7 percent declared no religion (Villalobos 2002, 236). There are traditional religious feasts in this country, the most important of these being La Tirana in Andacollo, a town in the north near Iquique. There, men disguised in colorful costumes representing devils, dance to the sound of drums in homage to the Virgin Mary. Of course the origin of this tradition is pagan and hundreds of years old, but it became Christianized after the arrival of the first colonizers. Another tradition is a pilgrimage on the eighth of December to a shrine of the Virgin Mary at Lo Vásquez, located on the road to Valparaíso. There people go by the hundreds to pay their respects or give thanks for a special favor, like recovering from an illness or finding a job. Young people are seldom part of these groups, mainly because they have distanced themselves from public expressions of devotion in spite of the fact that their elders still practice them.

Another picturesque, semireligious Chilean custom is the *animita* (little soul). *Animitas* are small, churchlike structures not higher than three feet, built at a site where a person has met a violent death. The name, date, and cause of death are engraved in one of the low walls or written on a brass plaque. People can visit the spot, leave flowers, light candles, say a prayer for the dead person's soul, and, of course, ask for a special favor. In return they make a *manda* or promise, in which the petitioner promises to bring a certain number of candles, to say prayers, or to hear Mass for the salvation of the *animita*'s soul if their requests are granted. Many times, at the end of the school year, female teens can be seen praying at one of these places, probably asking the *animita* to grant them the favor of getting good grades and passing the final examinations.

But generally speaking, teenagers in Chile feel that their churches have stayed behind the social changes that took place at the end of the last century (Villalobos 2002, 240). According to 18-year-old Andrés, there is more meaning in helping others than in attending religious ceremonies or practicing religious customs. This is why he participates in study groups sponsored by one of the Christian churches in order to help other youngsters who may have become addicted to alcohol or another drug. In spite of these feelings, Andrés, Natalie, and most teenagers agree on one thing: If and when they marry, they would like to do it in a church; they feel that that gesture would make their commitment more enduring.

CONCLUSION

Teenagers in Chile nowadays enjoy greater freedom than their parents and grandparents ever dreamed of, and much greater freedom that their peers in other Latin American countries, Asia, and the Middle East have today. They are allowed to decide on their future, on the career they want to pursue, on the use of their leisure time, on their attitude to religion, and on the clothes they want to wear, among many other aspects of their lives. Parents find it hard to discipline them or to control their comings and goings, even the friends they choose to see. One reason for this is that parents are seldom at home because they have demanding jobs and/or equally demanding social lives. Another reason is that teenagers at present are in direct contact with the outside world because globalization makes it accessible to almost everybody, even those in isolated villages.

The dark side of this situation is that teenagers show many signs of alienation from society, even a rejection of it. For example, they refuse to vote, to have anything to do with politics or the government. They have also lost faith in what their school can do for them and in what society will be able to offer them when they finish their studies.

These teenagers grew up in the 1990s, a period of great affluence, and the present crisis, which apparently has come to stay, will be their lot when they are ready to start working. Their perception is that there will be unemployment and fewer opportunities than their parents had. Some specialists agree that these unpromising prospects may account for the high levels of depression suffered by adolescents of both sexes, their use of alcohol and other drugs, the increase in early unplanned and unwanted pregnancies, their lack of definite goals, and the growing number of teens with eating disorders (Florenzano 1992, 24).

In spite of all these considerations, the picture is not entirely bleak. One of the most remarkable characteristics of Chilean teenagers is their great generosity. It only takes one of the national catastrophes that happen often in this part of the world, such as a flood or an earthquake, for young people of both sexes and all social levels to rush forth to help, even at the risk of their own lives. They have no qualms about shoveling mud; giving blood; collecting, classifying, and distributing clothes; and feeding babies, for example. Besides, they know very well how to get organized in these situations and how to recognize, choose, and follow a leader.

Another positive aspect of teenagers in present-day Chile is their strong commitment to the practice of conservation and caring for the environment. They are proud of their country's natural resources and feel responsible for the kind of world they will leave to their children. On Easter Island, for example, teenagers are taking active part in the collecting and recycling of waste. They are the most enthusiastic participants of a house-to-house campaign conceived to teach people to separate their refuse into plastic, metal, paper, and organic matter. They help carry this last element to specially prepared, compost centers on the island. The rest is ground into powder and sent back to the continent. Visitors to the island have reported that young people appear to be proud to have been given the chance to help keep their island clean for themselves, for tourists from all over the world, and lastly, for their children.

Finally, one of the most remarkable proofs of the generosity and sense of commitment that characterize Chilean teenagers nowadays is their participation in the campaign called Adopt a Brother. This campaign, sponsored also by the Hogar de Cristo, consists of having an older boy or girl become for a year the brother or sister of a younger child, who is usually from a low-income family. The older sibling visits the younger one several times a week, helps with homework, and gives advice and support on personal matters. On weekends they sometimes go out, to the zoo or to a park, or talk and plan for the future. Both youngsters are usually very sad when the year is over and they promise to continue meeting in the future. Many of the young ones who have enjoyed the benefits of an adopted brother are so grateful that they themselves become older brothers and sisters when they grow up. Acts of youthful generosity like these are always uplifting and confirm people's ultimate faith in the human race.

RESOURCE GUIDE

Aninir Antilef, Pedro. Personal interview, 13 December 2002.
Atica Consultores. "Uso y abuso del alcohol en la cultura juvenil." *Estudios del Instituto Nacional de la Juventud*, 1 November 1999: 1–8.

Chapell, David J. "Government Structure." *Spotlight on Chile*. November 25, 2002. http://www.localaccess.com/chapell/chile/govnmt.htm.

De la Lastra, Manuel. "Embarazo y Adolescencia." *Familia*, no. 23 (1992).

Downey, Ricardo. "Cayun: Autonomía territorial la busca solo una minoria." *El Mercurio* (Santiago), 13 October 2002, C5.

Duery, Lilian A. "Isla de Pascua sera un paraíso limpio." *El Mercurio* (Santiago), 6 May 2002.

Espíldora, Marcela. "El nuevo perfil de los adolescentes." *La Tercera* (Santiago), 6 May 2002.

Florenzano Urzúa, Ramon. "La familia como factor de riesgo." *Creces*, no. 7 (1992): 24–28.

González, Natalie. Personal interview, 12 November 2002.

Molina, Jorge, and Claudette Medina. "Críticas a Lagos caracterizaron las marchas mapuches en el Día de la Raza." *El Mercurio* (Santiago), 13 October 2002, C5.

Palma, Andrés. Personal interview, 15 November 2002.

UNICEF Chile. "La percepción de los niños acerca de la relación al interior de sus familias." *Indicadores sobre la infancia*, November 8, 2002. http://www.unicef.cl/indicadores/diversion.html.

Villalobos, Sergio. *Breve historia de Chile*. Santiago: Editorial Universitaria, 1979.

———. *Desarrollo humano en Chile 2002*. Santiago: Programa de las Naciones Unidas para el desarrollo (PNUD), 2002.

"Zona de Contacto." *El Mercurio* (Santiago), 22 November 2002, 4.

Nonfiction

Barros, Robert. *Constitutionalism and Dictatorship: Pinochet, the Junta, and the 1980 Constitution*. Cambridge, U.K.: Cambridge University Press, 2002.

Castillo-Feliú, Guillermo I. *Culture and Customs of Chile*. Westport, Conn.: Greenwood Press, 2000.

Dwyer, Christopher. *Chile*. Broomall, Pa.: Chelsea House, 1997.

Falcoff, Mark. *Modern Chile 1970 to 1989: A Critical History*. New Brunswick, N.J.: Transaction Publishers, 1989.

Mavor, Elizabeth, ed. *The Captain's Wife: The South American Journals of Maria Graham 1821–23*. London: Weidenfeld and Nicolson Ltd., 1993.

Politzer, Patricia. *Fear in Chile: Lives under Pinochet*. Translated by Diane Watchell. New York: New Press, 2001.

Fiction

Allende, Isabel. *The House of the Spirits*. Translated by Magda Bogin. New York: Knopf, 1987.

Web Sites

http://www.localaccess.com/chapell/chile/
Complete review of the country and its institutions.

http://www.sernatur.cl/
National Tourism Agency.

http://www.geographia.com/chile
Places of interest in Chile.

Pen Pal Information

http://www.injuv.gov.cl
Instituto Nacional de la Juventud.

http://www.pen-pal.net
Pen Pal Network.

Chapter 4

COLOMBIA

Juana Suárez

INTRODUCTION

Colombia is located in the northwestern region of South America. It is Latin America's fifth largest nation, with 440,000 square miles. Colombia has a rich and diverse geography that strongly influences its society and politics, as it shapes the particular characteristics and lifestyles of each region. Colombia borders Panama, Venezuela, Brazil, Peru, and Ecuador. It is the only South American country with both Pacific and Atlantic coastlines. On both coasts, fishing is an important economic activity. In the southeastern part of the country is a vast plain known as Llanos Orientales. Extensive jungles lie near the frontier with Brazil and where Colombia borders Peru and Ecuador. Lowlands near its Caribbean coast are used for agriculture and raising cattle.

Three famous cities lie on the Atlantic coast. Cartagena is a historic city with impressive colonial buildings, while Santa Marta is a favorite destination for young people because of the beach resort at Rodadero and the city's proximity to Parque Tairona, one of Colombia's most famous natural parks. Barranquilla is Colombia's most important port in the Caribbean. Two rivers separate the three main Andean ranges. The main population areas among these ranges are located on plateaus, in basins, and in river valleys. Colombia's most significant cities are located in this region.

Colombia has a population of nearly 40 million inhabitants. Bogotá is the capital city, a cosmopolitan town with a population of eight million. There are many social problems within the city, which have increased as a result of a lack of city policies to cope with the growing influx of citizens displaced from rural zones due to sociopolitical violence. However, Bogotá's last two administrations have made visible contributions to the city such as the implementation of a collective transportation system, the recuperation of public space, and the construction of local libraries, among others. Many of these programs have turned out to be beneficial to teens since this group is one of the main users of public services.

Medellín is the second most important city in Colombia. It is located almost 500 kilometers to the northwest of Bogotá and has a population of almost three million. Medellín might be remembered for the proliferation of drug-related businesses there in the 1980s. It is a negative image that extends to all of Colombia and which encapsulates the international image of Colombia as a place of drugs, violence, guerrilla and paramilitary groups, and corrupt politicians. It is impossible to describe the country and not mention these negative aspects, but it is also unfair to concentrate only on them. Medellín, for example, is a symbol of the enormous potential of the country. It is a beautiful city that preserves a balance between industrial development and its natural surroundings.

Despite the political turmoil and the violent situation within the country, Colombia has the oldest democratic tradition in Latin America. A president is elected every four years, with no immediate reelection allowed. The country is divided into departments that are similar to states in the United States. There is direct election of departmental governors. The other main branches of power in Colombia are the Senate and the House of Representatives. Two political parties traditionally run the country: the Liberal and the Conservative.

The official language is Spanish, but more than 180 Indian languages and dialects are also spoken. Colombian ethnic composition is 60 percent mestizo (mixed Indian-European descent), 20 percent white, 18 percent black or mulatto, and 2 percent indigenous population (Harding 1996, 74). Forty-one percent of the Colombian population is under 18 years old.

Colombia's currency is the peso. Its most famous export is coffee, which is grown mainly on the temperate slopes of the Andean ranges. Other important products from Colombia are oil, coal, and minerals, along with bananas and other tropical fruits. Colombia is an important supplier of flowers for the United States. On certain holidays, 80 percent of flowers sold in the United States come from Colombia. The success of this product is currently being taken as a harbinger to encourage investment in Colombia as a means of eliminating crops of coca leaves and opium poppies. Although the production of coca and opium poppies is illegal, these crops have obliterated possibilities for other agricultural products to do well in national and international markets. Colombia has a unique variety of plants as well as diverse animal habitats. It also has more species of birds than anywhere else on earth, with over 1,550 recorded.

Most of Colombia's contemporary problems are rooted in ancient social issues related to the distribution of wealth, social status discrimination, a history of government corruption, and regionalism, a result of the country's diverse geography. Although people often refer to Colombian violence, there is a difference between violence related to political causes and that related to social problems, such as robbery, assault, or other criminal activities. Armed guerrilla groups have been active in Colombia since the mid-1950s and have been receiving support from drug traffickers since the 1980s. The leftist revolutionary agenda of the guerrilla groups has disappeared, and most of the conflict has become a matter of control over national territory. Guerrilla groups operate in rural areas but the presence of urban militias has been growing; in many cases they are recruiting teens.

The economic situation of the country is hard and has had repercussions even in the upper class. In recent years, people from different social classes have taken flight, with the United States as their main destination. Since it is not always economically possible for a whole family to move together, they might be divided among countries. The possibility of moving with an entire family is easier for upper-class families. The increasing exodus has led some European countries to tighten immigration measures, making it more difficult for Colombians to enter. Because of the hardships, the number of families where both parents work has increased. Former stay-at-home mothers engage in small businesses in order to contribute to the home financial situation, and in the middle and lower sectors of the population, teens take jobs to help support their families or to provide for their own needs. Middle-class women may take part-time jobs or sell food, cosmetics, clothes, or crafts at home. The highest concentration of street vendors and people with nomadic jobs is in the lower class, where teens are expected to help their parents with either setting up a street buggy or taking care of customers.

Unemployment is high. In rural zones, working is not easy because of harassment of the local population by guerrilla and paramilitary groups. One of the biggest problems resulting from the violent situation in rural areas is displacement of the population and its migration to the cities, where jobs are difficult to find. According to the United Nations Agency for Refugees, women, children, and teens make up almost 72 percent of the displaced population and it is estimated that 54 percent of that number are children and adolescents. Displacement affects the personal development of children and teens since violent acts or harassment often precede it. Such strain is usually followed by a sudden change of location and, many times, leads to the separation of family members. According to the United Nations Children's Fund (UNICEF), there are some 5,000 adolescents, many of them from displaced communities, linked to illegal armed groups. These young people are often exposed to segregation and stigmatization affecting not only their development but also their self-esteem. There are also issues of health and malnutrition related to displacement (ACNUR 2001, 27).

Teens become adult citizens at age 18, when they must apply for the *cédula de ciudadanía*, the official identification card that entitles them to vote. The *cédula de ciudadanía* is not a driver's license but is required for every official procedure. Military service is mandatory for all males, who are required to sign up for training when they turn 18. Exceptions are made if they have not graduated from high school, and, in most cases, to avoid entering the military, they must pay a waiver based on their family's income. Paramilitary and guerrilla groups also recruit male teens. Teens from rural areas often join these groups either because they are fascinated with the idea of rebellion or simply because they have no other outlet for violence. For many rural families, allowing their sons to join the guerrilla movement translates into the end of their harassment.

Colombian teens show great concern for the situation of their country, although many are resentful of the ongoing bureaucratic and corrupted political environment and are apathetic toward political participation. As with most Colombians, teens feel that problems with drugs, guerrillas, and corruption have created a negative image of the country that obliterates Colombian national pride in, for example, its beautiful natural regions, the contributions of writers like Nobel Prize winner Gabriel García Márquez, painters like Fernando Botero and Alejandro Obregón, scientists like Manuel Patarroyo, and the growing visibility of outstanding Colombian athletes and artists. Many of them are aware that young people stand out (contradictorily) either in sports or in violence. Although statistics show that a high number of Colombian adolescents are involved in different kinds of criminal activities, in general they disapprove of violence and long for a better future where they can have jobs they like and feel satisfied with life (Office of the President of Colombia).

TYPICAL DAY

A family's geographic location, occupation, and social group, among other aspects, influence its typical daily routines. Routines are strongly linked to educational access. If a teen lives in an urban area and goes to school, the organization of his or her day depends on the school schedule. Even then, the schedule will depend upon whether the teen attends a public or private school. There is an evident difference in the way teens spend time outside of school since public schools do not offer as many extracurricular activities as do private schools. Most public schools have two shifts. Students attend school in the morning (usually from 7:00 A.M. to 12:30 P.M.) or in the afternoon (from 1:00 to 6:00 P.M.). Public schools do not have a lunch break and therefore most students go home after dismissal. Many attend sports practice in the hours of the shift in which they are not taking classes, but their performance on the field is not related to school.

After school, teens usually devote time to homework, TV, and chores at home. Many work, especially those from low-income sectors. Teenage girls and boys sell items on the street, help their parents in their occupations or businesses, or bus tables. Watching TV after school or work becomes the main entertainment for this group of teens since they might be too tired to do anything else. Most students who attend public schools work. The rate of those who do is so high that many schools offer evening and/or intensive programs to help teens complete high school. Students who go to school during the day and do not work can take a break in the afternoon to do homework, play sports, spend time with friends, or watch TV. TV is popular in every population sector since even those in remote areas have access. The upper and middle classes often have cable services that allow them to watch American TV. Spending time with friends from one's neighborhood is common. Male teens usually gather outside, on a corner or in front of a store. Girls tend to get together at somebody's house. In cities near water, aquatic and other outdoor activities are popular. Parties are common everywhere, since Colombians in general love music and dancing.

Many private schools run from 8:00 A.M. to 2:00 or 3:00 P.M. and they often have lunch breaks. Their education patterns are similar to schools in the United States or Europe. Most are bilingual. In such schools, teens might stay after classes and participate in activities such as sports, cheerleading, or music.

Students are admitted to universities at as young an age as 17. They may keep some of the routines they had in high school unless they have taken a part-time job in order to pay for university studies. Even if they are young adults attending universities, they continue to live with their parents. It is different, of course, for those students who have to move to a big city to pursue a university degree.

Regardless of social position, young adults in Colombia are expected to help with chores as part of their daily activities. This may differ in upper-class families with maids. Otherwise, chores such as cleaning and making beds are expected from teens. In middle- and lower-class groups, girls were traditionally assigned cleaning and similar domestic tasks but that is changing. With each succeeding generation of new families, responsibilities are increasingly divided up between both boys and girls. Teens also work with their parents if they own a business or if the main income of the house results from manual labor. They learn the family trade at a young age and are given duties to fulfill, in order to learn how to manage the family business step by step.

FAMILY LIFE

Traditionally, Colombian families were large but nowadays the average number of children in a family is three. Although divorces and legal separations have increased, most teens live with both parents. Domestic partnerships have also increased as well as families in which both parents work. Although housework is traditionally considered the woman's responsibility, the participation of men is increasing. As a result of the sociopolitical situation of the country, the number of women who are the head of a family has increased. Many women have become young widows or are separated because their husbands are involved, whether by choice or by accident, in the armed conflict. Also, many families from rural zones have been displaced to urban ones. It is easier for women than for men to find temporary jobs as maids or waitresses, or in service industries, when families have just arrived in a new city.

Family reunions are probably the only activity people of different social classes and geographical zones have in common. In general, families maintain close ties and weekends are opportunities to get together for lunch. Occasions of this nature include uncles, aunts, cousins, nephews, nieces, and grandparents. Teens' circles of friends often include their siblings and cousins. Although family members might have different schedules, spending time together and eating together at least once a day is central to the lifestyle of Colombia. Families might spend time together doing something as simple as talking or watching TV. Watching soap operas is a favorite activity for the whole family at night. Some Colombian soap operas have become popular in other Spanish-speaking countries as well as in U.S. cities highly populated by Spanish speakers. Family parties are common but there are also parties organized by teens and held at friends' houses.

Social class discrimination has always been a problem for Colombia and continues to be one of the main causes of friction and division. Upper-

Teen girl sits with mother and siblings on their porch,
San Andres, Colombia. © J. Monaco/TRIP.

class families own cars and big houses or apartments in exclusive neighborhoods. They have mobility and resources to spend vacations in the United States or Europe, and often have a vacation house in a town or coastal resort near where they live. Their kids have access to the best schools and universities, and they have the resources to get children involved at early ages in activities such as art and sports. While for these teens, moving to another country or securing income is easy despite the difficult times, paradoxically, there are high rates of drug addiction and alcoholism among them because their parents are too busy with their social obligations or business occupations.

Middle-class families in Colombia own or rent more modest houses. The American suburban lifestyle is in fashion these days. For this sector, opportunities to vacation away from home depend largely on their ability to visit relatives who live in other cities or on discounted plans offered by offices of human resources. Most businesses subscribe to *Cajas de compensación*, entities that allow families to book rooms or entertainment venues at special prices.

Unable to afford cars of their own, young middle- and lower-class teens rely on public transportation. Upper-class teens borrow the family car and usually get their first car upon beginning university studies. In any case, costs are high in Colombia and many people prefer not to have cars because they are easily stolen or may cause the owner to be the target of thieves. If teens from private schools or from upper-class families are engaged in extracurricular activities, school transportation is seldom provided. Parents must drive them or organize car pools with the other families involved.

Many people from the lower classes have little mobility or opportunity to enjoy the country's natural wonders. Plane tickets are rarely affordable. The situation has worsened for people of all social classes since traveling by car or bus is no longer safe due to the sociopolitical violence. Traveling by car carries a risk of being robbed or kidnapped.

Activities and festivals provide entertainment opportunities for teens locally, but in general social segregation and a lack of opportunities are strongly reflected in the situation of lower-class youths. In the absence of education, work, and entertainment opportunities, teens from the periphery and from misery belts are at high risk of becoming involved with gangs or criminal activities. The situation of these social groups usually results in broken families, teen pregnancy, drug abuse, and other social problems. Sociologists, anthropologists, nongovernmental agencies, and human rights organizations, among others, have placed emphasis on the dire situations of these teens. Contemporary Colombian literature and film have a common interest in the representation and portrayal of different sectors of society, but the government needs to offer more effective and immediate programs and alternatives to provide teens with opportunities for social reinsertion, education, and jobs.

Teens feel that their family is being replaced more and more by the relationships they form outside the house. They also feel they have more freedom to do whatever they please when they are with their friends (Office of the President of Colombia). This may be a result of reduced parental supervision given the increase in households in which both parents work. In many cases parents are too busy with their social and/or business occupations, and there are high rates of drug addiction and alcoholism among upper-class teens. Sixty-eight percent of teens feel that family troubles affect them. They rank the prevalence of these problems, from top to bottom, as due to economic difficulties, lack of mutual understanding, lack of communication, problems related to children and their education, and infidelity. They feel that major conflicts between parents and their teenaged offspring derive from the former's apparent disregard for, or opposing views on curfews, choice of friends, school, money, music, and drinking. They are aware that in most cases, their parents know their problems and show concern about their troubles and behavior. Although parents approach them in a friendly way, teens also feel that their parents frequently act out. Most of them manifest strong ties with their parents, love them, and show concern for their well-being but they would change the way their parents discipline them, and as (potential) parents, they think they will be less manipulative and promote better communication and more of an exchange of ideas (Office of the President of Colombia).

TRADITIONAL AND NONTRADITIONAL FOOD DISHES

In general, Colombian food reflects Spanish gastronomic traditions, indigenous cuisine, and heavy African influences on both coasts. Colombian food doesn't contain the hot spices associated with some Latin American countries. Instead, spices like cumin and combinations of herbs are used more frequently. Breakfasts and dinners are often light. Most teenagers have coffee or hot chocolate for breakfast, with bread or *arepas* (traditional Colombian corn cakes). On weekends, breakfast may be more complete since family members are not rushing to school or work. Larger breakfasts are more the norm in rural areas where teens work in agricultural fields.

Lunch is the most substantial meal of the day and is served around noon or 1:00 P.M. A typical lunch for upper- and middle-class sectors of Colombian society consists of homemade soup, a main dish with meat or fish, and rice and/or potatoes. For lower-income families, meat and fish are luxuries, so their diet is richer in carbohydrates. In the cold temperatures of the Andes, for example, the diverse kinds of potatoes of the region constitute the main food staple. *Panela,* a solid paste made of brown sugar that melts in boiling water and provides a lot of energy, is a food highly consumed among this sector. Often accompanied by bread, it is cheap and in low-income families it may be the only food that they will have.

In rural areas, diet depends upon which crops are in season. Colombia is rich in vegetables and tubers. Juices made from its wide variety of natural fruits are popular accompaniments to meals but sodas are also popular.

Besides fruit, items common to every geographical zone are yucca, plantains, rice, corn, and legumes.

Colombia does not have a national dish but there are numerous regional dishes that nowadays can be found not only in the region of origin but also in the most important urban centers. Although they vary from place to place, *arepas* are popular. In addition to their popularity as a breakfast staple, these corncakes may be served with meals or eaten as a snack. Like *arepas*, tamales can be found throughout the country but its ingredients and presentation vary according to region. Corn is the basic ingredient of tamales, which are wrapped not in cornhusks (as in Mexico) but rather in plantain leaves. *Ajiaco*, a soup typical of the highlands, is made with chicken, corn, and three different types of potatoes. It is served with cream, capers, and avocado. Antioquia is famous for its *bandeja paisa*, a hearty plate of red beans with pork skin, rice, ground meat, fried plantains, *arepas*, and fried egg. A stew called *sancocho* is popular in many parts of Colombia. It is always prepared with plantain and yucca but the meat item changes according to the specific production of each zone. It is made with saltwater fish on the coast, freshwater fish in the river valleys, and chicken or other meat in the highlands.

Traditional Colombian food is popular among teens, although international foods are increasing in popularity in the larger cities. Hamburgers, pizza, sushi, and foods from Mexico and the Mediterranean are becoming more visible but not affordable for everybody. Restaurants and bars that offer these foods are usually located in upper-middle-class zones. Pubs, coffeehouses, and soup and salad bars are popping up daily and it is common to see fast food places that look like some in the United States but that have adopted combinations that appeal to Colombians' tastes. A combo in one of these places may be a hamburger made with *arepas* instead of bread, or the side dish might be *papa criolla frita* (small, yellow potatoes), or yucca sticks instead of French fries. Other places offer tropical fruit and/or coffee milkshakes with delicious results. The adaptation of food extends to junk food, fried yucca, fried plantains, and pork skins. Other items are conveniently wrapped in small packages and can be found in supermarkets, convenience stores, and, of course, school cafeterias. However, Colombians consume their own food and international and fast foods are not replacing the traditional Colombian fare. Even in major cities, white-collar employees and office workers look for traditional restaurants for lunch.

In cities, food is purchased in supermarkets, local markets, and *tiendas* (barrio stores). Lower income families prefer the latter two because food is cheaper there. Middle- and upper-class families prefer to buy food at supermarkets. Supermarkets in Colombia are similar to those in the United States. There are different chains and it is easy for a family to spot which offer better prices. Many specialize in gourmet, precooked, or imported foods. Others feature basic foods for everyday consumption, while still others sell specialty foods from different regions of the country. Geography is again an important factor for food acquisition. In coastal cities, many families prefer fish to beef or chicken. In Llanos Orientales, raising cattle is the most important economic activity so that beef is a staple. Some indigenous groups in the Amazon jungle and other parts of Colombia still hunt for food. This is not necessarily linked to economic factors but to cultural heritage. In the same way, food items and preparation in these regions are different. Staples such as yucca and other tubers are common. In some rural zones, families grow their own crops since they have land for gardens and orchards. Depending on the geographical zone, they may produce potatoes, corn, onions, carrots, zucchini, tomatoes, and green peas. They may also raise poultry, or perhaps cattle if they are wealthier.

Colombian food continues to be a central part of family and other social gatherings. In urban centers, it is common to see teenagers meeting in barrio coffeehouses or in *fruterías* (juice and fruit salad bars) after class. These feature juices, *salpicón* (a nonalcoholic mix similar to sangria), Colombian pastries, and other bakery products and coffee, and many have added pizza, hamburgers, and hot dogs. Since malls have become popular, teenagers gather in food courts where they can find American food as well as Colombian traditional meals in fast-food versions.

SCHOOLING

The official education system includes six years of high school, known as *bachillerato*. However, Colombians receive an average of only seven years of education. When they are about 11 or 12, teens begin their first year of high school (junior highs and middle schools do not exist in Colombia).

Some schools are exclusively for boys and some for girls only, while others are coed. In special schools called *normales*, students may combine high school with a preliminary career in teaching. Many *normales* have traditionally been schools for women. There are also trade schools, or *escuelas vocacionales*, where, in addition to a high school diploma, students may acquire a certificate in a vocational technical career.

Public schools may be totally or partially funded by the state or by the department. Parents or guardians must pay for private schools, which are very expensive. Curricular content is standardized for every school, as well as for both shifts in public schools. The main core of courses includes math, human and natural biology, national and Latin American geography, history, and literature in the first four years of high school, followed by chemistry, physics, algebra, trigonometry, world geography, history, and literature in the last two. Foreign languages and computer classes are part of private school programs, although the implementation of these two specific courses into public schools is becoming more common since there is an increasing awareness of the impact of both in university careers as well as prospective employment.

Students take, at the very least, six to seven courses a day, each 45 minutes long. The academic year is divided into two halves. Students receive monthly or bimonthly report cards. The grading scale is given through a report that underlines the goals accomplished for each course.

Upon completion of the *bachillerato* students must take a national exam, the scores of which help regulate admission to universities. The national exam is a comprehensive test of subjects standardized for both private and public schools, and it covers Spanish, math, general sciences, chemistry, and physics as well as verbal and mathematical aptitude. The scores also provide indicators for administrators who plan the curriculum for Colombian schools. This is the most important exam students will take, although universities may require additional examinations as part of their admissions procedure.

In general, schools have strict policies regarding performance, attendance, punctuality, and overall discipline. Students are responsible for the content of classes that they miss, and makeup tests are given only in extreme cases. Most schools require students to wear uniforms. A standard uniform in public schools consists of a blue sweater, white shirt, jeans, and black shoes for boys. Girls wear a blue sweater, a white shirt, a blue-and-white plaid skirt, white socks, and black shoes. On days that physical education is scheduled, students wear blue sweatpants and sweatshirts along with white T-shirts and tennis shoes. Private schools also have uniforms, consisting of the same clothing articles but in different colors. Schools forbid smoking not only while at school but also anytime a student is wearing a school uniform, even if he or she is not at school but in another public place. There has been difficulty enforcing that rule. Schools do enforce strict rules prohibiting fancy jewelry and makeup with uniforms. Many have regulations limiting hair length for males. In general, they dictate that students' uniforms be clean and tidy. The idea of uniforms might seem extreme to U.S. students, but in Colombia, the uniforms help bridge gaps between social classes. If both middle- and lower-class teens attend the same school, the distraction and friction resulting from overt consumerism as expressed in clothing is somewhat regulated through the uniform. It does not mean that students gladly accept wearing it. Most teens see the regulation as a burden and have a hard time complying with it.

Although education is regarded as a way to improve one's life, the quality of education and the purpose of studying are currently under heated debate. Pursuing a university career has become difficult and expensive. Many teens no longer look forward to completing high school. Because of high unemployment rates, even professionals such as engineers, doctors, and architects can't find well-paid jobs or positions in their area of expertise, which discourages young people from pursuing further studies. In addition, the quality of education is itself severely questioned by many Colombian teens.

In general, students would like to see the school process as a dialogue among teachers, parents, and young people. They consider their own forms of art, such as graffiti and rock music, to be expressions of their reality. Many resort to artwork to participate in the construction of a national identity that revives Colombian history and national values as they interact with the rest of the world. They would like to see new school programs that target creation and research and that are less concentrated in the memorization or repetition of data (Cajiao 1996, 53–63).

SOCIAL LIFE

Teens meet other teens at school, in their neighborhoods, through family members, and in public places. There is a tendency for teens to associate with people from their own social class. It is the same at the university level. This doesn't mean that there are not permanent relations or strong friendships among people from different economic levels, but teens' circles of friends do strongly relate to social status.

Dates are not prearranged in Colombia. In general, teens can select their dating partners. Because family is central to Colombian society, it is common for adolescents to bring girlfriends and boyfriends home. Many parents do try to influence teens' decisions, not only in dating but also in their choice of friends. Parents usually welcome teens' friends if the friendships do not jeopardize performance at school and if the friendships seem to be a positive influence.

Teens choose their clothing themselves. Conflicts over dress are pretty much similar to ones that every generation experiences everywhere else:

parents try to divert teens from looking sloppy when trying new styles, hair colors, hair styles, piercing, tattoos, and so on. Even though Colombia is a big textile and leather producer and a large supplier of fabric and handiwork for the sewing industry, the clothing shows strong evidence of Americanization. Teens love American clothes, brands, and styles. Most of this tendency is highly related to consumerism as portrayed in magazines, TV, and film. Hollywood film is popular in Latin America, as it is in the rest of the world. Colombian brands offer shoes and clothes that look like those in vogue in the United States.

In general, teens dress casually, although sports clothes such as sweatshirts and shorts are devoted solely for use in sports activities. Flip-flops and extremely casual shorts are not worn to university classes or social events. Sports caps are popular but not worn all the time. Teens wear jeans, shirts, T-shirts, leather jackets, and wool sweaters in cold cities like Bogotá. In warm cities like Cali, Medellín, Barranquilla, and Cartagena, kids dress nicely yet comfortably.

Currently, many public service advertisements encourage teens to find their own style and not to be influenced by everything they see on TV. The ads are part of a larger campaign aimed at helping teens to develop safer consumer habits. Similar ads address issues such as keeping young people away from smoking, alcohol, and drugs. Others encourage teens to delay premarital sex, while other ads advocate practicing safe sex and being aware of the risk of AIDS.

The number of teens who engage in premarital sex has increased in recent years. The average age for a first sexual relationship is 14.4 years old (Office of the President of Colombia). Premarital sex is acceptable to teens but not to parents. As a result of the increase in premarital sex, the pregnancy rate among female adolescents has also risen. Finishing high school while raising a baby is difficult for girls and is a major reason that they drop out of school.

The average age at which people get married is 24 for women and 26 for men. Teens usually live with their parents until they marry. If a teen becomes pregnant and the couple decides to settle down together, they are likely to live with one of the two families. Lower-income couples often live with their families even after they wed, until they can afford their own housing. Free unions are becoming more popular. Schools, churches, and community organizations are implementing programs to better inform teens on issues such as birth control and peer pressure. These groups address homosexuality, bisexuality, and sexual education in general because there is an urgent need for teens to obtain accurate information on such issues. Love and steady relationships are important to Colombian teens. They regard communication, loyalty, and sharing home responsibilities as the keys to success for living as a couple (Office of the President of Colombia).

RECREATION

Although schools offer sports activities, participation in them is not central to school life. Schools support athletic curricula but academics are considered more important. There are many sports centers available for athletic practices. Soccer is the most popular sport but is only for boys. Male teens tend to be more engaged in sports activities, while music is a favorite pastime for girls (Office of the President of Colombia). Only in recent years have female teens taken more interest in playing. Males engage in rougher sports such as soccer, biking, and boxing. Many young Colombian women stand out in skating, tennis, and swimming. Upperclass teens have more opportunities to play sports through their schools or through membership in social clubs. Middle- and lower-class teens can take advantage of available health and recreation centers located around the cities. Teens who live near water are avid swimmers and love taking advantage of the natural resources. Because biking is a traditional transportation means in the Andes, Colombia has had prominent athletes in biking tournaments throughout the world.

Teens from rural areas do not share the same activities as do teens from larger or mid-sized cities. In the countryside, the school schedule is still important but sports and entertainment facilities are limited. Rural teens help with family chores such as farming, gardening, and caring for animals. Outdoor activities such as swimming, climbing mountains, and hiking are popular but are not necessarily performed for physical fitness or in a competitive way. Rather, they are done simply to connect with the surroundings.

Teens follow the performances of Colombian athletes closely. Much hope is devoted to the success of the country's soccer team every time the World Cup calendar is active. The Colombian soccer team has successfully performed in international tournaments but the achievement of the World Cup is still a dream. Some noted sports celebrities from Colombia are Juan Pablo Montoya, a Formula One race car driver; Santiago Botero, world cycling champion; Eileen Katherine Vargas, junior golf world champion; and Fabiola Zuluaga and Catalina Castaño, both tennis players.

Some main avenues close to traffic on Sundays and holidays so that people can participate in the *ciclovía,* an opportunity to hike and bike in the city. The *ciclovía* is a teen favorite and a great opportunity to exercise and mingle with people of the same age. This activity has also extended to cities like Cali, Medellín, and other, smaller cities.

Music festivals and traditional celebrations are popular. Bogotá features a summer festival that includes sports competitions, folk dance performances in public spaces, and free concerts. Also popular is a three-day gathering of national and international rock *en español* (rock in Spanish) bands. A prominent celebration in Cali is *La feria de Cali* that includes a reunion of the most famous salsa music bands. Street dances known as *verbenas* are organized in many neighborhoods. Barranquilla has a famous carnival that coincides with the Christian calendar that determines other world-famous carnivals. It depicts popular characters from the Caribbean lifestyle and traditional dances of the Caribbean coast, most of them keepers of strong African traditions.

Historically, Bogotá has always been an important cultural center with important events such as the Iberoamerican Festival of Theater that gathers famous ensembles from all over the world. The festival features activities for everybody and every budget, drawing teens to participate because of the many free shows in public spaces. Medellín hosts an International Festival of Poetry every year. Despite political turbulence, Colombians engage enthusiastically in cultural activities, and many of them provide teens with free entertainment as well as exposure to cultures from all over the world.

ENTERTAINMENT

Music, sports, watching TV or videos, reading, and going out with friends are the most popular activities for teens (Office of the President of Colombia). Music is central to entertainment in Colombia. Teens love parties. Most are big music fans and love to go out dancing, which is also the most popular way to meet people. Although schools sometimes have socials, spontaneous parties in somebody's house are more common, as are dance clubs and discos. Teens love Latin American rhythms. Salsa has increased in popularity over the past 30 years, especially in cities like Cali and Barranquilla and, more recently, in Bogotá. Colombian salsa bands and singers are among the favorites. Teens also listen to and dance to merengue and Colombian *vallenatos* (music from the lowlands in the Caribbean). There are many famous Colombian groups, bands, and singers in all these categories of music, and the country's teens are among the most devoted fans. These artists have become famous in most Latin American countries and among Spanish speakers in the United States as well as in some European countries, so Colombians are supportive of their work because they export a positive image of the country.

Colombian teens listen to a lot of American pop music. They keep on top of musical fashion through radio stations, TV, and newspapers. U.S. Latino pop is well liked. Currently the most popular singer in that genre is Shakira, who has become a national icon among teens. Rock *en español*, a hybrid resulting from a mix of Latin American traditional rhythms and American beats, is also common. More and more bands, mainly those from marginal sectors of the cities, have adopted genres such as hip-hop, techno, and rock to voice their opinions regarding different issues of contemporary Colombia.

TV shows and videos are popular among teens, too. Video rentals are common in cities and towns but not in rural areas. Teens enjoy Hollywood films, which are released almost at the same time as their premieres in the United States. However, other kinds of foreign film and art cinema are popular among people of different ages. In some cities, teens and young adults frequent film series organized by different cinema clubs or film aficionados around the works of European directors, U.S. independent film directors, or other topics.

Colombians are increasingly more aware and supportive of their national film industry. In 2001, *El Tiempo*, Colombia's leading newspaper, conducted an Internet poll to determine what Colombians thought to be the best Colombian film, director, and script. The poll was also conducted in universities so it greatly reflected teens' and young adults' preferences. Víctor Gaviria was selected as best Colombian director. His two most important films are *Rodrigo D. No Future* (1989) and *The Rose Seller* (1998), centering upon the lives of teens from marginal zones in Medellín and featuring nonprofessional actors. Raúl García's *Kalibre 35* (2001) was selected best Colombian film. A criticism of the state's lack of support for young talent in Colombia, it narrates the adventures of two young men who decide to rob a bank in order to finance production of their film. Luis Ospina's *Breath of Life* (1999), depicting how a young woman's life is shaped by the confluence of different forms of violence in Colombia, was chosen as best script. Results of that poll showed that preferences related to young people's stories and/or to a concern, on the part of the directors, to portray real life. In general, Colombian teens support forms of art that voice their concerns and pay attention to issues related to adolescent life in Colombia.

There is no legal drinking age in Colombia but that may change in the near future. Alcohol abuse is increasing among young people. Drug use, alcohol consumption, and smoking are less predominant in teens between 12 and 14 but are growing in other sectors of the young population. A high rate of drug and alcohol use exists in the 18 to 21 age group. Curiosity, peer pressure, and the desire to escape family and personal problems are the main reasons for drug abuse (Office of the President of Colombia). National prevention programs have called attention to the role played by families and have questioned the fact that minors can easily buy alcohol since they are not carded. Many bars have started designated driver programs to encourage responsible behavior by adolescents.

More drastic measures have been taken in cities like Bogotá. The mayor decreed a curfew for minors and the measure was subsequently extended to almost 20 Colombian cities. It is part of a program known as *rumba zanahoria* (healthy partying). Even though this has been a polemical issue, cities like Medellín have shown a 43 percent decrease in teen deaths. Although these measures have shown positive results, their total effectiveness is questioned because, as some adolescents report, "The early closing has merely pushed the party outside the city, beyond easy monitoring by the cops" (Day 2002).

Teens enjoy going in groups to movies, concerts, and parks. Attending soccer games on the weekends is popular. Fans closely follow the national cup and local tournaments. Shopping malls are becoming popular. Bigger cities have modern malls similar to those in the United States. They feature Dolby sound, multiplex cinemas, food courts, electronic games, and cyber cafés, the latter of which are increasing in popularity. Having access to the Internet at home is still a luxury for many teens; therefore, electronic cafés are appealing because teens can surf the Web, play computer games, and hang out with friends.

RELIGIOUS PRACTICES AND CULTURAL CEREMONIES

The predominant religion in Colombia is Roman Catholicism but it is no longer the official religion. Many teens identify themselves as Catholics because that is the religion practiced by their family, but few attend church regularly. There are some synagogues and mosques because there are small Jewish and Muslim populations in Colombia. A minority of Colombians, mainly those of European descent, practice Protestant religions and attend the Anglican or the Lutheran Church (Williams and Guerrieri 1999, 22). Protestant evangelicals such as Jehovah's Witnesses and the Church of Christ of Latter Day Saints, along with other denominational Christian churches, have gained ground in recent years. There is some concern from different sectors of society over the proliferation of satanic sects and the attraction that they hold for young people. In general, though, teens' participation in religious activities is not high.

Christmas is an important family celebration. Preparation begins on December 16 with the *novena de aguinaldos*, a traditional celebration that takes place every night until Christmas Eve. Families and friends gather around nativity scenes in relatives' or friends' houses, where they pray and sing Christmas carols and later, perhaps, dine and dance together. This tradition was disappearing but has been revitalized in recent years. On Christmas Eve, family members exchange gifts and have a special meal together. Families also celebrate New Year's Eve together.

Birthday celebrations are always special. Usually, families celebrate with cakes and small parties. *Quinceañeras,* observed when girls reach the age of 15, are similar to sweet sixteen parties in the United States. Although it has all but disappeared in the larger cities, *quinceañeras* continue to be common in small or remote towns and villages. Very traditional, wealthy families may still hold parties in selective clubs, where daughters are officially introduced to society in a manner similar to the debutante, coming-out tradition in the southern United States.

A popular celebration for teens is the *Día del amor y la amistad* (Love and Friendship Day) the third Saturday of September. It is similar to St. Valentine's Day but the focus is on friends as well as loved ones. Teens joyfully celebrate the end of the academic year. There are many class farewells; graduation from high school is the most important celebration for teens. Although teens continue living with their parents, graduation means a transition in roles, responsibilities, and freedom. Of course, since access to education in rural and remote areas is more difficult, turning 18 might be the rite of passage for this population. Also, teens in indigenous groups may have adulthood and womanhood rites of passage tightly linked to the ways of their society.

CONCLUSION

Given the geographical diversity of Colombia, the social class divisions, and the way violence has touched every sector of the population, it is difficult to formulate strict definitions of teens in Colombia. In general, family is very important to them. Friends and activities are largely dictated by the social group a teen belongs to and by the part of the country where he or she lives.

Soccer is popular throughout Colombia. Teens love dancing and listening to music and they are keenly aware of Latin American as well as U.S. musical trends. Although Americanization shows up in aspects such as clothing and music, most other facets of teens' lifestyles are shaped by Colombian traditions. Colombian teens constitute an important sector of the population for cultural projects rich in diversity that lead to national reconciliation. In spite of hard times in the country and teens' worries about the stability of their future, they want to be a decisive part of the shaping of a new Colombia.

ACKNOWLEDGMENT

Special thanks to Nikki M. Wilson for research and editorial assistance.

RESOURCE GUIDE

ACNUR (Grupo Temático de Desplazamiento). *Estado de situación del desplazamiento*. Bogotá: ACNUR/OCHA (United Nations), 2001.
Cajiao Restrepo, Francisco. "ATLANTIDA: una aproximación al adolescente escolar colombiano." *Revista Nómadas* 4, 53–64, 1996.
Chaparro Valderrama, Hugo. "La rockoteca del Divino Niño." *Gaceta*. 47 (June–December 2000): 106–110.
Day, Adrienne. "Colombian Club Kids, Grooving at the Edge of Apocalypse. 'The Bomb My Nation Has Become.'" *Village Voice*, February 13–19, 2002. http://www.villagevoice.com/.
"Farc están reclutando menores en Bogotá." *El Tiempo*, February 14, 2002. http://eltiempo.terra.com.co/.
Harding, Collin. *Colombia in Focus*. London: Latin American Bureau, 1996.
Jerez, Angela Constanza. "Menores más alcohol, más droga." *El Tiempo*, 23 December 2001, 1–2.
Meertens, Donny. "The Nostalgic Future. Terror, Displacement, and Gender in Colombia. Victims, Perpetrators, or Actors?" In *Gender, Armed Conflict, and Political Violence*, edited by Caroline Moser and Fiona Clark, 133–48. London: Zed Books, 2000.
Office of the President of Colombia. "Colombia joven: Encuesta Nacional de Jóvenes. Presidencia de la República." http://presidencia.gov.co/.
"Víctor Gaviria: el mejor para los colombianos." *El Tiempo*, December 5, 2001. http://eltiempo.terra.com.co/.
Williams, Raymond Leslie, and Kevin G. Guerrieri. *Culture and Customs of Colombia*. Westport, Conn.: Greenwood Press, 1999.

Nonfiction

Williams, Raymond Leslie, and Kevin G. Guerrieri. *Culture and Customs of Colombia*. Westport, Conn.: Greenwood Press, 1999.

Web Sites

http://www.advocatesforyouth.org/factsfigures/directory/c.htm#Colombia
Describes Colombian organizations featuring special education programs for teens.

http://www.hrw.org/reports/1994/colombia/genertoc.htm
A Human Rights Watch report of violence and children and teens in Colombia.

http://lcweb2.loc.gov/frd/cs/cotoc.html
The Library of Congress Colombia country study.

http://www.presidencia.gov.co/
Official Web site for the Colombian presidency. The section "Colombia joven" provides statistics on teens and describes specific programs for them.

Pen Pal Information

http://www.pen-pal.net
Pen Pal Network.

Chapter 5

CUBA

Gastón A. Alzate

INTRODUCTION

Cuba lies 90 miles south of Miami, Florida. The biggest island in the Caribbean, Cuba is situated at the mouth of the Gulf of Mexico. Cuba's nearest neighbors are Haiti to the east, the Yucatán Peninsula to the west, and Jamaica to the south. Consisting of the main island and around 4,195 smaller keys, quays, and islets, Cuba has 110,922 square kilometers of mostly flat territory. Its nature, diverse and prodigious, shows a wide variety of plants and animals, and includes 7,000 km of coastline and around 300 beaches.

Cuba was claimed for Spain by Christopher Columbus on October 27, 1492, 15 days after he stepped for the first time onto the new continent in the Dominican Republic. As in other Latin American countries, conquest and colonization caused the extermination of the aboriginal inhabitants. When this happened, the Spanish Crown imported slaves from Africa. Today Cuba has a population of more than 11 million, in a particular mixture of Spaniards, Africans, and Asians. In 1898, Cuba declared its independence from Spain after a long and cruel war. Victory over Spain left Cubans exhausted, weak, and vulnerable. *Los Yankees*, as the Cubans called the U.S. government, intervened. Armed intervention led to a military occupation. The Platt Amendment, a legislative addition, was inserted by the American government into the Cuban constitution. It sanctioned North American intervention for "the maintenance of a government adequate for the protection of life, property, and individual liberty" (Perez 1995, 57).

In 1933, Fulgencio Batista Zaldívar guided a rebellion, known as the Revolt of the Sergeants, indicating that he had taken control of the army from the administration. It also marked Batista's appearance as self-appointed chief of the Cuban armed forces and privileged U.S. man. As a result, rights and democracy for many Cubans were limited. Resistance to the government was rapidly and brutally crushed. American business interests and organized crime flourished under Batista. In the 1950s, Cuba became an important city for the American Mafia. Gambling became big business in Havana, and Batista and his cronies manipulated government power to enrich themselves. Within this corrupt political atmosphere Fidel Castro took power in 1959.

The Cuban Revolution was one of the twentieth century's most distinctive political triumphs for many underdeveloped and poor countries around the world. At the beginning of the 1960s, the Cuban Revolution had many challenges stabilizing the new government. Sweeping changes were taking place across the country. The U.S. viewed Castro as a threat to its national security and began an economic embargo, bringing the import of American goods to a halt and penalizing other countries who had business with the island.

In support of the new socialist island, the Soviet Union supplied Castro with economic aid and nuclear missiles for defense. In October of 1962, the United States and the Soviet Union almost came to nuclear war in a period called the Cuban missile crisis. The Soviets eventually capitulated, and peace was restored.

There is still debate among Cubans, but some scholars agree that the crisis pushed Castro into the Soviet domain. Whatever the reason, it is clear that after 1963 Cubans became part of a socialist experiment that many Latin American and Third World countries looked to with respect and affection.

Nevertheless, life inside Cuba was not as easy as many assumed. Thousands of educated Cubans fled, so skilled labor was scarce. The 1960s marked the beginning of political repression. Thousands of dissidents were jailed. Education and cultural policies became more extreme, trade unions were dissolved, and the media fell under total control of the government.

In the 1970s, the situation improved for some sections of the population. Economically, Cuba advanced. Cuba's health care system eliminated infectious diseases, drastically lowered the infant mortality rate, and illiteracy was eradicated.

At the beginning of the '80s, Cuba was still a Latin American symbol of independence from U.S. imperialism, but the quality of life in the country was beginning to decline. Almost 125,000 Cubans fled to the United States in the Mariel boat lift, adding to the several hundred thousand who had left the country in the early years of the revolution.

When the U.S.S.R. fell apart in 1991, the impact on Cuba was devastating. On an annual basis, the country lost over US$7 billion worth of imported goods ("Socialism or Death," 2001, 56). The Cuban government declared *el período especial*, a "special period in time of peace," which is a belt-tightening survival strategy. Millions of Chinese bicycles were imported because of the lack of oil for public transportation, oxen replaced tractors in the fields, and rations allowed just enough food for survival. Patients brought their own paper towels, bed sheets, and cotton items to hospitals. Although the situation has greatly improved since then, most of these difficulties are still challenging the lives of Cuban teens today.

TYPICAL DAY

Because all teens have to go to school, one can say that all Cuban teens begin their day at the same time. Education is compulsory in Cuba from age 6 through 15 (grade nine). At 16, students must either continue with their education or join the Youth Movement.

Although there are some exceptions, children and teens do not work. Some of them work after school, but only for a few hours. In many rural areas, students attend boarding schools. At these schools, they are required to perform agricultural or other forms of manual labor in addition to their studies. It is important to state that the special period, particularly as it pertains to tourism, has negatively impacted teens' enthusiasm for education.

In rural areas teens have to walk up to three miles to get to school. In urban areas what time they wake up depends on what transportation they take to school. There are few buses. Some teens even use flatbed trucks or horse-drawn carts. Cubans are masters at keeping old automobiles running: You can see many classic cars on the streets taking people to school or to work. Nevertheless, the most common form of transportation are bicycles. In many families, teenagers have to share a bicycle with their parents because the family cannot afford more than one. It is not out of the ordinary to see three members of a family riding the same bicycle. It is with humor and pride, although not far from reality, that Cubans say their health is the best in the world because of the daily exercise they are compelled to do on their bicycles.

Cuban teens usually spend five hours per day in school. They typically begin school at 7 or 8 and finish at 12 P.M. or 1 P.M. Some have afternoon schedules: 1 P.M. to 6 P.M., for example. If they have morning schedules they have lunch at home, and after a short siesta they do their homework. If they are from rural areas they usually help their parents with agricultural tasks. Before or after homework, teens spend a great part of their time outside playing baseball or volleyball. Sometimes they spend one or two hours just sitting down, chatting with neighbors or friends. Gossiping is the national sport, many Cubans would say.

In urban and rural areas during the afternoon, and also into the night, many teens watch TV. Although Cuban TV has limitations because of the economic emergency, a major difference between it and Western mass media is the fact that there are no advertisements on Cuban TV. Cuban TV has special programs for teens and children, such as soap operas where the main characters are teenagers. There are also contests in which teens from different schools compete on world history topics. Many of these programs are popular among the teen population. Cuban TV also offers special programs at night and on weekends that are attractive to the whole family.

On a typical night, teens usually have dinner between 6:30 and 7:30 P.M.—but this depends on blackouts. Cuba has dealt with rolling blackouts for over a decade due to a shortage of oil and other fuels. On some occasions Cubans experience as few as two hours of electricity per day. The situation seems to be improving, but the random schedule of these blackouts due to the energy shortage is a headache for many. Cuban teens go to bed between 9:30 to 10:30 P.M. except on weekends, when most are allowed to stay awake until 12 or 1 A.M., or longer if there is a party in the neighborhood.

FAMILY LIFE

In a typical Cuban family both parents work. The socialist system has provided women with all of the rights that are common in developed countries. In 1975, the Cuban Family Code declared gender equality in the family and ran a successful effort to incorporate women into the paid labor force at all levels. Nevertheless, Cuban culture is formed out of two powerful patriarchal cultures, the African and the Spanish, which is in itself a mix of the Arab, Iberian, Celtic, Jewish, and Gypsy cultures, all of which are typically *machista* (male chauvinistic) and homophobic. This has a deep impact on Cuban family life, especially the social roles of female teens. A focus on incorporating women into the workforce has produced a situation also common in other cultures: Women have two jobs, one at the workplace and the other at home. Females are in charge of cooking, shopping, cleaning, and caring for their younger siblings (although in urban areas men usually do the shopping). As a result female teenagers have tended to carry more of the stress of looking after the home during the special period in Cuba.

In Havana and Santiago de Cuba, the two largest cities, it is difficult for family members to eat at the same time because of differing schedules and blackouts. In rural areas it is easier. Nevertheless Sunday is the most important day, when the Cuban family usually congregates and eats together, especially if this is not possible during the week.

In the past 15 years Cubans have experienced substantial changes in family life due to rules the government has implemented in order to survive the U.S. embargo. Because of the economic crisis in 1994, the government allowed the once illegal farmers' markets, where rural residents may sell their products, to operate. In 1993 Castro authorized people to go into business for themselves, offering licenses for fishermen, mechanics, farmers, taxis, *bicitaxis* (bicycle taxis), and *paladares* (family restaurants). The same year, the state legalized the use of the U.S. dollar, of which only a few privileged, high-ranking members of the Communist Party had access to previously. This action democratized the Cuban market a bit, but at the same time divided the island in two new classes, those who had dollars and those who didn't. For those with dollars life greatly improved. *Tiendas de dólares* (dollar shops) sprang up everywhere. Like in any American or European supermarket, *tiendas* carry almost everything. Boys and girls from the age of 12 are hungry to buy anything from the dollar shop, due partly to the many restrictions they experience under the socialist system.

Decriminalizing the dollar had a devastating effect on the teen population, especially in a culture explicitly designed to produce egalitarianism. New generations are becoming more Americanized in their daily life. Teens in general express admiration for the American lifestyle and people. At the same time most of them are angry and perplexed by the continuing American economic embargo that has made basic living needs, and even medical supplies, scarce and expensive.

There are three ways for Cubans to acquire dollars: through relatives living abroad, through a family business, or underhandedly, in the black market or as prostitutes.

The minimum driving age in Cuba is 21, however in Cuba today cars are not only luxury objects but also an impossible dream for teens. Some teens have motorcycles, and the lucky ones have family abroad to send them money, not only to help with the cost of the motorcycle but also with the gasoline, which is very expensive. The average Cuban salary is 200 Cuban pesos per month, around $20, while a liter of gas may cost $2.

Schoolgirls walk down main street, Santiago de Cuba, Cuba. © K. McLaren/TRIP.

Most Cuban teens, especially those not directly involved with the revolution, are obsessed with Miami because many have family there, or their friends do, who tell them about American supermarkets and teenage fashion and music. This obsession reached a peak after the fall of the Soviet Union. At that moment people became so desperate to leave that they were willing to risk their lives on fragile rafts. Some teens attempted crossings with their parents, aunts, or uncles, and died. However, some survived and are now in Miami. During the great exodus in August and September of 1994, around 2,000 rafters a week were setting sail. Between 1989 and 1994, the worst time of the entire revolutionary period, over 10,000 rafters made it to Miami ("Dreaming of Miami," 73). Castro said that the United States contributed to the crisis by refusing to grant visas to people who were later welcomed as heroes after they risked their lives on rafts. Finally this great exodus stopped when the U.S. government agreed that all refugees picked up at sea would be returned to their homeland.

Relations between Cuba and the U.S. improved during the last decade (1990–2000). Before the terrorist attacks of September 11, 2001, in New York, Cubans had access to 20,000 American visas each year, many of them allocated by lottery. It was difficult to get one, since approximately 500,000 Cubans apply for these visas. Now relations between the two countries have changed. As an example of this new situation, the American Interest Office in Havana did not give tourist visas to Cuban winners of the 2002 Grammy awards, which would have granted them entry into the U.S. to receive their prize. In any event what this Cuban Miami dream has created in the imagination of Cuban teens is incredible. In general they believe that everything can be achieved in the U.S. When Tere, a 15-year-old young black woman, learned that in the U.S., as in Cuba, there were also lines to enter a rock concert or to buy a ticket for a football game, she said, "All my life I had had the idea that lines were Fidel's invention."[1]

This idealization of Miami contrasts with the ideas of other Cuban teenagers, particularly ones in secondary schools who participate actively in the revolution, with the Youth Movement, or as part of the Pioneers. The José Martí Pioneers Organization was formed in the 1960s and has 1.5 million young Cuban members. These revolutionary teenagers see the people of Miami as worms or *mafiosos*. For many Cubans, Miami is a terrorist city. The most dramatic act of terrorism was a 1976 bomb attack on a *Cubana de Aviación* airplane, on its way from Barbados to Havana. All 73 passengers and the crew died. Some Cuban government officials perished in the plane, but most of the dead were civilians; many were teenagers who had belonged to the national fencing team.

Generally speaking, all Cuban teens—both those who dream of Miami and those who do not—believe that terrorism against Cuba by the United States is not just Castro propaganda but a real threat to the island.

To further complicate this contradictory relationship between Cubans living in Miami and Cubans from the island, many who left the country as rafters have returned legally as tourists or entrepreneurs, helping friends and family to set up enterprises. A new law allows Cubans who previously left the island illegally to come back if they have enough money to spend in Cuba. These new businessmen and businesswomen have changed the face of many cities, especially Havana, and also have produced in many teens changes in the way they see their future in Cuba. At the same time, their particular contradictions and ambiguities have caused commotion in ordinary Cuban family life. Parents, as in all cultures around the world, tend to have a more conservative view, which in the case of Cuba is to embrace the government view. Teens tend to reject their parents' values, which are communist values, and have a sense for a more libertarian future, which in many cases is to embrace consumerism and capitalism.

TRADITIONAL AND NONTRADITIONAL FOOD DISHES

Cuban people have developed creative and unique approaches to food. Cuban cuisine traces its influences to Taínos and other indigenous peoples and to African slaves that Spaniards brought to the island. Root crops central to Cuban cuisine, like *malanga*, sweet potatoes, yuca, and various types of squash and beans, were cultivated by indigenous peoples. The arrival of Spaniards meant the introduction of pork and with the Africans came plantains. These are the basic elements of Cuban cuisine. As in many Caribbean cultures, although Africans were enslaved, their influence over Cuban cuisine was very strong.

A traditional Cuban meal is formed by *yuca con mojito* (a sauce of fried garlic and lemon), *puerco asado* (roasted pork), *moros y cristianos* or *congrí* (Moors and Christians), and a salad of cucumbers, tomato, carrots, and maybe avocado. *Moros y cristianos* is significant not only because it refers to Muslims and Christians, the two major religions in Spain at the time of Cuba's conquest, but also because it is a symbol of the mixture of races in Cuban culture (black beans for dark skin and rice for white). Cuban desserts are sweet, reflecting years of dependence on sugarcane. The most popular dessert is *flan de leche* (crème brulèe). A typical Cuban meal ends with a little cup of concentrated, sweetened coffee.

Unfortunately, nowadays Cubans rarely can have a meal like this unless they work in tourism or receive money from abroad. Officially they are limited to what they receive through the *libreta* (ration card). A Cuban's typical ration amounts to one piece of bread a day, three eggs a week, and a portion of fish or chicken once a month. A family of four is allotted one bottle of cooking oil four times a year, and milk is available only for children under eight. Many Cubans rarely enjoy the taste of beef or pork. Pork has been replaced by fried eggs or chicken. Sometimes they have canned sardines. Cubans' diets can vary considerably depending on their profession and access to dollars. Some people live mainly on their rations, purchasing little else, while others are able to afford a little more (Wetzel n.d., 17).

In urban areas, men (fathers and sons) do the shopping, which includes picking up rations as well as produce at the farmers' market, and also items like milk, meat, and eggs available at *la tienda de dólares* (dollar market).

Most Cubans like their food fried, thus the Cuban diet can be very high in fat although obesity is not as widespread as in the United States. There are some cafeterias, called *rápidos*, that offer fried chicken or *hamburguesas* accompanied by Tropicola (Cuban Coca Cola). *Rápidos* are visited by lucky teens who can spend two or three dollars on Saturday or Sunday. Nevertheless the presence of Cuban teens in these cafeterias is not challenging the presence of Cuban food at home. In rural areas teenagers have more opportunities for a better diet, because parents have their own land to cultivate. Solidarity between neighbors, friends, or family, even if they are not very close, is common, especially in rural areas. In urban areas everything depends on the *libreta* or dollars.

SCHOOLING

The Cuban education system consists of three types of schools: secondary and pre-university institutes in rural areas, polytechnic schools located near factories, and teacher-training schools in all regions of the country. Each school has its own dynamic, and is very particular in the way a typical school day is organized. Nevertheless in both secondary and pre-university schools, students work three hours per day in agricultural programs. Students who attend polytechnic schools and technological institutes spend four hours per day in industrial shops. In teacher-training schools, students learn to teach by practicing in local schools.

The Cuban government has been in the process of restructuring the school system. Schools, however, are still run largely under a system characterized by a rigid curriculum guided by the overarching goal of developing model, so-called socialist prototypes. It is important to note here that Cuba and North Korea are the only fully Communist countries left in the world. In Cuba the state needs to use education as a tool to reinforce its fight against tourism and its influence on children and teens. This has been the basis for the changes to the Soviet model in Cuba. Ironically, the state promotes tourism at the same time in an effort to save the economy.

Cuban classes are generally taught in a strict teacher-directed format, with some teacher-student interactions. Memorization is seen as the center of the curriculum while critical thinking is generally discouraged. Education is intertwined with community life through group projects, class chores, practical skills, and acceptable political thought.

The school year is 40 weeks long and goes from September to June. Each school provides instruction in Spanish, mathematics, science, the humanities, and farming technology and production. A school week typically involves 26 hours of instruction. Students must choose 9 or 10 subject areas designated by the curriculum, which is controlled by the Ministry of Education. Three or four years of high school then are open to students.

Every year, students must pass national examinations to proceed to the next grade. If a student wishes to transfer to another school, the student's adherence to socialist ideals is weighed heavily.

Castro's critics say that education in Cuba is used for political indoctrination. This tension between indoctrination and good quality education has had a definitive impact upon a teenager's education. The biggest collision is with the socialist ideology. By the late 1980s and the beginning of the '90s, Castro tried to resuscitate the revolutionary slogans *patria o muerte* (fatherland or death) and *socialismo o muerte* (socialism or death). It is evident that the appeal of these sentences that once expressed authentic communist ideas has now been lost ("The Cubans" 2001, 86). The only possibility for a teenager to believe in these slogans is to take an active part in the educational socialist order. Those who can incorporate themselves into their education are definitely within the system. The Lenin Vocational School, near Havana, is an excellent example because it is one of the most prestigious. This is a boarding school—at a level equivalent to high school in the U.S. Its 3,300 students are selected by exam scores and grades. The Lenin School emphasizes science but students are allowed to pursue a range of academic studies. According to a 16-year-old girl, Yuri, at that school, students follow a rigorous schedule of study, athletics, and cultural activities that begins at 6 A.M. and keeps them busy until bedtime at 10 P.M. She said, "We are allowed some television viewing in the evening, and home visits are possible on weekends." Ninety-five percent of graduates from these schools go on to attend a university.

Normally the high school graduation ceremony takes place in a plaza in front of the American Interest building. Many schools have their graduation ceremonies at the end of the school year, but the most significant is the Lenin ceremony because the Lenin school is for the most brilliant and revolutionary students in all of Cuba. Speakers blare through the neighborhood. Students wave flags at specified times and chant phrases in unison. The teens pledge themselves to socialism and raise their voices and fists against the U.S. *bloqueo*.

With funds gained from tourism, the government has begun to invest large amounts of money in reforming the educational system. It is publicly known that teenagers have started to lose interest in classes. The lack of interest in teaching is dramatic. The government now gives subsidies to students who register to be elementary school teachers. Other professions that were very prestigious in the past, such as medicine, nursing, economy, and law, do not make much sense in the new system, often because waiters and taxi drivers can make 10 times more money. On the other hand there are careers that are changing rapidly. The largest challenge for the Cuban government is that teens are abandoning professions in areas such as economics or law in favor of professions in the tourism industry.

English language training was not a priority during the first 35 years of the revolution; most teenagers studied Russian. Perhaps the paradox is that English is now a formal part of the school curriculum. Since tourism has begun to return as a source of income, many teens now have a desire to learn English. As in other places around the world, English is now seen as the gateway to the international community. So English is now part of the teacher-training programs in Cuba. Considering Cuba's situation, and the lack of resources, the program has done quite well (Robson 1996, 6).

Although the state has invested, and is still investing, a large part of the money from tourism in education, it is a common impression that the worst time of the *período especial* (1990–95) destroyed part of the ideological power of the educational system. According to 17-year-old Lázaro, from Cayo Hueso, a Havana downtown neighborhood, "Around half of the teen population do not have any hope for education, even if they go to school and do their homework." For teenagers, the future is hard to see when they have difficulty surviving from day to day. The following is a very well-known joke in Cuba today. A professor asks a 6-year-old boy, "What do you want to be when you grow up?" The student answers, "I want to be a foreigner."

Lázaro quit school when he was 14 and has worked since then harassing tourists. He is what Cubans call a *jinetero*. The system is simple. He goes to a prestigious hotel, where he picks a tourist. He prefers a man or a woman who is alone. He offers to take the tourist on a tour of the city, to a nearby beach, or to a *paladar* where the tourist can eat a good lobster for $7. Lázaro gets $1.50 per lobster from the owner of the *paladar*. If that does not work, Lázaro offers a cheaper hotel. If necessary, he will switch to more challenging topics (tobacco, rum, girlfriend, or boyfriend). Lázaro can get anything. If the tourist does not pay attention to him he follows the tourist for the whole day and waits for him outside of a restaurant, hotel, or theater. He takes it for granted that by the end of the day the tourist will buy something from him. When asked if he gets tired of this, especially when tourists do not want him around, he responded, "If you are poor, you have two brothers and a sister, and your father works and earns 200 pesos [$20 dollars] a month, you just don't care if the tourists are tired of your harassment, you need the money and that's it. If *yumas* [Cuban slang for foreigners] are tired of me, I am more tired of my situation." Sometimes Lázaro has become involved emotionally with some of his clients, but he prefers not to fall in love because he has a very jealous Cuban girlfriend. Working as a *jinetero,* he earns between 200 to 400 dollars a month, depending on the season. With this money he is a rich man on his block. He gives some money to his mother, but spends most of it at the dollar shop. Recently he bought a CD player, of which he is very proud. When asked if his father cares that he does not go to school, Lázaro says no, because his family needs his money. His mother does not have a job. He says also that his father considers himself very lucky because Lázaro is part of the tourism industry.

Other teenagers are not so lucky. There are many daughters and sons of doctors, lawyers, and engineers who, after 40 years of revolution, still do not have a house. Many married Cubans live with their children in a single room in their own parents' houses. Now that their children are teenagers and have girlfriends or boyfriends, and have been educated in a liberal society, the problem of *hacinamiento* (two or three people sharing the same bed) is very serious. In spite of the fact that Cuba is an egalitarian society, doctors earn less in a month than what waiters or taxi drivers earn in one day.

SOCIAL LIFE

On a first date, Cuban teenagers generally go to a social event where their other friends will be around, such as school excursions, discos, or neighborhood parties. After the first encounter, they may do something more private such as going out for ice cream, a movie, or a promenade. But all these activities depend upon permission from their parents. In general, parents do not allow female teenagers to have boyfriends until they are 15 years old. For males there is no such restriction unless they are going out with an older partner. Most female teenagers have boyfriends when they are 13 but they do not tell their parents.

Because of parents' restrictions most teens have their first date in boarding school. Many parents complain that the widespread separation of students from their homes has consequences in that many have emotional relationships before they are ready. Some complain that this practice weakens their authority over their children and promotes sexual experimentation at an early age. Others consider sexuality to be a normal part of a teenager's life. AIDS is one of the most serious concerns among parents when they talk about teenagers dating. Most of them think that tourists are responsible for the spread of AIDS in Cuba.

In Cuba, sex education and support groups, combined with a socialist focus on community, seem to have diminished challenges such as teen pregnancy, abortion, and domestic violence. In addition, when compared to other Latin American countries, the teen pregnancy rate is very low in Cuba.

Since Cuban teenage girls start their first love relationship when they are around 10 to 13 years old, they are forced to handle the unbalanced situation of women in Cuba. Teenage women alone on the street are always bombarded with sexual comments from men of all ages. These *piropos* (audacious remarks) are not always dirty or sexually connotative. *Piropos* vary from a courteous compliment to an invitation to have sex in a public restroom. It is important to clarify that in spite of this situation, rape is almost unheard of in Cuba, and violence against women is highly penalized by the socialist system; consequences include the death penalty.

On the other hand, it is important to understand that *piropos* are common in all Caribbean cultures and in many Latin American societies. The big difference is that Cuban girls feel that they can answer improper remarks without fear. They can express their anger because they feel that in a socialist country this behavior shouldn't be acceptable. In most cases Cuban men apologize. It is not rare to see female teens arguing with teenage boys about these topics on the streets. The ambiguity of this issue in a socialist country lies in the fact that more than 40 years of official policy designed to achieve the equality of men and women have not touched the culture's deep-rooted macho spirit.

Male teenagers, to fully accomplish their masculine role, are expected to have two or three girlfriends at a time. This dynamic in relationships frustrates many female teenagers. Some girls react to this imbalance by having many boyfriends themselves. As a consequence, many boys fear their girlfriends would prefer to date tourists, who obviously have more money than they do. In fact, nowadays many Cuban girls marry foreigners. At expensive hotels and restaurants it is common to see young Cuban women holding hands with their 40- to 50-year-old Spanish, Italian, German, and French boyfriends. Some find their way out of Cuba in this form, and come back for vacation to visit their families. Laura is a 19-year-old mulatto woman from Guanabo who married a 42-year-old Italian geologist. They met in Guanabo Beach, a favorite place of Italian tourists. In

Guanabo it is forbidden for unmarried Cubans to talk to foreigners, so Cuban policemen often stop to check IDs. If they are not satisfied with the explanation provided, police will write down their names. If it is the second time they are caught with a tourist, they can be arrested.

Laura married her husband, Bruno, two years ago, when she was 17. She says she was not a *jinetera* looking for a husband when they started to date. It was a very exciting situation because it was forbidden. When he was going to go back to Italy, he proposed marriage. They now live in Milan. She speaks Italian and is studying to be a hairdresser. She is happy because she can visit her family once per semester and can help her mother repair her house. When asked about Bruno's age, she says, "I really don't care. How I am not going to be crazy in love for the man who changed my life?"

Two fashion styles coexist in contemporary Cuba. One is based on socialist culture. The second is generated by the regularization of the dollar in Cuban economy and the influence of American culture in the world. Very often Cuban teens cross from one fashion style to the other without a smooth transition.

Socialist fashion has some essential icons: military uniforms from youth school, pioneers uniforms, Che Guevara pictures, and 26th of July flags, among others. These icons are still important and have a close relationship with socialist ideology.

On the other hand, if a teen does not belong to any Cuban socialist organization, these icons do not mean much, and he or she has a different scale of fashion values. On this scale, consumerism provided by dollar shops or by presents from family in Miami, Spain, or Mexico defines their outlook. For these teenagers the most precious element is gold in all imaginable forms: necklaces, bracelets, rings, earrings, and so on. It is important to note that this teenage predilection for gold is no different in other Caribbean cultures such as those of Puerto Rico, the Dominican Republic, Haiti, or Jamaica.

Another fashion element, common among teens throughout the island, is changing one's hair color. Blonde is preferred; red places second. Common fashion elements for Cuban teens parallel those among teens from any Caribbean society: blue jeans and colorful items for girls such as strapless tops, tight dresses, short skirts, and biking shorts. Boys may sport athletic shoes, baseball shirts, Bermuda (long) shorts, roller skates, and portable audio devices. All are similar to ones that Cuban teens see in American movies and, nowadays, are in fact part of the ordinary lives of many Cuban teens.

A large challenge for contemporary Cuban society is that not all teens can afford these expensive, often luxury, items, according to Latin American parameters. For this reason many teens get frustrated with their families and with a system that cannot provide the momentary happiness many teens in the world get to experience.

RECREATION

Officially, sports in revolutionary Cuba is seen as an integral part of one's physical and moral education. Fidel Castro has said, "Sport is an antidote to vice." (Fidel Castro Ruiz, cited in Geralin Pye 1986, 124). Half the population has participated in organized sports. Starting in elementary school, students compete in a variety of athletic competitions in the School Sport Games. Those who stand out are invited to the School for Sports Initiation, where students range in age from 11 to 16. Those who perform best will graduate to one of the Schools of Higher Athletic Performance. Although professional sports are illegal in Cuba, all athletes who participate in high competitions receive free housing, education, and medical care.

It took more than a decade for this system to make an impact on the sports world, but when it did, it did extremely well. In the 1992 Olympics in Barcelona, Cuba was the fifth-highest medal winner, surpassing larger countries such as France and Britain. In Atlanta in 1996, at the end of the worst time of the special period, it placed eighth. More than half of Cuba's Olympic triumphs are in boxing. Since the 1972 Olympic Games in Munich, Cuban boxers have won 27 Olympic gold medals. The total would be even higher if the country had not boycotted the 1984 and 1988 summer games.

Among teenagers, national sports heroes include Teófilo Stevenson, Alberto Juantorena, Ana Fidelia Quirot, and Javier Sotomayor. Stevenson, a heavyweight boxer, has won three Olympic gold medals. Juantorena won gold medals in the 400- and 800-meter races, the first man to win both events in one Olympics. Quirot triumphed in the 800-meter race at the world championships in 1997. Sotomayor, the greatest high jumper of all time, has frequently broken world records. He took the Olympic gold medal in 1992 and world champion gold in both 1995 and 1997.

The most popular sport among females is women's volleyball. The national team is the best in the world and has won three Olympic gold medals in a row. Among male teens baseball players are the most popular. Two who left the country in 1997, Livan Hernández and his brother Orlando "El Duque" Hernández, now play for the New York Yankees.

The government has free, amateur sports programs for people of all ages, held in special youth recreation centers. In these centers teenagers can practice rhythmic dance, ping-pong, badminton, or judo. With the disappearance of the Soviet bloc, all these programs have been having problems. Most of the facilities have peeling paint, dusty concrete floors, corridors that have not been washed for awhile, and playing fields where teenagers play without nets. Nevertheless they are always full of young people who want to practice for love of the activity, not for gain or greed.

Teenagers play volleyball and baseball everywhere, but especially in the streets and at the beach. Although baseball is considered more of a male game it is possible to see female teenagers playing baseball in their neighborhoods with male friends. In the neighborhoods, boys and girls also play volleyball together. As a professional sport female teenagers are more likely to play softball.

ENTERTAINMENT

Before discussing the activities young people enjoy in their spare time, it is necessary to explain first the impact of dollar legalization in Cuba. In turn, the impact of the legalization of the dollar on the Cuban economy cannot be understood without taking into account something else. To combat the U.S. embargo Cuba has allowed companies from Canada, Mexico, and the European Union to invest in the island. These countries are investing millions of dollars in the economy, especially to develop tourism. The relationship between the tourist industry and Cuba is a love-hate one. In the 1950s Cuba was an exotic getaway with a reputation for gambling, drugs, and prostitution. One of the goals of the revolution was to forever change the image of the island, especially in relation to issues such as prostitution. Nevertheless, because of the embargo and the failure of the system, the Cuban government had to make a pact with the devil, which in socialist terms means a pact with capitalism, its archenemy.

This pact has created many ideological problems. Among the teen population it is not unusual to hear bitter criticism of tourism, particularly from those who are not linked to the tourist industry. The situation reminds many teens of what they have seen in movies about life in Cuba before the revolution, and especially of what they have learned in school about the time of the Batista regime. The division between locals and tourists clearly suggests the idea of a tourism apartheid because some hotels, especially the most expensive, are like private country clubs. Locals are not allowed in unless foreigners accompany them. Therefore, Cuban teens do not have direct access to tourist facilities nowadays unless a foreigner invites them in. Under these circumstances, the only entertainment available to most young Cubans is homemade. A day sitting on the

Malecón, a long drive on the bay, chatting with friends, drinking home-made rum, and dancing to music from a tape recorder or car radio is entertainment for many. For many teens the most important entertainment is still the beach. On weekends, or even after an ordinary school day, teens will go to the beach with their families, girlfriends, boyfriends, or class-mates, in groups of 2, 5, or 20.

Cuban teens are never happier than when they are in front of the magnificent blue ocean that surrounds the island. On the beach they talk, cook, dance, and dream. Cuban teens listen to tropical music: mostly salsa, merengue, and boleros. But they also like rap and American pop music. The most popular group among all ages is *Los Van Van*. This 14-member dance band is practically synonymous with modern Cuban music. The group invented their own peculiar style, which they call *songo*. Particularly popular with teenage audiences in Cuba is the group *Orishas* (Cuban rap). The most popular singers are Pablito FG, Carlos Manuel, and Issac Delgado.

Cuban teenagers do more than listen to music; they like to dance to it. They dance at family parties, in discos, on the beach, in the streets, and everywhere. In this sense Cubans, teenagers, children, and adults are in harmony: all like to dance to Cuban music. The only music teenagers do not share with older generations is the American music that teenagers listen and dance to in discos for teenagers. The entry fee for these discos is around $1 to $2. The place is usually a big empty house or apartment. Sometimes dances are held with official permission from the Committee for the Defense of the Revolution, sometimes without. In these places teens are able to dance together outside the gaze of adults. Music in these discos is typically American and European pop music.

RELIGIOUS PRACTICES AND CULTURAL CEREMONIES

Officially atheist since the early 1960s, Cuba's government began softening its stance on religion in recent years. Catholics and other believers were granted permission in 1991 to join the Communist Party. Catholicism was the traditional religion before the revolution and is now recovering. The Pope visited Cuba in January of 1998, giving Catholics great inspiration.

Soon after the Pope's visit, Castro allowed the Council of Churches to have a large demonstration in the Plaza de la Revolution. The Council of Churches is an officially recognized body that represents most of the country's non-Catholic churches. Castro has told Methodists, Baptists, Presbyterians, Episcopalians, Pentecostalists, and Jews that their prayers are necessary to help solve the serious economic problems facing the country.

Cuba's principal religion is not Catholicism but rather Santería (Way of the Saint), a blended religion that mixes the rites and rituals of Catholicism and traditional African beliefs. Although it started as a religion among Cuba's blacks, Santería followers come today from all races and social conditions. Also known as Regla Ocha, it stems from the beliefs of the Yoruba people of West Africa. Cubans say that almost everybody on the island has participated in some form of Santería ritual. This is an incredibly high figure considering the many years that it was discouraged by the communist state.

With respect to religion there is not a particular generational conflict. In general teens follow parents in their traditions. At the beginning of the special period Catholic and Christian practices became more popular among adults. Parents were apprehensive about an activity that had been illegal in the past. With time, they have brought their children to church.

Teens are divided between those who go to Catholic or Christian churches and those who practice Santería. Some teens do both. Since Santería is a fetishistic and practical religion that some believe concretely helps its followers in their ordinary lives, it is more popular than Catholicism among teens.

Teens use Santería mainly to do witchcraft on another person, usually a lover. Yet some teens use Santería for more serious matters, such as to cure their health problems, succeed in school, or help their parents at work. Some teenagers just go to the Santería priest for guidance and counseling.

CONCLUSION

Cuban teens are warm, expressive, and affectionate. Some are also frustrated and dream of living in another country. Some are convinced that their parents' dreams did not fail with the communist system. Others, are getting rich, maybe richer than their parents with the money they earn from tourism, while yet others are extremely poor and do not eat at night nor have breakfast. Some are fun, spontaneous, and happy. Most are generous, while others want to take advantage of any situation. Teens in Cuba vary in their perceptions of life, their future, and their culture but all are struggling in one way or another for food and other goods. Cuban teens are growing up in the middle of a serious international conflict. They can do little to solve it, although they are the future of the island. The U.S. embargo against Cuba directly punishes children, teens, women, and the elderly, at least in one very important aspect: Cubans have to pay extremely high prices for medicine.

Cubans tend to be a generous people. This generous nature, closely linked to the gregarious spirit that characterizes the island, is becoming extinct. The beautiful hope of an equal society is slowly disappearing with tourism. The only sensible certitude in regard to the island is the natural candor still present in teenagers.

NOTE

1. All quotations from teens come from interviews conducted by the author in Cuba, May–July 2001.

RESOURCE GUIDE

Bethell, Leslie, ed. *Cuba: A Short History*. Cambridge, U.K.: Cambridge University Press, 1993.

Betto, Frei. *Fidel and Religion: Castro Talks on Revolution and Religion*. New York: Simon and Schuster, 1987.

Cabrera, Lydia. "Religious Syncretism in Cuba." *Journal of Caribbean Studies* 10, nos. 1 and 2 (winter 1994–spring 1995): 84–221.

Crahan, Margaret E. "Cuba: Religion and Revolutionary Institution." In *Socialist Cuba: Past Interpretations and Future Challenges*. London: Westview Press, 1988.

"The Cubans." In *Insight Guide: Cuba*, 85–91. London: Apa Publications, 2001.

Daniel, Yvonne. *Rumba: Dance and Social Change in Contemporary Cuba*. Bloomington. Indiana University Press, 1995.

Davies, Catherine. *A Place in the Sun? Women Writers in Twentieth-Century Cuba*. New York: Palgrave Macmillan, 1998.

"Dreaming of Miami." In *Insight Guide: Cuba*, 72–75. London: Apa Publications, 2001.

Ferrer, Ada. *Insurgent Cuba: Race, Nation, and Revolution*. Chapel Hill: The University of North Carolina Press, 1999.

Insight Guide: Cuba. London: Apa Publications, 2001.

Matibag, Eugenio. *Afro-Cuban Religious Experience: Cultural Reflections in Narrative*. Gainesville: University Press of Florida, 1996.

Matibag, Eugenio D. "The Yoruba Origins of Afro-Cuban Culture." *Journal of Caribbean Studies* 10, nos. 1 and 2 (winter 1994–spring 1995): 50–65.

Matthews, Herbert L. *Revolution in Cuba: An Essay in Understanding*. New York: Charles Scribner's Sons, 1975.

Moore, Carlos. "Race Relations in Socialist Cuba." In *Socialist Cuba: Past Interpretations and Future Challenges*, edited by Sergio Roca. Boulder, Colo.: Westview Press, 1988.

Pedraza, Teresita. "This Too Shall Pass: The Resistance and Endurance of Religion in Cuba." In *Cuban Studies* 28 (1999), edited by Enrico Mario Santí, 16–39. Pittsburgh: University of Pittsburgh Press.

Perez, Luis A. *Cuba: Between Reform and Revolution*. 2d ed. New York: Oxford University Press, 1995.

Pye, Geralin. "The Ideology of Cuban Sport." *Journal of Sport History* 13, no. 2 (Summer, 1986): 119–27.

Randall, Margaret. "Gathering Rage: The Failure of Twentieth Century Revolutions to Develop a Feminist Agenda." Monthly Review Press, 1992.

Robson, Barbara. "The Cuban Education System." In *Cubans—Their History and Culture*. Washington: Center for Applied Linguistics Refugee Service Center, 1996. Available at http://www.culturalorientation.net/cubans/CUBANS.HTM.

Smith, Lois M., and Alfred Padula. Preface to *Sex And Revolution: Women in Socialist Cuba*. New York: Oxford University Press, 1996.

"Socialism or Death." In *Insight Guide: Cuba*, 53–61. London: Apa Publications, 2001.

Tomas, Hugh S., Georges A. Fauriol, and Juan Carlos Weiss. *The Cuban Revolution 25 Years Later*. Boulder, Colo.: Westview Press, 1984.

Wetzel, Alyssa. *Food as a Reflection of the Cuban Experience*. Master's thesis, University of Minnesota, n.d.

Nonfiction

Insight Guide: Cuba. London: Apa Publications, 2001.

Luis, William. *Culture and Customs of Cuba*. Westport, Conn.: Greenwood Press, 2000.

Staten, Clifford L. *The History of Cuba*. Westport, Conn.: Greenwood Press, 2003.

Fiction

Arenas, Reynaldo. *The color del verano* (The Color of Summer). New York: Viking Penguin, 2001.

Guillen, Nicolas. *Por el mar de las antillas anda un barco de pape l*(Through the West Indian Sea Sails a Paper Boat). Edited by Keith Ellis. New York: Lectorum Publications, 1984.

Marti, Jose. *Versos sencillos* (Simple Verses). Houston, Tex.: Arte Publico Press, 1997.

Yañez, Mirta, ed. *Cubana: Contemporary Fiction by Cuban Women*. Boston: Beacon Press, 1998.

Web Sites

http://www.nnc.cubaweb.cu/
CUBAWEB NotiNet. One of Cuba's Internet portals. In Spanish and English.

http://www.granma.cu/
Granma Internacional.

http://www.prensa-latina.org/
Prensa Latina. A news bureau based in Cuba. Available in Spanish.

http://www.radiohc.org/
Radio Havana Cuba. Listen to shortwave broadcasts online. Reports-Transfer's
RHC Audio Archive in English.

More Information

Cuban Interests Section
Cuban Consulate
2639 16th St., NW
Washington, DC 20009
Tel: 202-797-8518, 8519, 20
Fax: 202-797-8521
Email: cubaseccion@igc.apc.org
http://www.geocities.com/Paris/Library/2958/index.html

Pen Pal Information

Although the situation is changing, there are still few junior or high schools that
use the Internet in Cuba. For this reason email service for Cuban teenagers is
limited. Nevertheless you can get information about this topic at CUBA-NIC-
Centro Cubano de Información de Red. Email: nic-staff@nic.cu. Fax: 537-24-8202.

Chapter 6

THE DOMINICAN REPUBLIC

Manuel García Castellón

INTRODUCTION

The Dominican Republic, a country of some 48,730 square miles (twice the area of New Hampshire), occupies two-thirds of the island of Hispaniola, which lies between the Caribbean Sea and the Atlantic Ocean. The country's eastern border separates it from the Creole-French speaking Republic of Haiti. The climate is tropical, with no significant variation in seasonal temperature. Deforestation has been a chronic problem for the entire island, but constant moisture brings fertility and glorious greenness to valleys of rich agriculture and permanent pastures. Nevertheless, a reduction in rainfall during recent years has produced a prolonged drought that has seriously damaged the agriculture and has caused water shortages in major cities, such as Santo Domingo with almost 2.5 million residents. Despite drought conditions, the hurricane season (from June to October) often brings severe flooding that destroys human settlements and arable land.

In the year 2000, the population count was 8.5 million, with an age structure revealing a large percentage of children and youths. In recent years birth control practices, a high infant mortality rate (some 36 deaths per 1,000 live births), and emigration to the United States have all contributed to an aging demographic. In spite of the hardships of life, life expectancy is high: some 74 years.

Dominicans are predominantly mulattos, a mixture of African and white ancestry. Only 16 percent of the population is white (mostly of Spanish and Canary Island origin), while 11 percent are black. The official language is Spanish and the literacy rate is 82 percent.

A legacy of nonrepresentative governments (some of them ruthlessly tyrannical) for much of the twentieth century came to an end in 1962, when free and open elections gave power to Juan Bosch of the Dominican Revolutionary Party. Other important political forces are the Dominican Liberation Party (PLD, center left leaning, winner in the 1996 and 2001 elections); the Dominican Revolutionary Party (PRD, left leaning); and the old Social Christian Reformist Party (PRSC, right leaning, issued from the old dictatorial political forces).

The gross domestic product per capita was estimated to be $5,400 in the year 2000, with 25 percent of the population living below the poverty line and with an unemployment rate of 13.8 percent. The real economy growth rate was 8.3 percent in the same year. Tourism, sugar, nickel, textiles, cement, and tobacco are the main industries. Agriculture is moderately diversified, but important products are sugarcane, coffee, and tobacco. The currency is the Dominican peso.

Historically, the country joined its destiny with that of Western civilization in 1492, when explorer Christopher Columbus landed on the island of Hispaniola during his first voyage. Today, the capital, Santo Domingo (founded by Bartholomew Columbus, brother of the navigator), is one of the richest sites in architecture belonging to the Spanish colonial age. Gothic-style ruins of its monuments are extremely well preserved, as are the first cathedral and the first university built in the Americas, as well as the impressive fort-palace that belonged to the Columbus family. The Dominican Republic's Spanish heritage is evident in the many churches built in stone, as well as the mansions with indoor patios decorated with tiles in the Moorish style. Not far from the town of Yuma, visitors can see the house that was the dwelling of Ponce de León, one of the first to explore North America.

People of the Taino and Arawak ethnic groups used to inhabit the island, originally called Quisqueya. They cultivated cassava, maize, peppers, and peanuts, offering gifts of such produce to deities they called *cemi*. According to the Spanish historian Bartolomé de las Casas, Tainos venerated and sang their ancestors memories in solemn hymns called *areito*. Archeology has discovered and preserved many samples of Taino art such as cave paintings, pottery, and idols in clay or wood. The youth played a game with a ball made of a certain resin called *copey*.

Spanish rule put an abrupt end to that civilization. The religious order of Saint Dominic was in charge of educating the people, whereas Columbus's clan dominated political life. Spain imposed the system of *encomienda*, a disguised sort of slavery given the fact that the natives had to pay with excruciating physical labor for receiving Christian indoctrination. Hunger (for the aborigines refused to cultivate land lest the Spaniards take their crops), suicide (as a way to escape slavery), self-induced miscarriages (to avoid having children live under tyrannical rule), and, finally, epidemics such as smallpox brought by the conquistadors contributed to the decimation of the native population.

The Spaniards mixed with the remaining natives. In order to replace the dwindling Indian peoples, who supplied the labor, Africans were forced to work in sugar farmlands, pearl fisheries, and mines. In time, the African race became overwhelmingly predominant.

In 1697, the French (who disputed the Spaniards' right to be sole colonizers of the island) started a successful sugar industry in its western part of the island. Since that time, the two colonies and future nations—French Haiti and Spanish Santo Domingo—have shared a relatively reduced geographical space. In 1795, a weakened Spain turned over the entire island's administration to France. Haitians proclaimed their independence from France in 1804 and so did Spanish Santo Domingans some years after, but in 1822 the Haitians invaded the Spanish side of the island, which they dominated until 1844. In order to prevent a new Haitian invasion, the Dominican elite and their military called Spain back for protection. Thus, in 1853 the old metropolis returned to rule its former colony. This new phase of Spanish control was a total failure. Spain imposed trade conditions unacceptable to the native elite. At the same time, the Spanish clergy aggressively tried to change many customs in the masses' rather African patterns of civilization. Therefore, a state of rebellion drove Spain to withdraw in 1865.

Between 1865 and 1916 there was a vigorous rebirth of the sugar industry, this time with Americans as the main owners of Dominican sugar farms. From then on, American influence was total in the political and social life of the country. Parliamentary government was a farce, for governments were vested autocracies serving U.S. commercial interests. The U.S. dollar became the official currency, and so it was until 1947 when dictator Rafael Trujillo, in a move to please the nationalistic trend, created the Dominican peso. This era brought problems inherent to modern industrialization, such as ruthless capitalism, labor unrest, and destitution of old small business owners, among other evils. Due to civil turbulence, in 1916 the American administration decided to occupy the island. What had been a virtual protectorate up to that date became absolutely real. The population suffered from the arrogance and frequent abuses of the U.S. Marines, who withdrew in 1924 due to popular and diplomatic pressure.

After that, Dictator Trujillo imposed a tyrannical rule, ruthlessly repressing all dissidence until he was assassinated in 1961 during an attempted coup. A year later, the first free and clean election gave power to Juan Bosch, an honest man and an intellectual, the leader of the Revolutionary Party.

Bosch's concern with the well-being of the poor and the use of island resources to benefit its masses brought a conflict of interests with U.S. landowners in 1965. That situation, as well as the fact that, at the time, neighboring Cuba was engaged in a socialist revolution, induced then U.S. President John F. Kennedy to send forces to occupy the island. Joaquín Balaguer, who had been vice president with Trujillo, was given presidential power through manipulated elections. Once again widespread corruption, disappearances, kidnappings, and murders of dissidents took place until President Jimmy Carter commanded Balaguer to carry on free and taintless elections in 1977, when Leonel Fernández (of the Revolutionary Party) became president.

The political class, paternalistic and eager to preserve the status quo, has always had a tendency to ignore youths' needs and, of course, youths' opinions. In reaction, youths have developed a disdain and indifference toward politics and politicians, accusing them of defending only their own personal interests. As for youthful organizations, they flourished in the 1960s and '70s, most of them distinguished by their leftist attitudes and radical opposition to the pseudo-democratic regime of Joaquín Balaguer. When the PRD gained power, all those organizations began to fade. Then, youths entered a phase of depoliticization and so it has remained up to today.

Tourism is becoming an important industry. Columbus immediately appreciated the incredible beauty of the island, sincerely believing that he had reached the biblical Paradise; in fact, it was as if he had traveled backward in history. "One would never like to part from these shores," he wrote in his diaries. Graceful coconut palms border the long beaches of fine, white sand. Extraordinarily plumaged birds fly over the peaceful jungle, where impressive orchids grow. The growing hotel industry has begun to disrupt this paradisiacal calm, but the progressive public opinion has spurred the government to declare some areas restricted as nature reserves. Large hotels, generally belonging to Spanish chains, rise among sophisticated holiday centers in several areas of the island. There are also exclusive resorts such as Club Méditerranée in Puerto Plata, managed by a French company, or the Dominicus Club near Bayahibe, under Italian management. Very often, foreign visitors stay in those tourist enclaves without venturing at all into the teeming urban life, thus missing the opportunity to mingle with Dominicans, some of the most fascinating, lively, easygoing, humorous, and friendly people on earth.

Tourism, nevertheless, does not suffice to rescue the country from its recession. Nor do the *maquiladoras*, such as foreign (mostly North American) manufacturers that enjoy large fiscal and financial benefits. In duty-free zones, work conditions are excruciating and trade unions are jeopardized. Women are paid less than men and anyone who becomes pregnant or sick may be laid off without any compensation. In recent years, the economy has progressed favorably, fueled mainly by the tourism industry and the free-trade zones. Nevertheless, the country's wealth is still very unevenly distributed. There have been political and social readjustments, with hard repercussions on the lives of the poor masses, in a country where only 30 percent of households can satisfy their basic needs. On the other hand, the economy's inflationary trend has cheapened the price of labor, and salaries have lost much of their acquisitive power.

A recession began abruptly in 1975, especially in the urban poles of growth, and continues today. As of 2002, there was an alarming 38 percent rate of unemployment, prevalent in both urban and rural areas and mostly affecting the youth. Unemployment, extreme poverty, and an uncertain future are all responsible for the high rates of emigration to Europe or North America, which are viewed by most Dominican teens as real lands of promise. In order to make their way into the United States, many youngsters attempt to cross the Mona Channel onboard *yolas*, or small boats. The Mona Channel is a highly treacherous passage that separates Hispaniola from Puerto Rico. There, storms are sudden and fierce and present serious dangers for small-craft navigation, but many teens do not hesitate to risk their lives to reach the shores of Puerto Rico, a U.S. Commonwealth. Once on the sister island, there are ways for them to obtain fake American IDs that have false Social Security numbers. Such documents are called *machetes*, which in figurative speech means something like a tool in the harvest of life. After that, jumping onto the continental United States is easy. Counting both legal and illegal immigrants, the concentration of Dominicans in New York and Miami is growing in number. Marriages of convenience are also a way to pass through the filters of the U.S. Immigration Service, resulting in legal permits to work. In the United States, Dominicans are known for their entrepreneurial talent, their reliability, and their strong family values. Of course, they easily establish bonds with other members of the Hispanic community in the United States.

TYPICAL DAY

Teens living in poorer conditions far outnumber those who enjoy more comfortable homes. The *bohío* is a humble peasant dwelling. It is a palm-roofed shack, held together by four pitchforks. Its floor is of well-trodden earth, with scarcely any interior divisions. Scant light enters through the chinks in the logs or driftwood. The home has neither water nor electricity. *Bohíos* are very exposed to the weather, especially during cyclones and torrential rains. Peasants plant limes, ginger, and geraniums around the *bohío*'s door, and the family eats outside while having placid conversation. *Bohíos*, along with country houses, are solemnly founded or inaugurated with ritual prayers.

In the slum districts surrounding the capital, where almost two million cram into an area barely 70 square miles, *bohíos* are known as *ranchos*. An overwhelming majority of the urban population lives under the hardest economic, social, and moral conditions. The appearance of the *ranchos*, made of wood, tin, rags, and other junk materials is appalling, in spite of the colorful house fronts painted during election time, when the political parties donate paint as part of their propaganda.

In the Dominican Republic, teens—both rural and urban—typically have overwhelming responsibilities, for they have to start contributing to the family's maintenance from a young age. In the fields, they help in the threshing of rice, the peeling of corn, or the cleaning of newly harvested kidney beans. Sometimes, they even cut sugarcane using machetes. They can lead mule wagons, cut and then hang meat to dry in the sun, or go fishing in *cocuyos* (carved-out, floating logs, of Taino heritage). In the countryside, impoverished youths live languid lives with lower rates of schooling and poorer diets, although, perhaps with a greater persistence of traditional values.

Employment—especially cheap employment—grew considerably in the years after the dictatorship with the inclusion of young women in the labor market. In the fields, mechanization and, alternatively, dispossession of the means of production and of land by masses of *campesinos* who sold their lands to the sugar industry, have destroyed a great deal of the traditional agrarian society, forcing youths to emigrate to the cities. Where small-scale agricultural exploitation still persists, many adolescents have to join the labor force, mostly during harvest time, in order to help their families. In urban areas, parents' lack of employment has sent many youths to seek jobs known as *chiripas* (e.g., as peddlers, cleaners, shoe shiners, ice cream, or fruit vendors). To those tasks one must add the growing numbers of young people who go into prostitution, for the Dominican Republic also has its place in the market of sexual tourism. In the nation's capital and in the beach resort of Puerto Plata together, there are more than a hundred establishments devoted to prostitution and employing mostly adolescents.

As for teen delinquency, there is always a category of youths who wish neither to study nor to work. They are victims of a subculture of despair produced by family disintegration, thus becoming early and easy prey of criminal nets. According to CNN en Español, in the last 10 years, teen drug use and crime have grown in alarming numbers, thus damaging the vital tourism industry of the country, which in 2001 experienced a 40 percent decline with respect to the previous year. Many hotels of the north zone of the country were forced to close down due to the increasing number of abductions, robberies, and murders. In recent years, most of these violent crimes have been committed by youths. The prison system mixes juveniles with adults, thus making jails true schools of evil for those unfortunate, first-offense teens.

FAMILY LIFE

Until the years of the Trujillo dictatorship, and before the explosion in the urban population, Dominican society was predominantly rural. In the countryside, market forces hadn't yet destroyed the small family farm. Many families lived in palm-roofed shacks and were united around the father as patriarchal figure with uncontested authority. Children would join the agrarian tasks as soon as possible, for schooling beyond elementary education was considered a superfluous luxury in the life of a country youth. In urban areas, only a minority of young people would reach the levels of higher education, but always in numbers that would not exceed market demands. Then, during the 1960s and 1970s, came the industrialization of urban peripheries and the migration of *campesinos*, or farmers, to towns in search of a better life, with a significant increase in birth rates. With this new situation, the family began losing its social importance. In fact, migration disrupted the traditional patterns of family life, either when only one of the two spouses set off for the city, leaving behind the rest of the family, or when the couple had to entrust the children to some relative's care until they were old enough to follow their parents. Therefore, when women and children were incorporated into proletarian life, fathers typically lost their importance as sole providers—and as patriarchs, too.

Nevertheless, the traditional *machista* (from Spanish macho [male], meaning male dominance and a derogative attitude toward women's opinions and values) patterns still prevail, thus causing conflicts not only among parents and children, but also between spouses, who are now equal and who must try to share authority and decision-making power equally. Today, the Dominican Republic has some of the highest rates of divorce, informal unions, and illegitimate children.

TRADITIONAL AND NONTRADITIONAL FOOD DISHES

The average Dominican youth of today does not go hungry, but certainly many children lack the necessary elements for a balanced diet. Although a primarily agricultural and cattle country, the Dominican Republic suffers from shortages of cereal and milk, necessary ingredients in a teen's diet. Responsible for such shortages is the decline of farming life in recent years, as well as monocultural trends in the agrarian sector. International agencies have to contribute much aid, with food supplies and nutritional programs for the youngest.

However, Dominican cuisine has developed great variety and exquisiteness throughout history. As a cultural product par excellence, the country's cuisine mixes European, native, and African elements. The *chenchén* is the typical plate of the southern regions, based on goat meat and corn. Other delicious courses are *mofongo*, with plantain as the main ingredient; *catibía*, or meat wrapped in cassava flour; and *sancocho*, made with mostly chicken and vegetables. Many dishes contain pork, such as *chicharrón* pie. A delicious dessert is *chacá*, which includes corn, coconut milk, and cinnamon. Rice and beans are prepared in many ways. An extremely popular dish, quick to prepare, is the combo known as Dominican flag, which invariably must contain four ingredients: meat, rice, beans, and salad.

Finally, as a test of the insertion of North American culture, Dominican cities now teem with Burger Kings, Wendy's restaurants, and Pizza Huts. These fast food franchises, not so popular among the youth during the '70s because of the U.S. Marine invasion, are now making a healthy comeback.

SCHOOLING

Schooling for a Dominican teen is very different depending upon his or her social status, geographic area, and other factors. Typically, the school day begins at eight o'clock in the morning and ends by one o'clock. In private schools, which offer more extracurricular activities, the school day may extend beyond one. The official school system seeks its model in the Americas and Europe. School begins with kindergarten and primary school, after which are eight grade levels. Passing from one grade to the next is based on test scores. Dominican sociologists observe a high rate of course repetition, as well as dismal rates in the number of dropouts, in all grades. In theory, all children in the Dominican Republic receive a basic education until the age of 14, that is to say, until the eighth grade. However, negative social factors often hinder youths from graduating. First of all, the public school system has lost its capacity to accommodate an exploding juvenile demographic. Schools are scarce, undersupplied, and overcrowded, and teachers often feel disappointed and discouraged. Meager pay also contributes to their social devaluation. A teacher's salary in the public sector barely reaches US$200 per month. A democratic system allows teachers to form unions and to go on strike.

Schools are often far away from young people's residences, without any available transportation for students to reach them. This problem, more pronounced in rural areas, is responsible for many youngsters reaching adulthood with only a rudimentary level of literacy. On the contrary, private schools, which educate youths of the wealthy class, provide transportation and generally have excellent materials and equipment. By means of competitive tests they also recruit the best teachers.

Catholic private schools have lost a great deal of their appeal or prestige, for they face competition from lay private institutions of American or European origin. These new schools have tough admissions criteria, and their bilingual programs are designed to educate youths to become future executives serving foreign enterprises.

Beyond the eight levels of basic education, four years of secondary school must be completed before a student may advance to the college level. Colleges and universities have experienced remarkable expansions during the last decades. Sociologists worry about the number of future graduates being produced, given the uncertainty of the job market. The National University has a central seat, with branches throughout the country. There are also some trade schools, but they are poorly equipped and have low rates of registration.

Many young Dominicans are dedicated to skillful works of craft, which they sell in tourist spots such as Puerto Plata or La Romana. Popular art and creativity arise spontaneously in architecture, interiors, jewelry, and so on. Toward 1939, after the Spanish Civil War, a few Spanish artists took refuge on the island and, understanding and respecting the true spirit of the people, contributed to the establishment of art schools with the intention of preserving and enhancing local styles. Thus, the National School of Ceramics and the National Center of Craft were created, utilizing advanced technology. In jewelry craft, the industry uses local amber, as well as famous *larimar*, a blue stone found only on the island.

The rate of illiteracy among Dominican youths has considerably decreased in recent years. Urbanization has certainly contributed to this improvement. The numbers of men and women who are literate are more or less even. The comprehensive literacy rate for the whole country is about

80 percent. Nevertheless, the crisis of the educational system will worsen if the demography does not stabilize and if the government is not able to devote larger sums of its future budgets to education (Cassá, 66).

SOCIAL LIFE

In today's Dominican Republic, teens socialize without any specific rituals of approach. Girls and boys mingle at the earliest school levels. The traditions of Christianity and Western civilization, deeply rooted, facilitate freedom of rapport of all sorts and there's never anything like a marriage prearranged by parents. Teens can select their own dates and decide to go together to discotheques or bars, either individually, as couples, or in groups. Generally, parents do not intervene in their teens' choice of dates. It may be said that Dominican society is remarkably liberal in that sense. The dissolution of the traditional prestige of conjugal unions has given rise to premarital sex and free unions. Traditional, moral sex education ingrained in Roman Catholic teachings and advice on prophylactics given by a few government and nongovernmental organizations do not suffice to keep the rates of sexually transmitted diseases and accidental pregnancies at acceptable levels, although it is possible to foresee that such rates will diminish in the near future.

Among young Dominicans, wearing designer shoes or clothing is a sign of status and social acceptance. Other than fashion and footwear, any manufactured product that is foreign—especially American—confers prestige: watches, perfumes, accessories, electronics, photography, music, and, obviously, cars. Of course, not all youths have access to these types of imported goods. Although poverty is generalized, there is some division according to the levels of income. Among a majority of have-nots, a few are considered the haves (called *jevitos,* in Spanish phonetic adaptation) and are ostentatious about their expensive Swiss watches, their leather jackets—obviously superfluous under the tropical sun—even their Impalas or Lexuses. These youths, with relatives or businesses in the United States, associate by social class. There is a certain degree of division by skin tone, but without the taken-for-granted apartheid that is customary in other places around the world. Until marriage, race doesn't really matter. Youths of all shades spontaneously mingle without prejudice.

However, when it comes to marriage, a youth of the white upper class will normally not marry somebody who is darker by a couple of shades. Race relations are not without complexity and prejudice. At the beginning of the nineteenth century, the white race accounted for 20 percent of the population, but many fled to Cuba, Spain, or the United States in large numbers during the days of the Haitian invasion. The remaining poor whites intermingled with blacks. Today Dominicans, although labeled on their identity papers as, for example, *claro* (light) or *indio oscuro* (dark Indian), prefer to be considered white. The country's black African heritage was for decades despised, even suppressed. Today some Dominicans harbor discriminatory feelings toward darker Haitians, as well as toward *cocolos*, as they call migrants from other islands of the Caribbean.

RECREATION

Female teens cherish the folk songs they learn together as young children. Making a round they sing old Spanish children's tunes that tell about castles, princesses, Moors, and Christians. Later on, as girls continue cherishing these folk songs, young males will begin to prefer games that need speed and physical skill.

Males, once they reach puberty, prefer sitting in the streets playing dominoes, chess, or Spanish cards. Another popular form of entertainment is the rooster fight, which is an occasion for substantial betting.

As for formal sports, baseball is the national sport par excellence, and it attracts all social classes and ages. Hispaniola has produced many baseball greats. Player Sammy Sosa is considered a youth hero of supreme stature,

Boys hang out with motorcycles outside shop, Costanza, Dominican Republic. © H. Rogers/TRIP.

both in the United States where he lives and plays and in the Dominican Republic, where he was born into a humble family.

ENTERTAINMENT

Teens also watch a great deal of television, either cable or satellite TV. Technology is more advanced than programming, but many shows are bought from the United States, Mexico, and Europe (especially Spain). Dominican teens also look to the United States for rock music. Due to youth interaction in black neighborhoods of the United States, folkloric forms have arisen that, on and off the island, try to recreate characteristics of African culture and music. Traditional rhythms have begun to fuse with jazz or American pop music. Besides, young Dominicans have learned to enjoy most present-day Hispanic folk music. Tickets for a concert by the Mexican pop star Luis Miguel, for example, typically sell out immediately, no matter how extravagant the price. As for music with a national heritage, the Dominican rhythm par excellence is the famous merengue, which is enjoyed by people of all ages, including the young. Merengue lovers tend to look down upon salsa, which they consider a commercial imitation. Merengue also expresses the cultural synthesis of Hispaniola: the native element is in the sound of the *güiro* (a dried pumpkin, with lines carved in it); the African element is in the *tambora* (made with goatskin); and the European element is in the accordion, introduced by Germans during the nineteenth century. Folk dances are also popular in town plazas during the holidays, with participation by old and young alike. Like all Antillean and West Indian peoples, most Dominicans develop, from an early age, an inimitable dancing style in which the body's movements gracefully adjust to a musical rhythm.

Important venues for entertainment include the famous carnivals of Santo Domingo and La Vega. Carnival was suppressed during the long dictatorship of Trujillo, but today it has been reborn with all its original brilliance. Around February 27, coinciding with the anniversary of the country's independence from Haiti (which occurred in 1844), carnival is celebrated with great fanfare. *Comparsas* (bands), each bearing a different theme, dance enthusiastically while parading. Throughout the previous year, the participants have spent a large amount of time preparing masks and costumes. Processions on the waterfront of Santo Domingo Avenue typically include more than 30,000 paraders, while the parade watchers may number more than a half a million. A famous parade is that of the *tiznados* (sooted), young men with the darkest skins who smear themselves with smut. Some say that in the origin of that custom lies a message of social protest against racism.

The parades that most attract the attention of youths are those with *diablos*, or devils, who dance and march to the beat of drums, disguised by masks with long horns and wearing cloaks with mirrors and sleigh bells. Some of these *diablos* bands may represent a drama in which the dead appear dressed in white robes.

RELIGIOUS PRACTICES AND CULTURAL CEREMONIES

Roman Catholicism is the predominant religion. Currently, under Roman Catholic patronage, some youthful organizations remain, but mostly with the purpose of educating teens on sexual abstinence and freedom from drugs. Data from a survey in the 1990s found that 47 percent of girls and 34 percent of boys declared their affiliation to be Roman Catholic, and some 5 percent (including both genders) declared themselves to be Protestants (Tejada Holguín 17, 29). Pastoral Juvenil, a group consequent with Catholic moral doctrine, is one of the religious organizations that attract most of the youths' participation. Pastoral Juvenil's essential activity is shaping the religious development of the individual, as well as giving free advice to youths in distress, or even economic aid to youths with scarce resources. In agreement with its creed, Pastoral Juvenil opposes contraception, abortion, and homosexual expression.

Catholicism, nevertheless, has to coexist with many other creeds, especially with forms of voodoo or Santería similar to those in Haiti, Cuba, or the other Antilles, although at a lesser level. Voodoo and Santería are both mixes of old African beliefs and Christian religion. While voodoo came from neighboring Haiti, Santería originated in the Spanish Antilles, including Hispaniola itself. Among the lower classes, both urban and rural, Anaisa, Ogun, Baron Samedi, or Olivorio—among other figures of the African pantheon—are worshiped under the appearance of Roman Catholic images. These are a sort of half-gods who live amid humans, described by those who claim to have met them as having all kinds of human weaknesses, including a taste for pure cane rum. Santería priests, known as *loases* (the men) or *metresas* (the women), raise small altars replete with votive offerings in any corner of the house. They perform healings or exorcism ceremonies, which often include convulsive states and incoherent babbling. Sometimes, these priests administer potions or utter incantations. Such cults lack both a hierarchy and institutional structure of any kind. In Holy Week, during the three days that Jesus is believed to have remained buried, *santeros* worship Gagá, who is entrusted by God the Father to maintain the good order of our world, thus keeping the devil at bay.

The *cocolos*, or West Indian immigrants, brought their *chorchas* (corruption for churches), mostly Methodist and Anglican, and are famous for their beautiful hymns. Freed slaves from the American south who were sheltered in Samaná brought with them their funeral customs, including the procession of a corpse to the cemetery amid chants and brass bands, just as in New Orleans.

Finally, Pentecostalism, charismatic churches, and all forms of non-Catholic Christianity have had many converts in recent years.

CONCLUSION

The Dominican Republic is, demographically speaking, truly a nation of young people. Its rate of birth exploded after the '50s. In the last several decades, many rural Dominicans left their farms in search of jobs in the city. Finding no jobs, they joined the city's dispossessed, thus seriously damaging the traditional sense of the nuclear family and, more than ever, favoring free unions that have precipitated high rates of unwanted pregnancies and abandoned children. Between 1975 and 2015, the country will havoubled its total population (from 5 to 10 million), according to U.N. United Nations data (http://esa.un.org/socdev/unyin/country3a.asp?countrycode=do).

While some Dominican youths now evoke the image of poor neighborhood youths, who may be drug addicts or delinquents who think only of emigrating to the United States where they might become rich by trafficking in drugs (Tejada Holguín, 5), little is said of the personal drama of interrupting youths' education with jobs that may last two weeks or a month, but that hold no future. On the other hand, there are many young people who, having completed secondary and higher education, rush into public life as promising women and men of politics, business, the sciences, or arts (Tejada Holguín, 5).

As for government policies concerning youths, the absence of a stable politics of youth development regarding employment, dwellings, education, health, diet, social security, and other governmental affairs. However, limited but important initiatives have been implemented such as the General Office for the Promotion of the Youth (*Dirección General para la Promoción de la Juventud*, with the Spanish acronym DGPJ), constituted in 1992, with the aim of including youths' needs in the plans of development for the republic. The sole legislative piece of some importance so far is the Youth Code, inspired by UNESCO's (United Nations Educational, Scientific, and Cultural Organization) Universal Declaration of Child and Youth Rights. Such a code recognizes factual couples, i.e., non-legitimized by legal or religious marriage. Obviously, it has encountered strong opposition by the Catholic Church. The code also regulates youth labor, but its rules are seldom applied (Tejada Holguín, 20).

The proportion of the public budget allotted to the comprehensive social needs of youths is among the lowest in Latin America. The per capita expense in education has experienced an alarmingly gradual reduction since 1980.

RESOURCE GUIDE

Bosch, Juan. *The Unfinished Experiment: Democracy in the Dominican Republic*. London: Pall Mall, 1966.

Calder, Bruce J. *The Impact of Intervention: The Dominican Republic during the U.S.A. Occupation of 1916–1924*. The Texas Pan American Series. Austin: University of Texas Press, 1984

Cassá, Roberto. *Los jóvenes dominicanos: Situación y tareas*. Santo Domingo, Dominican Republic: GRIPAC, 1995.

CNN en Español. "La violencia sume en crisis al turismo dominicanó." http://cnnenespanol.com/2001/destinos/07/31/santo.domingo_turismo/

Conrad, James. *The Cultures of the Hispanic Caribbean*. London: Macmillan Education, 2000.

Domínguez, Jaime de Jesús. *Historia dominicana*. Santo Domingo, Dominican Republic: ABC Editorial, 2001.

El Listín Digital. http://www.listin.com.do/antes/200801/opinion/opi4.html.

Friedel, Marion. *Dominican Republic*. Photographed by Michael Friedel. Steingau, Germany: MM-Photodrucke, 1999.

Gracía, Wifredo, Manuel Rueda, Ramón Francisco, and Ramón Oviedo. *De tierra morena vengo. Imágenes del hombre dominicano y su cultura*. Santo Domingo, Dominican Republic: Editora Amigo del Hogar, 1987.

Hartlyn, Jonathan. *The Struggle for Democratic Politics in the Dominican Republic*. Chapel Hill: University of North Carolina Press, 1998.

Moya Pons, Frank. *The Dominican Republic: A National History*. New Rochelle, N.Y.: Hispaniola Books, 1995.

Palmer, Bruce. *Intervention in the Caribbean: The Dominican Crisis of 1965*. Lexington: University Press of Kentucky, 1989.

Rodríguez, Ernesto: "Políticas públicas de juventud en República Dominicana 2000–2001." http://www.infoyouth.org/404files.php?fil=169.

Seminario sobre la Juventud: Situación y Perspectivas en la República Dominicana (Santo Domingo: 1985). Santo Domingo, Dominican Republic: Instituto Tecnológico de Santo Domingo, 1986.

Silvestre, Emmanuel, and Jaime Bogaert. *La neo-prostitución en la Republica Dominicana*. Santo Domingo, Dominican Republic: Ed. PAIS-UNESCO, 1991.

Tejada Holguín, Ramón. "Informe de República Dominicana." *Políticas de Juventud en América Latina, Evaluación y Diseño*. http://www.idrc.ca/lacro/foro/results/inf_rcadominicana.htm.

Nonfiction

Brown, Isabel Zakrzewski. *Culture and Customs of the Dominican Republic*. Westport, Conn.: Greenwood Press, 1999.

Fiction

Alvarez, Julia. *How the Garcia Girls Lost Their Accent*. New York: Plume, 1991.

———. *How Tia Lola Came to Stay*. New York: Knopf, 2001.

———. *In the Time of Butterflies*. Chapel Hill, N.C.: Algonquin Books, 1994.

———. *Something to Declare*. Chapel Hill, N.C.: Algonquin Books, 1998.

Alvarez, Julia, and Fabián Negrín. *The Secret Footprints*. New York: Random House, 2001.

Diaz, Junot. *Drown*. New York: Riverhead Books, 1997.

Web Sites

http://cnnenespanol.com/2001/destinos/07/31/santo.domingo_turismo/
CNN en español

http://www.the?dominican?republic.com/
The Dominican Republic

http://education.yahoo.com/search/fb?p=Dominican+Republic
Yahoo education. Search World Fact Book

http://esa.un.org/socdev/unyin/country0.asp?countrycode=do
Youth at the United Nations. Country profile.

http://www.hispaniola.com/
Hispaniola.com

http://www.presidencia.gov.do/English/welcome.htm
Presidencia de la República Dominicana

Pen Pal Information

http://www.pen-pal.net
Pen Pal Network

http://www.absoluteagency.com
Dominican Republic Pen Pal

Chapter 7

ECUADOR

Jason Pribilsky

INTRODUCTION

Ecuador, as one observer noted "defies every stereotype or generalization used to describe it" (Handelsman, xiii). Although a small country in Latin America—approximately the size of the state of Colorado, with a population of only 12 million—Ecuador contains a wealth of diversity in terms of ethnicity, culture, and geography.

Ecuador sits astride the equator, from which it derives its name. Geographically, the country is neatly divided into three distinct regions: the sierra (Andes mountains), the *costa* (coastal lowlands), and the *oriente* or *selva* (Amazonian jungle basin). The *costa* and *selva* can be swelteringly hot and humid, while the highlands—much of it over 9,000 feet—can be bone-chillingly cold. Ecuador also plays host to a number of volcanoes, including Pinchincha and Tungurugua, both of which had active explosions in 1999 and 2000.

Before the arrival of the Spanish in 1531, much of Ecuador formed the northern reaches of the Inca empire, the largest pre-Columbian state society. The Inca, though, maintained only a tenuous hold on the inhabitants of the region, which was loosely organized into individual chiefdoms and settlements. While the Inca demanded tribute in the form of a portion of the harvest and labor, they also allowed different indigenous groups of the region to maintain their own customs and grow their own crops. However, the Inca left as one of their greatest legacies upon the area the spread of the official imperial language, Quichua (or Quechua in Peru), spoken by Indian groups throughout the highlands and in many parts of the *oriente*. Today, indigenous peoples comprise approximately 35 percent of the total population of Ecuador (Gerlach 2003, 7–8). Most of its indigenous peoples (called *indígenas*) live in the rural areas of the Andean highlands and the Amazonian basin. In the past 30 years, *indígenas* have commanded a greater presence in Ecuador's largest cities—in Guayaquil, Cuenca, and the capital city of Quito. A small Afro-Ecuadorian population (between 5 and 8 percent of the population) inhabits Ecuador's northern highlands and coast. They are descendants of slaves brought to Ecuador as well as of a maroon population (escaped slaves) that fled colonial Colombia.

The Spanish invasion into the New World forever changed life in Latin America and what would become the Republic of Ecuador. Perhaps the most significant legacy of the Spanish was the emergence of mestizos, persons with mixed indigenous and Spanish heritage. Approximately 55 percent of Ecuador's population are considered to be mestizos. For all of the colonial period, the Spanish held indigenous peoples in a position of servitude, demanding from them labor and tribute. Many Indians in the highlands found themselves virtual slaves in mines; in weaving sweatshops, where they were forced to produce textiles for the export economy; and especially on haciendas, large farms that dominated the highland landscape. On the haciendas, Indians were treated as serfs, given miserably small plots of land to grow food for their families in return for the highly exploitative work they provided for the Spanish overlords.

Little changed for the original inhabitants of Ecuador when the country won its independence from Spain in 1822. In fact, it would be almost 100 years before President Alfredo Baquerizo Moreno would sign legislation freeing *indígenas* from the slavelike conditions that bound them to the Spanish. Even then, it was not until 1964 that the government went so far as to grant Indians their own lands, much of which had been taken from them hundreds of years before.

Ecuador still bears the historical stamp of its colonial past. People who claim to be of Spanish heritage continue to enjoy the highest socioeconomic and political status in the country, owning the majority of land and possessing the greatest amounts of wealth. In fact, the richest 20 percent of the population receive 53 percent of the income derived from the gross domestic product. Conversely, the poorest 40 percent of Ecuadorians receive only 14 percent of the household income. Increasingly, Ecuador's mestizos, the country's hope for a middle class, have felt the poverty that its natives have always known. However, there is hope that the status quo could change. Since the early 1990s, indigenous groups have commanded a strong presence in formal Ecuadorian politics, demanding that greater attention be paid to their ancestral and territorial rights and separate identities. In particular, The Confederation of Indigenous Nationalities of Ecuador (CONAIE), founded in 1986, has moved toward greater prominence, winning seats in local government races and in legislature. Indigenous activism has been instrumental in limiting the encroachment of oil exploration and development in the Amazonian basin and in designing and revamping national, bilingual education programs in addition to promoting land rights and aid to small farmers.

Despite these advancements, Ecuador finds itself in a paradoxical position. As one anthropologist notes, Ecuador has "the strongest indigenous-rights movement and the weakest economy in Latin America" (Meisch 2003, 14). In the late 1990s, Ecuador faced its worst economic crisis in over a century and weathered extreme political upheaval that threatened its national stability. After fighting a short-lived, but costly, border war with Peru in 1995, Ecuadorians removed corrupt President Abdalá Bucaram in 1997 and endured El Niño floods during 1997–98 that crippled banana exports and infrastructure, causing over $2 billion in economic damage (International Monetary Fund 2000, 8). These economic setbacks were compounded when prices for oil, Ecuador's most lucrative export, fell to a near-record low. By early 1999 the government of President Jamil Mahuad had consolidated, closed, or bailed out 16 financial institutions at a cost of nearly $2.6 billion (IMF 2000, 23). Inflation increased to 60 percent, and in September of 1999 Ecuador earned the dubious distinction of being the first country to default on its Brady Bonds international loans. By the start of 2000, the unpopular president tried to salvage the economy by announcing a plan to convert the economy to U.S. dollars (a process known as dollarization). Protests mounted and President Mahuad, forced to resign, was replaced briefly by a junta formed from an unlikely coalition of military and civil forces with the country's strong indigenous movement. Finally Vice President Gustavo Noboa assumed the presidency and vowed to continue the dollarization plan and other neoliberal austerity measures.

For young people coming of age in Ecuador, it is an understatement to say that the future for them is unpredictable. Ecuador, like much of Latin America, has a large youth population. In 1995, 32 percent of the population was estimated to be between the ages of 10 and 24. According to figures of the 1990 census, people under the age of 24 represented 59.3 percent of the total Ecuadorian population. Young people, more than others, feel the weight of these numbers as they enter into the job market as the country's most able-bodied workers but find few opportunities to employ their skills. Current unemployment hovers at around 15 percent

(Bolsa de Valores Guayaquil 2001) and over 40 percent are considered underemployed (unable to find enough work to make ends meet).

Unemployment has been blamed for a number of social ills that plague Ecuador. Elevated crime rates, youth gangs, and drug and alcohol abuse have been reported in association with a disillusioned youth culture in Ecuador. Still, many Ecuadorian youths continue to seek out alternatives to the evils of poverty and the lack of opportunities. Perhaps the most dynamic force has been the emigration of thousands of youths to the United States and, increasingly, to Spain and other parts of Europe. Since the late 1960s, over 400,000 Ecuadorians have emigrated to the United States, and the numbers are increasing. The majority of the new emigration is illegal.

TYPICAL DAY

There is no one, typical day for teenagers in Ecuador, just as the country has no one, typical kind of teenager. In fact, the category of teenager, as used in the United States to denote persons between the ages of 13 and 19 and more or less under the ward of their parents, cannot be neatly imported to describe Ecuadorian youths. Rather, Ecuadorians typically make a distinction between adolescents (10–17 years of age) and youths (*jóvenes*) (17–24). While in practice the line between the two is gray, one event that does separate the two is when young people marry. Ecuadorians of all regions frequently wed in their late teens, and by doing so they become adults, albeit *jóvenes* adults, in the eyes of their communities. For women, this status is reflected in their elevation from *señorita* to *señora* (the proper address for a married woman). Therefore, one can go very quickly from being a teenager to a fully functioning and identified adult.

A teenager's day in Ecuador depends largely on his or her social and economic position in the country. A typical day for an upper-class Ecuadorian teen living in a city—Quito or Guayaquil, for example—does not differ significantly from a teenager's day in the United States, including the type of schooling and the activities of playing sports, watching television, or spending time with friends at the mall. Many upper-class teens, in fact, come to the United States to attend school, visit relatives, and take vacations, and as such have cultivated a transnational teen culture that differs little from the American model. However, a typical day for a teen growing up in the rural highlands differs considerably from what might be described as mainstream, North American teen life. The descriptions given here attempt to capture the daily lives of teens living in the rural highlands and, when applicable, comparisons are made between social classes, ethnicities, and regional differences found in Ecuador.

For teens in the highlands, a typical day now often begins with getting ready for school. In the past, many rural households often had to make the choice between losing their children's help in agricultural work or investing in their children's future through education. As farming has diminished as the prime source of food in many parts of the Ecuadorian Andes, schooling has taken on an increased importance.

If rural teens attend school they often have to rise very early, by 4 or 5 in the morning, in order to have enough time to carry out their chores on the family farm. Many rural students must leave enough time to get to schools that are sometimes up to an hour away. The informal socialization and rearing of children in highland Ecuador, as many anthropologists have noted, takes place in the context of increasing responsibilities for children. It is an unspoken assumption that young children, as they progress through adolescence, should increasingly learn to consider their parents (*considerándoles*) by anticipating their needs and helping out as much as possible without being asked. The absence of having to be reminded of one's tasks rather than praise for tasks completed frequently demonstrates a parent's happiness with a child. For their part, teen girls may be expected to help their mothers prepare breakfast, while boys will have the task of feeding animals or another farm-related job.

Schools in rural Ecuador offer few of the resources to which their counterparts in the United States are accustomed. For example, teens can expect to spend their time in the same classroom, sometimes with the same teacher, for an entire school year. Nationally, the education system has faced significant financial cutbacks in the past decade, leaving most public schools with a shortage of teachers, outdated textbooks, and dilapidated classrooms. On any given day, the instruction begins with a morning lineup and call to order. To the shouts of "*¡Fórmense ya!*", entire student bodies form rows by class and wait for further instructions. In many ways, the morning ritual looks a lot like what would take place in a military setting. All children, allowing for male and female style differences, dress in uniforms, typically consisting of a pressed white shirt, a sweater in official school colors and school crest or name, and conservative slacks or skirts. There may be a flag raising, frequently a singing of the national anthem or other kind of formal reverence of the Ecuadorian nation. News of the day usually follows. After announcements, students adjourn to their classrooms for instruction in math, the natural sciences, social studies, and, increasingly, English as a foreign language. Schools servicing indigenous populations offer instruction in both Spanish and Quichua. At recess periods, students enjoy many of the same sports as schoolchildren in the United States, although soccer tends to dominate. School normally runs only until 1 or 2 P.M. in order to accommodate the family's central meal, the *almuerzo*.

The *almuerzo* is a cherished part of a family's day. It is the time when all members of the family, often including extended family such as grandparents and aunts and uncles, come together and share information about their day. For teens, the meal may be a chance to see other teen relatives who do not attend school. The *almuerzo* is the largest meal of the day, and it is not uncommon to eat multiple courses, even in the poorest of households (see section on food).

When the *almuerzo* is complete, teens usually rush to get out of their school uniforms to take care of chores, join friends, or both. Afternoon chores in the rural highlands can include taking animals to pasture or watching over the family store (*tienda*) while parents are away. Both teenage boys and girls are expected to look after younger siblings. Many rural households continue to cook their food over fires (even though gas stoves are now widely available and the price of gas is subsidized) and it is often the responsibility of youths to collect fuel—branches and grasses gathered in the hills around their homes. These gathering sessions often turn into social events, as teens frequently must travel far away from town (usually on foot). Away from the watchful eyes of parents, these are times spent reveling in being young.

Evenings are usually spent quietly at home. Sometimes teens will have additional chores to attend to, or homework to complete, or family members to visit. Many communities that have their own churches hold evening services called *rosarios* (literally, rosary). While these events are full of reverence, expressed in singing and prayers, they equally provide opportunities for teens to come together for conversation, and as is often the case, flirting with the opposite sex. Evenings almost always culminate in a small meal, the *merienda*, which consists of coffee, hot cocoa, and bread, or leftovers from the *almuerzo*.

By U.S. standards, people in rural Ecuador tend to retire early to bed. While this is partly a function of their early morning schedules, it is equally an accommodation to limited electricity. Many communities have their electricity use rationed, especially in the dry season when the country's few hydroelectric dams are running at capacity. Rural households may forfeit electricity after 8 P.M. at night in order to have it in the morning. However, electricity service is improving, and with it there is evidence that people are staying up longer, often enjoying hours of television viewing. (Televisions outnumber telephones in the Ecuadorian country-side.)

FAMILY LIFE

In Ecuador, as in all of Latin America, *la familia* reigns supreme as the locus of social relations. Indeed, many Ecuadorians are often amazed at what appears to be the casual stance North Americans take toward their families. At the core of Ecuadorian families are nuclear families: a mother, a father, and their children, but more often than not families in Ecuador are also extended. It is not uncommon for a single household to represent three generations, with parents, grandparents, and children functioning as a single-family unit. Many who consider themselves a family unit do not, in fact, live in the same house. Instead, families are defined by less ob-vious ties, such as who shares food with whom and who uses the same kitchen. Maintaining family ties through and across generations, includ-ing strong relations with aunts, uncles, and cousins, ensures greater access to all kinds of opportunities in society. These connections in particular are said to increase *palanca* (literally, a lever), as the more people one identifies as family, the more resources one has at his or her disposal.

Families related by blood also seek out fictive relationships with other families to strengthen community relations and opportunities through a system called *compadrazgo*, a form of god-parenthood. Common through-out Latin America, *compadrazgo* allows families to engage in relationships of reciprocity and mutual aid. Poorer families seek out those more power-ful than them, to make sure their children will always be provided with protection. As a rule, all children who have been baptized and gone through a confirmation have *padrinos* (godparents). *Padrinos* can be called upon to help pay for a child's school, for instance, or help finance a wed-ding. Overall, *compadrazgo* relationships persist to compensate where gov-ernment and other institutions fail to help people meet their needs. Indeed, *compadrazgo* relationships are as much about relationships be-tween parents and *padrinos* as they are between godchildren and *padrinos*.

Family life may be one of the areas undergoing the greatest amount of change in rural Andean life. Older generations have followed what might be thought of as an Andean model of family life—what Andean anthro-pologists call sexual complementarity. Both men and women, for in-stance, perform nearly the same work tasks in agriculture and artisan production. While men frequently migrate out of their communities to find work on the banana and sugarcane plantations on the coast or to work construction in the cities, both men and women are expected to contribute equally to the household economy. Many young people, from various sources including school and television, have come to see a different model—the Hispanic model—as more modern and desirable. In this model, men are often the primary breadwinners and providers, while it is the women's role to stay at home and see to domestic duties and childcare. Obviously, this model benefits men more than women, as the latter are confined, in their duties and decision making, to the household. Young men, though, find the Hispanic model equally difficult to follow, as diminished work opportunities make being the sole breadwinner a difficult position to attain.

In recent years, young men have responded to these challenges by seeking to emigrate illegally to the United States. For those who can marshal the resources to leave (up to $10,000 to pay a migrant smuggler is needed) and are successful in their entry into the country, the rewards can be enormous. With average daily earnings of a migrant laborer in the United States averaging $70, many rural youth question why they continue to attend school or toil in unproductive agriculture when they might make as much in one day in the United States as they would in a month in Ecuador. If successful, young Ecuadorian emigrants can hope to send between $100 and $400 a month to their families in Ecuador. For young, married couples, emigration is often one of the only viable routes to start their own households. Equally appealing for rural youth who lack opportunities for social mobility in Ecuador's national culture, going to the United States offers a powerful engagement with modernity. Many rural youth talk of going to YANY (a slang term for New York, derived from the slogan I♥NY, which, in Spanish, translates to *Yo Amo Nueva York*). Learning some English, adopting American-style clothing, and soaking up American culture are avenues through which they may escape their low statuses back in Ecuador.

The mass emigration of so many rural youth from Ecuador has had its reverberations on those who stay behind. Through the desires developed in presentations of a YANY lifestyle, many young people who will never go to the United States are nonetheless growing up with images of ideal futures that are patently out of reach.

TRADITIONAL AND NONTRADITIONAL FOOD DISHES

The diet and cuisine of Ecuador reflect the diversity of its people and regions. The coast, for instance, has a diet and cuisine heavily influenced by the availability of seafood and the bounty of fruits. Coastal cuisine also tends to be spicier and exhibits a wider range of flavors than either highland or Amazonian cuisine. Signature dishes from the coast (though found in all parts of the country) are a tasty salad made from marinated fish and shellfish mixed with tomatoes and onions (*cebiche*) and *bolos de verde*, a soup consisting of balls made from processed green bananas. *Cebiche* is enjoyed by young people throughout the country as a reputed pick-me-up after an all night session of drinking and dancing. To be sure, on any given Sunday, one can find youths congregated at *cebecherias* eating *cebiche* (and often drinking beer) as they regale one another with stories of the evening before. In the Amazon, diets are based around yucca (manioc), a starchy potato-like root vegetable that is boiled, fried, and used in soup.

For highland peoples, their diet is also centered upon starches, principally potatoes and white, parboiled rice. Almost no meal, even increasingly in indigenous households, is complete without one or both of these starches. A typical dish is the *seco*, a plate of food consisting of rice, a small side vegetable, and a small portion of meat (usually beef or chicken, but also perhaps goat or lamb). Restaurants throughout Ecuador serve inexpensive *secos* as part of the daily *almuerzo*, accompanied by a first course of soup and followed by dessert and perhaps homemade juice. *Secos* are also served with a small bowl of popcorn or *mote* (hominy-like corn). On weekends an outing may include visiting the open-air fruit and vegetable market to enjoy *hornado* (over-baked pork) served with *mote*, *llapingachos* (cheese-filled potato pancakes), and a ubiquitous spicy condiment known as *ají*. By far the most popular food served at celebrations is *cuy* (roasted guinea pig). Almost all rural households raise guinea pigs (they often live under people's beds and are fed table scraps and grasses). *Cuyes* are cooked whole over a fire, seasoned with garlic and cumin. In towns and cities of the highlands, Ecuadorians delight in taking late-afternoon coffee breaks where it is customary to eat a small snack. In particular, Ecuadorians either break for *humitas* (a kind of steamed corn cake made with cheese and cornmeal) or tamales (cornmeal snacks filled with chicken, pork, hard-boiled eggs, and vegetables).

For teenagers, snack foods are very popular. In larger towns and cities, vendors cluster near school entrances to sell snack foods to hungry students. Popular choices include charbroiled bananas, *chuzos* (meat on skewers), and *tostado* (toasted kernels of corn mixed with tomatoes and onions). For Ecuador's youth, the tradition of a late afternoon snack of tamales and *humitas* competes with what is easily the most popular snack option, *salchipapas*, American-style French fries served with a sliced hot dog on top accompanied by ketchup and mayonnaise. Young people also enjoy fruit shakes (called *batidos*) and a wide array of fresh juices (*jugos*).

Soda has been popular in Ecuador for a number of years, but does not seem to have quenched Ecuadorians' thirst for freshly made juices. Pizza and other American fast foods (Kentucky Fried Chicken, McDonald's, and Burger King) are available in all cities in Ecuador, but are prohibitively expensive for many youths. Less expensive, national fast-food chains such as Pollo Gus (Gus Chicken) provide Ecuadorian cuisine in an American fast food format and atmosphere. The appearance of a variety of ethnic restaurants is so far confined mostly to Guayaquil and Quito. Traditionally, the only non-Ecuadorian cuisine available has been that brought by its most prominent and successful immigrant groups, the Chinese, whose cuisine is represented in Ecuador by a unique hybrid called *chifa,* and the Lebanese, who introduced *schwama,* gyro-like sandwiches, to the national palate.

Rural households have experienced a number of changes in diet and cuisine in recent years, many of them catalyzed by the wishes and desires of teens. For many years, the percentage of food grown by families for their own consumption has dropped in the Ecuadorian Andes. In some parts, little more than corn and potatoes contribute to household consumption. In the place of traditional foods, families have become increasingly dependent on rice, noodles, bread, and other foods they must purchase at the market. One arguably disturbing trend is the growing consumption of processed white loaf bread to the exclusion of whole wheat and high calorie varieties of freshly baked bread. The introduction of these new types rivals the tradition of a weekly visit to the local bakery to pick up fresh loaves of bread.

SCHOOLING

Schooling in Ecuador is compulsory for all children through the sixth grade (between the ages of 6 and 14). In practice, though, there is little enforcement of this law and many children, especially in the rural areas, receive intermittent schooling or none at all. As mentioned earlier, the decision to send children to school often hinges on a child's economic worth. At a young age, children in the rural highlands begin to take on adult tasks and by the time they reach their early teens they are competent enough to help with most aspects of adult work. A second factor leading to parents' decisions to not send their children to school is also economic. While theoretically, all state schooling is free, a number of fees and ancillary costs make it prohibitively expensive. Parents must pay for matriculation, uniforms, supplies, and sometimes food, which together can total upward of $90 per year—an enormous expense by Ecuadorian standards. Because of its high cost and its poor investment for the future, secondary school attendance is far lower than primary school (56 percent for girls; 54 percent for boys of the population at large).

State schooling in Ecuador has fallen into disarray under the recent economic crisis. In the 1999–2000 school year, a number of strikes and protests initiated by Ecuador's teacher's union paralyzed schools and students went months without classes. Teachers continually push for the government to increase salaries that are barely enough to live on. Consequently, the country often faces shortages of trained and accredited teachers, as many abandon the profession altogether. Most public school teachers must rely on second jobs in order to make ends meet.

Students who follow through with school can attend a university. Ecuador has 12 national universities spread out among its major cities. The costs of attendance have traditionally been extremely low, making the university a glimmer of hope in democratizing the social hierarchies of the country. Under the current economic crisis, universities have been forced to raise costs or face the threat of having to close their doors. Once affordable university education has now become too expensive for the masses.

While universities have seen a decline in the overall number of students matriculating, they recently charted a new direction in options for degrees and professions. Fewer students each year elect to pursue advanced degrees in such fields as medicine, law, and engineering—once solid professions allowing for social mobility—as job prospects in these fields have dwindled. Instead, students who have the resources to do so are choosing more vocationally oriented associates degrees in, for example, computer technology and marketing. Ironically, in the midst of crisis, Ecuador has witnessed the proliferation of a number of expensive private universities and junior colleges available only to those who can afford them.

Among the upper classes of Ecuador's cities, there is an enormous movement among teens to learn English. Hundreds of private English schools operate in Quito, Guayaquil, and Cuenca as well as in the booming coastal towns, providing classes in English writing, conversation, literature, and test preparation for English-speaking university entrance exams. It is highly improbable that the great majority of students who receive English instruction will ever travel to an English-speaking country. Many young people who enroll do so instead to get jobs in tourism and international business and many others merely for the status symbol of speaking the most popular language in the world.

SOCIAL LIFE

Social life for teenagers in Ecuador again varies greatly depending on social class, ethnicity, and region. In the rural highlands, social life is not neatly divided from work life or the world of adults. With few options for recreational activities outside their own communities, teen life is sporadic and for the most part, public.

As teens mature, much of their socializing carries a pretext of courtship and the prelude to marriage. In the Andean societies of Ecuador, there are few explicit rules about social interactions between male and female teens. As children grow up, they are not separated from one another and often will do the same kinds of work. Within Hispanic-oriented families,

Girl embroidering at the market, Otavalo, Ecuador.
© T. Bognar/TRIP.

however, it is a different story. Young girls, as they reach dating age, are carefully monitored by parents. Girls, as opposed to boys, are expected to protect their family's honor by maintaining a good reputation and keeping their virginity. Young girls who engage in premarital sex and otherwise nonvirtuous behavior are perceived to have brought shame upon their families and, in particular, their fathers and older male siblings who are ostensibly in charge of them. While rules and regulations are changing as girls assume many of the same roles as boys and as positive images of more assertive women become standard through television and other media, traditional customs still abound.

Courtship in both Andean and Hispanic Ecuador continues to be taken very seriously. Courtship often begins earlier than it does in the United States, since it is common, and in some cases customary, for rural youths to marry in their late teens. There are few formal structures for courtship. In many rural villages, no traditional teen hangouts exist; instead, teens will often congregate informally at night in front of shops where they may drink alcohol (sometimes beer, but more often a strong sugarcane-based alcohol [*trago*]). This is customarily a male activity; while females may occasionally join in hanging out, it is only the males who drink. Planned fiestas provide one exception (see below). Often fiestas are accompanied by dancing that lasts through the night. Increasingly, traditional dancing is giving way to dance forms associated with popular Latino and North American music, thanks in large part to the many mobile disc jockeys who provide music and sound systems to the most remote Andean villages.

Meeting members of the opposite sex is informal and not frequently discussed. People in rural areas talk about courtship as *tupanakuy,* which translates from Quichua as "meeting and flirting," or *topar* (meaning "to bump into"). Rural youths in the provinces of Azuay and Cañar will say that flirtation and courtship often begin in the cornfields where, hidden in the thick foliage of corn plants, they may escape the watchful eyes of adults. For youths in northern Ecuador, where altitudes are higher, courtship and flirtation take place in the upper mountain regions called the *páramos.* These are also places where sexual experimentation occurs and is tacitly sanctioned by the community.

When a couple's flirtation gives over to true affection for one another, courtship often leads to a marriage proposal. Young men must initiate the process and seek permission to marry their girlfriends (*novias*). This stage, called *palabriar* (from Spanish, meaning "word"), includes the actual proposal of marriage and the setting of a wedding date. Customarily, the *palabriar* brings together various men from the future groom's family who visit the house of the potential bride with offerings of bread, bananas, and, more often than not, alcohol and cigarettes for her parents. If the young woman's parents agree to the marriage, plans move on accordingly. A civil wedding in the office of a parish registrar often will precede a church wedding, to be held later when enough financial resources have been secured to pay for the event.

RECREATION

Recreation for teenagers in Ecuador can mimic the recreation choices of American youth in the United States. Urban teens visit malls, surf the Internet, and go to movies. For rural youths, recreation is a constantly evolving area of life. In some areas where agriculture has been on the decline and teens are not needed for work, recreation has become a large supplement to the life of the student. Television viewing is on the rise.

Ecuadorians, like people of many cultures, are avid sports fans. In Ecuador, soccer (futbol) reigns supreme. Cutting across class, ethnic, and regional differences, soccer unites Ecuador and in many ways defines the national pride. During televised soccer games, restaurants and bars become packed with people glued to televisions. The Copa de Libertadores (Liberator's Cup), qualifying matches for the World Cup and the South American championships are much-anticipated events. Though Ecuador has never garnered a World Cup victory, many Ecuadorians can recollect important games when they beat longtime rivals like Peru and Argentina. Beyond the national team, provincial capitals have their own closely followed ball clubs.

Ecuadorians also enjoy playing sports. On any given weekend, in open fields of rural villages and urban parks alike, everyone seems to be playing soccer and volleyball. While teens may belong to a number of town leagues, they can also find spontaneous games of what young people call indor. Indor, unlike how it sounds, is played in the street, with the curbs and rocks used to set up boundary markers and goals. A smaller ball, much like a softball, is used in place of a regular soccer ball.

Both watching and playing sports are closely associated with male youth, but this appears to be changing. Most urban schools have extensive sports activities for girls. In the countryside, too, girls' soccer clubs have begun to proliferate.

ENTERTAINMENT

Teens' access to various forms of entertainment depends on where they live and, to some degree, how much money they have to spend. Cinemas are commonplace throughout larger towns and cities of Ecuador. Quito, Guayaquil, and Cuenca all boast state-of-the-art, multiplex movie theaters that show Hollywood blockbusters and, less often, films from other parts of the Spanish world. Prices, though, are high, excluding many teens. In rural areas and poor city neighborhoods, options for inexpensive public movie viewing are video parlors where young people can rent movies to watch on an establishment's television. The film copies are often pirated and the quality is poor, with incorrect subtitling and missing sequences.

Music also forms a large part of Ecuadorian teen entertainment. The enormous success of Latin pop, from Ricky Martin to Colombia's Shakira, is not lost on Ecuador. Radio remains a huge (and free) format for youths to listen to music. At the same time, the ability to digitally copy music from the Internet (albeit illegally) has meant that Ecuadorian radio stations can now release brand-new music from the United States to the ears of Ecuadorian youth almost immediately after it hits the American airwaves.

Despite a barrage of English-language rock and roll into Ecuador, it is a surprising relief to find the tenacity of young people in their quest to learn the country's popular music. Many young males know how to play guitar and are familiar with the songbook of Ecuadorian music, including the songs of the beloved Guayaquileño Julio Jaramillo. In particular, the *pasillo*, a kind of slow waltz with themes of romance and unrequited love, is a favorite of young crooners at parties.

RELIGIOUS PRACTICES AND CULTURAL CEREMONIES

Ecuador remains overwhelmingly a Catholic country. As much as 95 percent of the population claim Catholicism as their religion. The other 5 or so percent of the population are Protestant, mainly Evangelical and Pentecostal denominations. There are upwards of 260 Evangelical denominations in the country (Goffin 1994, xx). In recent years, the Church of Jesus Christ of Latter Day Saints has begun to make inroads into both urban and rural Ecuador.

Throughout Ecuador, everyday life, whether in neighborhood barrios or rural villages, is punctuated by fiestas in honor of Jesus Christ and the Virgin Mary, along with a throng of official and nonofficial saints. Each rural village recognizes a patron saint as well as many others who are celebrated in fiestas during the year. In indigenous villages, Catholic festivals often contain strong elements of Indian culture.

Fiestas, both religious and nonreligious, mark different stages in the lives of young people. In the teen years, confirmation of one's faith to the Catholic religion is an important and recognized event. Even in poor house-holds, parents may spend hundreds of dollars on a child's outfit for the spe-cial day and the preparations for a big party after the service. An additional coming-of-age celebration for girls, the *quinceañera,* is held upon their turning 15 years of age. Akin to a sweet 16 celebration in the United States, the event has historically served to publicly recognize a girl's pas-sage into young adulthood and her eligibility for marriage. *Quinceañeras* are often costly affairs. Besides the purchase of a traditional pink dress (from which comes the colloquial name Fiesta Rosada—Pink Party), fam-ilies may purchase expensive gifts for the girl and throw her a lavish party.

CONCLUSION

Despite its small size and population, Ecuador exhibits a wide array of diversity. Due to an unimaginable gulf between rich and poor in the coun-try, teenagers may have such different experiences that it might seem they are from two different countries. What does unite Ecuadorian teens, how-ever, is the unfortunate mystery of what the future of the country, and their personal future, holds. The economic crisis of 1999–2000 required all teens to rethink their future paths. The only difference among them was that some had options while the vast majority did not.

RESOURCE GUIDE

Bolsa de Valores, Guayaquil. August 2001. http://ww.4bvg.fin.ec/.

Fundación Internacional Para La Adolescencia (FIPA). *Investigación sobre la situacion socio-economíca y expectativas generacionales de los adolescentes y jóvenes Ecuatorianos, una visión panoramica.* Quito, Ecuador: FIPA, 1996.

Gerlach, Allen. *Indians, Oil, and Politics: A Recent History of Ecuador.* Wilming-ton, Del.: Scholarly Resources, 2003.

Goffin, Alvin M. *The Rise of Protestant Evangelism in Ecuador, 1895–1990.* Gainesville: University of Florida Press, 1994.

Handelsman, Michael. *Culture and Customs of Ecuador.* Westport, Conn.: Green-wood Press, 2000.

International Monetary Fund. *Ecuador: Selected Issues and Statistics Annex.* Staff Country Report No. 00/125, October. Washington, D.C.: International Monetary Fund, 2000.

Library of Congress. *Ecuador: A Country Study.* Washington, D.C.: Federal Re-search Division, Library of Congress, 1991.

Meisch, Lynn. "Crisis and Coup in Ecuador." *Against the Current* 15, 3 (2003): 14–16.

Miles, Ann. *Poor Adolescent Girls and Social Transformations in Cuenca, Ecuador.* *Ethos* 28, 10: (2000): 54–74.

Pribilsky, Jason. "*Nervios* and 'Modern' Childhood: Migration and Changing Contexts of Child Life in the Ecuadorian Andes." *Childhood: A Global Journal of Child Research* 8, 2 (2001): 251–73.

Rowe, Ann Pollard, ed. *Costume and Identity in Highland Ecuador.* Seattle: University of Washington Press, 1998.

Schodt, David W. *Ecuador: An Andean Enigma.* Boulder: Westview Press, 1987.

Suárez-Torres, José, and Delores López-Paredes. "Development, Environment, and Health in Crisis: The Case of Ecuador." *Latin American Perspectives* 24, 3 (1997): 83–103.

Tenorio Ambrosi, Rodrigo, María Soledad Jarrín S., and Paul Bonilla S. *La Cultura Sexual de los Adolescentes.* Quito, Ecuador: Ediciones Abya-Yala, 1995.

Whitten, Norman E., Jr., ed. *Cultural Transformations and Ethnicity in Modern Ecuador.* Urbana: University of Illinois Press, 1981.

Nonfiction

Handelsman, Michael. *Culture and Customs of Ecuador.* Westport, Conn.: Greenwood Press, 2000.

Fiction

Brenner, Susan E., and Kathy S. Leonard, eds. *Fire from the Andes: Short Fiction by Women from Bolivia, Ecuador, and Peru.* Albuquerque: University of New Mexico Press, 1998.

Icaza, Jorge. *Huasipungo* (The villagers: A novel). Translated into English by Bernard M. Dusley. Carbondale: Southern Illinois University Press, 1981.

Yanez Cossio, Alicia. *Bruna and Her Sisters in the Sleeping City* (in Spanish). Translated into English by Kenneth J. A. Wishnia. Evanston, Ill.: Northwestern University Press, 1999.

Web Sites

http://conaie.nativeweb.org/
The Confederation of Indigenous Nationalities of Ecuador.

http://www.cultura.com.ec/
Consejo Nacional de Cultura del Ecuador. Ecuadorian National Council on Culture.

http://www.ecuador.org/main.htm
Ecuadorian Embassy in the United States.

Pen Pal Information

Thompson Family Adventures
347 Broadway
Cambridge, MA 02139
Tel: 800-262-6255
Email: info@familyadventures.com

Chapter 8

EL SALVADOR

Cecilia Menjívar

INTRODUCTION

El Salvador is the smallest country in Central America (it is slightly smaller than Massachusetts). It is situated on the Pacific coast and is the only Central American country without an Atlantic Ocean coastline. It borders Guatemala and Honduras, and its capital city is San Salvador. The country has a total population of approximately 6.1 million people, of whom 43 percent are under the age of 18 and about 5 percent are over 65, making this a very young country. The majority of the population still lives in rural areas, and there are more women than men in urban areas (Center for Reproductive Law and Policy). In terms of ethnic composition, there are small percentages of European descendants and of indigenous people, but the overwhelming majority of the population are mestizos, that is, they have a mix of European (mostly Spanish) and Amerindian (indigenous) roots. There is not a significant black influence, as El Salvador does not have a Caribbean coast and it was not economically feasible for colonizers to bring African slaves to work on plantations.

The national language is Spanish, but there is a small population of indigenous natives who still speak Nahuatl. This group and its language have managed to survive in spite of aggressive tactics to eradicate them. One in four Salvadorans does not know how to read and write; in the rural areas the percentage of Salvadorans who are illiterate is higher. The literacy rate for women and men is different and reflects the lower status of women in Salvadoran society. For instance, whereas the literacy rate for women is estimated at 69 percent, for men it is approximately 74 percent. Violence against women in El Salvador is also a serious problem. The

Center for Reproductive Law and Policy reports that the Legal Medical Institute attended to almost 4,000 victims of rape between 1992 and 1996, of which the overwhelming majority were female. Also, it is estimated that among youngsters, rates of sexual abuse reach 22 percent, with the rate among those between 15 to 18 years in rural areas who work for a living or live on the streets reaching an astonishing 65 percent.

People tend to marry relatively young in El Salvador. The age at which more than half the people marry for the first time is 18.5 years. Such early marriages mean that many women become mothers at a young age. For instance, in 1995, 13 percent of adolescents between 15 and 19 years of age were mothers. On average, Salvadoran women give birth to three children in their lifetime. The Center for Reproductive Law and Policy reported that just over half of Salvadoran women use some form of contraception; the most frequently used is female sterilization. Abortion law in El Salvador is one of the most restrictive in the world. Abortion is not legal under most circumstances, not even to save the life of the mother, so many Salvadoran women, particularly the poor, the young, and those with little education (the more vulnerable women), resort to illegal abortions, which are dangerous. In the six months from January to June in 1996 alone, approximately 4,000 women were treated for complications from abortion procedures.

El Salvador is a poor country that has suffered a series of devastating events during the past decades. For about 12 years, from late 1979 until early 1992, the country was immersed in a civil war that led to tremendous destruction, with approximately 75,000 people killed and thousands who simply disappeared. The war had profound effects on many aspects of Salvadoran society. The economy was already poor, suffering from a weak tax collection system, lower coffee prices in the international market (coffee is the main export product), and factory closings, which only worsened with the civil war. In addition to the problems teenagers suffer in other parts of the world, Salvadoran teens of all social classes suffered the militarization of life manifested in bombings, the constant presence of soldiers, curfews, kidnappings, and crossfire during the war years. Many Salvadoran teens, mostly the poor ones in rural areas, were forcibly recruited by armies on both sides during the civil war. Therefore, many boys as young as 11 or 12 years old became soldiers in the war. In one case, two brothers, aged 9 and 11, joined the guerrilla forces to avenge the torture and death of a sister. After they were killed their 14-year-old sister also joined the guerrillas and, after she also died in combat, their 12-year-old brother also thought about enlisting with the guerrillas ("Caught in War's Web" 1990). The government army also enlisted very young boys in its ranks, even though the El Salvador's constitution does not officially allow recruits younger than 18 in the army. Thus, mainly poor teenagers fought the war.

As a result of the war many Salvadorans left the country; most headed for the United States. It is estimated that one of six Salvadorans lives outside El Salvador with the overwhelming majority in the United States. In 1986 there was a serious earthquake and in 1998 Hurricane Mitch left its mark on the country's already fragile infrastructure. Under these circumstances, Salvadorans living abroad, particularly those in the United States, have been sending money (remittances) to their families in El Salvador, thus providing the country with one of its most important sources of foreign currency. But Salvadorans living abroad have exerted much more than simply economic influence in their country. By remaining close to family members back home, Salvadorans abroad have contributed to the tastes, lifestyles, and aspirations of friends, family, and acquaintances in El Salvador. These social and cultural influences, mostly from the United States, can thus be found everywhere in Salvadoran society.

As a result of the war and of natural disasters the country's economy has been set back tremendously and the infrastructure has suffered billions of dollars in damages. There have always been marked social differences and profound imbalances in the distribution of wealth. For instance, it is believed that the richest 2 percent of the country own 60 percent of the productive land, account for over two-thirds of the national income, and, directly or indirectly, control all key productive sectors of the economy. One-third of the people live in misery and another third in poverty, and few have access to health care and other social services. Three-fourths of the population live in substandard housing—mostly in slums—and go to bed hungry, and only one-third of the people are officially employed. Thus, natural and man-made disasters have deepened social differences and worsened conditions for the vast majority of the population. Following a trend already in place in other Latin American countries seeking to ameliorate profound economic crises, El Salvador recently dollarized its economy: the colón was the currency until December 2000. It is now the U.S. dollar.

The country is sometimes known as the Land of the Volcanoes; it has frequent volcanic activity and sometimes very powerful and destructive earthquakes. Due to the frequency of earthquakes, the area where San Salvador is located is often referred to as the Valley of the Hammocks because the earth moves like hammocks. Temblors have destroyed the capital city more than once in its history; several times government affairs have been moved to other cities while San Salvador was being reconstructed. The latest of these earthquakes occurred on January 13 and February 13 of 2001, leaving huge devastation and incalculable losses. The actual number of deaths is believed to have surpassed several thousands, as entire towns disappeared and many were listed simply as missing. Schools, churches, and homes throughout the country collapsed to the ground. The school year, which normally begins in early February and ends in late October, was suspended at least twice because the infrastructure of many schools was too weak, and with strong aftershocks occurring daily, these establishments presented too much of a risk.

With a weak economy and a legacy of violence as a result of the 12-year war, it is not surprising, then, that today the statistics on violence in El Salvador are alarming. El Salvador has one of the highest homicide rates in the entire continent and gangs are rampant throughout the country. In particular, gang membership among youths has been growing, and some estimate that about 30,000 youngsters may belong to gangs. The United Nations Children's Fund (UNICEF) estimates that only 40 percent of youngsters between 13 and 18 years old attend school, and 29 percent work. The remaining 30 percent (or about a quarter of a million) spend their time in unknown ways (De Cesare 1998), and many speculate that they engage in illicit activities and/or gangs. There are many reasons gangs have spread so rapidly in this country. During the war, both the guerrilla forces and the government army recruited youngsters, sometimes as young as 11 years old, to join their ranks. Living in poverty and experiencing the violence of war on a daily basis, youngsters became easily attracted to gangs with their promises of a better life.

Many Salvadorans left the country, either fleeing direct persecution or because the economic situation had become unbearably difficult; many could not feed their families on their salaries. Thus, those who had either friends or family in the United States (or in other countries, mainly in Canada and Australia) went abroad to earn and send money to their loved ones back home. Many children stayed with relatives, grandparents, aunts, and siblings, oftentimes experiencing adult-size violence like bombings, the sight of mutilated bodies in the streets, and crossfire from fighting armies. Sometimes children would emigrate to reunite with their parents, but other times they stayed put and survived on the hard-earned money their parents sent. When the war ended in early 1992, many soldiers on both sides of the conflict, who had been trained to kill and were largely indifferent to violence, did not turn in their weapons and in the midst of rampant unemployment, they began to earn a living by engaging in crime. At this crucial point, the United States began to send back youngsters who had engaged in crime (and been in gangs) in the United

States and who did not have legal authorization to live there permanently (because they were undocumented). These youths, back in an environment where unemployment was high and where youngsters had grown indifferent to violence, were instantly able to recreate the same gangs to which they had belonged in the United States, often using the same names. There have been shootouts and homeboys killed; boys and girls as young as 12 years old have joined gangs, particularly in impoverished areas throughout the country, both in rural and in urban areas alike.

TYPICAL DAY

A typical day in the life of a teen in El Salvador can only be explained through the lens of social class because the everyday lives of teenagers of different social classes varies widely. In fact, the lives of upper-middle- or upper-class Salvadorans are much more like the lives of U.S. teens than are those of poorer Salvadoran teens. As remarked earlier, not everyone has an opportunity to go to school. Upper-, upper-middle-, and middle-class teens go to school, and they attend private schools. These teens do not work for a living; instead they are full-time students. In contrast to how work is perceived in U.S. society among teenagers (e.g., as a means to instill responsibility and good work habits in youth), Salvadoran teens with parents who can afford to spare their children from work will always do so. Thus, those teenagers who work do so as an economic necessity to help out their families.

Education is still a privilege, even when combined with work: Fewer than 60 percent of Salvadoran children reach the fifth grade, fewer than one in five Salvadoran teens are enrolled in high school, and only 6 percent of the total population has a college education (Nessan; "Spotlight: El Salvador"). In rural areas, children may attend a local school, sometimes nearby, but sometimes a few miles away. Usually these are elementary schools; for more advanced grades children need to go to the nearest town. Not all towns have high schools, in which case students have to travel to a larger city in order to further their education. If they want to attend college, they have to go to the main cities of the country, where these centers of higher education are located.

War and postwar conditions have disrupted life profoundly, and in rural areas there is widespread violence and fewer and fewer people now engage in agricultural production. But a typical day in the life of a girl in a rural area would include helping her mother out with cooking breakfast for the entire family in the morning, feeding the animals, and sweeping the (usually) dirt floors. She would probably get up at dawn, and if she attends school, she would probably walk quite a bit, at least a mile, but if her family is not too poor she may ride a horse to school. She would probably come home by noon to help her mother prepare the noon meal, care for younger siblings, carry lunch to her father or brothers in the fields, wash dishes, and so on. In addition, she may help in harvesting something the family might sell, such as corn, beans, or small animals. She would probably carry out these activities while listening to the radio. She would then participate in the preparation of the evening meal and help her mother out with other chores. Boys typically do not help inside the home; they are more likely to work alongside their fathers in the fields, planting and harvesting a range of products both to eat at home and to sell at market. However, in the many families headed by women, boys assume domestic responsibilities as well. At a young age, boys and girls learn that there are certain behaviors expected of boys and others expected of girls, and they also understand in what ways they are expected to contribute to the household. The few teens in rural families with means (usually owners of large landholdings) are not likely to have many chores, particularly the boys. Girls in these families would learn household chores, but it is likely that there are paid workers (mainly female maids) to carry out these activities. From an early age, boys in these families would be taught to manage the family's landholdings. In these families it is likely that the boys

Three generations in San Luis de la Herradura, El Salvador. © G. Fleming/TRIP.

will go to college, but the girls may be encouraged to marry instead, although some will also attend college.

Just as there are marked differences by social class in the rural areas, the differences between rural and urban areas are equally sharp. A typical day for a girl from a relatively poor, working-class family in an urban area would also include helping out at home, caring for younger siblings, washing dishes, and cooking meals. If she is attending school, it would be a public one, and she would probably travel a distance, just as her rural counterpart does, but in this case, she would likely take a bus. When she comes home, she would probably help to care for younger siblings and help out at home. She may help her mother sell a variety of products either in the street, at a small corner store, or at a market. She may also watch television at home (local stations do not offer programming throughout the day, so there may not be much on television in the afternoon to watch), but more often she would listen to the radio or a cassette player, and perhaps spend time hanging out with her friends in the neighborhood. A boy is likely to not engage in helping out at home (unless he is an only child or an older child in a female-headed household), and if he were attending school he would probably be required only to help his parents in whatever work they engage in to earn a living. That may range from selling items at a market to working as a mechanic or perhaps apprenticing at a carpentry workshop.

The lives of middle to upper-class teenagers in urban areas differ markedly. They attend private schools and are not expected to work in the home because there are maids to do the chores. While some might ride a bus to school, those of higher social class backgrounds would be driven by car. Upper-middle- and upper-class children may attend language-specialized schools such as French, American, German, or British schools, where tuition is the highest in the country. At the end of the school day their lives would be very similar to those of U.S. teens: they come home and watch television (usually cable TV), talk on the phone or visit with friends, listen to music, and, importantly, complete their homework, which children in poorer families often have difficulty finding time for. Less privileged children might try to do their homework while they are watching their mother's small business in the street or in the market, or in the work environment where their parents need them. Middle- and upper-class youngsters would have dinner prepared by a maid, continue to do what they were doing before dinner, and then get ready for school the next day. Many are driven to special lessons, such as art, ballet, swimming, music, and, often, English language instruction.

FAMILY LIFE

Family life varies not only by class, but also by location. Rural families, whether they are poor or with more means, tend to include members of the extended family, such as grandparents, cousins, or aunts and uncles. In urban areas this may not always be the case: there, smaller units tend to be the norm. Nuclear families (parents and their children only) are growing in urban areas, but very often a mother-in-law will live with a family to oversee the household while the mother is away working. That is an important phenomenon that needs to be kept in mind. Many urban households, and to a lesser extent rural ones, are headed by women, particularly among the working class and poorer social strata. In these households one will usually find other female (but sometimes male) relatives to help take care of children and with household chores. There are also female-headed households in rural areas, but these are less common. In general, in a home the division of labor is highly structured, with women performing most of the chores.

Both men and women work, in urban and rural areas alike, and in the working class as well as in middle- or upper-middle-class families. The kinds of jobs men and women perform differ by educational level (and thus, social class) and by geographic location. For instance, men in rural areas will likely work the land, either their own or others' plots. Women also engage in agricultural production, even working as hired laborers to till other people's land. But their presence is rarely acknowledged in official statistics because usually it is the man who is hired, and the rest of the family, even the children, are seen as helpers, so the man gets paid as the head of the family. In urban areas men and women work in different occupations depending on their educational levels. Those with few or no skills work in petty trade, as helpers in stores, and so on. Poor urban women tend to work as domestic servants or increasingly, in factories that manufacture products for export, mostly clothing. Women predominate in both domestic services and in export processing factories, but their salaries are low and the conditions of work are usually harsh. Men and women with higher educational (and social class) levels may find work as teachers, as nurses, as clerks, or in government offices. Both men and women work in professional occupations (as lawyers, professors, doctors, engineers, architects, and dentists, for example) but there are fewer of these jobs than of those requiring fewer skills.

Often poor children as young as six or seven years of age work, sometimes helping their parents, sometimes holding jobs on their own and contributing their wages to the family, but there are many children who have to fend for themselves because they are orphans from the war or because their parents do not have enough to feed them. Sometimes children run away from home because they have been victims of abuse. Many of them live and grow up in the streets, and quickly become exposed to drugs and the allure of illegal activities. These children and teenagers have been found to use different types of drugs; some of the most affordable are inhalants. Prostitution is not uncommon among both boys and girls. Also, many children find others in the same situation and bond with them, creating a feeling of the family they no longer have.

There are specific practices among city dwellers. City children who live with their families tend to eat at different times, not because of any customs that dictate who should eat first but because in urban areas almost everyone in the home has a different schedule. Traffic is a major problem, particularly in the capital city, so parents and children often leave home very early in order to get to their places of work or school on time. Schools usually start early, sometimes as early as 7 A.M., and if the children need to catch a bus or the parents need to maneuver through traffic to get them to school on time, they must leave the house sometimes around 6 A.M. Even those teenagers (usually boys from upper-middle or upper-class backgrounds) who own cars and drive themselves to school leave home early in the morning to get to school on time. They usually do not eat lunch at the same time, and dinner might not be a convenient time for everyone to get together because of tight schedules. On weekends, when everyone is home, the family will share a meal (usually the midday meal, or lunch, which is the most important meal in El Salvador), and among the middle or upper-middle classes it is often customary to invite friends or members of the extended family over to share this meal. In these cases, everyone eats together.

In sum, there is a great difference between rich and poor when it comes to family life in El Salvador, as there are between urban and rural households. There are marked differences between boys and girls as well, in all social classes. And there has been a tremendous change in family life in the past two decades or so, as more demands are placed on parents to generate incomes to purchase goods that the children are exposed to in the media and movies. In this sense, new generations are becoming more Americanized in their daily living than ever before.

TRADITIONAL AND NONTRADITIONAL FOOD DISHES

A person's diet depends on his or her social class and place of residence. For instance, among poorer groups both in rural and in urban areas, the diet consists of tortillas (thick cakes made of ground corn and cooked on a circular, clay surface) and beans, sometimes with rice and cheese. Once in a while they might add chicken or some other meat or make a stew of beans and pork. In rural and semirural areas people can add fruits and vegetables, but only if they grow them or find them within reach (like mango trees that people simply grab fruit from as they walk by). Since half of the people in the country are classified as poor, this diet is probably the most common among Salvadorans. However, since one-third of the population is classified as living in extreme poverty, many may not be able to eat much more than tortillas with beans perhaps only once a day. Among these very poor groups malnutrition runs high, and very often the children's calcium intake (in the form of dairy products) is quite low. Instead of drinking milk, children often drink instant or brewed coffee.

Among the middle and upper classes in both rural and urban areas, the diet is more varied. Although they also eat beans and tortillas regularly, their choices are considerably expanded because they can afford to buy meat, vegetables, and fruits. In some homes people eat elaborate dishes prepared with an assortment of ingredients, whereas in other homes dishes are simpler but offer variety. These groups are also able to afford more dairy products, and thus the children and youngsters in these families drink milk everyday. They also go to restaurants and fast food eateries, where they can eat anything from pizza to hamburgers, to steak to fine Italian, French, or Japanese food. Although going to McDonald's might be regarded as a special treat among the working class in the cities (there are no McDonald's in rural areas), teenagers with more means can easily eat there regularly. There are many American fast food eateries and restaurants, so in this sense, going out to eat (for people with more resources), especially in San Salvador, is not too different from going out to dinner in the United States.

People also consume traditional, or national foods, either at home or in restaurants. There are many such dishes, but those that teenagers eat most often, and foods that people eat regularly, are described here. Corn, a crop inherited from the natives who lived in the area before the Spaniards arrived, is used in many dishes. It is the primary ingredient of the main staple, the tortilla, which is used as bread.

A dish typically associated with Salvadoran traditional cuisine is the *pupusa*, a tortilla made out of corn and filled with beans, cheese, and pork, or a combination of these, and cooked on a surface (preferably made of clay, although nowadays metal is more often used). Although people can prepare *pupusas* at home (and many do), there are special places (called *pupuserías*) where women make them and where people go to buy them either to take home or to eat on the spot. Corn is used to prepare *atole*, which is made with mashed baby corn mixed with milk, water, and cinnamon; it is also used in tamales, which are cakes filled with meat, olives, and hard boiled egg, all wrapped in plantain leaves. Again, tamales can be prepared at home or may be purchased in places that specialize in making them (but places that prepare *pupusas* are much more common). The root vegetable called yucca is also eaten often, and it is served fried or boiled. Fried ripe plantains are also part of the traditional fare, as is a dish called *casamiento* (meaning "marriage"), which is a combination of beans and rice. Beverages are prepared using a variety of fruits, such as mango, tamarind, or guava. There is also a very popular sweet drink called *horchata*, made from ground pumpkin seeds, along with other spices, and mixed with water and milk. There are also many traditional snack foods, like fried yucca or green plantains, fruits to cut up like green mango, watermelon, or *jícama* (often sold in the street) served with salt and a spicy sauce, which teenagers typically eat after school.

More and more teenagers, particularly those who stay at school over lunchtime, take sandwiches to school. Ingredients in these sandwiches are sometimes similar to what you would find in the United States, but often they are made using French bread rolls (much more commonly consumed than American-style sliced bread) and filled with avocado, any variety of local cheeses, scrambled eggs, or beans. Given the variety of foods available to teenagers, one would assume that they would not want to eat at fast food eateries. But they do, and they love it, even though fast food meals are more expensive and less nutritious than traditional ones. However, because this does not ordinarily become a habit, parents do not usually frown upon kids wanting to eat at McDonald's or at Hardee's—provided that they have the money to afford it.

Women or young girls are overwhelmingly in charge of preparing the food, either at home or in restaurants or eateries. A recent study conducted in San Salvador found that in 95 percent of families women prepare all the meals, and in 90 percent women wash all the clothes (Colburn 1999). Women usually go to the marketplace or (in the upper-middle and upper classes in urban areas) to a modern supermarket to purchase food. Women in small towns may go to the marketplace every day to buy fresh produce, including live animals that they will prepare at home. At the market women have a chance to talk and to exchange news with others, and also to bargain with the sellers (who also tend to be women). In modern supermarkets, food, including fruits and vegetables, is

packaged like in the United States, and these places are not centers of social life like markets; bargaining would also not occur in these supermarkets.

SCHOOLING

A typical day in a school in El Salvador starts early in the morning; by
about 7:30 most children are already in the classroom. For a long time
children went to school all day, with a break of about two hours in the
middle of the day. But due to increased enrollments, schools implemented
a system of two shifts; half of the students attend school all morning until
1 P.M. or so, and the other half attends from 1 P.M. to about 7 P.M. Some
schools still have this double-shift schedule, while others have kept a
single-shift schedule in which students attend school for about 6 hours
straight every day. The school system is very demanding, so a typical day
is busy, and it is so for students of all ages. For instance, a typical day in
high school may include instruction in math, chemistry, physics, English,
literature, philosophy, biochemistry, and perhaps physical education only
once a week. In private schools students also receive religious or music instruction.

Up until about two decades ago, most private schools, except for a couple like the American School, were administered by different religious orders. These schools were also gender-segregated, and many were also
boarding schools. This has changed significantly. Several religious orders
still run schools, but except for a handful, these are now coed and the
overwhelming majority are no longer boarding schools. Public schools,
grades K–12, have always been coed and, except for a few specialized vocational ones, were not boarding schools. Children of all ages in most
schools, public and private alike, wear uniforms to school.

Not everyone in El Salvador gets to attend school, though. With about
3 million Salvadorans under the age of 21, there are approximately
200,000 school-age children who do not attend. These children may have
to work to help their parents, or they may have dropped out to engage in
a life of crime. In any case, these children do not attend school for reasons
mainly linked to the profound economic and political dislocations that
the country has suffered in the past few decades.

Of the children who are in school, not everyone goes to the same kind.
Social class may be the most important factor in the type of school attended. Wealthier kids attend private, expensive schools, where the curriculum includes many classes not taught in public schools (such as extra
foreign language instruction) and extracurricular activities that enhance
their lives considerably. Thus, the school a youth attends is not deter-

mined by intellectual ability, merit, or potential, but by the socioeconomic standing of his or her family. There are no tests to pass to enter schools, but children must pass rigorous tests at the end of each year in order to continue to the next grade. Up until about two decades ago, high school graduates needed to pass a series of very difficult exams in order to receive a high school diploma. These exams were given on the same day at the national level, and they also determined whether high school graduates would be able to enter the college (or study the major) of their choice. This is no longer the case. There are no national exams to pass in order to graduate from high school, but there are stringent requirements to enter college, so the education system remains very rigorous.

Up until the ninth grade, both private and public school students take pretty much the same subjects, following a national program designed for all schools by the Ministry of Education. High school, however, is not the same for everyone. Students can choose among different specialization areas, such as academic (further subdivided into a humanistic or a science concentration) or industrial and business (these function as vocational training but are also for students who want to study business or engineering in college), among other concentrations. In principle, then, students need to decide very early on what they want to study in college or what they plan to do after they finish high school. There are several vocational schools, such as teaching and nursing colleges that students can attend after completing ninth grade. There are also several schools where youngsters can learn different trades.

School is demanding, and often, very rigid. Students graduating from high school can speak with knowledge about a wide range of topics. In class there is a lot of lecturing, but more and more, children are taught through a combination of class activities, hands-on projects, and outside work. Homework is usually heavy, even for students in primary school. Unlike American schools, only in specialized or vocational high schools are students offered classes like wood workshop. In most Salvadoran schools, the educational program is heavily academic. Sports are encouraged, and many children—both boys and girls—play basketball, the most common school sport, and, to a lesser degree, volleyball, although boys regularly play soccer on school grounds. But students are not encouraged to become athletes as a way to enter college because college admission is based on merit and/or financial means.

School is important to everyone, and parents, in particular, recognize its value. However, sometimes children do not attend school because they are needed in other activities or their parents do not have the means to send them. Most children who attend school go to public schools where the education is free, but parents must still pay for school uniforms, books, and the like. Only a small minority of school-age children has the opportunity to attend private schools where parents must pay for everything including tuition, uniforms, books, and additional activities.

SOCIAL LIFE

Teens meet other teens at parties, friends' homes, and basketball games, among other places. They can choose their own dates, but parents usually keep a watchful eye on them, particularly those parents who feel their family has a reputation to uphold (typically among the upper-middle and upper classes). Although teens' dates are not prearranged in a strict sense, they tend to meet other youngsters of their same social status in the places where they hang out because so many of their social activities are class-bound. In this sense, the social environment in which teens live has the same function as formal arrangements for dates because usually, people tend to mingle mostly with those of their own social class. While marriages are not prearranged, parents do have a strong influence on their children's decision of whom to marry. Parents of higher social classes guard their children and oversee their choice of whom they socialize with. Teens go to parties regularly, where boys and girls have a chance to interact. Schools do not usually have social dances, but they sponsor events such as intramural games, where kids have a chance to interact with friends and to meet others.

More and more teenagers are adopting American cultural expressions, reflected in their dress, tastes in music, and food choices. Since there are close links between the United States and El Salvador at the individual, family, group, and institutional levels, styles fashionable in the United States reach Salvadoran youth immediately. Again, there are differences along social class lines, as teenagers of higher class backgrounds usually wear clothes, shoes, and other items acquired in the United States, to which they often travel to shop. Teenagers who have relatives in the United States also wear U.S.-purchased clothes, but these are not as expensive as the ones that higher class teens wear. In recent years, Salvadorans who live in the United States have been bringing used clothes for sale as well as electronics and a host of other items. Thus, poorer teenagers can wear American clothing as well. But many teens do not have the same means to even purchase such used clothes, and must wear clothes bought (and sometimes made) in El Salvador, though they usually long for American fashion.

Although teenagers are encouraged to say no to sex, and their behavior is closely monitored (and the Catholic Church plays a major role in shap-

ing these views), many do engage in premarital sex. Among the higher social classes, if teenagers become pregnant it may lead to forced marriages
so that the family does not lose prestige or honor in the eyes of others.
This is now changing, but there is still a stigma (at least on the surface) associated with premarital sex, mostly among the higher social classes. As
indicated above, in general, people marry at very early ages, which means
that many become parents while they are still teenagers. But in their efforts to become, or at least to appear, modern, many middle- and upper-
class parents are relaxing their strict rules toward teenagers.

RECREATION AND ENTERTAINMENT

Youths of all social classes, both boys and girls, go to parties (particularly after turning 15), usually at friends' houses, but those who live in
urban areas can also choose to go to clubs. In either case, they dance to all
sorts of music, including American tunes, which are popular among everyone. Urban teens with financial resources also hang out at video ar-
cades or dine out with friends or family. Youth in urban areas also
participate in organized activities such as hiking or camping. Many compete in organized sports, mainly through their schools, and the season of
school intramural games (particularly basketball) becomes very popular
nationwide. Teams are not coed; boys and girls play on separate teams in
different leagues. Basketball is very popular among both boys and girls, so
there are basketball teams everywhere in the country. Outside of school,
teens follow national soccer, the most popular sport in the country, and
boys love to play the sport.

One important event for teens in El Salvador, as in the rest of Latin
America, is when they turn 15. Teen girls who are celebrating their 15th
birthday are referred to as *quinceañeras*. There is usually a big party for
girls because it signals that they can go out at night (and negotiate their
own curfews); they have entered a new stage in their lives and are no
longer considered children. Turning 15 is also important for boys, but the
larger parties and celebrations are reserved for girls. So girls look forward
to turning 15 because they will have a big party, or their parents will give
them a special gift, such as a nice vacation or a nice piece of jewelry.
Those who cannot afford this still celebrate in whatever way they can.

RELIGIOUS PRACTICES AND CULTURAL CEREMONIES

In the past few decades there has been a substantial increase in religious
activity by Protestant groups. It is now estimated that up to 20 percent of

the population may belong to Protestant churches, many of which are Evangelical. Nonetheless, Catholicism is the main religion of the country, so Catholic religious celebrations and activities are well integrated into the cultural practices of most Salvadorans. Holy Week and Christmas are major holidays, and because stores close for a couple of days during Holy Week and at Christmas and the New Year, practically everyone becomes involved in the celebrations, whether Catholic or not. When a teenager turns 15, there is typically a religious celebration to accompany a party. It is a modified Catholic mass (called a *Te Deum*) said before celebrations begin. Again, this happens much more frequently among girls than boys. Those who are not Catholic (along with those too poor to afford it) do not celebrate their 15th birthday with the same ceremonies and festivities.

CONCLUSION

In general, the lives of teenagers in El Salvador are in constant change and youngsters often awaken to a new reality each day. Their lives have been much affected by war, the massive migration of their families and friends, and tragic natural disasters over several decades. They are not passive victims of all this, however. Through community organizations, teens have taken a remarkable role in reconstructing the country each time it has been hit. There is a strong sense of organization at the community level in El Salvador, and many teens actively participate in all kinds of community projects. For instance, several city halls throughout the country target teenagers as participants in community projects because they have abundant energy, along with a vested interest in seeing their communities return to normal. They also actively participate in church organizations that help the poor or that take religious teachings to others. In many ways, the events that have hit their lives negatively have made Salvadoran teenagers active participants in the betterment of their communities. In contrast to American teens, Salvadoran teens have to mature much more rapidly and become adults much earlier.

RESOURCE GUIDE

"Caught in War's Web." *Scholastic Update* 122, 11 (February 9, 1990): 1920.
Center for Reproductive Law and Policy. December 2000. http://www.crlp.org/elsalvador_1.html.
Colburn, Forrest D. "Post-Cold War Feminism in El Salvador." *Dissent* (winter 1999): 43–46.

De Cesare, Donna. "The Children of War." *NACLA Report on the Americas* 32, 1 (1998): 21.

Nessan, Craig L. "Give Us This Day Our Daily Bread." *Currents in Theology and Mission* 27, 3 (2000): 178–84.

"Spotlight: El Salvador." *Population Today* 26, 9 (1998): 7.

Nonfiction

Boland, Roy C. *Culture and Customs of El Salvador.* Westport, Conn.: Greenwood Press, 2000.

Web Sites

http://www.planrocca.org/psm/el_salvador.htm.
Contains a section called "Children and Adolescents First" and plans for reconstruction after the earthquakes of 2001. It also contains photos of adolescents.

http://www.geocities.com/iniciativa_civil/index.html
General Web site with a section on childhood and adolescence in El Salvador, and it contains social estimates.

http://www.ippfwhr.org/profiles/elsalvador_initSP2.html
Lists preventive measures against HIV/AIDS among adolescents, a problem that is becoming severe in El Salvador.

Chapter 9

GUATEMALA

Rose McEwen

INTRODUCTION

To appreciate teen life in Guatemala—and the way of life of all Guatemalans, for that matter—one might begin by reflecting on a popular tale that goes as follows: When God was in the process of creating Earth, the Creator dotted a relatively small region in Central America with spectacular scenery—towering volcanoes, Eden-like jungles, crystal-blue lakes, dense forests (Guatemala means "land of forests" in Maya-Toltec), and sun-drenched seashores.

"Why so much beauty in a single, tiny spot?" asked an assistant angel, to which God presumably responded: "Wait until you see the leaders I will put on that land!"

This tale embodies the serene attitude of a people whose history has been set in a paradisiacal landscape repeatedly defiled by rulers with oppressive hands. From the Spanish conquistadors and their progeny, who, from the sixteenth to the nineteenth century, virtually despoiled the land of its treasures and devastated its native populations, to the self-glorifying mestizos (persons of mixed European and Indian parentage), who as military dictators in the nineteenth and twentieth centuries were responsible for the genocide of hundreds of thousands of Guatemalans, most of them Maya Indians—indeed, the ecological splendor and biodiversity of the national panorama has been tarnished by the wickedness of the majority of its leaders.

Nevertheless, land and its cultivation are the kernels of the Guatemalan way of life. Most modern-day descendants of the Maya still harvest small plots of land for their own sustenance just as their ancestors did thousands of years ago. The Indians' connection to the land is as deeply rooted as the crops they cultivate: in Mayan culture no one person can possess the earth, which is worthy of reverence and ceremonies in which they ask her for permission to cultivate her and later thank her for the harvest she's given.

Yet, this same land has been regarded differently by those who held Guatemala's power after the Maya, who once ruled over a region of the Americas that stretched from the Yucatán peninsula through parts of Mexico, Guatemala, and Honduras. Guatemala's rich soil and extended rainy season render a highly coveted land most favorable for plantation crops such as bananas and sugarcane in the lowlands along the Pacific Coast, and coffee in the mountainous highlands. During colonial times, Indians who spoke only Mayan languages were forced by Spaniards and those of mixed Indian and European blood (mestizos) to sign documents in Spanish to relinquish lands that their families had revered for many generations. The new owners readily drafted titles that legally authorized them to exploit the earth—as well as its original inhabitants who had regarded it as sacred. Mayans became objects of possession among entrepreneurial European and mestizo capitalists.

Since the U.S. intervention (1954) prompted by President Jacobo Arbenz Guzmán's (1951–54) intended agrarian reform, which would have expropriated United Fruit Company's fallow landholdings that the Arbenz government offered to compensate at the value United Fruit had underassessed for tax purposes, little effort has been made by the country's rulers to respond to the lawful claim to land by its original owners. Because land ownership is an indicator of wealth, the historical relationship between the conquering rulers and the masses they command has remained practically unchanged since the time when Tepeu and Gugumatz, the givers of life, created the first Mayan lords over the land. In today's society, Indian peasants remain subordinate to a feudal class of elite landowners and the nation's economic power is held by a select group of perhaps 400 privileged families, who jointly own over 60 percent of the land. Guatemala has always been a land of contrasts and diversity, a nation known as the land of eternal spring and also as the land of eternal shootings, where a minority of well-to-do elites in the capital city guiltlessly enjoy all the conveniences of any developed European or American city, while most villagers in the city's outskirts and especially in the rural countryside don't have electricity, water, or food. Understandably, each year thousands of poor Guatemalans emigrate, legally or illegally, to Mexico or the United States. Those who do so illegally face numerous perils; many lose their lives on the way and the majority of the rest are captured and deported back to Guatemala.

Today, Guatemala's population of over 12 million is a mosaic of contrast and diversity, underscored by the nation's three major ethnic groups: Roughly 60 percent are full-blooded descendants of Maya Indians, 35 percent are mestizos, and the rest are white. (It should be noted that a mestizo in Guatemala is also referred to as a *ladino*, a term that speaks particularly about a person of mixed European and Mayan ancestry who intentionally rejects Mayan identity and instead identifies with the Spanish-speaking, Latin-based culture.) Some towns along the Caribbean coast are populated by small communities of Garifuna. Descendants of Africans who mixed with Carib and Arawak people of the Antilles, the Garifuna continue to hold ties to their African and indigenous American heritage.

Because the unequal distribution of land accounts for the disparate earning potential of the nation's three ethnic classes, these classes are distributed in a pyramidlike socioeconomic arrangement that closely resembles the divisions by ethnic race: At the bottom of the pyramid lie the approximately 70 percent of Guatemalans, mostly Maya Indians, who live in conditions of extreme poverty. Next are the 20 percent—mostly mestizos—who are poor. At the top of the pyramid are the 10 percent who are not poor, which is defined as being able to satisfy basic necessities; the majority of the wealthiest are white. There are middle-class whites as well as wealthy mestizos, just as there are a few Indians who have prospered enough to no longer be considered poor. They are the exceptions.

As can be appreciated, poverty punishes Mayan Indians most severely. As a congress of concerned Guatemalan bishops observed in 1984, the entire socioeconomic structure of Guatemala rests on the platform of an indigenous population who are subjugated and impoverished. The Mayan situation of desperate marginalization (that is, having to live outside the confines of the dominant sector of society) was markedly compounded by the institutionalized violence that characterized the history of the country during the second half of the twentieth century; from the mid-1970s on, Guatemala was led by a succession of U.S.-backed generals who effectively oversaw the destruction of over four hundred villages in the highlands. The Commission for Historical Clarification, appointed by the United Nations to investigate human rights violations and acts of violence that took place in Guatemala, released, in 1999, a report that recorded 669 massacres and concluded that more than 200,000 people died or disappeared as a result of the 36-year-old armed conflict between the nation's military and rebel forces. In the commission's report, the reign of terror was openly exposed as a deliberate staging of violence "fundamentally directed by the State against the excluded, the poor and above all, the Maya people, as well as against those who fought for justice and greater social equality" ("Historical Roots of the Armed Confrontation" 2000).

Extreme, generalized poverty is aggravated by one of the highest birth rates in Latin America. Together with poorly outfitted hospitals and a lack of medicines and good nutrition, these factors are almost solely responsible for the second-highest infant mortality rate in Latin America (after Haiti): of every 1,000 babies born, more than 80 die shortly after birth. For most Guatemalans, making it to adulthood offers 50:50 odds at best: almost half of the Guatemalans who die every year are younger than 14. Humanitarian agencies report that over 100,000 abandoned children wander the nation's streets—25,000 in Guatemala City alone. Yet, the elevated birth rate and the high incidence of death by homicide or war (11.3 percent) has led to an average age in Guatemala of only 22 years. In fact, almost 60 percent of the population is younger than 18 while nearly 50 percent is under 15. Teen life for the majority of Guatemalans can be best described as endurance, subsistence, and survival.

Despite the numerous obstacles faced by the majority of *chapines* (as Guatemalans are known throughout the Spanish-speaking world), unwavering determination and resiliency also characterize Guatemalans. In many ways, Guatemalans aspire to realize the American dream—self-sufficiency—just as Americans do. However, to fulfill this dream, the majority of Guatemalans—including teenagers—require a much earlier start.

TYPICAL DAY

There is no single, typical day in the life of teens in Guatemala for the simple reason that each of the three principal sectors of society—the extremely poor Maya Indian, the less poor mestizo, and the generally wealthy, white and upper-class mestizo—meets the day with entirely different goals in mind. It should be noted that 35 percent of Guatemalan children begin to work when they are only six years old. Additionally, male and female roles are distinct, particularly in the Mayan way of life.

Most Mayan teens—who reside mainly in the country's rural areas—wake up before sunrise. The majority of indigenous teens do not attend school; instead the young men work as *campesinos* (field laborers); girls take care of the house and of younger siblings, but often also work in the fields. After a scant meal consisting of a corn tortilla with salt and perhaps a cup of coffee or *atol* (a drink made of maize dough, water, sugar, and milk), peasant teens step out of their adobe ranchos (one-room, thatched-roof huts) and walk or catch a ride to the plantations where they are employed. Guatemala's Department of Labor acknowledged in 1992 that 31 percent of the coffee bean harvest was accomplished by children. Because fields can be a few blocks or several kilometers away, farm-worker teens may have to walk for a couple of hours before they can actually begin work. Rides might be obtained (usually for a small fee) in the back of a pickup or in the bed of a large, cattle-hauling truck; frequently, Indians of all ages can be seen sharing transportation quarters with cows, chickens, or pigs. Few Indians own bicycles, which at any rate can be hard to ma-neuver on unpaved, hilly roads, especially when transporting a machete (a large, heavy knife used for cutting underbrush or sugarcane) or a hoe. At noon, the young Mayan peasant may take a short break, sitting on the ground or leaning against a tree for shade. Lunch would most likely be a couple of tortillas, perhaps with some black refried beans.

It is estimated that 90 percent of landholders pay their laborers less than the minimum wage of 25.08 quetzales—about $3.20 per day. After working in the fields from sunrise to sunset, a teen peasant walks or rides home for dinner, which, most likely, would again be tortillas and beans and maybe broth prepared by a sister with the vegetables she has culti-vated in a small plot adjacent to the family hut. While a few *indígenas* (In-dian females) may move to larger cities to work as maids, most female Mayan teens stay at home until they get married, spending their free time perhaps embroidering blouses, weaving a *tejido* (cotton fabric), or making handicrafts. On market days young *indígenas* will take crafts, *tejidos*, blouses, and/or vegetables to the nearest large town, hoping to earn a few quetzales; customers may include American or European tourists. In the rancho, daily personal hygiene is minimal due to the lack of running water in most rural homes; a teen may wash his or her face with water that was likely brought home from a nearby stream or waterfall in large clay or plastic pots by a female family member. On weekends and especially on religious or special holidays, teens will take a dip in the river for a full soap-and-water bath.

For a mestizo teen, a typical day can be quite different from that of a Maya, however, the daily routine of all mestizos is not necessarily the same; it depends on the economic status of the family. Like most Indians, extremely poor teens may have to work for a living instead of going to school. Poor, male teenage mestizos may work as blue-collar factory labor-ers, bricklayers, gardeners, bus or truck drivers, waiters, garbage collectors, street vendors, or store clerks, or they may shine shoes on street sidewalks. Poor, female mestizas as young as 12 often work as street vendors, store clerks, waitresses, laundresses, seamstresses in *maquilas* (export processing plants), or hired servants of richer mestizo or white families, in whose homes they will reside most of the week. Servants usually have only one day off a week, when they either return to their villages to visit their families or go shopping or strolling along a *parque central* with girlfriends whose work situations are similar to theirs. Some male teens own motorcycles. The method of transportation of most poor mestizos is the state-subsidized public bus system; powered by diesel fuel, this principal means of transportation in Guatemala profusely emits toxic fumes that have succeeded in making Guatemala City—the hub where the majority of buses concentrate—one of the most polluted cities in the world. Whether male or female, poor mestizo teenagers dream of moving up the social ladder and bettering their life; a number of those for whom the dream becomes a frustration resort to a life of prostitution, pornography, or other delinquent behaviors.

Affluent mestizo and wealthy white teens do go to school. Their daily routine would start with a hot shower, followed by breakfast, most likely prepared by a mestizo or Indian maid. Less-affluent students may have to travel on a public bus, while the more well-to-do use school transportation, are chauffeured by a parent, or drive themselves (Guatemala's minimum legal driving age is 16). After school, again depending on the family's economic status, a teenage student may either hold a part-time job, do household chores and homework, do as he or she pleases while a servant caters to his or her needs at home, or go to a mall or a friend's house to kill time.

FAMILY LIFE

The average Guatemalan family has five members, although a poor, indigenous family can be twice as large, due in part to the fact that few Mayan women use birth control. Machismo—the propensity of some Latin men to assert their masculinity at all cost—may be in part responsible for the higher number of children born to poor Mayan and mestizo families, since a macho believes that the more offspring he fathers, the more his virility is confirmed.

Family life—like the typical day of a teenager—is determined by a family's socioeconomic status. For example, both parents of Mayan families must work, whether to contribute income to the household's earnings, or to bring to the table food cultivated in their small garden plots. The roles of Mayan men and women are distinct and have been inculcated since early childhood. Women are homemakers and care for their children, home, family garden, and the few barnyard animals (typically chickens and pigs) that the family may own. In their spare time, Indian women do handicrafts, embroider blouses, or weave *tejidos* to sell on market day. Men work mostly in the fields, as hired hands for neighboring landowners; some join the military as low-ranked soldiers. For special occasions when an entire Mayan community gets together, such as for a fiesta honoring the patron saint of the community, women and men may congregate away from each other and the two groups may not intermingle for the duration of the feast. However, indigenous families are very close-knit and often pool their resources together. It is fairly common to find large, extended families of grandparents, great-uncles, and great-aunts—and a widowed sister—living under the same roof.

Among most middle-class mestizos and less-affluent whites, both parents typically work outside the home while their toddlers are cared for by a relative. Common professions for women include store clerk or cashier, beautician, waitress, secretary, and schoolteacher. Men might also teach, or perhaps work as taxi drivers, policemen, tour guides, pharmacists, waiters, bookkeepers, or office workers for the state.

After work, women are in charge of caring for children and the home, while men are largely responsible for mechanical chores and repairs. Middle-class households may employ an inexperienced maid to help with menial household chores. These families strive to find time to spend together as a family—one reason many teenagers are given a curfew—and the incidence of divorce among this sector is rare.

In well-to-do households usually only the fathers work; having received an excellent higher education, often in the United States, their ranks include physicians, dentists, lawyers, educators in private colleges or high schools, business owners, bank executives, high-ranking military officers, government officials, and industrialists. Affluent women are the movers and shakers of high society. They host catered soirees in their elegant estates, distinguished tearooms, and exclusive halls, holding everything from first communions to wedding receptions. Some ladies volunteer with nonprofit organizations or organize fundraisers for charities. Their principal role, however, is to manage the household, which mostly entails shopping and giving instructions to a staff of two to four maids, a chauffeur, a full-time gardener, and in some cases a lady in waiting and a bodyguard or two. A fact of life, in Guatemala City and other urban centers, is that the wealthiest families have to live under the watchful eyes of a well-armed battalion of trusted henchmen whose chief duty is to prevent a family member's abduction by the well-organized gangs of kidnappers who operate practically unchecked. Some teens have curfews due to the fact that the majority of kidnappings take place during the night. Since the early 1980s, kidnappers have indiscriminately held for ransom hundreds of the wealthy. After paying extravagant ransoms, most hostages have been returned to their loved ones; others were never seen alive again—the high price paid by an opulent society that for centuries has ostracized the poorest socioeconomic groups, especially the Maya. Many full-blooded Maya shed their *traje* (traditional clothing), refrain from speaking their indigenous language so as to appear more Latin, and migrate to cities, where they hope to have a chance at a better life by blending in. For rejecting their Mayan identity, these Indians are pejoratively referred to by their indigenous counterparts as *ladinos*. What the Maya have found in the nation's urban centers is that opportunity favors the mestizo and white, that is, the middle and upper socioeconomic classes. There are exceptions, of course, but most well-to-do ride around city streets in expensive, European cars with black-tinted windows—ostensibly so that they aren't recognized by likely kidnappers, but conceivably also so that they don't see the misery and poverty that adjoins them. The resentment of the poor toward the rich has ironically contributed to deepen the chasm originally forged by the moneyed classes to marginalize the native indigent.

Perhaps as a consequence of a life of conflict, contrast, and distrust, 99 percent of the adult population consumes alcohol, with 15 percent reported to be problem drinkers. Due to its low cost, the Maya favor *aguardiente* (literally, "burning water"), a rumlike liquor made from fermented sugar. Rum and beer of excellent quality are substantially produced in Guatemala and constitute the beverages of choice of the middle class, while those who can afford it prefer imported scotch. There is no established minimum, legal drinking age.

Beginning in the 1970s, Guatemalans of all races and socioeconomic classes embarked on a process of Americanization that accelerated from the mid-1990s on, posing an obvious contrast to the human and physical landscape of Guatemala. In the 1970s this contrast manifested itself in Mayan peasant farmers who wore denim Levis with handwoven, traditional shirts. In the 1980s, when modern U.S. franchises such as McDonald's and Dairy Queen materialized practically overnight next to Catholic churches or other structures dating to colonial times, the contrasts appeared to be anachronistic (that is, occurring at a point in time not consistent with history). In the 1990s, Americanization became evident in the gradual disappearance of centuries-old traditions such as taking a siesta and celebrating *quinceañera*, a formal dance and/or party that marks the rite of passage of 15-year-old girls into womanhood. The vanishing siesta may be attributed to tight schedules and traffic congestion, making eating lunch at home impractical in larger cities, but it is the 15-year-old girls of modest or well-off means who decided that a chaperoned trip to the United States, for example, was preferable to the antiquated tradition of a formal dance.

TRADITIONAL AND NONTRADITIONAL FOOD DISHES

Thanks to the spread of modern trade, in Guatemala all the foods of the world are available to those who can afford them. In the capital city, restaurants offering Chinese, Argentinean, Cajun, French, Mexican, German, Spanish, Italian, and Greek food can be found as easily as the American fare offered by the local Friday's, Subway, Dunkin' Donuts, or Pizza Hut. Yet, if anything unites Guatemala across its cultural and socioeconomic divide it is its people's predilection for indigenous foods. The great stone cities of the Maya may now lie in ruins, but food traditions of the once-great pre-Columbian civilization have survived the centuries and nowadays dominate what is the nation's everyday cuisine.

The most common of foods is the tortilla, served at all meals in most Guatemalan homes, regardless of economic level. In rural Mayan villages, the homemaker makes tortillas from scratch, just as her ancestors did millennia ago, milling the corn, which she probably cultivated and dried herself, on a grinding stone and making a dough that, with a clapping motion, she shapes into flat circles the size of the palm of her hand. These circles of life-sustaining corn—a main staple in the diet of indigenous Guatemalans—she cooks over a thin, clay disc that rests over a wood-fed cooking fire. In larger villages and cities, tortillas are purchased at markets or from corner vendors or enterprising women *tortilleras*, who walk neighborhood streets balancing on their heads baskets weighted with the tortillas they peddle from home to home.

In the poorest Mayan households, tortillas are, of necessity, the main course. Black beans, eggs, tomatoes, fruit, vegetable soups, peppers, squashes, rice, yucca or cassava, and occasionally chicken, turkey, or pork complement the Mayan diet. When the family can spare money for beef, every cut of meat is fair game to the Indian homemaker, from a steer's tail to its tongue and brains. Seasoned with tomatoes, ground squash seeds, and aromatic herbs like cilantro and epazote (which grows wild in most of the highlands), and colored with bright-red/orange *achiote* (food coloring made from the seeds of the annatto tree), these cuts of beef—which would often be discarded by American taste buds—could easily pass for a delicacy concocted by an accomplished European chef. Unfortunately, meat and other protein sources (only 18 percent of the population has access to milk) are seldom consumed in poor households. A low-protein diet accounts for the fact that at least 75 percent of Guatemalans consume less than 1,500 calories daily. Infant malnutrition oscillates between 75 and 85 percent; in the highlands, where the population is almost entirely indigenous, the index is higher still. Malnourished children often exhibit slower growth rates and are underweight (it is not uncommon to discover that a young person who appears to be 12 or 13 years old is actually 17 or 18). Of the 75–85 percent who are undernourished, 7 percent suffer mental retardation. Malnourishment also causes eye disease in 15 percent of children; of these, one in six is irreversibly blind.

Middle- and higher-income families fare better at the table: their diets include edibles from all the food groups. Their menus could pass for typical American meals, such as orange juice, scrambled eggs, and bacon for breakfast; a lunch of oven-fried chicken, mashed potatoes, and steamed green beans; and lasagna and Caesar salad for dinner. What betrays the menu's nationality are the dependable tortillas (Guatemala's bread), black refried beans, and other pre-Hispanic accompaniments like *agua de tamarindo* (a sweetened beverage made from a tart, local tropical fruit), and the many varieties of chiles—from mild to the super-hot *chiltepe*—that may be served with a meal. And nothing is more Guatemalan than a dessert of *platanitos rellenos*—flat, egg-shaped sausages made from refried beans wrapped in a dough of cooked, mashed plantains, browned in corn oil, sprinkled with sugar, and served hot with coffee or tea.

Religious occasions are distinctively marked with traditional dishes. The most anticipated social and culinary event is the preparation of *fiambre* on All Saints' Day (November 1). While this unusual salad traces its origins to the Convent of Capuchinas in the town of Antigua, Guatemala's colonial capital until earthquakes destroyed it in 1573, today its preparation is a ritual shared by the female members of an extended family. Each family prepares its own variation of one of two principal styles (sweet-and-sour or vinaigrette), but common to all *fiambres* is that the basic recipe is served at room temperature and calls for 40 or more ingredients as diversified as peas, shredded cabbage, boneless pork, green peppers, cooked beets, farmer's cheese, celery, pickled beef tongue, chopped gingerroot, asparagus, stewing hens, orange juice, salami, radishes, hard-cooked eggs, grated Parmesan cheese, and the edible flower pods of the *pacaya* palm tree.

Special festivities are more commonly celebrated with a painstakingly prepared, pre-Hispanic dish. Most children and teenagers may opt for hamburgers and French fries for weekend outings, but for their birthdays they will beg for a Guatemalan *tamal*. Unlike Mexican tamales, the Guatemalan *tamal* is made of rice dough wrapped in glossy, green *palmyra* palm tree leaves. Tamales can be seasoned with a sauce whose main ingredients are ripe tomatoes, peppers, and *achiote*, or with a sauce of squash seeds, toma-toes, and bitter chocolate. They are an essential element of Christmas Eve and most religious feasts. For a true Guatemalan, nothing tastes better than a *tamal*. Guatemalans living abroad are famed for traveling back from Guatemala with frozen tamales carefully concealed inside their suitcases.

SCHOOLING

The contrasts that shade Guatemala are especially highlighted by the divergent educational opportunities available to school-aged children of each socioeconomic class. A blatantly discriminatory education system privileges the education of school-aged children who reside in Guatemala City. Although the capital city accounts for less than one-fourth of Guatemala's population, 33 percent of the nation's elementary schools, 61 percent of its secondary schools, and 90 percent of its universities are con-centrated there.

As explained earlier, the majority of indigenous teens do not attend school: the majority of Mayan Indians grow up without the opportunity to receive an education for the simple reason that schools do not exist in their sociogeographic realm. The few schools available to Mayan school-aged children in the nation's rural areas are state-run, public elementary schools staffed by teachers who, with limited academic preparation and scant pedagogical training, teach in conditions inadequate for the fulfill-ment of their jobs. To make matters worse, in the 1980s, when Guatemala witnessed the destruction of over 400 villages in the highlands, more than 600 rural-area teachers were assassinated or kidnapped and disappeared. To further complicate the situation for the Maya, in a society of plural cul-tures in which they are a clear majority of the population (70 percent), with many speaking only one of the nation's 21 indigenous tongues, edu-cation is mostly offered in Spanish, the nation's official language. The re-sult of this system of institutionalized discrimination is that up to 75 percent of Guatemalans older than 15 years are illiterate, one of the high-est rates in Latin America. This is especially prevalent among Indians (83 percent) and among women (higher than 85 percent); among Mayan women, 95 percent are functionally illiterate. As can be deduced from these sobering statistics, illiteracy predominates in the rural, peasant areas where the poorest Maya subsist.

By contrast, in the nation's capital and the largest cities, educational opportunities abound for the middle and upper classes. Mestizo, *ladino*, and white students can attend either a cost-free, state-administered pub-lic school, or, for a tuition ranging from modest to high-priced, any of a variety of private educational institutions, some run by religious orders of clergymen or nuns, whose caliber of education ranges from inferior to first-rate. Most private schools offer bilingual (Spanish-English) education.

Top-rated private schools are noted for their high standards, great expectations of student performance, and strict discipline; comparable to an American preparatory school, many offer education in grades K–12 and students are required to wear school uniforms. In secondary school, students study anywhere from 8 to 12 subjects. During the academic year, which in Guatemala runs from January to October, homework can be demanding and may consume most of the free time high school students have on weekdays. Final exams can be very stressful: if a student fails three subjects, he or she automatically has to repeat the grade. If he or she fails one or two courses, the pupil can retest in those subjects in early January before the new school year starts. In the latter situation, well-to-do parents customarily hire tutors to coach their children during the November–December school break. If a child fails the second test, the grade will have to be repeated. However, money is key to educational success in Guatemala: less-than-scrupulous institutions have been known to make special concessions to wealthy parents who, for a charitable contribution to the school, have secured their child's advancement to the next grade. When all else fails, affluent parents will switch their misunderstood child to a different school to save him or her the embarrassment of staying a grade behind his or her classmates.

Because poverty is prevalent in this nation, only 13 percent of all Guatemalans over 15 years old complete elementary school. Of every 100 children who start first grade, only 27 finish the sixth grade; in rural areas the number is only 15. Of those who do complete their elementary education, 85 percent go on to secondary schools and, of these, only 36 percent finish high school. When the education received by all Guatemalans is averaged, the median is 1.7 years.

SOCIAL LIFE

Outside of the working relationship between employer and employee, the social paths of the Guatemalan rich and indigent seldom cross. Toddlers of whites or mestizos may play with the infants of their Mayan servants, but children and teens of different socioeconomic levels rarely fraternize. In fact, although they are one-half Mayan, most mestizos consider socializing with an Indian equivalent to stepping down the hierarchical social ladder. Indeed, the term *indio* not only describes the full-blooded Maya, but it is also inordinately deployed as an insult sure to spark the ire of mestizos uneasy with their Indian ethnicity. In Guatemala's plural cultures society, the innocence of childhood is soon replaced by racial prejudice.

Because Guatemala's rich and poor exist in radically different spheres of society, their customs and rules of behavior essentially differ. In general, indigenous people are more traditional than whites and mestizos. Most of today's Indian traditions are steeped in the mysticism and mythology of a Maya past and have been fiercely preserved through the collapse of the Maya empire, the Spanish conquest, and colonial times. Today, the past finds expression in the present, in a continuum of Mayan identity that manifests itself in many elements of daily life. One such element is indigenous clothing or *traje*. *Trajes* are made of *tejidos*—cotton fabric tightly handwoven by women, who can weave perhaps two inches of cloth an hour on a back-strap loom. Distinct weaving designs have been found in over 150 different Mayan communities; in fact, the home village of any *traje*-dressed Mayan Indian can be determined by the patterns woven in the fabric of his or her clothing. Clothes worn by most Mayan teens today are a close reproduction of what their ancestors wore many generations ago. In most towns throughout the highlands, female indigenous clothing consists of a wrap skirt, a belt, a *huipil* (embroidered loose blouse), and a

Miss Maya is chosen, Guatemala. © ASK IMAGES/TRIP.

shawl. In more conservative villages, males wear a brightly colored shirt, knee-length pants, and a short, woolen coat. In the poorest villages, shoes are a luxury; children go barefoot, and those who own shoes wear them only on Sundays or for special affairs. Among urbanized Maya, however, most indigenous men do not wear *traje;* instead, having yielded to the pressures of a racist, Latin-ruled society—with which they wish to identify—urban *ladinos* wear Western-style clothing.

The coexistence of the past in the Maya present is also affirmed in the ingrained traditions associated with courtship and marriage. Mayan teens may look at each other in public spaces such as a park, market, or church; however, girls and boys will rarely speak to each other or mingle openly. As one observer notes, "If a girl is seen in the street with a boy, she loses her dignity and breaks the customs of our forefathers" (Menchú 1984, 63). Perhaps because at the age of 10, Mayan boys and girls are initiated into adulthood—with all its responsibilities—marriage can happen as few as four or five years later. While marriages are not arranged, they must receive the express approval of the parents of both bride and groom. Courtship is a ritualized process that advances through three stages under the monitoring eye of a girl's father, who gives a young man permission to call on his daughter only on Sundays, when there will always be someone in the house. A Sunday suitor will never be empty-handed; he will arrive with a present (perhaps bread or *aguardiente*) for the parents of his intended bride. Oftentimes, the initial Sunday visit is the first occasion in which a young couple actually talks to each other; if a girl does not like her suitor, she will indicate this by simply not replying to him. Successful courtships will continue until a pair has proven it is ready for the serious commitment to the Mayan community that marriage constitutes: the newlyweds will have to "preserve... traditions, and act as an example for their brothers and sisters and for their neighbors' children" (Menchú 1984, 62). Among the Maya, divorce is rare, birth control is negligible, and abortion is regarded as a sin.

Mestizo and white teenagers, on the other hand, strive to appear modern, cosmopolitan, and un-Guatemalan, which entails rejecting Mayan clothes and dressing just like American teenagers. Whether they favor a rapper-ragged look or a smart-casual wardrobe, their clothes look American—and are, ideally, U.S.-made. Not surprisingly, girls show off belly buttons punctuating stomachs clearly anorexic-gaunt—a paradox in a nation where 5 percent of the wealthiest consume 60 percent of the food, since it means that well-to-do Guatemalan teenagers are choosing to starve themselves, while poor children die of starvation against their will.

Dating protocol has also been modernized in the past two decades; teenagers meet in much the same manner and in the same places as teens do in the United States: at school, fast-food restaurants, movie theaters, a mutual friend's home, shopping malls, church, or through the Internet. Formalities among the middle and upper classes have particularly relaxed in recent years, especially among the wealthiest families. Stricter parents may still impose curfews on their children younger than 18 (Guatemala's legal age of majority) or may require their daughters to go on dates accompanied by a girlfriend, but children of most well-to-do parents often enjoy more independence than American teenagers. Premarital sex, while not prevalent, occurs among older, white and mestizo teenagers. If a teenage girl becomes pregnant, the course of action is directly dependent on her family's purchasing power: if marriage is out of the question, a wealthy girl may be sent abroad under the pretense of education, while the less affluent may spend her pregnancy at a distant relative's home. The poorest will face the relentless censure of a female, professedly Catholic sector of society that hypocritically reproaches other young women for doing what many of them do or have done. Abortion is rarely an alternative; unwanted babies of mestizo or white teenagers are either put up for adoption or raised by a female member of the family.

RECREATION

The spectacular landscape with which this Central American nation is endowed provides ample opportunities for recreation for all sectors of society. Rain forests and protected biospheres have sparked a booming ecotourism industry that caters to birdwatchers from abroad. Boating, water skiing, and jet skiing are favorite weekend pastimes of Guatemala's affluent, most of whom own vacation homes. These homes may be anything from two-bedroom condominiums to palatial estates with indoor swimming pools on lakefronts or along the black lava beaches of the Pacific coast. A modest income, however, does not preclude anyone from enjoying a swim; public beaches are open to everyone and on holidays, seashores are packed.

Guatemala's national sport is soccer. Males and females of all ages and all socioeconomic levels enjoy this sport, but especially poor *ladino* boys, who play in dirt lots or dusty, unpaved side streets—feet bare but hearts laden with dreams of joining one of the two finest men's soccer teams: the creams or the reds (the nicknames by which the teams are known owing to the color of their uniforms) and following in the footsteps of their idols.

When championship games are played, the nation seems to stand still: the majority of poor and middle-class men tune in to a radio or TV broadcast.

Guatemalan men also distinguish themselves as long-distance runners; many have proudly represented their nation at renowned races around the world. This sport's economics renders it accessible to males of any socioeconomic bracket, ethnicity, or age. It isn't uncommon, while driving up a remote, mountainous roadway, to glimpse indigenous runners, with glossy nylon shorts and callused bare feet, effortlessly darting past one's trudging automobile while training for an upcoming race. The main coliseum in Guatemala, the capital's Mateo Flores where principal soccer matches and track meets take place, was named in honor of legendary *ladino* Doroteo Guamuche Flores, who in 1952 won the Boston Marathon.

Less-popular organized sports, played by most high school students of both genders, include basketball, volleyball, baseball, and softball. Weight lifting and wrestling are favored by young men. In the most prestigious high schools, rivalry among teams can be fierce. These organized teams—as well as professional ones—are gender-specific, although both genders may play together in a practice match or a friendly game.

Gaining popularity among wealthy teenagers is the game of golf. Children—mostly boys—often accompany their fathers for a round at one of several exclusive golf courses that take advantage of the naturally verdant scenery.

Physical activities for female teenagers include those with aesthetic movement, such as ballet or flamenco dancing (for those who can afford private lessons). In public and private schools in the capital and larger cities, *gimnasia* (a form of aerobic exercise with some acrobatics) and/or swimming are frequently required. Gym clubs offering aerobics classes, weight training, and quick weight-loss alternatives (massages, diets, or creams), abound in Guatemala City.

ENTERTAINMENT

In the twenty-first century, with satellite TV and the Internet bringing American society into most middle- to upper-class Guatemalan homes, mestizo and white Guatemalan teens follow the same fads as do their American counterparts. For example, most teenagers are infatuated by NSync, Britney Spears, and the Barenaked Ladies, and they religiously watch popular American TV programming like *Friends*.

Like everything else in Guatemala, forms of entertainment are diverse and vary according to ethnicity and socioeconomic level. One source of entertainment enjoyed by most is the radio, which delivers music, news, and talk shows. Music favored by indigenous-run radio stations—which in the highlands may be broadcast in one of the principal Mayan languages—includes *música ranchera* (Mexico's country music, or mariachi) but particularly marimba, Guatemala's national music, played by *traje*-clad Indians or mestizos with a percussion instrument of that name. Akin to a xylophone, the marimba is composed of a sound box made of gourds, with wooden-slatted keys that are hit with rubber-tipped sticks; its origin has been traced to Africa. For their part, mestizo teenagers of the middle class prefer *música ranchera*, pop Hispanic music (the same Enrique Iglesias and Shakira melodies that today are top-ranked in the U.S.), and contemporary rock in both English and Spanish. Affluent teenagers forgo marimba and *ranchera*, preferring exclusively music popular in the U.S. Many distinguished rock bands have been formed by middle-class or wealthy teenagers; local idols include Guatemalan-born and internationally acclaimed Ricardo Arjona, who has released several hit CDs. Regardless of their Americanized tastes, however, no wealthy 15-year-old girl's birthday is complete without a traditional mariachi serenade.

For Mayan Indians and poor mestizos, diversion is usually community oriented. In rural villages, for example, on religious or national holidays, Mayan Indians and poor mestizos may trek to a neighboring town during the local municipal fair. There they might enjoy amusement park rides, the coronation of that municipality's queen, perhaps an open-air concert by the town's marimba band or the local military unit's band, and definitely every type of gastronomic indulgence locally produced. More commonly, after Sunday mass and lunch with family, men and women of all ages, in their best Sunday suits, saunter to the town's central park and either sit on a park bench or lean against a *ceiba* (Guatemala's national tree) and watch others stroll by. Vendors walk by or set up stands in strategic locations, peddling delectable morsels such as sliced green mango with hot pepper or cashew nuts. Faint sounds of transistor radios, whispering voices, and warbling birds fuse into a muted cacophony soothing to the ears. The lull may be occasionally interrupted by the clatter of a bolting old pickup truck, the laughter of children splashing by the park's fountain, or the wail of a ravenous child. Curiosity may stir a few park visitors away from their perches, drawn toward the crowd that hovers around the occasional soothsayer, the ambling merchant of magical emollients, or the proselytizing evangelist; few will buy anything. When the sun begins to set, everyone returns home: the few hours of placidity are a modest reward for the previous six days of toiling, for meager wages, from four in the morning until late at night.

By contrast, the privileged classes have at their disposal every form of diversion available to teenagers in the United States, including water parks; movie theaters offering the latest Hollywood releases, dubbed or subtitled in Spanish; satellite TV with American programming; theater productions; motocross, horse, and car races; and live concerts and discotheques. Traveling abroad, especially to the United States and the Caribbean, is also popular among the well-to-do.

RELIGIOUS PRACTICES AND CULTURAL CEREMONIES

If Guatemala's ethnic diversity is comparable to a mosaic, the character of its religious practices is analogous to a palimpsest, that is, a parchment manuscript that, after being written upon, is imperfectly erased and then written upon again, with the result that the earlier writing is still more or less visible. Roughly 65 percent of Guatemalans are Catholic and 30 percent are Protestant. Mormons, Jehovah's Witnesses, and Jews add up to 5 percent, while Mayan spiritualism accounts for 43 percent. That the percentage exceeds 100 corroborates the palimpsest comparison because practically half the population—namely the Maya—practice a blended form of religion consisting of pre-Hispanic, indigenous beliefs combined with Western, Christian doctrines.

Mayan religion was never entirely erased by the Catholicism imported by Spaniards to the New World. In fact, in the early stages of the colonial period, religious blending became an essential weapon of Indian self-defense: given the choices of either converting to Catholicism or receiving the conventional punishment prescribed by the Spanish Inquisition to heretics—death at the stake—indigenous people resorted to outwardly observing Catholic practices, camouflaging with Christianity their own Mayan beliefs. Mayan and Christian religiosity fused so well through the centuries that today it is impossible to determine the true origins of some religious beliefs.

Today, in many regions of the highlands, *costumbre* (literally, "custom") refers to the now traditional practices of blended Maya-Catholic religion, at the heart of which are the burning of candles and incense at altars established hundreds of years earlier by Mayan priests.

For the Maya, daily existence entails the observance of mystical rituals inherited from a pre-Columbian past. Fields are sowed according to the Mayan sacred calendar (renowned astronomers, the Maya also devised a solar calendar as accurate as ours); all forms of the self-existing universe are revered as manifestations of God (a doctrine known as pantheism); and daykeepers (diviners who keep count of the 260-day sacred Mayan calendar), shamans (tribal priests who the Maya believe possess magical powers, are in touch with the spiritual world, and can explain signs or look into the future), and medicine women are consulted for their ancient knowledge of divination, natural medicine, and healing rites. Because orality sustains age-old traditions, Mayan *costumbre* is grounded not so much on written documents as on the spoken word. In the Mayan world order, the advice of elders has more authority than do civil and religious laws. Thus, cultural practices and *costumbre* are scrupulously handed down from one generation to the next, leaving an imprint upon an Indian's consciousness from a very early age. Most of today's Maya and teenagers—in essence tomorrow's daykeepers, medicine women, elders, and shamans— know the vital role they play as preservers of the Mayan way of life.

But many Maya are also fervent Catholics, as are 65 percent of all Guatemalans. During Easter Week (the most solemn religious celebration in Guatemala) Mayan Indians, *ladinos*, mestizos, and whites come together to shoulder enormous platforms that move slowly down the streets of Guatemalan cities bearing statues of the Virgin Mary or Christ carrying the cross. Christmas, celebrated the midnight of December 24, is equally significant in Guatemala's religious liturgy.

CONCLUSION

Guatemala is a mosaic of cultural, economic, and ethnic diversity. Teen life in Guatemala cannot be generalized. In an earthly paradise where some teens struggle to survive while others enjoy privileges of aristocratic proportions, the only constant is contrast. Extreme poverty dwells alongside superlative wealth, vast social injustices are exacerbated by the impunity that shields the corrupted elite, and illiteracy limits the possibilities of a majority while boundless educational opportunities are reserved for a few. Until Guatemalans are able to put into office honest leaders, the story of Guatemala will remain unchanged. This means that the future of Guatemalan teenagers is practically predestined by their socioeconomic status at birth.

Yet, that the past survives despite the present confers an encouraging sort of poetic justice to the story of Guatemala yet to be written. The facts are that a spiritual conquest of the Maya never really took place and that, since 1985, a Maya-led movement pressuring for equality in Guatemala's social order has gradually been gaining strength. Demanding an end to religious, military, economic, and educational discriminatory colonial forces that are still functioning today, the movement has gained needed support from international organizations such as the United Nations and the

Organization of American States. Progress is slow, but some Mayan politicians are already winning popular elections in medium-sized municipalities. Perhaps Tepeu and Gugumatz, the givers of life according to Mayan religion, have a better future planned for beautiful Guatemala.

RESOURCE GUIDE

Barry, Tom. *Guatemala: A Country Guide*. Albuquerque, N.M.: Inter-Hemispheric Education Resource Center, 1990.

Fisher, Edward F., and R. McKenna Brown, eds. *Maya Cultural Activism in Guatemala*. Austin: University of Texas Press, Institute of Latin American Studies, 1996.

Hawkins, John. *Inverse Images: The Meaning of Culture, Ethnicity, and Family in Postcolonial Guatemala*. Albuquerque: University of New Mexico Press, 1984.

"Historical Roots of the Armed Confrontation," *Report: Conclusions and Recommendations*, February 24, 2000, http://hrdata.aaas.org/ceh/report/english/.

Lovell, W. George. *A Beauty that Hurts: Life and Death in Guatemala*. Austin: University of Texas Press, 2000.

Menchú, Rigoberta. *I, Rigoberta Menchú: An Indian Woman in Guatemala*. Edited by Elisabeth Burgos-Debray. Translated by Ann Wright. New York: Verso, 1984.

Moser, Caroline O. N., and Cathy McIlwaine. *Violence in a Post-Conflict Context: Urban Poor Perceptions from Guatemala*. Washington, D.C.: World Bank, 2001.

Perera, Víctor. *Rites: A Guatemalan Boyhood*. San Diego: Harcourt Brace Jovanovich, 1986.

Schlesinger, Stephen, and Stephen Kinzer. *Bitter Fruit: The Untold Story of the American Coup in Guatemala*. New York: Doubleday, 1982.

Shea, Maureen E. *Culture and Customs of Guatemala*. Westport, Conn.: Greenwood Press, 2001.

Warren, Kay B. *Indigenous Movements and Their Critics: Pan-Maya Activism in Guatemala*. Princeton, N.J.: Princeton University Press, 1998.

Nonfiction

Cameron, Ann, and Thomas B. Allen. *The Most Beautiful Place in the World*. New York: Knopf, 1988.

Malone, Michael. *A Guatemalan Family*. Minneapolis: Lerner, 1996.

Menchú, Rigoberta. *I, Rigoberta Menchú: An Indian Woman in Guatemala*. Edited by Elisabeth Burgos-Debray. Translated by Ann Wright. New York: Verso, 1984.

Shea, Maureen E. *Culture and Customs of Guatemala*. Westport, Conn.: Greenwood Press, 2001.

Films

El norte. Director: Gregory Nava. U.S./U.K., 1983. http://www.popmatters.com/
    film/reviews/n/norte.html
El silencio de Neto. Director: Luis Argueta. Guatemala, 1994. http://members.aol.
    com/tikalan/
Rigoberta Menchú: Broken Silence. Video recording. Director: Felix Zurita, 1993.

Web Sites

Portals, General, and Cultural Information about Guatemala

http://www-personal.si.umich.edu/~rlwls/andcent.html#guat
Central America, a useful list of sites compiled by the University of Michigan
Reference Librarian.

http://www.lanic.utexas.edu/la/ca/guatemala/
Latin American Network Information Center, affiliated with the University of
Texas at Austin, is the most complete directory of links to Internet information
on Latin America.

Guatemalan Folk, Pop, and Rock Music

http://www.quetzalnet.com/marimba/
Download Marimba.

http://mi-guatemala.tripod.com/Cantantes.html
Grupos & Cantantes, a site in "Mi Guatemala en el Internet." Lists links to URLs
posted by Guatemalan musicians and their fans.

Guatemalan Recipes in English

http://food4.epicurious.com/HyperNews/get/regions/16/3.html

Travel Information

http://www.lonelyplanet.com/destinations/central_america/guatemala/
Lonely Planet. Online travel guide that includes maps and pictures of
Guatemala; background information such as history, culture, and environment;
suggestions on how and when to travel to the country; and recommended activities and events upon arrival.

More Information

http://travel.state.gov/guatemala.html
State Department Consular Information Sheet.

http://usembassy.state.gov/guatemala/
U.S. Embassy in Guatemala.

Guatemalan Embassy in the U.S.
2220 R Street, NW
Washington, DC 20008
Tel: 202-745-4952, extension 102
Fax: 202-745-1908
Email: embaguat@sysnet.net

Pen Pal Information

http://clubs.yahoo.com/clubs/guatemalaenelinternet/
Guatemala Chat Room.

Chapter 10

HAITI

Maude Heurtelou

INTRODUCTION

Haiti is located in the Caribbean, where landscapes and seascapes are spectacular. It shares the island of Hispaniola with the Dominican Republic. Cuba, Jamaica, and Puerto Rico are its closest neighbors. In Haiti, enormous mountains appear to defy the sky while protecting the plains and the valleys and looking down upon the coasts. It is a country of geographical contrasts that bears all the diversity of a tropical nature that one can imagine on a West Indian island. The coastal communities are flat, hot, and rich in seafood and coconut trees. The inlands are composed of smooth hills with curvy roads. Inland soil is best for planting coffee, grains, and tropical fruits. Higher lands are mountainous and cool: They are known for exotic flowers and fresh produce.

To get a picture of the unique topography of Haiti, imagine squeezing a big sheet of paper in the palm of your hand and then examining it from a flat perspective. All the lines and curves of the squeezed sheet could easily be compared to the unexpectedly rugged shape of the country. It is little wonder that "Haiti" is an Amerindian word for mountainous.

Life in Haiti is sunny and bright almost every day. The sun never misses its rendezvous with the sky unless it is hurricane season. Days are long and hot in the plains but temperatures cool down in the evenings. Nights are often dark in most cities and especially in rural areas when there is no electricity. In mountainous regions, it is cool and humid during the day although it can get chilly at night. Nature is ever present, everywhere, in all the senses. At any time one can smell a variety of plants, hear mangoes or breadfruit falling from tree branches and rolling like speedy drumbeats over sheet-metal roofs, see colorful bougainvillea leaning on fences, touch the dew on a papaya tree's large leaves, or taste the powerful flavor of wild cherries.

Haiti is also a land where the royal palm tree grows tall and strong. It is one of the rare places on earth where rhinoceros iguanas have thrived until recent decades.

With the arrival of Christopher Columbus, who landed on Hispaniola in 1492, Haiti became a colony of Spain. Because the Spaniards wanted to exploit the land's riches, they submitted the indigenous Amerindians, the first occupants, to a regime of hard work that they were not used to. This caused an almost complete extermination of the Indians in a very short time. To replace them, the Spaniards introduced Africans to the island. It didn't take long for slavery to become the destiny of thousands and thousands of Africans deported from that continent.

After repeated attacks, in 1625 Spain surrendered the western part of the island to France. The French quickly organized to exploit it, intensifying plantations of coffee, cotton, and indigo, and expanding sugarcane fields. The colony became known as Saint Domingue. Sold, enslaved, and colonized, Africans experienced brutal treatment and inhumane conditions under the vigilant control of French settlers. The French maintained control of this part of the island until the war for independence.

The independence of Haiti is the first-known organized, successful, antislavery revolution. With far fewer arms, and less organization and education than the French armies, African slaves victoriously fought and freed themselves after over 400 years of struggle against extreme abuse. A new red and blue Haitian flag was born during this period. After the pivotal Battle of Vertières, on November 18, 1803, liberated blacks were ready to build a new nation that would be known from then on as Haiti. The new nation's motto was "United We Are Strong."

Haiti is about 27,750 square kilometers in area. Its population is mostly black with less than 5 percent mulattos and 0.5 percent immigrants, the latter mainly from the Middle East. There are about 8,000,000 Haitians in the world, a million of whom live abroad, largely in the United States and Canada. The population is about 70 percent rural and 30 percent urban. Traditionally, a majority of the population's revenue comes from agriculture. In socioeconomic terms, its people can be roughly separated into the rich (1 percent), the middle class (29 percent), and the lower group (70 percent).

While the rich live like most rich people around the world, with access to technology and a high standard of living, the middle and lower socioeconomic classes better reflect the reality of Haiti, where most live with only the essentials and many times with much less. Like other countries in the developing world, Haiti's population is mostly young, poor, and illiterate. Money and education are luxuries for them. Daily life affords only limited technology. Haiti is still close to nature and bears strong similarities to Africa.

The people are strong, joyful, and determined even if many are poor. It is estimated that 50 percent of the population are unemployed. Consequently, those people live on a day-to-day basis, never really knowing if they will get food on their plates the following day. Sometimes they are evicted from their rental homes and become homeless, or they may have a stable place to live but don't have spare clothes and what they wear may look like rags. Many children may spend their free days in their backyard with only a shirt, or with shorts only, because the only outfit they own is being laundered. To many, the basics are food, shelter, and clothing. Fortunately, there are only occasional cases of starvation in Haiti. It is a poor country that gets its strength from the challenge of its own destiny. Most people find reasons to live, to have fun, to dance, and to be proud even though they have very little hope for economic advancement. In large part, this is due to the fact that the value system is not materialistic and people share among themselves the little that they have.

Despite the fact that the middle and lower socioeconomic classes represent the reality of the country, those two groups live in very different worlds that sometimes contrast with each other. It is important to understand these contrasts and similarities to better visualize the life of Haitian teens. In fact, teens from urban areas have little in common with teens from the countryside, largely because most of the material resources available in bigger cities are unknown in the rural areas.

Although Haiti is a small country, its people differ, through accents and facial features, according to their regions of birth and the racial mix in their ancestry. Those from the north have melodious Creole accents, influenced by geographical proximity to the Dominican Republic. Those from the south often have physical features that remind one of the previous European mix in those areas.

Haiti is a republic. During the dictatorship of well-known Papa Doc Duvalier, the country experienced an apparent stability because public opinion was controlled. Poor people had no influence, so their suffering was kept out of sight, while the middle and upper-middle classes were either forced to be silent for fear of retaliation or else were brainwashed into cooperating directly or indirectly with the status quo. Many, however, chose to leave the country instead. Some spoke out or challenged the situation and paid the ultimate sacrifice. As one observer noted, "Almost everyone I know can tell the story of a neighbor who has been killed or assassinated for his or her political ideas during that period. I was in elementary school when one of my classmates lost her entire family because the *'tonton macoutes'* [literally, "boogey man"—Duvalier's paramilitary] walked in her parents' house, vandalized and killed everyone including the servants. My classmate was [away] visiting her godmother...that weekend and that is the only reason she is still alive today. This traumatic experience was to such a proportion that we, the children, were scared to talk to her in school, fearing to be associated with someone from a 'dangerous family.' During that same period, Numa and Douin, two activists who were against the [dictatorship], were killed in a public park, under the eyes of adults and children invited to watch their fate. This was one of the most intimidating experiences the population went through collectively and individually. I believe the whole country turned mute after that and nobody felt at ease to even look at each other in any way that could have been interpreted as a disagreement."[1] Now the country is governed by Jean-Bertrand Aristide, a former priest who is an advocate for the poor, and Haiti is still searching for the path to democracy. While it appears to be unstable now, one can say for sure that nobody is mute anymore and everyone can look at each other and say what they think. This is a great step toward hope and real democracy. In Haiti there are executive, legislative, and judicial branches but the political infrastructure is still fragile and sometimes worrisome. Under dictatorship, the poverty of the country was silenced and covered up, and the country presented an apparent stability that was comfortable for the middle and upper socioeconomic class. Today, the lower socioeconomic class is rightly using their new freedom of speech to protest their lack of access to social, political, and economic opportunities for advancement. Often, these struggles are not conducted in an orderly way and the chaotic shifts are now causing discomfort in the middle and upper socioeconomic class. This discomfort and chaos are not allowing the country to advance. Haiti has a long way to go toward achieving a peaceful democracy.

Haiti is divided into nine departments, each with its own headquarters. Port-au-Prince is headquarters of the west department. The northwest is a more arid area, known for frequent droughts. The south is flat and prone to flooding during hurricane season, while the west is right at the center, facing the small La Gonave Island.

As in any other country, Haitians occupy different positions in their society depending upon their profession. Among the traditionally better paying positions are those of physician, industrialist, agronomist, engineer, lawyer, administrator, businessman, and other professionals. People in these positions represent the upper-middle class by their income and level of education. Teachers, nurses, and state middle-management staff are examples of the center-middle class, educated but with average incomes. Blue-collar workers and retailers with limited incomes and with middle- to high-school levels of education make up the lower-middle class. Beyond these groups are many more workers who may not occupy career positions or hold steady jobs but who do take care of the basic needs of their families. Some women, not educated at all but with a talent for business, are as successful as the professionals. It has been reported that market women, for instance, will travel all the way to Japan to buy and resell goods.[2]

Haiti is primarily an agricultural country, and the majority of its population still makes a living from agricultural labor and products. Unfortunately, agriculture is becoming less of an option for peasants, forcing many to abandon their lands to search for jobs in the manufacturing industry. Agricultural production has been deteriorating partly because the soil has eroded; trees have been ruthlessly exploited either as fuel for domestic use or for lumber and furniture. Agricultural production has been maintained on a very small scale, using little or no machinery and consuming a lot of manpower. This reality can partly explain the fragility of the nation's economy. For generations, peasants have proudly cultivated their lands, but with distribution of inheritances from generation to generation, and with land erosion worsening with time, life in rural areas has become more difficult and less attractive and there has been an exodus of inhabitants to larger cities, especially Port-au-Prince.

Peasants as well as urban dwellers face the challenge of a small country that offers limited employment options and opportunities for training. Educated Haitians are already competing for the few opportunities available and they have to stay on their toes to update their knowledge, get regular training, and maintain professional growth. Because the majority of the workforce is unemployed, it creates a system of dependency among children and parents, partners, family members, and so on.

This situation has created a gap in lifestyles between the poor and uneducated and the educated middle to upper classes. Those born into families whose parents and grandparents were educated and hold good jobs usually have a better chance of personal success. They can rely on the inherited worth and knowledge of their educated parents to secure their own comfort and opportunities. Those who are not educated or have inherited few or no assets from their noneducated parents cannot find jobs unless they are uniquely skilled in something. There are success stories occasionally, but it is not the case for the majority. Haiti is a country of contrasts and this is reflected in the lives of teens.

TYPICAL DAY

Teens in urban areas have a completely different reality from that of teens in rural areas, so it is expected that their typical day is very different. In urban areas, teens get up and get ready for school. Their day starts with a cold shower that is very pleasant since the sun rises early and it gets hot very soon. After a quick stop in front of the mirror to fix a teen hairstyle, it is time to wear the school uniform, usually impeccably starched, with shined shoes. It is good manners to kiss one's parents good morning. The parents usually set the table and fix breakfast since all they expect from their children is that they go to school and learn at least from the morning until they return from school. Many parents assign no responsibilities to their teens, not even to take care of their room, so they can focus on being in school on time. Of course some parents make them fix their bed to teach them some order and discipline.

After a quick breakfast, boys and girls are ready to walk to school if mom or dad has not ordered them to go back and redo a hairstyle that is not appropriate for school or to change out of a skirt that ends above the knees. Most teens must pass their parent's approval before leaving the house. Boys, for example, must wear their shirt tucked inside their pants to go to school.

Most students walk two to five miles from home to school. Walking from and to school is a special time when friendships are built and confidences made to best friends. This long walk is frequently taken as a social opportunity to walk with a friend, share personal ordeals, or just talk about hot teen topics that might be censored by parents. In groups of two or three, boys and girls walk most of the time in an orderly manner to go to school. It is not the time for arguments or fights: the school uniform is sacred and the mood is subdued. Some parents might drop their children at school on their way to work and others go in taxis or with a contracted driver.

Students gathering outside the school to wander, fight, or play before the morning opening is almost always prohibited so they must arrive just on time to enter the schoolyard by 8:00 A.M. sharp; arriving late is a breach of discipline. Therefore, every school day, by 7:30 A.M., just thirty minutes before each school's bell rings, there is a traffic rush around each school's neighborhood when groups of students in uniform clog the streets to enter their school yard and report on time. It happens, however, that some students get in trouble with their principal for misbehaving on the streets while in their school's uniform. Needless to say, they take the risk of being punished twice, at school and at home, once their parents are informed by their school's administrator. Students who are to school on time line up to sing the national anthem and to watch the flag raising in the most respectful behavior. Promptly thereafter, they will walk toward their classroom and stay there until the morning break around 10:00 A.M., which lasts about 15 minutes. By 12:30 they will have lunch. One hour later, they will be back in their classroom until 4:00 or 5:00 P.M. depending on what grade they are in.

When students return home from school they change quickly into comfortable house clothes to do their homework. Some may watch television if they have access to one but definitely after doing their homework. Many may go play soccer in their backyard or go do some errands for their parents. The time from 5:00 to dinner is the break that teens wait for. Dinner is served around 6:30 P.M. and homework must be completed by then or before bedtime. Students who have no electricity at home study and do their homework under the streetlights of the nearby park, sometimes when it's late. Responsible parents might walk all the way to the park to check to see whether their children are really doing their homework or just chatting.

On weekdays, teens have little social activities but on weekends they may go for a picnic in the midmorning. They may pack a snack and walk to the beach or to the mountains. Under the heat of the sun and breezy winds, between intermittent games in and around water, they may drink coconut water instead of soda while singing love songs, youth hymns, or oldies. Teens who are out with friends must come back home before dark, especially girls. Boys may be allowed to stay out later but no parents would go to sleep with their teens on the streets unless they know where they are, whom they are with, and who is bringing them back.

Teens don't usually work and their routine tends to be set around going to school and learning.

In the rural areas, girls and boys wake up early, at the call of a rooster nearby, as early as 4:30 in the morning. While girls may go fetch water to make the family's big pot of coffee, the boys may start getting the mule ready or may start sharpening their father's machete, which will be used in the field. Life starts with work. Teens who go to school always have a couple of assignments to complete before leaving their house. Since their family lives day by day, teens' responsibilities are important and might be more important in the short term than going to school. Going to school may even be a barrier to their lifestyle, which includes so many responsi-

Young teen boys ride horses in rural Haiti. © ASK IMAGES/TRIP.

bilities. Even getting a shower prior to going to school requires that teens walk to the river or go fetch the water first.

After that they will walk many miles in narrow and escarped mountain alleys toward their schools. By then, it is midday when they arrive at school. Because the rural population is sometimes spread all over and school can be far away for some students' houses, many students walk hours to reach school, which can be physically exhausting. Classes start later and end earlier than in the urban areas. When teaching is not relevant to the rural lifestyle, many teens in rural areas drop out.

After school, teens are back to work, the girls helping their moms in house chores and the boys, their fathers, in the field. The day ends early, with sundown. Unless there are cockfights, folk dances nearby, or voodoo ceremonies in town, most teens in rural areas will listen to stories from elders, go for a walk under the moonlight, or already be in bed by 8 o'clock.

On weekends, teens still work at home or in the fields but they may stay up late because of a social event, harvest season, or a *combite*,[3] or just because the neighbor next door is salting a pig that he plans to sell in the market the next day: anything is a valued experience and is a lot of fun for teens living in rural areas.

FAMILY LIFE

Haitian parents may love their children but they do tend to be strict with them. The tendency is for parents to be coaches, constantly reinforcing values and urging youths to focus on studying and graduating. Parents make sacrifices for their children. They often live in tight conditions to pay for private school or to send their children abroad for further education. Sometimes parents take opportunities away from other siblings to give a better chance to the oldest or smartest. This is a calculated move, because if one makes it, the whole family will benefit. Too often, these opportunities are automatically awarded to males, putting females in a disadvantaged position.

Sometimes parents make a choice to push boys instead of girls because not only do boys have a better chance of obtaining a job in a market dominated by males, but also because they tend to make more money than do their female counterparts. Educated children almost always contribute to the education of their siblings as soon as they start working.

Haitian family members are supportive of each other. It is expected that parents give the best they have to their children and it is also expected that the oldest help the youngest in any manner possible, including financially. Older siblings may postpone important decisions in their lives, such as weddings or other important engagements, in order to assist the youngest in finishing school. The same phenomenon is observed among Haitians who have settled in North America.

It is not common to see public demonstrations of affection among family members. Love and care are mostly demonstrated through actions or unspoken sacrifices. While reprimands or punishments might be expressed in public, hugs and kisses in public occur rarely.

The traditional family includes parents and their children but it is also common for grandparents to live with them and to participate actively in their grandchildren's lives. In many cases, uncles and aunts may live under the same roof with the nuclear family before they are married or move out to build lives of their own. This may appear overwhelming for people from another culture but it is perfectly acceptable, in Haitian society, for someone to marry and have children and at the same time to accommodate his or her parents and siblings in the same house.

Older parents expect to live with their adult children in old age. The extended family stays together even when roles change and parents become dependent on their adult children. It is not only a financial convenience; it is also a tradition of love, care, and responsibility that has existed for many generations. It is inconceivable that a Haitian parent would want his or her offspring to leave the family nest just because that offspring has reached a certain age. If that were to happen, there must be an important reason, such as because the child is going to school elsewhere, going to work far away, or getting married. Some parents remain available for assistance or to welcome their children back if they need to return.

An extended family is a plus in the Haitian culture. Uncles, aunts, and cousins around a teen are complements to his or her parents. Teens can confide in an uncle or an aunt. They can get support from grandparents when tensions rise with mom or dad. They can get assistance for their homework from an older cousin. They can see role models in all these people and, finally, it is priceless to be loved, spoiled, or coached by so many people who care. In a country where counselors and specialists are out of reach for most teens, growing up with lot of family support prevents teens from facing a crisis alone.

The immediate neighborhood also plays an important role in a teen's life. Parents of other children in the neighborhood naturally volunteer to keep an eye on all the teens in the block. It is as if all adults assume responsibility for all children. A neighbor's involvement is not as deep as the parents' or the extended family's but teens can count on the intervention of a neighbor if something happens, especially in dangerous situations. Of course, neighbors will also reprimand teens if necessary. Misbehaving in the presence of an adult implies that you would misbehave in front of your own parents. If a teen acts out, adults feel free to report it to the youth's parents. Children are somehow always under adult supervision.

It is understood that children represent not only their parents but also the future of their neighborhood and the standard of their school. There is silent pressure on teens to respect and honor their family name, to represent their neighborhood, and to act as ambassadors of their school even outside of its walls. It seems that armies of people are waiting to be proud of the growing generation.

Neighbors and friends do not congratulate parents for well-behaved teens, though. To behave is the norm. Parents would be embarrassed if an adult were to be offended by their teen's behavior and report it to them. Such situations may carry serious punishment. Sometimes it is not clear if the punishment is for the embarrassment or for the behavior.

Punishments vary in style and intensity but the most traditional is corporal punishment, an issue that clashes seriously with North American tradition. This subject is still actively debated in Haiti and abroad. There have been cases of misinterpretation where the love of Haitian parents for

their children was questioned because of their use of corporal punishment. Although there have been reported cases of excess, these are isolated incidents.

TRADITIONAL AND NONTRADITIONAL FOOD DISHES

During summer, teens living in or visiting the countryside enjoy waking
up when a next-door rooster gives the signal, or arising to the smell of
fresh, locally grown coffee. Breakfast consists of freshly harvested food,
since much of the food consumed in the countryside is harvested on the
same day or the day before. Some have been sun-dried, salted, or preserved with traditional spices. Frozen or canned foods have almost no part
in the rural diet.

On January 1, almost everyone in Haiti will have squash soup. This is a
tradition that even Haitian emigrants keep. Squash soup is made with
squash, meat, carrots, celery, potatoes, and noodles. It has a creamy, yellow appearance and is a complete dish and a delight for people who like
soup. They may top it off with Haitian cake and homemade anise liquor.
Many people make an extra large pot of squash soup to offer to visitors
who come and go throughout the day. On New Year's Day, one can have
visitors from early that morning until the following dawn. Visits are kept
short because everybody has a long list of friends, relatives, and neighbors
to visit. Usually, the youngest visit the oldest. It is rude not to visit your
elders and superiors on New Year's. This day is also Independence Day in
Haiti and provides opportunities for many teens to meet relatives who
live far away, to attend emotional family gatherings, and to be acquainted
with their families' history, secrets, or glorious past. Sometimes the visits
continue on January 2, Forefather's Day, which is also a holiday.

During carnival, people enjoy beignets. They are sweet, ripe, banana
fritters, sprinkled with powdered sugar and sold on street corners. One can
smell them from a block away. Teens enjoy walking around eating
beignets with their friends as they wait for the traditional parade where
fans of different musical bands show off their costumes while dancing and
singing.

The Haitian diet is based mainly on vegetables. Rice, corn, millet,
beans, plantains, and *boniato*, along with roots like yucca and *malaga*, are
the most common foods. People also enjoy rice and beans with fried pork
and fried plantains.

As in most of the West Indies, food can be spicy. The best-known pork
recipe, *griyo*, is a dish of fried pork marinated in a sour orange base, then
prepared with green onions, thyme, pepper, and cloves. People enjoy *griyo*

with fried sliced green plantains, topped with *pikliz*, a spicy vegetable mix of chopped onions, scallions, and hot pepper, marinated in lemon juice. People enjoy goat and beef as well. Although Haiti is located on an island, fish is expensive and not accessible to the majority. Most animal foods are expensive. Meat, eggs, fish, and cheese are not on the daily plate of the poor.

Tasty, traditional, homemade desserts include sweet potato pie and cornmeal pudding. Haitian cake tastes like pound cake with a twist of almond essence. Sweets and candies are popular, too. Children and teens like caramel-like treats, such as *tito* and *mayilov*. Some enjoy coconut-based candies, like *kòk graje, tablèt kokoye, or kòk griye*. The latter is prepared with ground coconut, which is sweetened and browned until it gets all dry and fluffy. Others prefer powdered corn served in a cone, called *chanm-chanm*. Some snacks are salty, like plantain chips, cashew nuts, and grilled peanuts. Some are refreshing, such as the crushed ice and ice cream that one can buy from itinerant sellers.

Haitian cuisine is a blend of African and French traditions. Breakfast varies from light, traditional oatmeal to a solid dish of steamed fish, green plantain, watercress, and sliced tomatoes accompanied by fresh grapefruit juice. Lunch is the heaviest meal, most likely rice and beans, steamed vegetables with beef, steamed conch, chicken, or fried pork. Dinner also varies from a light porridge of corn, rice, or yucca to a complete meal like lunch. Some people enjoy bouillon, a vegetable soup topped with meat and sliced roots, steamed slowly with fine herbs and fresh spices.

SCHOOLING

About 50 percent of Haitians are 18 or younger, and teens represent 25 percent of the population. Elementary school is mandatory. Education is free in Haiti from first grade to the university level. However, not every parent can afford books and uniforms. Besides, the state program has limited capacity, especially at the university level.

Before starting secondary school, which is equivalent to middle and junior high school in the United States, students must pass a national test called *Certificat*. Similarly, before attending university, students must complete a seven-year secondary program and pass two national tests called *Baccalaureat* 1 and 2. Until the last few decades, the Haitian school program was inspired by the French educational system. Books and education materials were imported from France. This has gradually changed toward the development of Haitian-Creole materials more adapted to the country's reality. American influence is also becoming strong. Parents who can afford to send their children to schools that have adopted American curricula into their program.

School hours are usually from 8:00 A.M. to 4:00 P.M. with a break from 11:30 to 12:30. Advanced classes like the *Baccalaureat* 1 and 2 may have classes as early as 7:00 A.M. or as late as 7:00 P.M. In traditional Haitian schools, classes are taught in French, but Haiti is bilingual: All Haitians speak Creole or Haitian Creole, and about 30 percent or so also speak French.

The school year starts around the beginning of October and ends in June. It is divided into three trimesters, ending around Christmas, Easter, and summer, respectively.

In addition to state education programs, there are many private schools and a few universities in the most important cities: Port-au-Prince, the capital, Cap Haitien in the north, and Les Cayes in the south. These institutions cover programs from kindergarten to university. In recent decades there have been a growing number of private universities covering several specialties, especially computer-based and business administration ones. They offer an alternative to the limited state institutions. However, there is still a lack of schools in small towns and in the countryside.

Education is the passport to success for teens in Haiti. Even teens from the middle or upper-middle class feel the consequences when they don't pursue a university degree. Thanks to education and determination, the history of Haiti is rich with examples of very smart children from the countryside who have succeeded not only in the capital but abroad. It is a fact that Haitian parents push their children through the educational system, even when they cannot afford the cost and even if they are illiterate themselves.

SOCIAL LIFE

Older teen boys spend time in long courtships with girls the same age. A long time ago, it was the tradition that a girl should not give in too quickly to the interests of a boy even if she were dying to go out with him. Courtship was long and sensual. Even today, most Haitians do not date the way Americans date. Usually, when a boy starts showing a privileged kindness toward a girl, he either wants to test his ability to get her attention or he is really attracted to her. It is a long journey for a teen boy to get to a point where he can express his love to a girl. Most proper boys wouldn't just stand and declare their love just like that to a family girl. There is a lot to be read between the lines before two teens even speak to each other, much less kiss.

The boy may try to just be nice at first. He may even voluntarily show more kindness toward the girl he is particularly interested in. The girl may start by ignoring him. Then she may give him a questioning look. Weeks, or perhaps months later, she may smile back at him. Or she may just accept a poem from him. And this may go on and on until they touch each other's hands for the first time. The Haitian middle class has been very strict about teens being sexually involved before marriage. Parents believe they have failed if they have not been able to prevent this from happening. Unfortunately, sexual education is also taboo. In the matter of active sexuality among teens, urban areas are much more conservative than rural ones.

Girls from the countryside may become mothers at very young ages, and rural lifestyles and traditions allow it. There is little planning and no long-term goals among rural girls, compared to their urban counterparts, who may wait until they graduate or accumulate enough resources to marry and move with their spouses into a house or apartment, to buy a car, or to travel. Life in the countryside is simple: Boys and girls meet, like each other, and become common-law partners. Marriage is too expensive. If a young man asks for the hand of a girl in a formal way, both parents pitch in to help the young couple build a small house. If lucky, they may also get a piece of land and a few cattle from relatives. As soon as they move in together, they will probably start a family.

But, many times, girls start living with their common-law partners because they are already pregnant. While their partners will have to travel from one farm to another to make a living for the new family, new mothers will be alone most days and will raise their babies by themselves. New fathers usually care very much for their children. If a relationship doesn't last, children remain with their mothers, while fathers visit occasionally and send money and goods when they can. The father is considered the main provider and the authority figure. Later on, the girl may meet another man and sustain a long-term relationship. This type of common-law union is called *plasé*.

RECREATION AND ENTERTAINMENT

Life after school is relaxing for most youths in urban areas. They watch television, talk on the telephone, or play soccer or volleyball. Teens go for walks with friends some afternoons. Many friends visit and do their homework together. Tradition states that girls are to be at home before dusk but boys may stay out later and parents worry about them less. There is, however, a progressive change toward more freedom and autonomy for youths of both genders. Access to U.S. television programs, the Internet, and globalization have brought new values, models, and alternatives to youths who want to live as if they are in America. Dress codes, hairstyles, music preferences, and role models are imported from North America and Europe and conservative parents are seeing dramatic changes before their eyes, as compared to ones in their own time.

During summertime, middle-class, urban teens often want to visit the United States or Canada. Many already have parents, uncles, aunts, grandparents, or cousins established in those places. With a round-trip ticket, they are ready to spend the summer with relatives, blending North American influences into their Haitian reality. After three to four consecutive summers in North America, they speak English and understand perfectly most American television and radio programs. These teens are challenging Haitian traditions and are setting new horizons for their generation. Although a minority compared to their rural counterparts, they are ambassadors of American style in Haiti and they are becoming role models for the majority. Jennifer Lopez, Ja Rule, and Dr. Dre, all well-known singers in America, frequently receive the attention previously given by teens to local or Latin American singers.

But most urban teens stay home during summer. Some may take summer classes or extracurricular activities such as dance, computers, painting, or music. Others might be sent to relatives in the countryside for nature experiences such as frolicking in rivers, on beaches, and in forests. Sometimes, they are sent to their parents' birth towns. It is not uncommon for people to keep the family house in their birth town while they move to a nearby, larger city with more commodities and better schools for their children. However, many remain close to their birth towns, since they bear memories that they want to share with their children, or maybe the grandparents still live there.

RELIGIOUS PRACTICES AND CULTURAL CEREMONIES

Haitians are collectively religious. Although Catholicism is the national religion, a large proportion of the population is Protestant. Most recently, the Jehovah's Witness, Mormon, and other religions have been openly promoted, creating an interesting diversity. Many Haitians are also voodoo practitioners. Voodoo is a pagan religion, born from the mixing of African religions and Catholicism. Under slavery, newly deported Africans brought with them religious traditions from their different countries and cultures. Those traditions became intertwined with Catholicism because many slaveholders wanted their slaves to convert to that religion.

In their new status as slaves, they forged a common ground in mixing their different beliefs and traditions.

Eventually, these beliefs helped them to consolidate their strength and even aided in the sparking of the 1789 revolution that would lead to the abolition of slavery some years later. In that sense, voodoo had a positive impact on the collective Haitian destiny. After independence, there was a trend toward the belief that voodoo practitioners were noneducated people. Voodoo was put down and was rejected especially by defenders or adepts of Catholicism and Protestantism. Those actions never really crushed voodoo and now, more than ever, people and some scholars are affirming their affiliation with, interest in, or validation of voodoo. Today no one knows how many Haitians are voodoo practitioners or believers.

Of course not all Haitians are believers or practitioners. Some perceive it only as part of folklore. Many traditions in Haiti are linked to religion. They include Christmas, Corpus Christi, Easter, All Saints' Day, Day of the Dead, and each town's dedicated saint's day. However, carnival and New Year's Eve are also important opportunities for celebration. New Year's traditions are very special. People visit each other to wish them the best in health, happiness, and prosperity. Adults share their wishes only, but teens' and children's visits call for gifts. The most common gift is money. Teens never have more money than on New Year's Day. Neighbors, uncles and aunts, grandparents, and family friends all give a little something in change. By the end of the day, the change amounts to way more money than teens or children usually have in their hands.

Youth hymns are patriotic songs that promote the joys of being young, healthy, and hardworking or of being the future of the country. Many schools encourage the learning of these songs because their messages stay in the minds of teens and contribute to the development of civic-mindedness and a love for the land. Many schools teach their own youth hymns, sung during parades on Flag Day or Labor Day, for example.

CONCLUSION

The future of Haitian teens is as challenging as the future of other teens in the world. A Haitian teen who focuses with discipline on learning will do fine in Haiti or abroad. Libraries and the Internet have opened doors to teens in the major cities of Haiti as anywhere. The frontiers of the island no longer separate Haitian teens from the rest of the world. However, a large majority of Haitian teens in rural areas have yet to gain access to basic knowledge, let alone to higher technology.

Haitian teens, despite that country's status as a poor, developing nation, face the same problems as teens all over the world. Studious teens represent the majority and they still believe that education is the key to better lives for them and their families. The political and socioeconomic context of Haiti doesn't easily allow a second chance and those who drop out of school and miss learning opportunities will most likely regret it forever. That is motivation to seize the present with a sense of responsibility. That sense of responsibility is one, if not the most, important ingredient in the future success of Haitian teens. They may not know it today, but soon they will face it: They are the most important assets of Haiti.

NOTES

1. Interview by author, Port-au-Prince, April 1995.
2. Interview by author, Port-au-Prince, 1999.
3. Traditionally, the word *combite* refers to an organized workload in a rural area and during harvest time, called for by one or many farmers to do farming work on a specific property. *Combite* participants volunteer their time, working for free until the work is done. Every participant will have an opportunity to benefit from that collective work. Some *combite* are so well organized that they include one or more people to cook for the laborers and one or more people to sing to encourage the laborers. Big *combite* can be well structured, with lines of authority well defined. Participants have a title, an assignment, and someone to report to. The beneficiary of the *combite* provides meal and entertainment.

RESOURCE GUIDE

Anglade, Georges. *L'Espace Haitien*. Les Presses de l'Universite du Quebec, Montreal, 1974.

Bastien, Remy. "Haitian Rural Family Organization." *Social and Economic Studies* 10, 4 (1961): 478–510.

———. *Le Paysan Haitien et sa Famille: Valle de Marbial*. Paris: Karthala, 1951

Cauna, Jacques. "Au Temps des Iles a Sucre, Histoire d'Une Plantation de St Domingue au XVIII ième Siècle, Paris, Ed. Karthala, 1987, 288p. Condensé de la thèse de doctorat de III ème Cycle: *Une Habitation de St Domingue à la Fin du XVIII ième Siècle: La Sucrerie Fleuriau de Bellevue*. Université de Poitiers, 1983, 765p., 2 vols.

Cyprien, Jean M. *History of Haiti*. Edited by Shannon K. Bolding, West Palm Beach, Florida 1999.

Farmer, Paul. *The Uses of Haiti*. Monroe, Maine: Common Courage Press, 1994.

Freres de l'Instruction Chretienne (FIC). *Histoire d'Haiti*. Port-au-Prince. Editions Henri Deschamps, 1942.

Grunwald, J., L. Delatour, and K. Voltaire. "Offshore Assembly in Haiti." In *Haiti—Today and Tomorrow: An Interdisciplinary Study*, edited by C. Foster and A Valdman, 231–52. Lanham, Md.: University Press of America, 1984.

Gutierrez, Gustavo. *The Power of the Poor in History*. Translated by Robert Barr. Maryknoll, N.Y.: Orbis, 1983.

Hurbon, Laennec. *Comprendre Haiti: Essai sur L'Etat, la Nation, la Culture*. Paris: Editions Karthala, 1987

Lawless, Robert. *Haiti's Bad Press*. Rochester, Vt.: Schenkman Books. 1992.

Moreau de St Mery, Mederic Louis Elie. *Description Topographique, Physique, Civile, Politique et Historique de la Partie Francaise de l'Isle de St Domingue*. Edited by B. Maurel and E. Taillemite. New ed. 3 vols. Paris: Societe de l'Histoire des Colonies Francaises and Librairie Larose, 1984.

Secretairerie d'Etat du Tourisme d'Haiti. *Haiti*. Paris: Guides Gallimard, 2000.

Shahin, Jim. "Island of Hope." *American Way* 24, 19 (1991): 54–61, 92–102.

Nonfiction

Dash, J. Michael. *Culture and Customs of Haiti*. Westport, Conn.: Greenwood Press, 2000.

Myers, Walter Dean. *Toussaint L'Ouverture: The Fight for Haiti's Freedom*. New York: Simon and Schuster, 1996.

Weddler, Ken. *Haiti in Pictures*. Lerner Publications Co., Minneapolis, 1995.

Fiction

Danticat, Edwidge, ed. *The Butterfly's Way: Voices of the Haitian Diaspora*. New York: Soho Press, 2000

Green, Graham. *The Comedians*. New York: Penguin, 1991.

Temple, Frances. *Taste of Salt: A Story of Modern Haiti*. New York: Orchard Books, 1992.

Web Sites

http://www.educavision.com/
Educavision/Haitian education/culture

http://www.gohaiti.com
Radio Haiti Amerique

http://www.port-haiti.com
Port Haiti: Haitian culture/travel/links

http://dir.yahoo.com/regional/countries/Haiti/
Yahoo: Haiti overview and links

Chapter 11

JAMAICA

Barbara Bailey and Michelle Davis

INTRODUCTION

Jamaica, located 600 miles south of Florida, is the largest English-speaking island in the Caribbean. It is 146 miles long and between 22 and 25 miles wide. Jamaica's landscape varies from world-famous, white sand beaches to coastal wetlands, rolling plains, and extremely mountainous terrain. The island has a maritime tropical climate, with average daily temperatures varying from a low of 63 degrees in the mountains to a high of 86 degrees at sea level. The months from July to September are the warmest, while May and October are traditionally rainy. The island is also subject to hurricanes and the months from June to October are considered to be hurricane season. Jamaica has two cities: Kingston, its capital, and Montego Bay, a well-known tourist resort area. Ocho Rios however, is the tourist capital of the island. Most hotels are located there and it is a major port for cruise ships.

Jamaica, largely due to its history of slavery, has a population in which the vast majority is of African descent or of mixed race. Other groups include East Indians, Chinese, Europeans, Lebanese, and Jews: hence the national motto, "Out of Many, One People." The current population of Jamaica stands at approximately 2,621,100 and in 2001 there was a gender ratio of 99.8 males per 100 females.[1] Population growth has been modified by emigration, primarily to North America and the United Kingdom.

Jamaica gained independence from Great Britain in 1962 but continues to be a member of the British Commonwealth of Nations. The head of state is the governor-general, who is the queen of England's representative. The government of Jamaica is a democracy based on the Westminster parliamentary model used in Britain with two major political parties: the ruling People's National Party (PNP) and the opposition party, the Jamaica Labor Party (JLP).

The official language of Jamaica is English, but patois (pronounced patwa), the language of the people, is more widely used and varies from one part of the island to another and even from village to village. Patois is used in many of the island's cultural productions involving speech, music, and drama. Jamaica's culture is rich and vibrant in the areas of dance, music, and drama and Jamaicans are known to excel in these art forms, in which traces of the African and British heritage of the island can be easily identified. Jamaicans are particularly well known in the pop world, especially in reggae music, which is indigenous to Jamaica. The late Bob Marley, a Rastafarian, was the most famous reggae singer Jamaica has ever produced. His single, "One Love," was voted song of the (twentieth) century and his album, *Exodus*, album of the century.

Jamaica is an extremely religious country and is said to have more churches per square mile than anywhere else in the world. The predominant religion is Christianity. Major denominations introduced during colonization by Britain include Anglicans (Episcopal), Baptists, Methodists, and the United Church, formed by the merger of the Presbyterian and Congregational groups. The Roman Catholic Church also has a strong presence and dates back to the time of the Spanish occupation. Traditionally, Christian festivals such as Easter and Christmas are times when families come together and, as in many other countries, these events have become highly commercialized.

There are also religious groups with a strong African tradition and influence. The Revival or Pukumina church is more than 200 years old. The Rastafarian religion is the most recent of the African derived groups and emerged in 1930 with the coronation of Ras Tafari, the crown prince of Ethiopia, as emperor of that country. Rastafarians believe in a supreme creator god, Jah, who is black. There are elders but no priests. The sacramental use of the weed of wisdom—marijuana or ganja—and the hairstyle—dreadlocks—are not articles of faith because ganja is not universally used and dreadlocks did not become common until the 1960s.

Hindu and Muslim religions were introduced when Indians arrived as indentured laborers in the late nineteenth century. There is also a small Jewish congregation that meets in the only synagogue located in the capital city of Kingston.

Historically, the Jamaican economy has had an agricultural base, dependent on a few staple export crops, primarily sugar and bananas. After

1952, the economy diversified with the introduction of bauxite mining that is now, after agricultural exports, the second highest foreign exchange earner. Since the 1990s, however, tourism has become the major earner of foreign exchange.

Unemployment and crime are Jamaica's two greatest problems today. Statistics indicate that for 2001 the average unemployment rate was 15.0 percent with the rate for females (21.0 percent) being twice that for males (10.3 percent). Unemployment rates for male and female youths (under 25 years of age) were 24.6 percent and 44.2 percent respectively and were higher than those of their adult counterparts.[2]

Jamaica has established and maintained a remarkable sporting record over the past half century. Since 1948, athletes have won many medals at the Olympic Games. Jamaican track-and-field athletes are acknowledged to be among the best in the world and Jamaica has even entered a team in the bobsledding competition in the Winter Olympic Games. Its best performance was at the 1994 Games at Lillehammer, when the team finished 14th in the four-man event. This was phenomenal considering that Jamaica is a tropical island that has never seen snow. This accomplishment brought further fame to the island through the 1998 film produced by Disney entitled *Cool Runnings*.

Jamaica's national football team, the Reggae Boys, also made history by becoming the first team from an English-speaking Caribbean nation to qualify to play in the prestigious World Cup. They won one match in that meet.

TYPICAL DAY

A typical day for teens varies considerably depending on their socioeconomic situation, the type of school they attend, and the groups to which they belong. In the 12 to 14 age group, 97.2 percent of males and 93.1 percent of females are enrolled in an educational institution. By ages 15 to 16 the percentages drop, and by ages 17 to 19 only 2.4 percent of males and 3.9 percent of females in the population age cohort are involved in formal schooling.[3] Those attending schools that start at 7:00 or 7:30 A.M. have breakfast between 6:00 and 6:30 A.M., while those who attend schools that start at noon don't have to get up or have breakfast as early. Schools with very large student populations have two shifts, or sessions: the first from 7:00 A.M. to noon, and the second from noon to 5:00 P.M.

Mealtimes are dependent on the proximity of home to school as well as on whether students use public transportation or are driven by parents. In a minority of cases, some college and university students and a few students in grades 12 and 13 drive themselves to school. Students below this level are not usually allowed to drive cars to school. The minimum age for holding a driver's license in Jamaica is 17 years.

Breakfast varies depending on socioeconomic status and whether the teenager lives in an urban or rural location. Those from poorer families may eat a bowl of porridge and a slice of popular Jamaican bread called hard dough along with a hot beverage. Those from more affluent homes tend to eat cold cereal with sweetened condensed milk and perhaps a glass of orange juice. Teens from rural areas tend to have a heavier breakfast, consisting of agricultural products such as boiled yams (root tubers) or green bananas, along with salted codfish or pickled mackerel, or vegetables such as cabbage or callaloo (a green leafy vegetable similar to spinach), which are seasoned and steamed.

Regardless of whether a school is public or private, school begins with a period of worship, generally conducted in keeping with the Christian religion. Non-Christians and others who do not wish to participate are excused with a written request from their parents.

Prior to leaving their classrooms to go on their lunch break, students in many high schools pray before eating. For those on the early school shift, lunchtime can be as early as 10:00 A.M., while for those on the second shift in a double-shift school, lunch may be as late at 2:30 P.M. Most schools are equipped with canteens that provide cooked meals or tuck shops, which provide snacks, so in high school very few teens carry packed lunches. Lunch often consists of a beef or chicken patty (a baked pastry shell filled with cooked meat), a sweet bun or other pastry, and a soda or a fruit drink. Few students eat a hot lunch, but for those who do, a favorite is fried chicken and rice with vegetables.

In many schools, students say an evening prayer. Some stay late for sports or extracurricular activities such as Key Club, Girl Guides, and Scouts and other interest-based clubs. Many teens, especially those preparing for school exit examinations in grades 11 and 13, are tutored after school and on weekends to prepare for these examinations in which success or failure is a strong determinant of future pursuits.

On returning home, many teens relax by watching television for an hour or two or by talking to friends on the telephone. Almost every home in Jamaica has at least one television set, and cable access is readily available in city areas and is also spreading to rural ones. Most homes in urban Jamaica have telephones and before doing homework both girls and boys spend a lot of time talking to friends. In rural areas, telephone usage is less, as there are not as many landline phones. Cellular phones, however, are very popular and many teens from all economic groups own these. With middle- and upper-class teens, computer games are also a popular activity during free time.

Following this period of relaxation, teens are expected to do whatever chores have been assigned to them. Boys tend to have fewer chores to do during the week after school, except perhaps to put out the garbage, and they have more free time to hang out with friends than do girls. Girls are likely to do household chores such as tidying the house, washing dishes, and, in some instances, starting dinner. In some households boys may wash dishes after dinner. In middle-class homes teens rarely have chores since many of those families employ a domestic helper.

Dinner usually consists of a meat dish eaten with rice and peas, or plain white rice, boiled dumplings made from a mixture of flour and cornmeal, and/or yams and vegetables. After dinner, homework is completed before bedtime. In Jamaica, the amount of homework given in high school may vary among schools, but all teenagers complain that they are given too much homework.

FAMILY LIFE

In Jamaica, legal marriage is very much a middle-class institution, endorsed and encouraged by the church, and is viewed as the ideal marital form. In 2000 there were 23,704 registered marriages, or a mean of 9.1 people per 1,000 in the population who are married.[4] In addition to the nuclear family structure with married parents and two or three children, two other family forms are prevalent in Jamaica and the wider Caribbean. These are visiting relationships, known as friending, and common law, or consensual unions.

Visiting unions most typically occur among the lower class, and one partner, most often the male, visits the other for companionship and sexual relations. This may take place in the family home, with parental consent, and the male is expected to contribute to the female's support and to that of any children that may result from the union. Although fidelity is expected of women in these unions, in many cases the man may have several visiting unions or may even be married. These unions often result in female-headed households with a number of children fathered by different men. In fact, a common family form in Jamaica is the female-headed household where women are the sole economic providers. In 2001, women headed 44.7 percent of all households.[5]

Common law unions, on the other hand, are more permanent residential, nonlegal but stable unions in which two individuals live together and pool their resources to support the family unit. Studies on the Caribbean family show a progression from one type of union to another, for example, from visiting union to common law to marriage, where the type of union depends on a number of factors including race, ethnicity, class, and age. Legal marriage is desirable by the poor and working classes but depends on a male's ability to provide suitable housing and the large, grandiose wedding that indicates one's move up the social ladder.

Many Jamaican homes, particularly in rural areas, have maintained an extended family structure. It is not uncommon to find a household that, in addition to parent(s) and children, may also consist of a grandmother or grandfather, aunt or uncle, cousin, and even unofficially adopted children who are not blood relatives. According to the Jamaica Reproductive Health Survey report of 1997, the average number of children per woman (total fertility rate) in Jamaica was 2.8.[6]

In general, most Jamaican teens live at home with their families. They do not usually leave home until their mid-twenties and because of the economic situation many remain for much longer. The high rents charged for housing, particularly in cities and tourist areas, is the chief factor that prevents teens from leaving home to live on their own. The only teens who typically live away from home are those who attend boarding schools. In rural areas, some single-sex high schools provide boarding facilities. All government-operated colleges and the three universities in Jamaica also have boarding facilities. In these cases, however, priority is given to foreign students and to local students who live far from the particular institution.

Another effect of the economic situation is that many mothers and sometimes fathers emigrate to the United States, and to a lesser extent to Canada or England, in an effort to improve the lot of their families. Their intention is usually to sponsor their children to join them within a short time but often years pass before this dream is realized and for some it never materializes. Children are therefore often left in Jamaica under the care of a grandmother or other close relative. Out of this situation has come the phenomenon of barrel children, so called because their overseas parents send them designer clothes and shoes and other items shipped in barrels. This is one way in which Jamaican teenagers are exposed to American fashions and acquire a desire for them rather than for goods produced locally.

The advent and introduction of cable television into many Jamaican homes has also facilitated teenagers' familiarization with American culture and ways of life. Jamaican teens love American music and fashions, and many of them dream of living in the United States one day. Jamaicans who can afford to do so send their children to American colleges and universities and thus contribute to the Americanization of Jamaican youths.

Although it is generally accepted that the emigration of Jamaican parents improves the economic situation of children and of the country as a whole through remittances, this comes at high personal cost. In many instances, because of a lack of parental control and guidance, the children—who are teenagers before they can join their parents abroad—often become delinquent. In some cases they actually drop out of school and may join gangs and/or become hooked on hard drugs, such as crack cocaine. Police reports indicate that most crimes committed in Jamaica today involve youths in their teens and early twenties.[7]

Unintentional pregnancies are of major concern to girls, a number of whom become mothers while still in their teens. Data from the 2000 and 2001 *Economic and Social Survey Jamaica* support this concern. Females aged 10 to 19 made 25 percent of all visits to antenatal clinics, an indication of the high incidence of pregnancies among teens.

One result of teenage pregnancy is the interruption or termination of education. Several programs are offered to minimize the impact of teenage pregnancy. They provide services for pregnant teenagers, teenage mothers and fathers, parents of teenage mothers, and young men at risk. These include opportunities for continuing education, counseling, skills training, provision of day care facilities, and an afternoon program for 9–18 year olds who have either dropped out or are at risk of dropping out of school.

Data also show that adolescents between 10 and 19 have the highest rate of sexually transmitted infections (STIs) and that at least one in every four sexually active adolescent in Jamaica has contracted an STI. There is also evidence that the mean age for the initiation of sexual activity for females is 15.9 and 13.9 years for males.[8] Surveys show that adolescent females have a up to three times higher risk of HIV infection than their male counterparts and that in the 10–24 age group there were therefore more females than males living with AIDS. Between 1982 and 2000, there were 84 reported cases of adolescents with AIDS and the 20–30 age group showed the highest number of reported cases.[9] Given that HIV has an incubation period of 10 or more years, it means that persons in the latter group would have been infected when they were adolescents.

Teenage pregnancies and growing rates of STIs and HIV/AIDS among adolescents have serious repercussions not only for the teenagers but also their families, which have the additional financial burden of caring for them. These problems point to the fact that adolescents are at risk and need to be targeted for health education programs through both formal and informal channels.

Youth.Now, a nongovernmental organization, has partnered with the Ministry of Health to address issues of adolescent reproductive and sexual health. Youth-friendly health clinics have been created and partnerships with the Bethel Baptist Church and the YMCA, both in Kingston, have been formed. Issues of confidentiality and privacy arise in addition to the stigma, ridicule, and condemnation that teens, particularly girls, face when trying to get access to condoms and other contraceptives at clinics.

Two growing concerns are the prevalence of child labor and the involvement in child prostitution of those ranging from 10 to 18. A 2001 study showed that most children involved in prostitution and related activities were girls and that the most common activities teenagers engaged in were

1. Boys living and working on the streets and having sex in exchange for the means of basic survival;
2. Girls who engaged in formal prostitution and solicited clients on the streets;
3. Girls who were employed as exotic go-go dancers;
4. Girls who were employed as masseuses in massage parlors and;
5. Girls and boys fulfilling arranged sexual encounters for economic exchange.

Factors identified as accounting for this situation included, among others, poverty, poor parenting, poor family values, peer pressure, limited education, and inadequate monitoring of laws.[10]

In many Jamaican families the typical nurturer/provider division between females and males is still fairly intact. It has been noted that

In Jamaica and the rest of the Caribbean, males and females are socialized to identify domestic work as female and work outside the domestic sphere, but supportive of it, as male. Cooking, laundry, childcare, housework and the like are seen as responsibilities of females, while chores related to household economy, such as animal husbandry, artisan skills, farming, wage labor and other outdoor forms of income-earning are the responsibilities of males. The fact that many boys are required to perform some 'female' tasks, as happens in a family of all or mostly boys, or that many girls are required to undertake 'male' tasks in a family of all girls, is of little consequence as far as the behavioral norms are concerned.[11]

In addition to being the nurturer in the family, most women work outside of the home in jobs that are really extensions of their nurturing roles, such as nursing, teaching, secretarial work, and child care. Traditionally male jobs include construction, engineering, architecture, medicine, and law. Although in recent years girls leaving high school have been entering these traditionally male occupations, the reverse is not generally the case. Few males, for example, enter teaching and even fewer go into nursing.

Because of the economic situation, teenagers, especially those from lower socioeconomic families, help supplement the family income or earn transportation and lunch money for school. Some help their parents in the markets on Fridays and Saturdays, resulting in poor Friday attendance in many rural schools. It is not uncommon to see teenage girls offering seasonal fruits, packaged in transparent plastic bags, for sale to passing motorists and pedestrians. Boys are more often seen at traffic intersections, washing windshields while others sell small household articles or car accessories. These activities occur mainly in the uptown business areas of Kingston and St. Andrew.

Due to varying activities and schedules in the average household from Monday to Saturday, in many families Sunday is the designated family day and is usually the only day that most families manage to spend time together and share a meal. A major activity for many is attending morning worship and some go back for an evening service. In many cases, however, men are not involved and boys often drop out of church in their later teen years.

Going to the beach is a favorite weekend pastime for many Jamaicans from all walks of life and teens will often go with friends rather than their family. Long, holiday weekends are times when families who can afford it go to hotels on the north coast. In general, Sunday afternoons for many families are times for visiting friends or relatives or just relaxing at home. In recent years, many sporting and entertainment activities have taken place on Sundays and some family members may attend these.

In rural areas, family activities tend to be more community related: football or cricket matches between neighboring districts; village fairs or concerts; and school or church fundraising activities. During holiday periods, it is popular for lower income groups in both urban and rural areas to charter buses and go far distances on outings, to spend the day at well-known beaches or other places of interest.

Family life in Jamaica has undergone many changes since the 1980s and is challenged by several factors including a fluctuating economic base, violence, an inadequate education system, and poor or absent role models.

Urbanization and Americanization have also influenced family relations. In some affluent homes children are overindulged and may not receive the attention and time of their parents but get money to spend on clothes, shoes, food, and sometimes drugs.

TRADITIONAL AND NONTRADITIONAL FOOD DISHES

There are several traditional foods associated with particular meals, days of the week, or seasons of the year. The traditional Saturday meal in most Jamaican homes is soup, made from either beef or chickens' feet blended with pumpkin, carrots and other vegetables, dumplings made from flour mixed with cornmeal, yellow yams, and other ground provisions. Teens who do not care for soup opt for beef patties, pizza, fried chicken, hamburgers, or other foods provided by fast food restaurants.

Sunday morning breakfast among Jamaican families includes a local fruit called ackee that, when prepared, resembles scrambled eggs and saltfish (salted cod). Together they make up Jamaica's national dish (ackee and saltfish). Still others prefer to have cow or goat liver and onions or a steamed green leafy vegetable (callalo) with saltfish. Each of these dishes is usually served with other fares such as roasted breadfruit, fried flour dumplings, boiled green bananas, and fried ripe plantains. Breakfast also typically includes a hot beverage such as coffee, tea, chocolate, or a local herbal tea.

A traditional Sunday dinner varies according to socioeconomic status. Most Jamaican families eat chicken cooked in one form or another or roast beef. Popular methods for cooking chicken are barbecuing, baking, roasting, currying, stewing, and French-frying. Whatever the choice, Sunday dinner for the average Jamaican family is eaten at about 4:00 P.M. and usually consists of a meat dish, rice and peas (kidney beans cooked together with white rice in coconut milk) or plain white rice, potato salad, and a tossed vegetable salad. A punch made from a variety of local fruits and/or vegetables is also a part of Sunday dinner. Dessert is eaten in some households and is usually banana or carrot cake or potato, cornmeal, or bread pudding.

Other weekday dinner favorites are steamed or brown stewed fish, stewed pork, baked or barbecued pork chops, curried goat, oxtail stewed with broad (lima) beans, and stewed red peas (kidney beans) cooked with pig's tail or salted beef. Rastafarians, some vegetarians, and some religious groups on the island do not eat meat of any kind, while some do eat fish.

An all-time Jamaican favorite is the Jamaican patty, consisting of a crust in which is enclosed a filling made from minced beef, chicken, shrimp, lobster, or vegetables. By far the most popular is the beef patty. The patty was the first type of fast food available to Jamaicans long before the advent of hamburger chains such as Burger King, McDonald's, and Wendy's. It is affordable as well as filling and is school lunch for many students.

Jerk cooking originated in Jamaica and refers to a particular method of cooking where the meat is sliced and soaked in a marinade of pepper, vinegar, scallion, pimiento, and other spices. The meat is then smoked over charcoal on a grill covered with strips of wood from the pimiento tree. Jerk goes back to Jamaica's slave history when a means had to be found for preparing food so that it would last the number of days that it would take to move from one village to another. Chicken, pork, fish, and lobster are prepared in this way and jerk is a favorite with both locals and tourists.

Chinese and Indian people who came to Jamaica in the post-emancipation period have influenced Jamaican culture and traditions and their foods are quite popular in Jamaica. Roti, an Indian bread made from flour baked on hot flat stones, is popularly eaten with curried mutton or chicken and is a popular Indian meal. Most Indian meals tend to be cooked with a special curry powder made from spices not normally found in Jamaican households. The most common Indian dish is curry goat and mannish water, a soup so named because it is made from boiling the head and entrails of a goat and is believed to increase sexual prowess in those who drink it. Chinese cooking is also popular among Jamaicans and can be found across the island.

At Easter and Christmas, Jamaican families eat special foods. At Easter, a family favorite is "bun and cheese." Heavily spiced and fruited buns, some homemade, are eaten with a popular brand of cheese throughout the season, beginning on the Thursday before Easter and continuing through to Easter Monday. It is also customary for many families to eat only fish on Good Friday.

If at no other time of the year, Jamaican families eat a lot of food at Christmas time. For many, Christmas dinner will consist of all the different types of meat eaten by the family. It is therefore not uncommon for the meal to include turkey, ham, roast pork or beef, fish, and oxtail, all served at the same time. The remainder of the meal consists of rice and peas, made with green *gungo* (pigeon) peas, sweet or Irish potato salad, a fresh garden salad, and/or coleslaw. At the end of the holiday season, a special *gungo* pea soup is made with leftover ham and turkey/chicken bones, along with the usual vegetables and produce, particularly yellow yams. Christmas dinner is usually shared not only by the immediate family, but also with other relatives, particularly elderly ones.

Dessert is Christmas pudding, a heavily fruited cake made with rum and wine and baked to the consistency of a pudding. It is eaten with practically every meal throughout the Christmas season. Some families send these puddings abroad to their relatives during this season. The Christmas drink for all Jamaicans is sorrel, called sorrel wine by some. It is made from the red flowers of the plant, which bloom at Christmas time. The juice extracted from the petals is blended with ginger and sweetened with sugar. The various variations to the ingredients that go into sorrel are closely held family secrets.

SCHOOLING

The Ministry of Education, Youth, and Culture has overall responsibility for policy that directs education. Tuition in government schools is heavily subsidized at the primary and secondary levels. At the latter, there are single-sex as well as coeducational schools and there are special schools for hearing, visually, and/or mentally challenged students. Students in all secondary public schools wear uniforms. There are 597 schools across the island catering to almost a quarter of a million students. Of that number, 49.2 percent are male.[12]

Jamaican students at a private school. © *The Gleaner Company Limited*. Used with permission.

There are different types of high schools in Jamaica and the placement of students in those schools depends to a great extent on how they perform in selection examinations. The Grade Six Achievement Test is taken at 11+ years, the point of exit from the primary level, and students who earn the highest scores are placed in traditional and newly established high schools. Those who scored next highest are assigned to comprehensive high schools, while those placed in junior high schools or the upper grades of all-age schools have typically attained low scores and often require remediation. Junior high schools and all-age schools end at grade 9, at which time a few students are given a second chance to obtain entry to the other types of high schools. There is also a selection examination for entry to technical high schools taken by students in grades 7 and 8 at all-age and junior high schools.

At traditional and comprehensive high schools, students are prepared to sit for either a regional examination, set by the Caribbean Examinations Council (CXC) or the General Certificate in Education (GCE) O (Ordinary) Levels, a British exam. The CXC exam taken at this stage is set at two levels: basic and general, with general being the higher of the two levels. Success in a combination of approximately five CXC (general) and/or GCE O level subjects permits students to go on to the sixth form in high school or to a community college, if they so desire. Those who go on to sixth form (grades 12 and 13), take the GCE A (Advanced) Levels, administered by Cambridge University, which is gradually being replaced by the Certificate Advanced Proficiency Examinations administered by the CXC. Many students who leave high school on completion of grade 11, particularly those who were not successful in their exams, pursue skills training. The HEART Trust/National Training Agency offers a range of programs that are government funded and are sought after by a number of students who leave school because training is free and students are given a small allowance during the period of training. Areas of study include accounting, computer studies, cosmetology, hotel/hospitality training, plumbing, masonry, and maritime studies, to name a few. Many HEART academies are residential and, for the most part, the choosing of programs by males and females is very much in keeping with typical sex-linked patterns. Males are predominately clustered in areas such as automotive trade skills, construction, and hospitality skills and females in apparel and sewn product skills, beauty care, and services and commercial skills.

There are also private schools that offer academic courses that allow school dropouts to repeat subjects that they failed in high school or in business and computer studies. These schools tend to be expensive and so are attended mainly by students from the middle and upper socioeconomic classes. As a result of increasing opportunities to work in fields related to the new information technologies, computer studies is a popular choice among both female and male teens.

Success in the A Levels qualifies students to enter the most highly recognized university on the island, the University of the West Indies, a regional institution with campuses also in Barbados and Trinidad and Tobago. Other tertiary level institutions offer a variety of programs, the majority of which do not require A-Level qualification for entry. Only about 3 percent of teenagers in the 17–19 year cohort have an opportunity to attend a tertiary-level institution. These include two universities, one college of visual and performing arts, one agricultural college, one college of physical education and sports, six teacher-training colleges, and five community colleges. Others take the Scholastic Aptitude Test (SAT) and, if successful, pursue studies in the United States.

High schools across Jamaica provide a number of extracurricular activities for teens. There are organized groups such as Boy Scouts, Girls' Guides, Boys Brigade and Cadets, to name a few. Teens, mostly those from rural areas, also participate in 4-H Clubs, which provide leadership training and agricultural skills.

Sporting activities are popular among teenagers at school and some school sports are very competitive. Both males and females participate in athletics and there are annual, national boys and girls championship competitions among schools.

Other national high school events include an annual debate competition and a highly contested event is the Schools' Challenge Quiz, a knockout competition held on national television each year. Teenagers, mainly from grades 12 and 13 take part in the quiz, which tests academic ability in various subject areas. Both competitions yield valuable prizes to both the winning schools and team members. There is also a relatively new, national schools' competition related to the tourism industry, in which teens are tested on their knowledge of the industry.

High school students are given a voice in governing through representation on their school's student council. The council is made up of class representatives from each grade in the school. Teens as a whole also get a chance to express their views through various teen-focused magazines, local newspapers, and other media. Call-in radio and television shows are also popularly used by teens to express their feelings on various matters.

The majority of school dropouts have no option but to look for jobs. There is, however, a high level of unemployment in that age group, especially among females, and many continue to live at home, even for extended periods. In some cases, older teenagers may even attempt to start their own business venture. Many of those who find jobs eventually finance the continuance of their education at evening institutes.

Sometimes teenage boys, particularly from the lower socioeconomic class and mostly in urban areas or from inner-city communities, drop out of school and become involved in gangs and criminal activities. A majority of them leave home and become street children. They can be seen in shopping plazas, begging, or at stoplights, offering to wash car windshields in exchange for coins. Life for these teens has little structure; they eat when they have enough cash and sleep on pieces of cardboard in various nooks and crannies. This type of life leaves them open to physical and sexual abuse. Currently, there are programs designed to provide these teens with opportunities for continuing their education, counseling facilities, and a daily meal.

Some teenagers try to make money by engaging in less acceptable activities. In recent years, Jamaica has seen a significant increase in the relatively new phenomenon of drug mules, of which a vast majority is female. These drug traffickers are paid to transport cocaine, packaged in small sachets, in their body parts either by ingestion into the stomach, hidden in body cavities, or stashed in luggage. Mules usually take their merchandise to the U.K. and, to a lesser extent, to the United States, Bermuda, and other Caribbean islands. Some mules die when hidden sachets rupture before they can be removed or expelled from the body. Many are arrested when they disembark, as their inability to eat or drink during the flight attracts the attention of airline personnel, who are trained to look out for such passengers and to notify local police prior to landing.

The police report that drug dons target students for use as drug mules. Teenagers are known to disappear on the weekends, when they go on all-expense paid trips to Miami or other U.S. destinations. The teenagers involved in these weekend trips travel mainly to Florida, unknown to their parents, who are usually under the impression that they are spending the weekend studying with a school friend. Their employers pay for their accommodation in hotels in the States and they usually earn US$2,000 per trip. The teenagers usually do extensive shopping, buying the latest designer fashions, before returning home to Jamaica. In addition to cocaine, drug traffickers also traffic in marijuana.[13]

SOCIAL LIFE

At coeducational schools, teens tend to socialize with their peers within the school. In single-sex high schools, there are traditional, informal links among particular schools and girls and boys from those schools form friendships. Teenagers begin dating at about 15 and school proms associated with graduation at the end of high school provide opportunities for teens' first formal dates. Private dating does not often occur among younger teens, as they tend to form groups rather than hang out as couples. Teens, particularly those who use public transportation, meet after school at places such as bus depots and taxi stands, and shopping malls and plazas to a lesser extent. Church, athletic events, social clubs, and fetes also provide opportunities for teens to meet.

In spite of these generalized dating patterns among teens, data from a survey carried out in 1997 revealed that the average age of first sexual activity for females is 15.9 years and for males, 13.9 years. The data further showed that 38 percent of females and 64 percent of males from 15 to 17 are sexually active.[14] Significant numbers of adolescents (50 percent of girls and 33 percent of boys) report, however, that their first sexual encounter was forced.[15]

Early sexual activity among teens has contributed to teenage pregnancy and sexually transmitted infections. As in other countries with a strong religious influence, teens in Jamaica are discouraged from engaging in premarital sex and are encouraged to practice abstinence but this conflicts with messages conveyed by mass media and peer influence.

RECREATION

Jamaican teens take a lot of time out for recreation. Soccer is the most popular sport and is played primarily by males, while netball is popular among females. Basketball is another favorite sport among Jamaican teens. Tennis, too, is popular but training is costly so the sport is pursued primarily by teens from middle- and upper-class homes.

Track-and-field activities are highly developed and competitive among both female and male students in Jamaican high schools. At annual athletic championships for secondary schools, popularly called Champs, athletes from high schools across the country enter the various events and vie not only for individual awards but also for points for their school. After Champs there are various school celebrations that are held at popular teen spots immediately following an announcement of the year's top girls' and boys' teams.

Each year a number of Jamaican athletes receive athletic scholarships to attend colleges in the United States. Scholarships provide a chance for many students to pursue tertiary education and to compete in track meets in the United States and elsewhere, opportunities that they may not have been afforded otherwise.

Beyond involvement at school, some teens are also members of swim clubs and participate in national, regional, and international meets. In the capital city some students, through their schools, have access to the pool at the National Stadium for training so that even if their school does not have its own swimming pool, they can be prepared for high school swimming competitions. Unfortunately, teens in rural areas are not as privileged.

A popular pastime for those who can swim is to go to the beach to participate in various water sports. At some beaches, fried fish, festival (a fried dumpling made from cornmeal, flour, and a little sugar), and *bammy* (a flat cake made from cassava) are available and these are all-time favorites among teens.

Badminton, less popular than tennis, is played by teens of both genders, but like tennis, is expensive to pursue. Some teens, however, participate and do well in international competitions. Cricket, though quite popular in Jamaica and the Caribbean, is not popular among teens, particularly those living in urban areas. Except for occasions on which their particular school team is involved in the local annual high school competition, urban teens are hardly ever found at cricket matches. However, cricket is a popular sport in rural areas where both boys and girls play at the high school level.

Another form of recreation for teens is hiking. Hikes to one of the peaks of the Blue Mountains are exciting adventures for many teens from church and other youth groups.

Church groups also hold functions that provide recreation for teens. These include singles' socials, Bible quizzes, Valentine's Day suppers, visits to plays, and various sports competitions.

Friends might also meet at someone's home and hang out there for the day. They sometimes order in pizza, jerk chicken, or some other fast food but, often, they run a boat. This means that they pool their money to buy meat (usually chicken), rice, and flour and then cook a meal themselves. Their day is not complete without their boom box belting out the latest local and American hit songs. Rural teens engage in similar activities and the principle of running a boat is the same, complete with boom box music but they tend to cook different foods, like corned pork and green bananas. Teens also play indoor games, such as dominoes, Scrabble, and cards.

Gaining popularity among teens is drag racing with cars or motorbikes. Unfortunately, in recent times teens and other young adults have taken drag racing to the streets of Kingston. The teens involved usually belong to upper-income families and use their own cars for the sport. Drag racing is illegal and police officers make a concerted effort to curtail it.

High school students across the island participate in the annual Schools' Festival Competition, which includes art forms such as dance, drama, speech, music, and song. They perform on behalf of their schools and are awarded gold, silver, and bronze medals and certificates of merit and distinction. Teens who participate in these events, as well as others who attend the participating schools, look forward to this event each year. The festival culminates with a showcase concert, called Mello-Go-Round, of the best performers in each category.

Increasing numbers of teenage girls have entered beauty and modeling contests in recent years. Several do very well, particularly in modeling, even to the extent of signing contracts with international agencies and receiving international acclaim.

Some teens participate in the annual carnival, held mainly on the streets of parishes in Kingston, St. Andrew, and, more recently, in Ocho Rios, the island's tourist capital. Carnival music and celebrations originated in the eastern Caribbean and have only recently been adopted by Jamaica.

ENTERTAINMENT

The most current music idiom is referred to as dancehall, an outgrowth of reggae music.[16] Dancehall parties are held both in homes and at clubs. Dancehall has a unique culture consisting not only of a particular musical rhythm but also of sexually explicit language and dance routines and a unique style of dress and crowd behavior. It is not a culture embraced by all levels of society but is the type of music liked by teens, regardless of social background.

Teens who dance to dancehall music rarely dance with partners, but rather individually or as one or more groups. An important feature of dancehall is showing off the latest dance moves that go with particular rhythms and/or songs. Teens may also attend the annual, internationally acclaimed, local reggae music festivals held mainly in tourist areas.

Many Jamaican teens of all social classes, particularly boys, aspire to become DJs (originally a shortened term for disc jockeys). DJs are improvisation artists who use a song's rhythm track, without its lyrics, to create rhymes, social commentaries, or jokes to entertain an audience. Their function is equivalent that of American rap or hip-hop artists. Many boys have aspirations to become DJs with the dream of quick and easy money, but only a few Jamaican DJs have gained international fame, won Grammy music awards, and made a lot of money.

An interesting trend in recent times is that a number of musicians who are popular with teenagers have converted to Christianity and now sing only gospel music. This has influenced many teens to become Christians, particularly since these former pop singers typically use reggae and DJ styles in their music. Many of the churches to which teens flock are equipped with the kinds of musical instruments used in pop bands and this helps to both attract and sustain their interest. Teens are also attracted to dance when used as an art form during worship at many of the modern, charismatic churches. There are also a number of gospel musical groups to which teens belong.

American rappers as well as certain ballad singers, called soul singers by teens, are popular in Jamaica. The BET, MTV, and VH1 cable music stations, also popular among Jamaican teens, provide up-to-date releases by American artists. Cable television is not as popular in rural areas as it is in cities, but rural teens listen to the same types of music through radio broadcasts or on portable cassette or CD players. Jamaica's 10 radio stations play a variety of music and some teens enjoy listening to alternative, dance, calypso, and soca music. On weekends, teens also enjoy parties, dances, and clubs that specialize in local music. Teens idolize American pop singers and groups but most prefer local dancehall music along with American-style rhythm and blues, rap, and hip-hop.

Schools, also, have various fetes and barbecue suppers at which popular, local pop/dancehall singers and DJs perform. Students take advantage of these functions to socialize with members of the opposite sex who attend other schools.

Some teenagers, especially boys, play computer games with friends in game shops, while those who can prefer to invite friends over to enjoy an evening of computer games at home. The Internet is also popular with some teens and is used primarily as a research tool for school assignments and for emailing friends and participating in chat rooms. Many teens enjoy hanging out at shopping malls where they patronize fast food restaurants or go to the movies. Schools usually have rules preventing students from engaging in these activities while in school uniforms, so those are generally Saturday activities.

Fashions are similar to those in the United States. Jeans, baggy pants, T-shirts, and sneakers are popular among boys. More conservative girls wear jeans and T-shirts but many girls wear styles that are more current such as miniskirts, or capri pants with tops that leave the midriff exposed, accompanied by sandals or slippers.

Some teens and young adults have a dress code influenced by both Jamaican and American pop cultures. Revealing dress styles are coupled with false fingernails and toenails with sculpted, intricate designs. Hairstyles consist mainly of long, flowing synthetic or human hair extensions sewn, glued, or braided into the hair.

Many teens, particularly those from more affluent homes, receive allowances for school lunches as well as movies and parties. Others may have weekend jobs in a family business. Some try to save by joining what is called a partner. Five or more people who trust each other agree to contribute a certain amount of money each week and at the end of the week, one gets to draw the entire amount. This continues until each has received a draw and then the cycle starts again.

Drug use is also a cause for concern. In 2000, adolescents accounted for 12.9 percent of clients who visited treatment or rehabilitation centers across the island.[17] It is interesting to note that a majority of Jamaicans, including teenagers, do not consider ganja (marijuana) a drug. Many therefore experiment with it while in high school and continue the practice into adulthood. Results of a survey of students in 64 schools show that marijuana represented 80 percent of illegal drugs used by teenagers and its use had increased from 19.8 percent in 1987 to 26.9 percent in 1997.[18] Ganja is also used in the Rastafarian religion as a part of worship, which may be one reason that teens are attracted to that religion.

RELIGIOUS PRACTICES AND CULTURAL CEREMONIES

Many churches hold annual campaigns, crusades, or conventions in an attempt to convert Jamaicans to Christianity. American evangelists, particularly those with television ministries, are often invited to be guest speakers at these annual events. Some American preachers, particularly those who promote a healing ministry, come to Jamaica and have their own crusades, which are always well patronized.

Weddings are both religious and social events. Wedding ceremonies are usually performed in a church even if the bride and groom are not church members. Receptions may be elaborate with food, drink, and cake. Funerals are also big affairs in Jamaica. There is the nine-night tradition, meaning that the ninth night after a person dies the family of the deceased will provide fried fish, hard dough bread, and hot coffee, chocolate, and cold drinks for the many friends and relatives who visit. Men usually play domino games and drink white rum and other strong drinks at these affairs.

In rural villages, mourners sing traditional songs that, along with the food and drink, may help to comfort the bereaved. Christian families in particular may organize prayer meetings in their homes. In cities and in many towns burials take place primarily in private cemeteries, while in rural areas internment is more likely to be in family plots. After a funeral those who attended traditionally return to the family home for refreshments.

Various ethnic and religious groups have different ceremonies for weddings, funerals, and other milestone events. For example, some Indian families in Jamaica practice arranged marriages. The Chinese Benevolent Association organizes celebrations for the Chinese New Year and the German Society celebrates with Oktoberfest.

Christmas and Easter are celebrated as religious holidays, but, as in other parts of the world, they have also become greatly commercialized. Independence Day, National Heroes Day, Labor Day, and Emancipation Day are holidays associated with significant historical events or persons.

Emancipation Day marks the end of slavery in Jamaica and is celebrated on August 1 each year. Independence Day signifies the end of colonialism. It occurs on August 6 but celebrations usually last for a full week. Street concerts are held across the island, as well as many fairs, particularly in rural areas. In earlier years, street dancing was a common event in which many teens would have participated but this practice is not as prevalent today.

National Heroes Day, occurring each year in October, is celebrated in schools throughout Jamaica. During the preceding week, students are reminded of the achievements of Jamaican national heroes and prepare skits to honor one or more of them. High-ranking officials place wreaths at the National Heroes Park. On that day national awards are announced at a grand ceremony with a full military parade.

CONCLUSION

Teens in Jamaica are on par, academically as well as in sports and cultural endeavors, with teens elsewhere in the world. Teens such as Tiffany Butterfield who completed the University of Pennsylvania's Introduction to Calculus course for gifted children and finished among the top three, and Jamaican Rhodes Scholars such as Nadia Ellis (in 1999) and Gyanprakash Ketwaro (in 2001) give credence to this. Athletes such as Janelle Atkinson, who placed fourth in the 400-meter freestyle swimming event at the 2000 Olympic Games also show the determination and commitment to excellence of many of Jamaica's teens.

There are, however, many teens in crisis. Social issues such as street children, sexual and reproductive health, violence and other crimes, and drug use and trafficking are causes for great concern. Poor economic conditions and community violence play a large role in the lives of many teens, particularly in inner-city areas of Kingston. This situation impacts greatly upon the achievements of these youths and ultimately on the contributions they will be able to make to national life.

American influence upon Jamaican teens is apparent. This is evidenced by their mode of dress, their diet (in particular, their preference for fast foods provided by American-operated chains), and their music. Local culture is also a strong influence, as represented by popular and traditional music and other art forms, along with customs and traditions such as dance, speech, and drama with which many teens identify and in which they actively participate.

NOTES

1. The Planning Institute of Jamaica, *Economic and Social Survey Jamaica 2001* (Kingston, Jamaica, 2002).

2. The Planning Institute of Jamaica, *Economic and Social Survey Jamaica 2001*.

3. *Jamaica Education Statistics 1999–2000.* Annual Statistical Review of the Education Sector, Ministry of Education and Culture. (Kingston, Jamaica, 2001).

4. Statistical Institute of Jamaica, *Demographic Statistics 2000* (Kingston, Jamaica, 2001).

5. Planning Institute of Jamaica and Statistical Institute of Jamaica, *Jamaica Survey of Living Conditions 2001* (Kingston, Jamaica, 2002).

6. The Planning Institute of Jamaica, *Economic and Social Survey Jamaica 2001*.

7. The Planning Institute of Jamaica, *Economic and Social Survey Jamaica 2001*.

8. The Planning Institute of Jamaica, *Economic and Social Survey Jamaica 2001*.

9. Ministry of Health, *Jamaica AIDS Report 2002.* http://www.jamaicanap.org/.

10. L. Dunn, *Jamaica, Situation of Children in Prostitution: A Rapid Assessment* (Geneva, Switzerland: International Labor Organisation, International Program on the Elimination of Child Labor, 2001).

11. B. Chevannes, *What We Sow and What We Reap: Problems in the Cultivation of Male Identity in Jamaica* (Kingston, Jamaica: Grace Kennedy Foundation, 1999).

12. *Jamaica Education Statistics 1999–2000.*

13. *Daily Gleaner*, 22 February 2000, D3.

14. The Planning Institute of Jamaica, *Economic and Social Survey Jamaica 2000* (Kingston, Jamaica, 2001).

15. *Daily Gleaner*, 12 June 2000.

16. For more on dancehall and DJs, see chapter on music in M. Mordecai and P. Mordecai, *Culture and Customs of Jamaica* (Westport, Conn: Greenwood Press, 2001).

17. The Planning Institute of Jamaica, *Economic and Social Survey Jamaica 2000*.

18. *The Daily Observer*, 20 July 2000.

RESOURCE GUIDE

Chevannes, B. *What We Sow and What We Reap: Problems in the Cultivation of Male Identity in Jamaica*. Kingston, Jamaica: Grace Kennedy Foundation, 1999.

Dunn, L. *Jamaica, Situation of Children in Prostitution: A Rapid Assessment*. Geneva: International Labor Organisation, International Program on the Elimination of Child Labor, 2001.

Leo-Rhynie, E. *The Jamaican Family: Continuity and Change*. Kingston, Jamaica: Grace Kennedy Foundation, 1993.

Mordecai, Martin, and Pamela Mordecai. *Culture and Customs of Jamaica*. Westport, Conn.: Greenwood Press, 2001.

Morris, Margaret. "Tour Jamaica." http://www.jis.gov.jm/information/.

Planned Parenthood Federation of America. "Jamaican Teens." http://www.teenwire.com/views/articles/wv_19990611p007.asp.

Reddock, R., ed. *Women and Family in the Caribbean: Historical and Contemporary Considerations with Special Reference to Jamaica and Trinidad and Tobago*. Prepared for the Caricom Secretariat for International Year of the Family 1994 by the Women and Development Studies Group/Centre for Gender and Development Studies, The University of the West Indies, St. Augustine, Trinidad.

Nonfiction

Mason, P. *Jamaica in Focus: A Guide to the People, Politics, and Culture*. New York: Interlink, 1999.

Mordecai, Martin, and Pamela Mordecai. *Culture and Customs of Jamaica*. Westport, Conn.: Greenwood Press, 2001.

Sherlock, Sir Phillip, and H. Bennett. *The Story of the Jamaican People*. Princeton, N.J.: Markus Wiener Publishers, 1998.

Fiction

Heymans, Donna. *River Woman*. New York: Washington Square Press, 2002.

Senior, O. *Summer Lightning and Other Stories*. Harlow, UK.: Longman, Caribbean Writers Series, 1986.

Web Sites

http://www.electionworld.org/election/jamaica.htm
Elections in Jamaica.

http://www.emjam-usa.org/
Embassy of Jamaica in Washington.

http://www.usembassy.state.gov/kingston/
Embassy of the United States—Kingston.

http://www.jcdc.org.jm/
Jamaica Cultural Development Commission.

http://www.jamaica-gleaner.com/
Jamaica Gleaner Newspaper.

http://www.jamaicaobserver.com/
Jamaica Observer Newspaper.

http://www.jamaicatravel.com/
Jamaica Tourist Board.

http://www.ncst.gov.jm/
National Commission on Science and Technology.

http://www.nce.org.jm/
National Council on Education.

http://www.nlj.org.jm/
National Library of Jamaica.

http://www.nrca.org/
Natural Resources Conservation Authority.

http://www.un.int/jamaica/
Permanent Mission of Jamaica to the OAS.

http://www.src-jamaica.org/
Science Research Council.

http://www.statinja.com/
Statistical Institute of Jamaica.

http://www.usimona.edu.jm/
University of the West Indies.

More Information

Permanent Mission of Jamaica to the OAS
Permanent Representative
His Excellency The Hon Seymour Mullings OJ

1520 New Hampshire Avenue, NW
Washington, DC 20036
Tel: 202-452-0660
Fax: 202-452-0081
Email: jamaica@oas.org
http://www.emjam-usa.org/

Permanent Representative, New York
His Excellency Stafford Neil CD
767 Third Avenue, 9th and 10th Floors
New York, NY 10017
Tel: 212-935-7509
Fax: 212-935-7607
Email: jamaica@un.int

Pen Pal Information

Youth Link
The Gleaner Company
7 North Street
Kingston, Jamaica, W.I.
Fax: 876-922-6223
Email: ylink@go-jamaica.com
http://www.youthlinkjamaica.com/

Chapter 12

MEXICO

Roberto Campa-Mada

Translated by Javier Ochoa and Kanishka Sen

INTRODUCTION

Mexico is a country rich in natural and cultural diversity. In its territory of almost two million square kilometers there is a complex canopy of land and aquatic ecosystems (deserts, jungles, savannas, woodlands, mountains, rivers, lakes, etc.) that shelter 10 percent of the world's flora. This great natural diversity offers conditions for the growth of thousands of animal species, many of which are unique to Mexico.

But Mexico is not just a great natural museum; it is also living history. Its territory bears testimony to the great civilizations that thrived on the continent before the arrival of the Europeans. Every year, thousands of tourists visit archeological areas that house the ruins of former ceremonial centers, temples, pyramids, and cities of the great Olmec, Teotihuacan, and Maya civilizations. Its museums of history and anthropology contain great collections of historical specimens, sculptures, murals, and artifacts. The majestic buildings of the colonial cities are derived from baroque art and architecture.

The monetary unit of the country is the peso, whose symbol is $. Mexico maintains commercial relations with many countries in different parts of the world. However, its principal partner is the United States, since that nation buys approximately 85 percent of Mexico's exports—including oil and metals like silver, copper, and zinc, as well as a great variety of agricultural and industrial products. Commercial exchange also occurs in the opposite direction, since among other items, Mexico buys considerable quantities of machinery and electronic equipment from the United

States. Important trade partners are Japan, Canada, China, Germany, Great Britain, Holland, Belgium, and other Latin American countries.

Another essential bastion of the Mexican economy is tourism. Along its more than 11,500 kilometers of coastline, which is second in length only to Canada's, there are many beautiful cities whose beaches enjoy international prestige for their natural beauty and the variety of activities that they offer, in addition to their hotel and services infrastructure. Cancun, Acapulco, Mazatlán, Manzanillo, Puerto Vallarta, and Ixtapa Zihuatanejo are only a few of the many ports on the Pacific or Caribbean coasts, which together receive several million visitors each year (many of whom are North American).

Mexico, officially named the United Mexican States, is a federal republic that consists of 31 states and a federal district, which is the seat of the national executive, legislative, and judiciary institutions. In the year 2000, Vicente Fox Quezada, a leader in the National Action Party, took office as president. His election ended an uninterrupted period of over 70 years of rule by candidates of the Institutional Revolutionary Party. Mexican laws do not allow reelection of a president, who exercises power during a six-year term.

Mexico is known to many for its ethnic and cultural diversity. The official language of the country is Spanish, but more than 50 native languages still exist, some with dialectal variations of their own. The Amerindian population is significant. Approximately 29 percent of Mexicans are indigenous; they constitute 49 percent of the total indigenous population of Latin America. There is also an important Afro-mestizo population, both in the Caribbean and on the Pacific coast.

Under conditions of obvious inequality, two Mexicos coexist. Whites and mestizos (mixed indigenous and white) constitute a predominately urban Mexico, in which they speak Spanish. Indigenous Mexico is multiethnic, multicultural, multilingual, and profoundly rural. It speaks ancestral languages and keeps alive the traditions, beliefs, and worldview of its forebears. Many of them belonged to advanced cultures whose evolutionary development was cut short and their survivors were left floating, like small islands in the middle of a foreign world: marginalized, exploited, and having to adapt in order to survive.

There are many worldviews to be encountered in a country with over 50 languages and hundreds of dialectal variations. Nevertheless, the worldviews, belief systems, and rituals of Mexico's cultures share common traits. Similarities include their social and economic organization as well as their perspectives on universal concepts such as time and death.

The reality is that the indigenous peoples of Mexico continue to be marginalized. Not only do they tend to be ignored, they are also regarded as strangers who resist assimilation. As a result, a number of armed uprisings of indigenous peoples, supported by the international community, have recently taken place. With these uprisings, Mexico's indigenous peoples seek to defend their ethnic rights as well as to create awareness about issues of diversity and the detrimental impact of globalization.

The current descendents of the pre-Hispanic peoples survive on the basis of a subsistence economy. There are small groups in which only a few hundred native speakers survive. Others are quite numerous—hundreds of thousands of people. In spite of the heterogeneous nature of these groups, most of their members engage primarily in agriculture. Almost all harvest the same crops: corn, squash, chile and beans. To a lesser extent, they keep some livestock and raise domestic animals (pigs, goats, chickens, and turkeys). Producing handicrafts is also a traditional activity and every group makes its own handicrafts using distinct materials. With world economic trends and the neoliberal model, subsistence agriculture has been losing ground, and many indigenous people (especially young males) have been forced to migrate to cities to survive. But due to their lack of technical skills and the fact that many don't speak the dominant language (Spanish), they are forced to find employment in the most unrewarding jobs (as loaders, day laborers, brick-layers, or seasonal farm workers, for example). Therefore, the never-ending cycle of exploitation continues.

Military service is compulsory for men. It doesn't typically represent a great concern for young men because Mexico is a diplomatic country that has not participated in any international conflicts in decades. Furthermore, it maintains a noninterventionist and self-determination policy. Mexican politicians have boasted about the country's continual social peace. Nevertheless, in January of 1994, a group of indigenous people, the Zapatista Army for National Liberation, raised up in arms in Chiapas. The relativity of Mexican social peace and well-being became self-evident. Since then, there have been uprisings of other groups. The undeniable underlying reality began to emerge and climaxed in the currency devaluation of 1994, which plunged the country into its worst recession in 50 years.

Unemployment and underemployment have reached deplorable proportions. Moreover, they have resulted in urban violence and crime. Robberies (even while driving a car), holdups, and kidnappings are a part of everyday reality in the major cities. The country's youths are forced to grow up and to survive under those difficult conditions.

A common misconception is that young people in Mexico are not interested in politics. However, widespread participation by youths in demonstrations and public acts claiming their rights or supporting other groups (ecologists, indigenous support groups, human rights groups, etc.) demonstrates exactly the opposite. According to results from the most recent national survey (*Encuesta nacionel de la juventud*), Mexican youths trust neither their politicians nor the police. The corruption and false promises of politicians justify this attitude. The government faces the challenge of regaining the credibility of its institutions.

Unlike most other Latin American countries, voting is not compulsory in Mexico, so the IFE (Federal Electoral Institute) continually embarks on intense campaigns to make people aware of the importance of voting. To awaken a civic sense of duty from childhood, IFE establishes special booths on election days, at which children can express their opinions on diverse social and ecological topics. Moreover, the voting ID is one of the official documents of personal identity that allows teens to prove their coming of age.

Major urban centers have recently experienced a boom in cultural offerings for youths. Female teens face much pressure in trying to define their personality. While their parents dictate how their teens should dress, how to behave, and whom to be, the media entices them into being aggressive and rebellious. Teens are an enticing market for multinationals but most Mexican teens are unable to acquire all that fashion dictates is hip. Conversely, male teens are confronted with the official image of the juvenile delinquent. Though teens react to these stimuli by redefining themselves, police repression exacerbates a vicious cycle. Teens face a variety of enticements to join gangs and other spontaneous associations, which are appealing because they offer a stable ideology that acts as a point of reference in terms of who to be and how to act during the chaotic quest for self-identity.

TYPICAL DAY

Given Mexico's diversity, a typical day for a teen depends on class and where he or she lives. At 5:30 A.M. a typical middle-class teen would be awakened by his or her mother so that he or she might get dressed before having a light breakfast (cereal or eggs and coffee, milk, or juice). At 6:30 he or she might take a (public transit) bus to school, which is generally nearby because the sector program places students according to residential area or to the school previously attended. Classes begin at 7:00 A.M. and end at noon. Public middle school is held in two shifts: morning and afternoon. Usually, working students are placed in the afternoon shift.

Male teens with girlfriends would probably accompany them home before heading home themselves. They may then change from their formal school uniforms into more informal clothing and have lunch with the other members of their family present at that time. They would probably walk to the closest *tortillería* to buy tortillas, since it is customary to eat fresh tortillas at mealtimes. Girls do the dishes.

After a meal, male teens might watch some TV and relax. They may take a brief nap before doing homework. If they have to do research for a school project, they will have to take a bus to the public library. Otherwise, they may meet their friends from the block and play a little soccer (sometimes against kids from another block) or some other sport. Later, after taking a shower, they might gather in various friends' homes to listen to music or chat. Once or twice a week they might go to the movies with a group of friends (although this is more typical of wealthier teenagers).

Lower-middle-class teenagers, on the other hand, have to get up to go to work in order to help support the family. There is not much room for relaxation. They might have oatmeal or *atole* (a hot beverage thickened with corn dough, milk, and sugar) for breakfast, or a glass of milk with a piece of bread, and off they go to work. They know that after work they will have to go to school, at least through middle school, which is mandatory. Some teens sell newspapers on the streets. They begin their shifts early in the morning, at 5:00 A.M. They are often found working on the streets, sometimes under extreme weather conditions, calling out local news headlines in the middle of traffic.

FAMILY LIFE

In Mexico the basic social institution is the family. Although with globalization the number of divorces and disintegrated families has increased, in general, people are taught that marriage is for the rest of their lives and that the family should be kept together at all costs. A nuclear family generally consists of a father, mother, and three or four children. The concept of an extended family, however, includes grandparents, uncles, cousins, in-laws, nieces, and nephews, among others. Close ties are maintained through constant visits, mutual support, trips taken together, family reunions, and so on. Weekends are an ideal time for these family activities.

Among several indigenous groups, extended families share the same housing complex (or live in nearby homes), and carry out domestic and subsistence chores together. All family members participate, including small children who help out from an early age with household or field chores, depending on their gender. Training comes with practice.

In the traditional Hispanic family, the father is the provider and the mother's role is to raise the children and carry out domestic chores. In other words, women are generally responsible for the unpaid work. This structure works against women since it makes them economically dependent and places them in a position subordinate to men. This type of family organization has also fostered a favorable context to perpetuate the retrograde macho mentality often associated with Mexicans. On the other hand, children receive greater attention by having one of their parents with them on more of a full-time basis.

Women's roles, however, are changing. In recent decades, women have gained access to professional activities. More women are completing their professional education and working at well-paid jobs that were formerly considered masculine. In young, middle class, married couples, it is also common for both partners to work. Given the condition of the Mexican economy, it is difficult for a family to make a decent living by relying on just one income. One downside to this is that most women still have to fulfill domestic chores after returning home from work.

Unfortunately, in many marginalized families, the prevalent mentality is still that women should do all the housework as well as bear misery and abuse. Some women have to work strenuous, 10-hour shifts in the *maquiladoras* (assembly line factories) and still return home to do the housework and suffer domestic violence.

In general, families try to keep their children from working so that it will not interfere with their education, but there are many instances in which the need to help support the family takes precedence. This has contributed to school dropouts and/or to poor scholastic performance. In upper-class families, some teenagers work over the summer, usually in the family business, in order to acquire discipline and economic independence.

In general, the customs of upper-class teens are similar to those of their American counterparts. Cable or satellite TV systems expose them to North American channels, they learn English in private schools, and they take several trips a year to buy clothes, shoes, and electronic items in the United States.

In rural areas, one can routinely see how crafts are handed down from generation to generation. From an early age, kids learn the tasks of their parent's trade. Therefore, the period of adolescence is cut to a minimum, since assuming adult responsibilities and becoming economically independent tends to coincide with the advent of puberty (or the phase of sexual development), at which time they are prepared to start their own family. This is one reason it is common to see married couples of relatively young ages in rural areas, whereas in technologically advanced societies, a longer preparation time is required and adolescence is extended until the completion of one's university education. Marriage, in those cases, is postponed. Due to current economic conditions, and in contrast to their counterparts in the so-called First World, it is rare for Mexican urban youths to become economically independent before completion of their studies, so they continue to depend on their families, becoming something like incubated adults.

Thus, even though the legal age in Mexico is 18 years of age, regardless of gender, coming of age is not accompanied by economic independence. Nevertheless, 18 is considered the legal age to begin exercising actions associated with adult life, such as buying alcoholic beverages, voting in public elections, or acquiring a permanent driver's license. However, as early as age 16, teens can obtain a permit allowing them to drive legally under their parent's oversight. Generally, only rich kids have cars. The income levels of middle- or lower-class families rarely allow for children to have their own cars. Therefore, public transportation (by metro or bus) plays an important role in the daily lives of urban teens.

In general, Mexicans live with their parents until they marry. It is rare for young, unmarried people to have lives apart from their families. Even some young married couples (especially in those marriages that are the result of unplanned pregnancies) sometimes continue to live with their families until they save enough to go out on their own.

TRADITIONAL AND NONTRADITIONAL FOOD DISHES

Food is an important part of Mexican culture. Many traditional dishes date from pre-Hispanic times and the recipes have been handed down from generation to generation through oral tradition. After the conquest, Mexican staples reconfigured European cuisine. What would Italian cuisine be without tomatoes—and what would the Swiss do without chocolate?

Discussing traditional dishes in Mexico would be exhaustive since every region has its own exquisite culinary specialties. According to traditional beliefs, corn (maize) was not only the main ingredient in Mayan dishes, but also the basic element from which humans were made. From corn, native peoples developed elaborate dishes ranging from *menudo* (a soup made of tripe, hominy, and chili, stewed for hours with garlic and other spices), tamales (packets of corn dough with a savory or sweet filling wrapped in corn husks), and *gallina pinta* (a broth with maize and beans) to delicious desserts. They also created exquisite drinks such as *atole*, *champurrado*, (similar to *atole* but made with chocolate and water), and *pinole* (ground, toasted corn with cinnamon). Other notable foods are *frijoles* (beans), *calabaza* (squash), and chile (peppers). Together with maize, they form the basis of Mexican cooking. The great diversity of chiles produced in Mexico (of different colors, tastes, and textures) contributes to the rich variety of salsas and dishes characteristic of Mexican cuisine.

Although many teens drink bottled drinks (especially sodas) many Mexican families still follow the lively tradition of drinking fresh water flavored with a great variety of seeds, flowers, and fruits, which grow naturally in the country.

People are ever more aware of the importance of a balanced diet, so the more fortunate include fruit, fresh vegetables, dairy products, fish, and cereals, among other products, in their diet. The economic situation of many forces them to continue to rely on the agricultural foods, such as corn, beans, and chile that Mexico grows in abundance.

There are sources for buying prepackaged and frozen foods. In urban areas, there are many national and international supermarkets, some of which are open 24 hours. People go once or twice a week to stock up. Nevertheless, for daily purchases, people prefer the *abarrotes*, small family-owned stores that operate in homes. *Casetas* or *changarros*, tiny stores that sell only basic items, are also commonly found. Roofed and open-air markets are also options for buying fruit and vegetables. These markets are known for the haggling over prices that takes place. Initially, a vendor quotes a price considered high given the city's standards. The customer then pretends to be uninterested and offers an amount under what he or she believes to be the fair price. After some give and take, people usually come to an agreement regarding cost. This practice doesn't take place in formal establishments such as convenience stores or in supermarkets, where prices are fixed. The informal commerce, however, is popular in Mexico. Some claim that this type of commerce is harmful to the overall economy. Nevertheless, it has become necessary given the economic conditions. The government has tried to prohibit it, especially in tourist or historic areas, but the pressure of the street vendors has prevailed.

In every area of the larger cities street vendors offer a great variety of products including food, clothing, artifacts, toys, and domestic or imported articles. In some of these markets piracy is openly practiced and it is not uncommon to see a spectacular dismantling of stalls and concealing of items in the face of a police raid.

Another form of small business endeavor related to food is the traditional *cocinas económicas* (economic cooking), where one can find a wide variety of traditional Mexican dishes prepared by expert cooks and with a homemade taste, at very affordable prices.

Mexican teens in general prefer fast foods (hamburgers, pizzas, French fries, soft drinks, etc.) and canned soft drinks, which they purchase from multinational companies like McDonald's, Burger King, and Domino's or at domestic and local businesses. *Tortas,* which are like sandwiches (though the bread is different), are also very popular. Every region has its own special type of *torta.* Guadalajara, for instance, is famous for its *tortas ahogadas* (sandwiches dipped in a thick soup, or *caldo*). Young people also like to go out for tacos. There are *taquerias* (taco shops) at about every corner of Mexico's cities, both in booths as well as carts, which are open until late at night. A great variety of tacos are available, including ones made with beef eyes and tongue.

Like other teens around the world, Mexican teens show a certain addiction to junk food such as *frituras* with *chamoy* and chile (fruit treats with tamarind pulp and chile) that when eaten in excessive quantities can alter normal bodily functions. Due to this, and due to the recurrence of gastrointestinal diseases detected in schoolchildren, the sale of these products near schools has been prohibited. Popular dishes among youths include *pico de gallo* (fruit and vegetable combinations) such as mango, coconut, watermelon, jicama, cucumber, and other ingredients dipped in chile sauce, salt, and lime juice. This taste for chile also appears in the ice cream industry. Mexican establishments (such as Michoacana and Tepoztlán, among others) in the ice cream industry are successful with various branches throughout the country. It is a highly evolved industry and includes mango *paletas* with chile, or cucumber and chile, or *chamoy*. Establishments also sell flavored water with an array of flavors from fruits cultivated within the country.

Mobile street vendors selling food items are also very popular. They can be found (pushing their carts or riding their bicycles) in parks and close to churches and other public places. They are diversified into *paleteros* (ice cream vendors), *eloteros* (vendors of corn on the cob), *taqueros* (taco vendors), and *raspaderos* (vendors of *raspados*, i.e., desserts made with crushed ice and syrup). In the northern part of the country, hot dog carts (following the American tradition) are very popular. However, Mexican hot dogs (*jatdogueros*) are not mere imitators of their American counterparts, since

Mexicans prepare their products in different ways and garnish them with multiple ingredients (tomatoes, pickles, onions, sausage, refried beans, potatoes, etc.) besides the regular ingredients.

SCHOOLING

Mandatory education in Mexico includes preschool from ages three to five, six years of elementary school (first through sixth grades), and then three years at the secondary level, which is the equivalent of the American middle school and one year of high school. In Mexico, preparatory (high school) lasts three years. The length of time required to earn a college degree depends on the field of study, with four to five years being the norm. Postgraduate studies include masters in sciences or in arts and doctorates (Ph.D.s).

On a typical school day, middle school students go straight to their first class, except on civic Mondays, when there is a brief ceremony to honor the flag, which is escorted by a group of six students. The ceremony includes the singing of the national anthem and the recitation of a pledge of allegiance and patriotic poems. The school principal may make announcements before students go to their classroom. In middle school, students at every grade level take classes with up to 11 different teachers due to the variety of subjects required in their curriculum. A class period consists of 50 minutes of instruction and 10 minutes of recess. The school day begins at 7:00 A.M. and ends at 2:00 P.M. In addition to the usual academics, subjects include physical education, music, dance, and workshops.

In major urban centers, children and teens with physical disabilities receive special education. That kind of instruction requires specialized teachers. There are also night schools for those who cannot attend school during the day or need to catch up. In open enrollment schools, students organize their schedules to meet, alone or in groups, with their instructors.

Educational opportunities also include private schools, accessible to those who can afford tuition, which is usually high. Students with high marks can benefit from scholarships offered by private schools, state, and federal governments and/or foundations.

Public schools throughout the country follow the same curriculum, updated periodically by the Secretariat of Public Education, a federal organization responsible for the administration of public education in Mexico. Every year, secondary students receive textbooks free of charge.

It is best for teenagers to be focused exclusively on their studies, but many young people, given the precarious condition of their families (or their lack of a family to support them) are forced to work the streets. Some are jugglers, others clean windshields. Some beg or perform dangerous acts like inhaling fire. All of this takes place in the middle of a busy intersection, and they risk being run over. Teens are easy victims of dangerous practices such as sniffing glue, paint thinner, or gasoline. In response, the government has issued a law prohibiting the sale of such products to minors.

In cooperation with many important companies, the government has also implemented a program to create part-time jobs for young people while encouraging them to continue their education. In order to be hired, and in order to keep their jobs, students have to present school documents to prove they are indeed studying. They perform a wide range of activities for these companies. Some bag groceries at supermarkets, others are movie theater or fast food restaurant employees, or work as newspaper hawkers in the main intersections of a city. As part of this collaborative effort, these companies provide areas designed especially for studying.

In cities, especially in Guadalajara and Mexico City, teens will work in urban places and on public transportation. Music students, for example, sing songs accompanied by their guitar or another instrument on public buses. Passengers give them tips to help them continue with their studies. Theater and mime students also perform in parks to earn money.

In recent years there have been efforts to extend education to every part of the country. Elementary and middle schools have been built in remote rural areas, so that students may receive instruction through satellite communication (the high school's TV system). That instruction is designed to reflect a student's reality by basing it on the economic activity of the relevant region, so that, for example, in agricultural areas the instruction is geared toward technical, agricultural, and livestock facilities. In an effort to make sure that all of the country's youths receive an education, governmental departments like the National Office for Educational Development send teachers to coastal and agricultural areas to teach indigenous families who work the fields, teaching in a relaxed atmosphere during rest breaks. Classes are taught in the students' native language, while they are encouraged to perfect their Spanish. When the harvest is over and it becomes necessary for the family to move to another region to harvest another crop, the teachers accompany them to continue their education program without interruption.

Notwithstanding these efforts, schooling has failed to meet its goal as a social equalizer. On the contrary, it increasingly accentuates preexisting social differences. The educational programs that the government designs periodically to improve education are not realistic and, though they sound wonderful in theory, efforts to implement them are met with a different, restrictive reality. Excessive enrollment affects space availability and classes are held with too many students. The budget is still too meager to pay teachers decent salaries; many are forced to look for additional jobs to survive.

The well-defined stratification of enrollment increases the gap between public and private education. Businesses further encourage the distinction by choosing to accept applicants from private schools over those from public ones. At times you even find job postings that note no graduates from specific institutions public institutions need apply.

Nevertheless, there are efforts underway to modernize public schools by installing computer equipment and offering foreign language instruction, for instance, but these efforts always turn out to be inadequate. Private schools are able to offer programs designed to foster leadership skills, such as the Young Entrepreneurs. They also offer instruction in languages, art, workshops, and other areas. Furthermore, these schools sell their image as shapers of future leaders. And indeed, as flaunted in the advertisements of these institutions, upon graduation alumni gain access to the best positions.

The good intentions of state educational policies are exemplified by bilingual projects aimed at indigenous communities, predicated on the notion that bilingual speakers who know the culture will teach in the native language. These initiatives have remained utopian ideals due to a great many barriers (the great diversity of languages, the lack of bilingual individuals in the teaching professions, the lack of textbooks in the different languages, etc.) encountered upon implementation. Therefore, these programs are usually reduced to teaching Spanish and a few basic math skills to indigenous peoples.

Since the nineteenth century, the liberal faction (most notably represented by President Benito Juárez) established that education should be secular, free, and managed exclusively by the state. Nevertheless, the lack of resources resulted in the state giving up a significant sector of the educational initiative to private interests, chiefly to religious institutions. The church thus reclaimed its historic control over Mexican education. In today's Mexico, there are a great many religious schools—Catholic for the most part—that offer a different perspective on the educational curriculum.

SOCIAL LIFE

In Mexico one's teenage years can be difficult. As teens feel like they are already adults they want to do things they associate with adult life (drink, dance, smoke, be sexually active, for example). However, in addition to the many social and legal restrictions that exist, they depend on their parents (who still view them as kids) for economic support. Only once they turn 18 are they allowed into bars and discos. Thus, teens frequently organize well-attended parties in their homes, patios, or even in the streets. During these parties, some teenagers show off their skills as deejays by playing (Spanish or international) rock and pop music. They also dance and chat.

Teens also get together in *tardeadas*, afternoon dances (*tarde* means afternoon or early evening) that schools organize two or three times per year for fundraising purposes. During these *tardeadas* students can dance, chat, and, most importantly, consume soft drinks and junk food sold by the school's fundraising committees.

Like many other teens throughout the world, Mexican teenagers have a curfew. If they stay out past it, their parents may ground them. Nevertheless, there is one night a year when they are allowed to stay out with friends until all hours. On the 10th of May (Mother's Day) some may not return until morning. During the early hours of this day, teens usually get together and serenade their respective mothers. (Mexicans hold their mothers in very high regard, almost as sacred beings.) Teens who have the means may hire a mariachi band to help with the serenading.

In general, like most inhabitants of the global village, Mexican teens wear jeans, T-shirts with slogans or designs, tennis shoes or comfortable shoes, and accessories such as caps. Most schools require uniforms, but out of school, teenagers try to wear (according to their taste and purchasing power) the brands and styles dictated by TV. Whether from Mexican commercial TV broadcasts or cable from the United States, teens are bombarded with ads on how to be hip. According to the 2000 National Youth Poll, teens follow these messages as irrefutable truths because most think that appearance and fashion define what it means to be young.

The election of a school's queen is a deeply entrenched custom and many different areas of social and economic activity have their own representative. Organizing the election involves substantial student mobilization. Prior to election day, female candidates organize public demonstrations. Fellow students drive in the parade. Publicity campaigns to secure votes are held at *tardeadas*. All female teens dream of being elected queen so, in general, they try to keep their figures trim. However, cases of anorexia and bulimia have not reached epidemic proportions as in other countries where extreme slenderness is an obsession.

Expos are becoming increasingly popular. They are exhibits showcasing activities ranging from ranching to farming, education, industry, and

Girls outside Guadalajara's cathedral, Mexico. © A. Tovy/TRIP.

commerce. In addition to visiting expo booths, youths enjoy amusement park rides, take part in typical fair games, visit the hall of mirrors, or watch the *Voladores de Papantla* (traditional Indian dances, in which dancers fly through the air in circular paths suspended by ropes from a central pole). Daily activities tend to conclude with a performance by a singer of national or international reputation.

The favorite activity of teens is going to the movies with a group of friends. All main urban centers have many multiscreen theaters where national and international movies are shown. As in most Latin American countries, most of the films shown are Hollywood movies. It is also common to have one screen showing a national or Latin American production and another showing an international release (usually European or

Asian). Foreign films are usually shown with subtitles. Sometimes very successful movies will be shown on several screens and viewers can choose between dubbed or subtitled versions. After a movie, teens will usually go out to dinner, or to a soda shop or ice cream parlor, to keep the fun going.

Mexican society isn't as strict as it was in prior generations. Today's teens enjoy many more liberties. They are much freer to choose both their friends and girlfriends or boyfriends. In urban centers teens tend to have several boyfriends or girlfriends before settling down. Courtship is no longer viewed as a step toward marriage as it continues to be in rural areas. In Mexico, prearranged marriages have all but disappeared. Young people are free to marry when and whomever they want.

In many respects, however, Mexican society is still very conservative, and traditional values are the norm. Some schoolteachers have been expelled because they have assigned students to read indecent material (as judged by very narrow standards). Religious organizations tend to exert pressure on theaters to censor movies with a controversial subject matter; however, their strategy backfires because they generate larger box-office revenues. Conservative organizations see themselves as the guardians of public morals. They try to encourage teens to practice abstinence, but a high percentage of them engage in premarital sex. The most recent National Youth Poll showed that 53.5 percent of young, sexually active people had their first sexual encounter outside of marriage.

RECREATION

Soccer is without a doubt the most popular sport in Mexico. Although it is not officially taught in schools, there are always regional and state soccer championships in which public schools compete against each other. In general, though, little importance is given to sports in education. In middle schools, sports are reduced to informal physical education classes, held once or twice a week. Students may run, do a few sit-ups, and play basketball or volleyball, the sports most commonly played in middle school. Most secondary schools are equipped with basketball courts. Nevertheless, when physical education classes are not being held or after school, students will play soccer. Kids and teens play on all types of courts, in vacant lots, and even in the streets. The two networks that control Mexican television broadcast the Mexican league's games as well as special programs related to the sport.

As in the rest of Latin America, soccer has always been considered a male sport, and females are left out of the ritual. This has begun to change in recent years, since soccer is now promoted among groups of female players, and in Mexico today there are several women's teams and inter-scholastic tournaments.

ENTERTAINMENT

Entertainment options for teens depend on socioeconomic status, since in Mexico, as in many other Latin American countries, the gap in wealth distribution is enormous. Wealthy youth enjoy access to a world of luxury and excess. Options range from golf and horseback riding to swimming, scuba diving, and yachting. Teens may take trips abroad or to summer-houses on the beach or in the country. They may also opt for private les-sons in various arts and disciplines.

Options diminish as one descends the social ladder. Youths whose sur-vival is contingent on work have little time for entertainment. For the many who live in the so-called lost cities, a TV set offers escape from their miserable predicament. Wealthy teens can enjoy the worlds and things that the poor can only access through their TV sets.

During the summers, through several agencies like the Casas de la Cul-tura (literally, Houses of Culture), state governments promote reading and the use of libraries. They also offer classes on painting, music, theater, and other arts at reasonable prices (which are still unattainable for the poor). Since cultural activities are associated with conservatism and the status quo, they generally attract small groups of kids and teens. Youths prefer more popular activities like going to the movies or listening to music. In recent years, rock music in Spanish has enjoyed a great boom among teens. Many excellent Mexican bands have emerged. Among teenagers, Café Tacuba, Molotov, Plastilina Mosh, El Gran Silencio, La maldita vecindad y los hijos del quinto patio, Maná, Santa Sabina, La Lupita, and Control Machete are especially popular. After many decades of decline, domestically produced Mexican movies are being revitalized. A new generation of important Mexican moviemakers has begun to win awards in the most important film festivals in the world, especially in Eu-rope. Their films express their viewpoints on Mexico's current political and social realities. They explore issues of Mexican identity in *Amores perros*, *Cilantro y perejil*, *El callejón de los milagros*, *Todo el poder*, *La ley de Herodes* and *Y tu mamá también*. This last movie offers an interesting de-piction of the conflicts faced by Mexico City's middle- to upper-class teens. Furthermore, behind its seemingly frivolous dialogues and atti-tudes, the movie offers an X-ray picture of Mexico as it is currently. Al-though director Alfonso Cuarón (*Sólo con tu pareja*, *Great Expectations*) stated that the movie was made with teenage viewers in mind, in Mexico it was shown only to adult audiences.

Many of the most important urban centers celebrate their own traditional festivals, attended by teens countrywide. These festivities range from carnivals (especially in the port cities of Veracruz, Mazatlán, and Guaymas) and fairs (the Feria de San Marcos in the state of Aguascalientes is the most famous) to festivals and even cultural events such as the October festivals in Guadalajara. The most prestigious internationally is, without a doubt, October's festival Cervantino at Guanajuato, a beautiful, mysterious colonial city with many tunnels and underground passageways. There are two different programs to the festival. The formal, printed one involves a price tag. The informal, spontaneous festival takes place free of charge in Guanajuato's streets, parks, and other public places. That international festival is so well attended that the city's main streets are completely flooded by a sea of people from all over the globe. The official program always includes world-renowned writers, theater companies, and orchestras. The unofficial program has become a forum for diverse artistic manifestations. The callejonadas (events taking place in narrow alleys called callejones) are significant because they involve youths following the bands of students who sing traditional songs while playing stringed instruments who parade along the alleyways of Guanajuato.

RELIGIOUS PRACTICES AND CULTURAL CEREMONIES

Though religious freedom is granted by the Mexican constitution, as in all other Latin American countries, a high percentage of the population (89 percent) is Roman Catholic. Protestants have begun to make inroads and now comprise 6 percent of the population; the rest practice other religions. Nevertheless, although the vast majority claim to be Catholic, the most recent National Youth Poll (Encuesta nacional de la juventud) indicated that most teens and young Catholics do not practice their religion, but rather that their religious affiliations result from a tradition passed on by their parents.

For historic reasons most traditional festivities are associated with the Catholic calendar. Before the arrival of the Spaniards, the indigenous peoples had complex rituals and religious systems but, after the conquest, the so-called universal religion was imposed on them by force. Nevertheless, indigenous peoples continued to practice their animistic and polytheistic rituals clandestinely. When they were forced to embrace a new religion, they continued to honor their gods, who were thinly veiled as the saints offered by the Vatican. This practice gave rise to a peculiar religion blended from rituals and beliefs from both worlds.

One festivity that has arisen from the mixture of theogonies is the Day of the Dead. November 2 is a day in which colorful fiestas are held with plenty of flowers, food, and drinks. What is strange is not the festivity itself but the place where it is held: the cemetery. That custom is based on the pre-Hispanic belief that once a year, the dead return from beyond to live with those they hold dearest and who are still living in this world. On this occasion, many Mexicans take favorite foods and beverages to their loved ones' graves, which they have previously adorned with wreaths and flowers (especially with a variety of large marigolds). Prior to the Day of the Dead, markets will display items associated with the celebration, which varies greatly depending on region and ethnic group, but which typically includes flowers, coffins, and miniature skeletons and skulls made of sugar. They also offer *pan de muerto* (literally, bread for the dead) as well as other ritual breads.

Indigenous groups usually practice Catholicism, although their interpretations of it may be interwoven with their ancient beliefs. Many believe in the existence of a *tona* or *nagual,* which is a guardian animal whose fate is tied to their own. They believe that whatever affects their companion animal will affect them too. On the other hand, sickness is generally interpreted as punishment attributed to abstract maladies like fright or chills or the evil eye (*mal de ojo*). Cures are sought through healers, or shamans may consume hallucinogenic mushrooms to decipher the causes of their illness and the appropriate treatment. All indigenous groups practice *temazcal* baths, similar to Native American sweats, which simulate the experience of being in the womb and are believed to cleanse the body and soul.

Most indigenous groups follow similar rituals when someone dies: there is music at the wake; guests are offered food, drink, and cigarettes and an ash cross is placed on the floor facing the family altar. A meal is served after the burial. Prayers are said for nine days (*novena*). On the last day, a friend (usually the deceased's best friend), picks up the ash cross and takes the ashes to the grave. If the deceased is a child, the wake is more like a party with music and dancing because deceased children (little angels) are believed to go straight to heaven.

Many tourists ask whether the crosses found on the sides of roads and highways mark actual gravesites. The practice is associated with an indigenous belief that those who die violent deaths (in automobile accidents, for example) are left to roam the Earth without knowing they have died. A cross with the deceased's name is placed at the scene of a fatal accident so that the victim may peacefully begin his or her voyage to the place of the dead.

As in the rest of the Western world, Christmas is also celebrated in Mexico. Celebrations include nativity scenes, *posadas*, *pastorelas*, piñatas, Christmas Eve, and Christmas Day. Every region has its own songs, ceremonies, and rituals associated with the season. *Posadas*, which commemorate Mary and Joseph's difficult journey from Nazareth to Bethlehem in search of a place to stay, are held during the eight days prior to Christmas. In a given neighborhood a party is held at someone's house on each of the days. Fruit punches are served, kids break open piñatas to get bags filled with seasonal fruit (sugarcane, oranges, Mexican hawthorn fruit, etc.) and an assortment of candies. *Pastorelas* are theatrical performances focusing on the shepherds who are said to have received the news of the birth of Jesus. During the Christmas season both professional and amateur theater groups stage plays similar to the ones the clergy staged to indoctrinate Indians who did not speak Spanish.

In Mexico there are many festivities throughout the year. Many are rooted in the Catholic calendar of saint's days. During Holy Week and Easter, many communities stage Passion plays. The most spectacular productions take place in San Miguel De Allende, Ajijic, and Iztapalapa.

In indigenous communities, festivities are also related to the calendar of saint's days but the most significant is the celebration of the town's patron saint. Every town has its patron saint. A certain person is chosen to organize the festival. To be charged with this duty is considered an honor. Sometimes that person becomes an authority figure in charge of solving internal issues only, since the authorities of any given indigenous community are subject to municipal authorities, and mainly to the mayor, who is usually either white or mestizo.

In Mexico there is a conscious attempt to preserve traditions. To celebrate the Day of the Dead, students compete making altars focused on famous historical figures or dead acquaintances such as teachers or classmates. In addition to pictures and objects related to them, traditional items include candles, sugar skulls, and *papel picado* (paper cut according to special designs). Traditions passed on from generation to generation include sharing a *Rosca de Reyes*, a ring-shaped sweet bread, which includes a little figure, made to celebrate the Epiphany on January 6. Families also encourage participation in other traditional activities, such as *posadas* and *pastorelas*.

CONCLUSION

In Mexico, destiny hinges on social class. The lives of upper-class teens are similar to those of their American counterparts. They study in private schools and travel abroad. Middle-class teens go to school, watch TV, play soccer, gather at friends' homes to listen to music, or go to the movies. Lower-middle-class teenagers will go to public school while working to help support the family. In rural areas, youths marry young. In urban areas, marriage is postponed until after college.

A common rite of passage for Mexican male teens is compulsory military service. Being able to vote and drive a car are also considered coming-of-age events. A fierce economic recession has led to widespread unemployment and underemployment. Some urban youths experience violence daily and learn how to deal with it; some find support in gangs. While a significant number of Mexican youths actively participate in demonstrations to support ecological issues or indigenous and human rights groups, most consume messages from the media on how to be hip.

Mexican youths reflect the country's ethnic and cultural diversity. While white and mestizo youths are predominately urban and speak Spanish, indigenous Mexican youths speak ancestral languages and maintain the traditions of their forebears. Most of them eke out a living from agriculture and raising livestock, and some continue the tradition of making handicrafts.

However, the imposition of the neoliberal economic model and the effects of the North American Trade Agreement in Mexico, among other factors, have forced many male indigenous teens to migrate to cities, where they have to work in dead-end jobs as loaders, day laborers, bricklayers, or seasonal farm workers. Mexican leaders have a mandate to rethink strategies to confront globalization in order to ensure universal social and economic well-being and provide youths with opportunities to bear a degree of control over their future.

ACKNOWLEDGMENT

This chapter was translated by Javier Ochoa and Kanishka Sen.

RESOURCE GUIDE
Nonfiction

Hadden, Gerry, ed. *Teenage Refugees from Mexico Speak Out*. New York: Rosen, 1997.

Paz, Octavio. *The Labyrinth of Solitude; Life and Thought in Mexico*. Translated by Lysander Kemp. New York: Grove Press, 1985.

Poniatowska, Elena. *Massacre in Mexico*. Translated by Helen R. Lane. New York: Viking Press, 1975.

———. *Tinísima*. Translated by Katherine Silver. New York: Farrar, Straus, Giroux, 1996.

Poniatowska, Elena, and Kent Klich. *El niño: Children of the Streets*. Translated by Katherine Silver. New York: Farrar, Straus, Giroux, 1996.

Suárez-Orozco, Carola. *Transformations: Immigration, Family Life, and Achievement Motivation among Latino Adolescents*. Stanford, Calif.: Stanford University Press, 1995.

Taylor, Lawrence J. *Tunnel Kids*. Tucson: University of Arizona Press, 2001.

Fiction

Arreola, Juan José. *Confabulario and Other Inventions*. Translated by George D. Schade. Austin: University of Texas Press, 1964.

———. *The Fair*. Translated by John Upton. Austin: University of Texas Press, 1977.

Garro, Elena. *First Love and Look for My Obituary: Two Novellas*. Translated by David Unger. Willimantic, Conn.: Curbstone Press, 1997.

———. *Recollections of Things to Come*. Translated by Ruth L. C. Simms. Austin: University of Texas Press, 1969.

Pacheco, José Emilio. *Battles in the Desert and Other Stories*. Translated by Katherine Silver. New York: New Directions, 1987.

———. *You Will Die in a Distant Land*. Edited and translated by Elizabeth Umlas. Coral Gables, Fla.: North-South Center, University of Miami, 1991.

Traven, B. *The Bridge in the Jungle*. New York: Hill and Wang, 1967.

———. *The Creation of the Sun and the Moon*. New York: Hill and Wang, 1968.

———. *The Kidnapped Saint and Other Stories*. New York: Hill, 1975.

———. *The Night Visitor and Other Stories*. New York: Hill and Wang, 1966.

———. *The White Rose*. Westport, Conn.: Lawrence Hill, 1979.

Web Sites

http://www.cia.gov/cia/publications/factbook/geos/mx.html
CIA

http://www.conafe.edu.mx/
Consejo Nacional de Fomento Educativo

http://www.imjuventud.gob.mx/
Instituto Mexicano de la Juventud

http://www.mexconnect.com/
México Connect.

http://www.mexico.com/
Mexico.com.

Pen Pal Information

http://www.penpalsnet.com.ar/es/index.php4
Pen Pals Net.

Chapter 13

PERU

Lydia Rodríguez

INTRODUCTION

Peru is a multilayered civilization, which makes the country and its people fascinating. Remains of the past are evident in the surviving colonial architecture of the lowlands and the Incan ruins in the highlands. Peru's 796,836 square miles are divided into coastal (lowland), mountainous (highland), and jungle areas. Peruvian personalities vary from one area to another. In the coastal region Peruvians are cautious of what they say and do; in the mountains, people also tend to be somewhat reserved; but in the jungle regions people are more open and daring. Jungle dwellers were not subject to the *mestizaje* of the Incan and Spanish mixture, hence their openness.

The country's official name is República del Perú; its government is a constitutional republic. Peru's current president is Alejandro Toledo. A president is elected for a five-year term, and the 1993 constitution allows for one consecutive reelection. The constitution also allows for and provides two vice presidents; currently they are First Vice President Raúl Diez Conseco (July 2001) and Second Vice President David Waisman (July 2001). The vice presidents are popularly elected, too. The Prime Minister is Roberto Danino, although he does not execute any power. All power is in the hands of the president.

Unemployment and underemployment are presently at their highest levels ever, and women are the most affected by the lack of jobs. The greatest areas of unemployment are in the cities of Arequipa, Chimbote, Piura, and Trujillo. The unemployed urban population is at 7.9 percent and underemployment is at 42.6 percent ("Peruinfo").

Peru's economic and finance minister is Pedro Kuczynski Godard. As of 1999, Peru's major trading partners were the United States, Japan, Germany, and fellow Latin American countries. Its major exports are gold, copper, zinc, fish, fish by-products, and textiles. In 1998, El Niño's impact on agriculture affected financial growth; then, in 1999 the aftermath of El Niño created another financial burden on Peru's economy. Peru's currency is the *nuevo sol* (abbr. *ns*).

Most Peruvians are mestizos (37 percent), Spanish or white (15 percent), indigenous (45 percent), or else black, Japanese, or Chinese (3 percent). Peru has two official languages: Spanish and Quechua. Aymara is also spoken. Roman Catholicism is the predominant religion: approximately 90 percent follow that faith. Virtually all Peruvians aged 15 and over are literate. In all, 88.7 percent of the population can read and write; within this number, 94.5 percent are male and 83 percent are female. The last census was taken in 1995 (Central Intelligence Agency).

Also in 1995, a war broke out between Peru and Ecuador over a portion of their border. A peace treaty was signed in October of 1998. Terrorism is still an issue. Peru has two active terrorist groups: Sendero Luminoso and Movimiento Revolucionario Tupac Amaru. Sendero Luminoso frequently attacks areas of Lima and the coca-producing Huallaga Valley, despite the fact that the group's leader has been captured. In 1996, the revolutionary group Tupac Amaru took more than 500 hostages at the Japanese ambassador's residence in Lima. After 126 days, 71 hostages were rescued; approximately 429 hostages had been killed. Tumultuous times in Peru are difficult for all. However, young Peruvians are indoctrinated to be politically well informed and to defend their country. The first is a given for all Peruvians. The second becomes a reality for those called to active duty. All Peruvians, males and females alike, must sign up for military training when they turn 16 years old. Although being called to duty may cause fear, Peruvians go with a national spirit.

Peru is the world's largest coca leaf producer. Most coca leaves are shipped to Colombia, Bolivia, or Brazil for processing into cocaine for the international drug market. Peru has worked to reduce coca cultivation by destroying labs, prosecuting officers involved in drug activities, and narrowing in on air, land, and river routes to conduct searches and seizures.

TYPICAL DAY

In Peru, adolescents fall into two distinct social groups: young teens from ages 13 to 16 who attend high school, and those from ages 17 to 21 who go to university and are considered young adults.

On a typical day, a young Peruvian teen gets up in the morning and eats a simple, light breakfast—bread, sometimes with butter, and a glass of milk. Breakfast depends on what time classes start, but normally it's eaten at about 7:00 A.M. After breakfast, the teen rushes off to school. Generally, teenagers take a packed lunch to eat during the 30-minute lunch period that starts at 1:00 P.M. Lunch may consist of a sandwich (bread with avocado, cheese, or meat), juice, and fruit. At 3:00 P.M. classes are over for the day, and teens go home to eat a more hearty lunch. This lunch is usually rice and a vegetable or meat dish, sometimes accompanied by soup, depending on the weather.

When teens arrive at school in the morning, the first thing they do is recite a prayer or, if in military school, the national anthem. Even though there is religious freedom in public and private schools, there is a tendency to pray before classes begin.

All Peruvian teens go to school, even those who live in the jungle. The time of day they go depends on their economic situation. Those who have limited economic resources work mornings and attend school in the afternoons. The number of hours teens spend in classes varies and starting times may vary, too—between 6:30 A.M. and 8:00 A.M.

Besides morning sessions, afternoon and evening classes are also offered. Typically, teens of low economic resources work mornings, selling products on the street, working as traveling sales representatives, or helping their parents at their jobs. Afternoon classes are from 1:00 P.M. until 6:00 P.M. Teenagers who work in the morning must return home quickly to eat lunch and get to school on time.

Teens who study in the afternoon cover the same academic material as the others. When the morning students return home, though, they have the luxury of watching TV, doing homework, playing with friends—or doing domestic chores. Young Peruvians are programmed to do housework as a part of their daily routine. Domestic duties may include cleaning windows, washing dishes, and making beds. If the family has a maid, then the teen is given other duties. Peruvian children always help out around the house. If a teen's parents own a small business, then the teen must help out there for several hours on weekends. Even if there's no real work for the teen at the family business, he or she is expected to be there to learn the trade.

Teenagers spend their time at or near home. After morning classes and lunch are over, boys may go outside to play soccer. Female teens don't go out as much as males. If their homework has not been completed, they're busy working on it, because in Peru lots of homework is assigned. On average, Peruvian teens have about two hours of homework daily. After homework has been completed, they may watch TV for an hour, telephone friends, or go outside to play.

The routine described above is typical of middle- and upper-class teens. There is a gap between the social groups because opportunities for extracurricular activities are so varied. Almost all watch a little TV. Even the poorest families have a television, no matter how remote their village may be.

Young adults from 17 to 21 are already university students. They maintain much the same routine as the young teens described. The difference is that many university students have to work part time in a business or start their practicum. Much depends on their parents' social status.

During these years, teens still live at home and depend economically on their parents. If parents need help supporting the household, these young adults will contribute. Some may even work full time to help their families. Students from privileged backgrounds don't have to work and are free to concentrate on their studies. This, in their parents' eyes, is their job. Nonetheless, all teens are obligated to work upon completing their university degree. This is what is termed the practicum.

FAMILY LIFE

Ideally, the whole family eats together at the main meal—lunch. Family members may have different schedules and families tend to be large, so that different school schedules are the norm. For example, by the time teens in junior high or high school come home to eat lunch, younger siblings in elementary school will have already eaten. Parents' schedules vary as well. In the evening the family may sit down together to watch a soap opera.

Weekends are when families come together—particularly in Lima, the country's capital. The family eats breakfast and lunch together. They talk about what they did during the week, joke, and maintain an informal atmosphere. On weekends the extended family may drop by. Normally, the teen is with his or her family until about 1:00 P.M. on Saturdays. After teenagers share this time with their families they may go out to play, take in a movie, or do homework. On Sundays, families usually go to church or mass together.

A high percentage of both parents work, since the economic situation in Peru is not strong. Stay-at-home mothers routinely take on extra jobs to make ends meet. Even the upper class has been affected by the high cost of living in Peru. In response, these women create businesses at home. For example, they may sell clothes or cosmetics to their friends. In other social classes women work as much as men do. This is true in all three regions of Peru. In mountainous areas women sell produce or crafts in the markets, while men work in agriculture. The situation is similar in the jungle areas.

In the lower classes, females and males have different responsibilities. Working in the fields, for instance cultivating and sowing, are regarded as masculine jobs while selling or preparing food is considered a female chore. Middle-class women frequently sell cosmetics or clothes to friends, while lower-class women sell food on the streets from small wagons. Items other than food—clothes, for example—are considered to be neither masculine nor feminine, so both men and women may sell them.

Education is seen as a way to improve one's lot in life. Many families have worked their way up to the middle class by obtaining university degrees—especially those who specialized in engineering: "Peru is one of the Latin American countries [with] the largest number of female engineers" (Morote). However, some areas of engineering are problematic for women. One example is the country's mining industry. Few women work in the mines due to a widespread belief that that is men's work. Nonetheless, the number of women in this field is increasing. Women have entered this field because they can earn more money. They're no longer looking for traditional careers; instead, they are looking for careers that will bring them more money and mobility. Another field attractive to women is medicine.

Nursing is definitely considered to be a feminine career, and it is rare to see males study nursing. Women also work as stewardesses, hotel hostesses, and kindergarten and day care workers. There are no written regulations on what males and females must study, but there are cultural rules governing the career paths females and males should take.

Peruvian work schedules and school schedules are fairly rigid. If a parent has his or her own business there is some flexibility, but a parent would not typically leave a job to watch a child's soccer game. School schedules are just as inflexible. The student is either present at school to take an exam or quiz, or he or she doesn't take it at all. There is no exception to the rule. If the student is an athlete and misses class due to a sports obligation, it is his or her duty to catch up on school material. The idea behind this rigidity stems from the different schedules at the elementary, junior high, and high school levels. At the university level there does tend to be more flexibility.

There is no minimum legal drinking age, and young teens can routinely be found drinking a beer or two after soccer games. Peru does not have much of a problem with teenage alcohol abuse. The minimum legal driving age is 14 years with the permission of one's parents. However, no one at the age of 14 owns his or her own car, unless the teen's family is wealthy.

Peruvians might buy their first car by the time they are 25. It's very hard to buy and maintain a car in Peru, especially for teenagers, because of the costs. Typically, teens use their parents' cars. Parents are more likely to lend their cars to their teenagers when they reach university age rather than while they're still in high school. The norm in Peru is that parents will lend the family car to a teen if he or she is attending university. If a high school teenager has a party to attend, then the parents will drive the youth and pick him or her up after the party. Should the teenager have a boyfriend or girlfriend, the parents will frequently pick him or her up too. In other words, the parents function as chauffeurs for those youths still in high school.

There is a distinct difference between rich and poor when it comes to family life. A poor family will vacation at a nearby beach and take their food. A rich family will vacation in a more exotic place, such as Miami or Europe. Poorer teenagers have to work in order to help out the household. Rich teens have a lot of free time. One of the few activities all have in common is watching television. They watch the same national programs—soap operas. Another similarity is school activities. There is uniformity in what is being taught to the two groups. In 1972, there was a socialist reform in Peru. This implied that all schools were to have the same quality of teaching, even the private schools.

In 1994, the schools started to differentiate themselves but they still maintained consistency. Up to 1994, rich and poor teens wore the same school uniforms. In 1999, private schools insisted upon special attire to differentiate private schools from state, or public, ones.

In recent years economic pressure has led to significant changes in family life. Since the early 1990s, women have entered the paid work force. The mother was once at home during meal times, but now she is not always present. In lower classes, young, single girls from the mountainous regions worked as maids. They worked during the day and attended school at night. Nowadays, married women with children dominate this realm. They take positions as maids to the upper-middle classes, working from Monday until Saturday. The economic situation of the last few years has affected all. Those struggling hardest are members of the lower classes, for example, those working as maids. Previously, when young maids got married they would leave their jobs to become housewives and attend to their own families. This traditional situation is no longer possible for some.

Another change since the socialist reform occurred in secular education. Until recently, anyone who employed a maid was required by law to allow time off for her to attend night school. In 1994, when the laws changed, employers were given the freedom to decide whether to send maids to school or not. In this manner, economics have altered the females' roles in the family structure, particularly in the lower classes.

There hasn't been a fad among Peruvian teens to Americanize themselves. Perhaps the only Americanization, if any, can be seen in the clothing, which is bought in the United States. There seems to be more influence by Japan or the Asian countries rather than from the United States. Asian influence can be found in food and clothing styles.

TRADITIONAL AND NONTRADITIONAL FOOD DISHES

For breakfast, most Peruvian teenagers eat bread and milk, but if the family is poor, they will substitute tea for milk. Those in the jungle areas normally eat yucca and plantain in the morning. In the mountainous regions, they might eat bread with sweet potato (a particularly popular combination) and *atole* (oatmeal porridge) for breakfast. Breakfasts are hearty compared to those on the coast—in Lima, for example—because extra energy is needed for agricultural work.

Lunch may consist of rice and a dish with meat and/or vegetables, such as *estofado de pollo*, chicken with vegetables. Those who can't afford meat eat legumes such as beans and lots of potatoes. In all Peruvian dishes, the potato is an important element. There are more than 3,000 types of potatoes in Peru. Potatoes are prepared differently depending upon their shape, size, and color. For example, small yellow ones are cut into pieces and eaten with meat, while red ones are boiled and white ones fried. The potato is a staple in all regions of Peru for every meal.

Eating meat (beef, pork, fish) is common in all three social classes. Those who cannot afford meat as often increase their intake of legumes to obtain daily iron and protein. Legumes are normally boiled with salt, potatoes, and a piece of bacon or herbs for flavoring.

Tamales—beef or chicken rolled in a corn flour patty, then wrapped in a cornhusk for cooking—are a traditional food eaten only on weekends. Peruvian tamales are identical to Mexican ones except for the spicy flavoring of the latter. Peruvians substitute a tomato sauce. Peruvians eat tamales topped with chopped onions and accompanied by a cup of coffee, something that most Mexicans might frown upon. Another traditional food is *anticucho a la parrilla* (grilled bull's heart). This dish is only eaten in

October (when *Cristo morado* is honored; see the section Religious Practices below) and on a few other festival days. Other than those traditional food dishes served on certain days or months, the Peruvian diet is consistent with white rice and chicken with vegetables.

Peruvians on a budget go to open markets because food is much cheaper there. Those who are more well-off go to supermarkets. Depending upon where people live, they may also go hunting for their food. There are indigenous groups in the jungles that are not poor but rather want to preserve their cultural heritage, part of which is to hunt for food in the wild. They may hunt monkeys, alligators, turtles, and other animals. Some Peruvians raise animals such as chickens to eat.

The Peruvian diet is well balanced even though it's high in carbohydrates. There may be a scarcity of milk or of meat due to high prices, but protein and iron are provided in legumes. Teens in Peru enjoy the foods that make up this balanced diet and have not been tempted by the fast food industry. American-owned hamburger and pizza chains have cropped up in Peru, but teens have not really substituted fast foods for their Peruvian dishes. They may eat fast food as a snack when out with friends, but they will still return home for a real meal. There isn't an appetite for international foods. Young Peruvians prefer traditional, homemade meals like white rice and meat. Therefore, there are few conflicts among teens and parents about diet.

SCHOOLING

Schools in Peru are different from those in the United States. Students must arrive on time for classes; otherwise the doors close and they are left outside. Inside the classroom, the teacher's ideas are respected without question. All students are quiet, in their seats, taking notes and asking questions only when the teacher grants permission.

At the high school level, the teacher constantly checks homework. At the university, the professor thinks nothing of doubling or even tripling the amount of homework. It's a student's obligation to find time to complete it. Homework at this level is not checked. Students are more self-motivated, in particular those attending national universities. A university professor arrives for class and discusses the material without correcting homework, so it's the student's responsibility to read the material and understand it. Students are on their own once at the university.

Since attendance is considered the student's obligation, teachers do not have to make an effort to entertain students or worry whether they are having a good time in class. Strategy games are not practiced in the classroom since students are required to learn the material as presented. As one Peruvian noted, "The professor's idea is you work hard and learn the material. The professor could care less if the student is bored. They are very domineering" (Maguiña-Ugarte; Morote). Some teachers are less rigid and do incorporate group activities.

Students are obligated to complete, at a minimum, five grades. Junior high and high school are grades 6 through 10. There is one exam for each course every two months. If a student fails two classes he or she can take a makeup exam during summer months. Should a student fail a summer makeup exam, he or she repeats the entire year. If a student fails three classes, he or she also repeats the academic year. Exams at the end of the academic year determine whether teenagers pass to the next grade as well as whether they enter university after completing 10th grade.

There are two kinds of schooling systems: national (public) and private. National universities have high academic ratings and offer a variety of career choices. Examples are the Universidad Católica del Perú and the Universidad de Ingeniería del Perú. These two institutions are prestigious and known for their good academic programs, thus there is a mixture of rich and poor teens who attend. It would be hard to decide which system is better—the privatized or the national schooling system, since both offer a good education. Teens choose based upon economics and career needs.

The state pays for all public school education. If the school is private then the parents pay. There are also scholarships for private schools, based on academic performance and economic necessity. Private schools are obligated by the Peruvian government to have at least 10 percent of their student body on scholarships.

Students may enter a university at age 16 if their grade point average is high enough. If a student with a high grade point average decides to attend a private university, he or she can apply for a scholarship. A teenager graduating from private school and entering a private university will pay more without exception; however, if a teen comes from a national high school and enters a private university, the tuition may be lowered or eliminated entirely. Much depends upon economics. The differentiation in the price gives all, rich or poor, an opportunity to go to a university if they have a high grade point average.

There are some schools for teens with special needs. For example, while there are not a vast number of schools for children with Down's syndrome or other challenges, some do exist. There are also schools offering adult education, which is very popular. Special programs for gifted students are new in the Peruvian curriculum.

Between 1972 and 1994, a socialist system was implemented in the schools, and acknowledging or rewarding a student for academic merits was not allowed. The socialist idea was that all students were the same. No individual academic awards were given; however, group (classroom) awards were handed out. Today, academic rewards are awarded to deserving individuals.

Peru also has a number of trade schools or, as they are sometimes called, technical schools. These train students to become secretaries, technical nurses, mechanics, translators, interpreters, and so on. All trade schools require a student to have completed elementary school. Technical courses of study vary from one to three years depending upon the type of certification desired. Students receive certificates upon satisfactory completion of their coursework.

There are specific requirements for each career. To be an elementary or high school teacher, the applicant must have a university degree. It takes five years to get a degree to teach elementary through high school. In general, those teaching at these levels are Peruvian, but at the university level there are many professors from other Latin American countries.

Peruvian parents of all economic levels view education as valuable and important. Some see it as a gateway to riches while others view it as a status symbol. It's the norm for parents to urge their children to continue their education. This demand is not only at a nuclear family level, but also at a social one. In Peru, there is a special type of police for students who are spotted playing hooky. When spotted, police pick these students up and take them to a detention hall where parents must come to claim them. Before the police release a youth to his or her parents, parents must explain why the child was not in school. Sometimes, the parents are even punished.

SOCIAL LIFE

Peruvian teens meet other teens at parties on Saturdays or Sundays, at school, or at soccer games. If they are from the upper-middle class, they may meet others in a social club or at a society barbecue. Teens of all social classes meet each other at parties.

Teenagers are allowed to choose their own dates. There may be certain influence from parents in their teens' choice of dates. Should parents be totally against their teens' dates, then parents and their teens will negotiate or these teens will see their dates behind their parents' backs. Females have more restrictions because "Parents usually don't like any of the boyfriends [a] girl brings home. They suggest that the female teen not have a boyfriend until she is in the university" (Morote 2000). Once in university, females have more freedom.

As do most teens around the world, Peruvian teens love to go to dances; however, parents insist upon knowing where a dance will take place and with whom their teen will be going. Since teens do not own cars, parents will drive teens to and from dances. Parents give their teens freedom to participate in different activities with different acquaintances, but they are always vigilant from a distance: "If it's a public party, parents insist teens go in a group. Thus, parents can watch with whom the teen goes out. Parents definitely prefer that teenagers go in a group rather than in pairs or by themselves" (Morote 2000). In the last couple of years there has been a boom in cellular telephones in Peru; the telephones are imported from Japan and are so cheap that everyone has one, even those who are poor. "It's the 'thing' to have a cellular phone if you're a teenager. Parents, of course, enjoy this new technology because they can constantly check on the whereabouts and associations of their teen" (Morote 2000).

Rich teens do not mingle with poor teens unless there is a celebrity performing in town like Ricky Martin or Michael Jackson. Then they mingle assuming tickets are affordable to all.

Socially acceptable behavior for teenagers in Peru depends on where a family lives and a youth's age. For example, in the jungle areas, it's common to see female teens in a miniskirt and a light, short blouse. This attire would be inappropriate for someone living in the mountains. On the coast, teens tend to be bolder in terms of clothing, although not to the point of vulgarity. Parents prefer that their teenagers dress more modestly, but teens are teens. There is no great difference in styles of dress from styles in the United States. Teenagers wear jeans, T-shirts, blouses, dresses, and tennis shoes. Hairstyles vary according to the fashions.

The behavior of males when socializing with each other is to use much slang, including swearing, but they are more cautious of language when female teens are around. The same is true for females. In mixed groups they tend to use a more standardized language.

In public, young couples may be seen holding hands or holding each other around the waist. This is not viewed as being in poor taste. However, they must look for a private place to kiss. If a couple is out in public "kissing themselves out of control, people see that as bad taste. There is a certain social pressure [in regard to what] people do not like to see in public, such as kissing that goes beyond a peck on the cheek or lips" (Maguiña-Ugarte 2000; Morote 2000).

In all social groups parents monitor their teenagers' behavior, even if from a distance. One of parents' greatest fears is that their daughters might become pregnant. Some social groups promote abstinence before marriage. Parents are open-minded about the female and male bodies, and they teach teenagers about sexual relations and implications. This education is extended to the national and private schools, which also encourage teenagers to abstain from sex before marriage. Parents caution their children to use condoms if they do plan to have sex, but they do not actively and specifically promote birth control. Gynecological visits and birth control are not often practiced in the country because parents either trust that sex is not being practiced or they turn a blind eye to it. In the last few years, school education programs have addressed birth control. Birth control devices such as condoms are free from any health center, but parents and professors continue to preach about abstaining from sex until marriage.

In some sectors, premarital sex is taboo. It is not accepted socially, and unfortunately it's females who suffer the social pressures. If a female teen becomes pregnant, parents are disappointed, angry, and worried about what her future might bring. About a generation ago there was a certain social pressure for a young couple to marry if a girl became pregnant. Parents do, still, advise couples to get married before signs of a pregnancy appear. Although marriage is not obligatory, should the female not marry she becomes an element of shame to her family. She is viewed as a failure. A teenaged, single mother in Peru endures social criticism along with a tarnished reputation: Many men will invite her on a date hoping only to have sexual relations with her. Her chances of establishing a serious relationship are remote.

A young, single mother reverts to a stage of adolescence in which she goes out only with a chaperone and parents become much more vigilant of the teen's whereabouts. At this stage, they fear she may become pregnant again. After a time there is a possibility a teenaged single mother may get married, but the chances are slim. Social pressure to abstain from sex before marriage ties into Catholicism. It is one of the oldest and strongest religions in Peru; thus, its ideologies have long penetrated the country with a doctrine of the female as pure and sacred.

RECREATION

Male teenagers play sports much more often than female teenagers, but all have fun when they go to parties, watch TV, or go to the movies. Organized sports include soccer for males and volleyball for females. At school they may organize their own teams to play against other classes or schools. Organized teams can also be found in neighborhoods, where one neighborhood team may play against another. This is true for both soccer and volleyball. Popular sports that all Peruvians—adults, too—follow are soccer, for men, and volleyball, for women. Sometimes men may play volleyball with women, but hardly ever does one see females playing soccer with males. Volleyball has been a national sport since Peru won a world championship in female volleyball.

Women and men play basketball together. However, teens do not play this sport as often as the others mentioned. Basketball requires a special court to play on and many schools do not have this, while soccer and volleyball can be played anywhere without special equipment. Teenagers do form teams in basketball, but there are no official games. It is more of a leisure sport for those who have a basketball court. Usually, the schools that offer basketball equipment are private. Only the higher social classes have access to this kind of sport.

Teofolo Cubilla is one of Peru's national soccer heroes, while Cecilia Tait is the female national hero in volleyball. As in any country, all keep up with their favorite players and the positions they play: in Peru, this means volleyball especially, due to their championship title. There are really no other recreational activities besides those mentioned above. Some teens practice swimming but there are no teams or competitions for this sport.

Female teens in the upper-middle class take aerobic classes for exercise. Some are preoccupied with their physical image. Male teens of all classes play soccer purely for exercise. They are not as concerned with their appearance. Females belonging to the lower classes either play volleyball or do no formal exercise at all. Taking aerobics at a gym requires money and therefore it is something women in the lower classes cannot afford. Jogging or exercising at home or in a public gym, to let off steam or tension, is not popular in Peru. Teens have little free time due to the quantities of homework they have from school, but tension and trauma are not issues. If these conditions exist, they are manifested differently than in the United States.

ENTERTAINMENT

It's in vogue to do what Peruvians call chatting. There are computer centers where teens can surf the Internet as well as chat with teens from all over the world. In all locations, even in remote areas, *centros de cómputos*, *cafés cibernéticos*, or *cabinas de Internet* may be found. A teen pays 25 cents to use a computer for an hour and then the teen can have fun communicating with strangers. This is a new entertainment for Peruvians. All classes of teens go to the *centros de cómputos* because the vast majority of

Teen bandmembers march in a parade, Peru. Courtesy of Olivia Rodriguez Morales.

them do not have personal computers. Some upper-class teens do have them at home, but they don't use them for the Internet. The phone system in Peru is very expensive. Teens with home computers surf the Internet only for quick reference because of the high costs of using the phone. Teens also go to where their parents work to use the computer for homework, in order to economize on telephone bills.

In the 1970s in Lima, teens listened to American music—disco—yet with a large migration of people from the mountainous and jungle regions into Lima, *chicha* music and mountain music can now be heard all over Lima. *Chicha* originated in Peru's jungle regions. The music is a mixture of salsa and *cumbia* (a popular dance of Colombia and Panama). Music from the mountainous areas is classified as *huaynas* or *huayno* (also known as *música serrana*). Many people characterize it as typically Peruvian. Some instruments include indigenous flutes (*quenas*), drums, and trumpets. The dance that accompanies this music is a *zapateo*, which requires fast stomping and pounding of the feet. *Chicha* and *música serrana* have vigorously penetrated all social classes. Teens delight in Peruvian music—*chicha* and *música serrana*—rather than international music. It's possible to hear such musicians as Luis Miguel from Mexico, but without a doubt Peruvian music has taken the country by storm. The music is viewed as a folkloric music of Peru. *Chicha* music may be folkloric, but it is at the top of the billboard charts as the hip music of the twenty-first century among teens of Peru. Another wave of music that has hit Lima very strongly is African music. This music comes from the Peruvians of African origin. It is sensual and includes a lot of movement.

Peruvian dance clubs are differentiated by age. There are plenty of dance clubs operating especially for teenagers and offering all kinds of music. Anyone can go to any dance club, but signs outside clubs advise people on what certain age group they will find inside. For example, a club may have the ages 15 to 20 years old posted. Those who go in are sure to find that the majority of the crowd is within that age range. No one is restricted to any one type of dance club, and in all dance clubs there is a variety of music to please most, if not all, tastes.

Boys and girls are allowed to dance in public; it is also common for females to invite males to dance. However, if a couple is dancing to a slow rhythm and they are hugging each other so closely that the two bodies seem like one, it's interpreted as crude and in bad taste and is heavily criticized. Peruvians tend to be reserved when it comes to slow music. Dancing is for Peruvians a form of diversion; it doesn't imply anything sexual. Couples may switch partners without restriction because teens are merely entertaining themselves.

Another form of entertainment particular to Peru is politics. Teens become interested in politics while very young. In Peru, families look forward to talking about politics during meals or after a game of soccer, and they will "drink a beer and talk, particularly, about politics...The jokes and atmosphere are very politicized" (Maguiña-Ugarte; Morote). Another form of entertainment is drinking small amounts of alcohol. Perhaps because it's not forbidden, teenagers tend to set their own, reasonable limits for drinking.

RELIGIOUS PRACTICES AND CULTURAL CEREMONIES

Eighty percent of Peruvians are Catholic, 10 percent Evangelist, and the remainder follow a variety of religions. Many fiestas revolve around Catholicism. Typical are national festivals such as the October ritual of honoring the *Cristo morado*, the dark-complexioned Christ. In this festival, there are processions, parties, and traditional foods. On the 31st of August, in Lima, there is a national fiesta in honor of *Santa Rosa de Lima*. Celebrations on these two occasions are similar.

Teens practice religious fiestas but in a pagan way. The mixture of the Inca culture and Catholicism has created a hybrid manifested in these practices.

Religious masses are more loosely interpreted than traditional Catholic ones. There is more discussion and even singing. University students attend if they want but are not obligated to. Holy Week is one of the traditions in Peru that deviates from normal Catholic practices. For young Peruvians, Holy Week is viewed as a time to take a vacation—to go camping or travel through the country. Teens view Holy Week as fun rather than as a time of penitence or prayer, as people in many other Latin American countries view it.

In general, teens are not strong practitioners of any religious customs. Teens have their religion and if they feel the need to visit church they know where to go. Some teens follow the Catholic religion passionately; others appear to rebel against the Catholic order. Rebels distance themselves from the system, but they may return after a certain age.

Evangelical Christianity is growing. One reason for evangelists' success in luring some away from Catholicism, especially those among the lower classes, are their programs offering food and housing. Some who convert do so in order to relieve economic pressures. Members of the lower classes may feel that help from the Evangelists will pull them out of poverty. There is apparent conflict among Peruvians today as to whether or not to abandon traditional religious practices. Evangelists try to disrupt Catholic masses, for example. As one observer noted, "During Holy Week when the Catholics give their masses, the young Evangelists create chaos in front of the Catholic churches. Their intentions are to bother and upset the Catholics" (Morote 2000). This is very predominant in Lima. Teens living in the mountains comply with their Catholic obligations because they view religious activities as sacred.

The traditional ceremony to introduce a female into adulthood occurs on her 15th birthday. The *quinceañera* celebrates a girl's reaching the threshold of adulthood in society. She is now old enough to date. The *quinceañera* in Peru consists primarily of a girl dressing up in a pink dress and is more of a cultural ceremony than it is religious. In the upper-middle classes, this celebration is slowly dying out because some view it as degrading to females: "Here's my product, who will marry her?" Instead, on their 15th birthday females in the upper-middle classes receive special presents from their families. The gift may be a trip to Europe, an intensive English course abroad (usually in the United States), or something else the young teen can use. No corresponding ritual for male adolescents exists.

CONCLUSION

By and large, teens in Peru are like other teens around the world. They go to school, do their homework and chores, and perhaps work at part-time jobs. Some points to consider about this group are its strong dedication to academic studies and a zest for traditional food along with a reluctance to fall prey to American fast food chains. What defines the young Peruvian population is its preference for national rather than American or other international music, and its interest in politics. Moreover, teens of both sexes willingly accept their required enlistment for military training at the age of 16.

When examining social and cultural aspects of Peru one must take into consideration the violent political impact of the 1980s, the imprint of which is still felt. The family structure of the 1980s was that of a solid harmonious family, and the ideals of Karl Marx and other socialists were held in high regard. In the 1990s, group projects and activities disappeared while individualism and capitalism emerged. Such characteristics are noted in society and encapsulated in literature as in the Peruvian plays "El día de la luna" by playwright Eduardo Adrianzén, or "Vladimir," by Alfonso Santisteban. The latter author's intentions are quite obvious: to criticize Peru's liberalism. There seems to be nostalgia for the conservative socialist years.

RESOURCE GUIDE

Amnesty International. *Peru, Open Letter to Presidential Candidates*. London: International Secretariat, 2000.

"Background Notes: Peru, October 1998." 29 April 2001. http://www.state.gov/www/background_notes/peru_1098_bgn.html.

Birdsall, Nancy, and Carol Graham, eds. *New Markets, New Opportunities? Economic and Social Mobility in a Changing World*. Washington, D.C.: Brookings Institutional Press, 2000.

Bowles, Ian A., and Glenn T. Prickett, eds. *Footprints in the Jungle: Natural Resource Industries, Infrastructure, and Biodiversity Conservation*. Oxford: Oxford University Press, 2001.

Burt, Jo-Marie. "Martin Pumar: Interview with a Peruvian Activist." *NACLA Report on the Americas* 31, 1 (1997): 47–50.

Cadena, Marisol de la. *Indigenous Mestizos: The Politics of Race and Culture in Cuzco, 1919–1991*. Durham, N.C.: Duke University Press, 2000.

Castro de la Mata, Ramiro, and Maritza Rojas Albertini. *Los jóvenes en el Perú: opiniones, actitudes y valores-1997*. Lima: CEDRO, 1997.

Castro-Urioste, José. "Modernidad y teatro en el Perú." Literatura peruana contemporánea. The 21st Annual Cincinnati Conference on Romance Languages and Literatures. Kingsgate Conference Center, Cincinnati, Ohio 10 May 2001.

Central Intelligence Agency. "Peru." *The World Factbook*. http://www.odci.gov/cia/publications/factbook/geos/pe.html (accessed April 29, 2001).

Chanfreau, Maria Francoise. "La vivienda en los pueblos jóvenes de Arequipa y Trujillo: creación de una nueva tipología regional." *Bulletin de l'Institut Francais d'Etudes Andines* 17, 1 (1998): 37–64.

Cisneros, Luis Jaime. "Peru's Child Workers Stake Their Claims." *UNESCO Courier* 5 (1999): 39.

CNNenEspanol.com. "Planean Segunda vuelta en Perú para el 20 de mayo, pero la fecha puede cambiar." 25 May 2001. http://cnnenespanol.com/2001/latin/04/11/peru.elex/.

Cooper, Marc. "Peru and the Post-Fujimori Future." *The Nation* 272, 14 (2001): 13–17.

Energy Information Administration. "Peru." http://www.eia.doe.gov/emeu/cabs/peru.html (accessed April 29, 2001).

The Europa World Year Book 2001. Vol. 2. London: Europa Publications, 2001.

Flindell Klarén, Peter. *Peru: Society and Nationhood in the Andes.* New York: Oxford University Press, 2000.

González-Cueva, Eduardo. "Conscription and Violence in Peru." *Latin American Perspectives* 27, 3 (2000): 88–102.

Henderson, James D, et al. *A Reference Guide to Latin American History.* Armonk, N.Y.: M. E. Sharp, 2000.

Higham, Robin, ed. *Official Military Historical Offices and Sources.* Westport, Conn.: Greenwood Press, 2000.

Hünefeldt, Christine. *Liberalism in the Bedroom: Quarreling Spouses in the Nineteenth Century Lima.* University Park, Pa.: Pennsylvania University Press, 2000.

Ilon, Lynn, and Peter Mook. "School Attributes, Household Characteristics, and Demand for Schooling: A Case Study of Rural Peru." *International Review of Education* 37, 4 (1999): 429–52.

Lonely Planet. "Peru." http://www.lonelyplanet.com/destinations/south_america/peru (accessed April 29, 2001).

Maguiña-Ugarte, Adriana. Personal interview, 28 November 2000.

Morote, Sofía. Interview with author, 5 December 2000.

Payne, Johnny, ed. and trans. *She-Calf and Other Quechua Folk/Tales.* Albuquerque: University of New Mexico Press, 2000.

Ravas Belloso, Jairo. "Juventud y actitud política." *Revista del Instituto del Pastoral Andina* 116 (September–October 1997): 2–4.

Sessarego, C. F. "Peru: Toward Equality in Marriage." *Journal of Family Law* 32, 2 (1994): 395.

Skoog, Don. "Peru Negro: Coastal Music and Dance in Peru." *American Visions* 12, 3 (1997): 24–28.

"Toledo y García captan por igual voto en blanco." *El Comercio.* http://noticias.rcp.net.pe/noticiaelec.phtml?NID=EK250501114843 (accessed May 25, 2001).

U.S. Government Printing Office. http://www.gpoaccess.gov/index.html (accessed January 24, 2004).

Nonfiction

Ferreira, César, and Dargent-Chamot, Eduardo. *Culture and Customs of Peru.* Westport, Conn.: Greenwood Press, 2002.

Fiction

Arguedas, José María. *Yawar Fiesta*. Translated by Frances Horning Barraclough. Austin: University of Texas Press, 1985.

Brenner E. Susan, and Kathy S. Leonard, eds. and trans. *Fire from the Andes*. Albuquerque: University of New Mexico Press, 1998.

McGahan, Jerry. *A Condor Brings the Sun*. San Francisco: Sierra Club Books, 1996.

Payne, Jonny, ed. and trans. *She-Calf and Other Quechua Folk Tales*. Albuquerque: University of New Mexico Press, 2000.

Pineda, Cecile. *The Love Queen of the Amazon*. Boston: Little Brown, 1992.

Scorza, Manuel. *Requiem for a Lighting Bolt*. Translated by Anna-Marie Aldaz. New York: Peter Lang, 2000.

Vallejo, César. *Tungsten*. Translated by Robert Mezey. Syracuse, N.Y.: Syracuse University Press, 1988.

Vargas Llosa, Mario. *Death in the Andes*. Translated by Edith Grossman. New York: Farrar, Straus and Giroux, 1996.

Wheeler, Kate. *When Mountains Walked*. Boston: Houghton Mifflin, 2000.

Web Sites

http://www.peruemb.org/
English. Peruvian Embassy.

http://www.best.com/~gibbons/index.html
English. Poetry, music, photos, etc.

http://www.travel.state.gov/
English. Travel tips to Central and South America.

http://www.rcp.net.pe/usa/
English. U.S. Embassy in Peru.

http://www.cultura.com.pe/
Spanish. Cultural information.

http://www.blythe.org/Perú-pcp/
Spanish and English. Peru's communist past.

http://www.peruonline.com/
Spanish and English. Variety: government, tourism, education, arts, etc.

http://www.cultura.com.pe/gastronomía/recetas/cocina/index.htm
Spanish. Food.

http://www.congreso.gob.pe/
Spanish. Peru's government.

http://www.peru.com/
Spanish. Variety of info: sensationalism, news, government, sports, chat, etc.

Pen Pal Information

http://www.hispaniconline.com/chat/
Hispanic Online—Chat.

http://74/http://www.geocities.com/MadisonAvenue/7293/
International Pen Friends—Americas.

http://www.argonet.co.uk/users/ed.morris/pals/
The Pen-Pal Group.

http://www.amigos.com/cgi-bin/w3com/start?ffe+guest
Spanish. Amigos.com.

http://www.pen-pal.com/
Student letter exchange.

Chapter 14

PUERTO RICO

Amarilis Hidalgo de Jesús

INTRODUCTION

The culture of Puerto Rican teens is complex. Puerto Rican teens come from a different social and ethnic background, which makes their culture unique when compared to the rest of the teen population in Latin America. The ethnic mix of Puerto Rican teens can be traced from the times of the Tainos to the arrival of the Spaniards and African slaves. During the nineteenth century, immigrants such as the French, Irish, Germans, and Italians settled down and combined with the already mixed population of Puerto Rico. Along with the Europeans came Chinese, Lebanese, and Venezuelan people who also married Puerto Rican women. Long after Spain lost political and economic control of Puerto Rico, Spanish immigrants continued arriving at the island.

At the end of the nineteenth century and after the Spanish American War in 1898 the accelerated Americanization of the island began. This resulted in a large migration of Puerto Ricans to the United States. The sons and daughters of Puerto Ricans who moved to the United States married whites, blacks, and Native Americans, adding a new racial and cultural component to the already diverse background of Puerto Rico. Cubans fleeing from the Cuban Revolution became the new immigrants to the island during the second half of the twentieth century. Dominicans and Haitians, in search of a better lifestyle, later replaced them.

Christopher Columbus came in 1493 to the island of Borikén—the native name given to Puerto Rico by the Tainos, which means "the great land of the valiant and noble Lord." This was his second trip to the Americas. He named the island San Juan, in honor of Saint John the Baptist, and the city of San Juan was named Puerto Rico because it was rich in ports. Years later the two names were reversed. Thus, Puerto Rico became the name of the island because of its great potential, and the capital city would come to be known as San Juan. By the time of the European discovery of Puerto Rico, Tainos already inhabited the island. They were descendants of the Arawak tribe that migrated from South America (more specifically the area of what is today known as Venezuela and Brazil) to the Caribbean. Tainos lived in small villages ruled by a chief and had a rudimentary culture and spent most of their time fishing and hunting. They were peaceful people who also believed in several gods. They called themselves Tainos, which means friendly people in their native tongue. At the beginning of the Spanish conquest, both Spanish and Taino cultures coexisted. The Spaniards took the natives as brides, conceiving mixed children called mestizos (racial mix of white people and indigenous people). Later, Spaniards mixed with the female black population brought as slaves to the island. Their children were called mulattos. Furthermore, the indigenous population mixed with the black population conceiving children known as sambos.

With the political and economic advances of the Spanish conquest, Spaniards subjected Tainos to slavery. They were also exposed to European illnesses, which contributed to the extermination of their culture and ethnicity. By the sixteenth century most of the indigenous population of the island had disappeared due to starvation, hard working conditions, suicides, epidemics, infant death, and a diaspora to other Caribbean islands. To replace Taino workers, the Spanish government brought African slaves to the island. They came after Catholic priest Father Bartolomé de las Casas wrote a letter to the Spanish government requesting the protection of the Taino people. However, the working and living conditions of the newcomers did not change. Black slaves were exposed to the same inhumane treatment and European illnesses that exterminated the native population.

A plantation system began to develop with the importation of black slaves. This system brought new changes to the Puerto Rican ethnic compound. More and more, colonizers mixed with the indigenous and black populations. The Puerto Rican people were born from those interracial marriages or partnerships. During the eighteenth century new immigrants arrived. Chinese and Lebanese immigrants, who worked as indentured servants in the construction of railroads, also combined with the already mixed population. By the middle of the nineteenth century came Irish, Italians, and Germans in search of fortune or better living conditions. Some French people came from Louisiana, while others, who escaped from the Haitian and other French Caribbean revolutions, entered as political exiles.

When Americans arrived in 1898, a new cultural and ethnic element was added. Before the invasion, Spain had controlled Puerto Rico politically, economically, and socially for four centuries. In 1898, with the Spanish American War (also known as the Cuban War) Spain lost all of her remaining possessions in the Caribbean and the Pacific. By that time, there was already a developed culture and social structure in the country. This culture was suddenly trapped within the new American culture. It was imposed on the islanders since the first moment of the invasion that occurred on July 6 and lasted through July 25, 1898. After the war, Spain revoked her authority over Puerto Rico and the United States did not recognize Puerto Ricans as legal citizens. It was not until 1917, with the Jones Act, when the United States gave Puerto Ricans American citizenship. Since then, political, economic, and social ties between Puerto Rico and the United States have expanded.

Before 1940, American governors were imposed on the people of Puerto Rico by the United States. In 1940 the United States granted the islanders the right to elect their own government. However, it was not until 1946 that the first Puerto Rican governor was elected by popular vote. From 1940 to 1946 the American government appointed Don Jesús T. Piñero as the first Puerto Rican governor of the island. Following his term, Luis Muñoz Marín became the first governor to be elected by popular vote. Under his leadership Puerto Rico became an industrialized country that economically and politically depended on the United States. As a way to stabilize the Puerto Rican economy, Muñoz Marín—guided by the U.S. government—promoted a mass migration of Puerto Ricans to the United States. This forced migration was historically known as Operation Bootstrap. With it, cultural ties between Puerto Rico and the United States increased. Consequently, the Americanization of the island accelerated, bringing along a hybridization of Puerto Rican culture that was formerly a homogeneous Latin culture. For example, Puerto Ricans adopted some American cultural traditions and holidays celebrated in the United States. Thus, cultural ties between both nations expanded and complemented each other.

The official languages of Puerto Rico are Spanish and English. The majority of Puerto Ricans, however, refuse to learn English for historical, political, and ideological reasons. More and more, however, the majority of Puerto Rican teens have been forced to learn English as their second language. In certain ways Puerto Rican teens have an adequate knowledge of English. They have a better proficiency in reading and listening comprehension than in speaking and writing skills. English is a mandatory subject in public and private schools. The American federal government, in conjunction with the Puerto Rican government, sponsors intensive English language training for teens in summer camps and in study abroad programs. They also support special public-language, immersion schools, such as the one located in the town of Aguadilla. There are also opportunities for teens to study and improve their English skills in private language academies such as the Berlitz Academy in San Juan. Programs like these allow students to be totally immersed in the English language.

Due to the political relationship between the United States and Puerto Rico, Puerto Rico has been known as a commuter nation. This denotes the fact that Puerto Ricans travel and move constantly between Puerto Rico and the United States. Some Puerto Rican teenagers are born in the United States and raised on the island, while others are born on the island and raised in the United States. This migratory pattern is also known as the cycle of transmigration, which makes the culture of Puerto Rican teens distinct from those in the rest of the Hispanic world. Puerto Ricans express themselves through the Afro-Caribbean culture of the region, and at the same time, they integrate into their culture the white and black cultures of the United States. This explains new Puerto Rican dances and rhythms, which are a mix of Afro-Caribbean music with jazz, pop music, and rap. This blend of cultures is also seen in Puerto Rican teens' daily language, which is completely mediated by English taken, in most cases, from American music, movies, and videos.

TYPICAL DAY

The typical daily life of a Puerto Rican teen varies according to the kind of school he or she attends. They may wake up around 6:00 A.M. on school days and 10:00 A.M. or 11:00 A.M. on weekends. In Puerto Rico the majority of students are at school from 8:00 A.M. to 3:30 P.M. Other kids attend school either from 7:30 A.M. to 12:30, or from 12:30 to 5:30 P.M. The teens who begin at 7:30 A.M. or 12:30 noon attend a school program called interlocking. They are supposed to leave school premises immediately following the school day. However, some of them—especially those who study in the morning—will hang around school property or go downtown before they return home. Some children rely on their parents for transportation, while others use public transportation or the school bus (when it is provided by the school district; private schools are not entitled to provide this service—parents usually have a contract with a private bus company). While private schools charge for breakfast and lunch, each public school district offers those free of charge.

Normally, a lunch period lasts from 11:00 A.M. to 11:50 A.M. for Puerto Rican teens. During this time they have lunch in the school cafeteria or leave school premises to eat at home or buy lunch in a nearby cafeteria. This type of school program is called full term. When school is over, Puerto Rican teens go home, hang around town, or go to the music school called Escuela Libre de Música (Free School of Music), where they can learn to play an instrument, join a band, or sing in a choir.

FAMILY LIFE

There is no such thing as a typical family life in Puerto Rico. The structure of the family varies according to social and economic circumstances. There are four kinds of family structures on the island: the extended family system; the nuclear family; father, mother, children, and stepchildren; and the mother-based or single-mom family. In the city, most parents work in industries, professional jobs, or odd jobs. In the suburbs, the mother traditionally stays home while the father works outside. In some cases parents do not have any income. The government helps these families economically. They live in housing subsidized by the government.

In Puerto Rican society, the roles of women and men are clearly defined. Traditionally, women are in charge of housework and children. Men perform odd jobs around the house (when there is a man in the household). The education of children is usually the mother's responsibility. She is the person who supervises school duties and monitors extracurricular activities. She is also responsible for cooking, organizing, and planning daily family activities as well as social activities in and outside the home. Fathers are mainly in charge of providing the income. Most families spend time together after work or when school is over.

Puerto Rican family members eat at the same time but some family members may eat at the dining room table while others may eat on the couch in the living room. Traditionally, the last person in the house to eat is the mother because she is busy preparing the meal. Dining hours fluctuate between four and six o'clock in the evening. Some families do not eat at the same time due to conflicting work schedules. Sundays are usually family days, however. Sunday is a day when most families gather at the grandparents' or another extended family member's home.

In Puerto Rico the legal drinking age is 18 and the legal smoking age is 16. However, teenagers are allowed to drink at home on special occasions without being penalized by legal authorities. Teens are permitted to drive at the age of 16, which is similar to the laws in most American states. They take a written test that grants them the right to apply for a driver's permit. After six months, teens are allowed to take a driving test that, if passed, gives them their driver's license. However, it is not common in Puerto Rico for a teen to own a car. Only some wealthy teenagers have that privilege.

TRADITIONAL AND NONTRADITIONAL FOOD DISHES

Although Puerto Rican cooking is similar to both Spanish and Mexican cuisine, it is a unique, tasty blend of Spanish, African, Taino, and American influences. Puerto Rican dishes are characterized by indigenous seasonings and ingredients such as coriander, papaya, cacao, kumquat, celery, plantains, and *yame* (a root). Native Puerto Ricans call their style *cocina criolla* (Creole cuisine). This cooking style can be traced back to the eating habits of Tainos, blacks, and Spaniards. The Taino diet was mainly composed of seafood, tropical fruits, and corn. Spaniards added beef, pork, rice, wheat, and olive oil to that diet. Sugar, okra, and taro (a starch known also as yautia in Puerto Rico) came with the arrival of African slaves and gave new food components to the Puerto Rican diet. The combination of these ingredients, along with other ethnic dishes and ingredients brought by new immigrants, created what is known today as *cocina criolla*. For example, the Venezuelan *ayacas* (a kind of white corn tamale dish with pork) became the culinary inspiration for Puerto Rican *pasteles* (a kind of tamale made of plantain, green banana, taro, pork, and Spanish spices). Italians brought pasta and tomato sauces. The Lebanese probably added Middle Eastern spices and falafel, a Middle Eastern dish that resembles *alcapurrias* (a blend of green bananas, taro, and meat). Chinese people developed the Chinese-Creole cuisine. Cubans brought *yuca frita* (fried manioc) and *mojito cubano* (Cuban rum drink). Dominicans brought their *morir soñando* drink (made of milk and mango or orange) and *mangú* (the equivalent of the Puerto Rican mashed plantains better known as *mofongo*). The Americans introduced meat pies and fast food. Ingredients and dishes passed from generation to generation resulted in the exotic combination of today's Puerto Rican cuisine.

Puerto Rican teens typically eat rice and beans and/or chickpeas (cooked with potato or pumpkin, tomato sauce, sausage, smoked ham, or pigs feet). *Tostones* (fried plantain), *mofongo* (mashed plantain), chicken, beef, stews, pasta, meat pies, seafood, roots such as taro, potatoes, yams, and vegetables such as lettuce, tomatoes, and breadfruit are all part of a teen's diet, as well. Due to the Americanization of the island, it is more and more appealing to teenagers to eat hamburgers, fries, pizza, and other American fast foods. Traditional foods are eaten on holidays and special occasions. These include rice with pigeon peas and pork, blood and rice sausages, *pasteles*, potato salad, and green bananas marinated in olive oil and onions.

A Puerto Rican teen's breakfast is usually a sandwich made of ham or *mortadella* (a kind of Spanish salami), cheese, and egg. This is accompanied by milk, juice, *malta* (a kind of sweet beer), or coffee. Lunches and dinners tend to be large in Puerto Rico. For these meals, a teen may eat a heavy plate of rice and beans, meat or chicken, ripe plantains or *tostones* and salad. They usually drink water, juice, or soda with their meals. It is more common for a teenager to drink soda instead of water, just as it is in the United States. Desserts are not commonly eaten at regular meals. Instead, Puerto Rican teens will have them for snacks. Most Puerto Rican desserts are made with coconut milk, cloves, and cinnamon. Tropical fruit jams like guava paste with white cheese are also popular.

In Puerto Rico, ingredients for meals are bought in supermarkets or at farmer's markets. There is a tendency to buy groceries weekly but mothers also like to shop daily for fresh vegetables, milk, bread, and meat. Frozen dishes are not very popular. However, Puerto Ricans frequently purchase frozen native foods such as *alcapurrias*, *pastelillos*, and *rellenos de papa* as snacks.

SCHOOLING

As in other Hispanic countries, education is mandatory in Puerto Rico until the age of 16. Although a free, public education is available to all, most middle- and upper-class parents tend to send their teens to private schools. Churches of different denominations sponsor most private schools in Puerto Rico. The most predominant ones are Catholic, Baptist, and Adventist. The curriculum of private Catholic schools is typically more academically rigorous than that of other schools. In most, the language of instruction is Spanish. English is taught as a second language. Nevertheless, there are bilingual schools where the language of instruction is English and Spanish is taught as a separate subject.

As in any other Latin American country, teachers are an important component in the life of a teen. They have a tendency to be strict. Sometimes they overextend their rules and power in the classroom but, at the same time, are also caring and loving with their students. Most believe in strong disciplinary actions that they enforce in and outside of the classroom. Still, teachers are seen as role models and figures of authority in the lives of students. Most parents will take a teacher's side, even if that teacher is not right in his or her demands. However, there are some parents who will take their child's side and some will interfere directly with learning and disciplinary measures required or administered by a teacher in his or her classroom.

A Puerto Rican teen's day at school is well organized. The first 30 minutes of the school day are dedicated to classroom announcements, class organization, and a small prayer or reflection session. In some schools, a pledge of the Puerto Rican and American flags is mandatory; in others, reciting or listening to the national anthems of Puerto Rico and the United States is required also. After that, teens go to the next period, which lasts for about 50 minutes. From 11:00 A.M. to 11:50 A.M. they have lunch (if they are in the full-term school program). They return to classes at noon and go until 2:50 P.M. From 3:00 P.M. to 3:30 P.M. they usually attend a club or a school activity or go back to their homeroom.

Teens study a variety of subjects at school. For example, in 10th grade they typically study general math and algebra, biology, health, English grammar and conversation, and English literature (American and/or British). They may also study Spanish grammar, Spanish literature (Spain, Latin American, Puerto Rican), music or art, the history of Puerto Rico, gym, and an elective. In 11th grade they study geometry or trigonometry, chemistry, health, English grammar and conversation, and English literature. They also study literature in Spanish, music or art, American history, gym, and an elective, as well. In 12th grade math and science subjects include pre-calculus or calculus and physics, while other subjects remain similar to those in prior grades. In religious schools students might study religion in addition to their basic courses. Some examples of electives a student might take are French, advanced courses in art or music, band, theater, driver's education, home economics, business courses, and photography. Gym classes are similar to those in the United States, with such sports as volleyball, basketball, baseball, softball, gymnastics, fencing, and track and field. School authorities promote field trips, especially those that focus on topics related to science or the social sciences. Students visit geological, historical, and environmental places in Puerto Rico and on the surrounding small islands. Some science-related field trips take place in Lajas (where the shining lagoon is located), Arecibo (home of the largest radio telescope in the world), Luquillo/El Yunque (where the only American rain forest is located), and Camuy (which has the third largest underground river in the world).

Sometimes private schools sponsor school field trips to the Caribbean islands, Mexico, or the United States.

Puerto Rican teens do not have study hall periods at school. They are expected to do their homework at home and bring it to school the following day. Those with poor study habits or learning disabilities may attend tutorial sessions in an after-school tutorial program sponsored by the government. When students exhibit behavior problems and are suspended from school, they are sent home. Puerto Rican schools do not have in-school or partial suspensions. Expelled students are not permitted on school premises until their parents reinstate them at school the following day. However, this system of punishment poses a problem to society because most of these teens end up staying at home, unsupervised.

Being creative is important in the education of a Puerto Rican teen. Students are encouraged to participate in theatrical plays, music performances, bands, choirs, and art exhibits. They constantly compete in science fairs, spelling bees, forensics, and choir competitions at the regional and national level, in which they apply knowledge and experience that they have acquired through their education. In art or industrial art classes they routinely build their own floats for the field day.

Puerto Rican teens may choose one of three high school concentrations when they attend public schools. They can major in general studies or business or attend a vocational school. If they choose the general studies concentration, their curriculum is oriented toward the sciences and liberal arts. If they choose a business concentration, they can major in accounting, marketing, or business administration. They may not have many literature courses, and they will have more flexibility with math and science courses in their last year of high school. Students who attend vocational schools study basic subjects (math, science, history, English, and Spanish) in the morning. Afternoons are dedicated to vocational training in the following areas: mechanical services, refrigeration, sewing, floral services, carpentry, nursing, food preparation, secretarial sciences, health services, drawing and graphic arts, drafting, beauty technicians, and many other technical programs.

In Puerto Rico, teachers, along with school and government authorities, constantly evaluate teens at school. Students take several tests and quizzes throughout the school year. In contrast to the education system in the United States, in Puerto Rico regular homework does not have a great impact on a student's grade because it is assumed that it is already a big component of the student's learning process. Students are evaluated more on their daily classroom performance and on class projects and exams

Happy high school graduates in Puerto Rico. Courtesy of Amarilis Hildalgo de Jesús.

than on homework. Grades, especially in private schools, are not inflated and the concept of extra credit is not well accepted in Puerto Rican schools. To be promoted to the next grade, a student has to have a D average in all subjects. If at the end of a school year a student has failed two subjects, he or she is not promoted to the next grade. This school policy creates educational problems among some teens, who become frustrated with the system and end up dropping out. On the other hand, teens who succeed and achieve an adequate score on the college entrance test will attend public colleges and universities. Others with lower grade point averages (GPAs) or lower scores on the college entrance text will attend private colleges and universities. A number of wealthy teens will attend colleges in the United States. The rest of the high school population will join the Puerto Rican skilled or nonskilled workforce or will migrate to the United States in search of better job opportunities.

It is mandatory for Puerto Rican teens to wear uniforms, including badges, to go to school. They are not allowed in schools without their uniforms. Uniforms mainly consist of jeans or casual pants (black, green, navy blue, brown, or cream) and a shirt (white or sky blue) for boys. Girls usually wear skirts or pants with dark-colored plaids or red. They also wear white or blue blouses. The most common school shoes for boys attending public school are black or blue sneakers. Boys who attend private schools only wear black or brown leather shoes. Girls attending private schools, on the contrary, wear white socks with low boots, moccasins, or other typical school shoes. Only girls who attend public schools are permitted to wear sneakers. Girls always want to be fashionably dressed at school, within the limits provided by their school's uniform code. If they attend public school, they may use make-up and their hair may be well styled. Girls who attend private school modify their make-up and hairstyle according to their school's dress code.

Puerto Rican teens dress casually outside of school. Jeans, T-shirts, shorts, skirts, and sandals are the daily attire. Girls and boys who are engaged in traditional religious practices dress more conservatively than do Catholic kids. Nevertheless, the tropical climate of the island invites teens to wear cotton, comfortable, and colorful clothes. As with teens in the United States and most Latin American countries, fashion influences how Puerto Rican teens dress. Boys tend to follow the *rapero* (rap) and rock style looks of the American casual teen fashion. Girls more often choose European fashion styles for formal events, but they also follow the American pop singer style when dressing casually. What is common to both genders is that they pay a lot of attention to their physical appearance.

SOCIAL LIFE

Puerto Rican teens socialize a great deal, much like teens in the United States. They get together with friends after school. They also chat on the phone, email friends, or surf the Internet and they have their own teenage coded language. On weekends, teens get together at friends' houses, attend dances and parties, go to a mall, or watch movies. It is trendy to go to San Juan, Ponce, or Mayaguez to walk or to dance in a disco. It is not typical of Puerto Rican students to stay after school to participate in sports or in a school club. Clubs usually meet during the last period of the school day. If students want to join a sports team, they do so with teams that play near their homes. Important activities for Puerto Rican teens include the science fair, dance club, choir, band, theater, and leadership activities on some school teams.

The most important activities during the academic year for a Puerto Rican teen are the Turkey Day race, field day, the prom or class night, and class day. In schools, a Thanksgiving Day or Turkey Day running competition is part of the American celebration of Thanksgiving in Puerto Rico. The competition takes place the Wednesday before Thanksgiving Day.

The prize for winning the competition is a turkey. Another important school activity is field day. During that day, track teams compete in local stadiums. Before the competition, a parade begins at school and ends in the stadium where track-and-field competitions are held. Cheerleaders carrying flags accompany the parade. School authorities and faculty members monitor students during these activities.

Graduation ceremonies are important to teens. Graduation is one of the busiest times of the year for high school students in Puerto Rico. School authorities, in conjunction with the graduating class's government association, sponsor class nights (in public schools) or prom (in private schools) along with class days. These social events are extremely important to Puerto Rican teens. Activities resemble junior high and high school graduations. Class nights are held in urban hotels or nightclubs, while proms are held on school premises or in small clubs. Class days are celebrated in places located in the countryside. Famous salsa and merengue singers or groups sing and play their music at the dance. Girls dress in expensive gowns that are usually made by a dressmaker. Boys wear sports jackets or formal suits. It is the custom for a male teen to invite his favorite girl to the prom. Boys invite the their prospective dates formally and even go to a girl's house to ask her father for permission to take her to class night/prom. In this patriarchal society, rules are different for girls than for boys. Girls are allowed to go to class night or prom if they go in groups, with an older sibling, or with a chaperone. On very few occasions, parents may allow a daughter to go alone to an event.

Previously in Puerto Rico, it was not common for junior high or high school students to engage in premarital sex, but as time goes by the statistics show that more and more teens are engaging in premarital sex. In Puerto Rico, 25 percent of the female teen population and 36 percent of the male teen population have engaged in premarital sexual intercourse (Teen Pregnancy Organization).

Just as in the United States, Puerto Rican society pressures males to have premarital sex. Peer pressure is a big component of a teenager's life. Boys in Puerto Rico are encouraged to be aggressive while females are taught to be reserved and are encouraged to remain virgins until they marry. There are, nonetheless, a high number of teen pregnancies. Statistics show that 29 percent of female teens between 15 and 19 years old have already given birth (Teen Pregnancy Organization). Most girls between 15 and 17 who get pregnant neither finish school nor get married. Forty-one percent live with a boyfriend or relative or stay at home with parents. Most also become trapped in the welfare system (Government of Puerto Rico Office).

Drugs are a constant dilemma in the lives of Puerto Rican teens. Fourteen percent of boys and 5 percent of girls reported that they used drugs or alcohol before their most recent sexual intercourse. Approximately 30 percent of the teen population in Puerto Rico have used or are presently using drugs (Government of Puerto Rico Office). Boys are more often the targets of drug dealers than are girls. Dealers introduce teens to marijuana and then later involve them in habit-forming drugs such as heroine and cocaine. It is probable that a Puerto Rican teen who uses such drugs will drop out of school and end up in a cycle of drug abuse and crime. It is important to mention here that Puerto Rico has a higher population of young boys than young girls. Due to a high mortality rate among boys, after the age of 16 there are more girls than boys in the population. Boys are more exposed to criminal activities related to drug use, drug overdose, and car accidents associated with alcohol or excessive speeding than are girls. Other societal problems that affect the lives of some less privileged Puerto Rican teens are family violence and lack of family discipline. Lower-class families face more societal challenges in raising their kids than do those of the middle and upper social classes. The former are more vulnerable to poverty and may be welfare recipients due to their lower educational and income levels. Most of these families are headed by single mothers, who are physically abused by their partners or addicted to drugs, which results in the family being yoked to a cycle of drug abuse and domestic violence. Most of the families of these teens live in public housing, inadequate housing in the countryside, or low-income barrios in cities that are corroded by violence, alcohol, and drugs.

RECREATION

Puerto Rico has a tropical climate, which provides conditions for outdoor activities throughout the year. In summer, Puerto Rican teens like to go to the beach and salsa concerts for recreation. During the school year they camp, hike tropical forests, and ride bikes. They also attend car races and boxing and wrestling matches.

Puerto Rican teens practice sports geared toward their gender. The favorite sports of most males are baseball and basketball. Swimming and track and field are practiced by both females and males. Gymnastics and softball are popular among girls. Upper-class teens from both genders play tennis and racquetball. Golf is mainly played by upper-class males. Ballet and modern dance are popular among upper- and middle-class girls. Due to the massive Americanization of the island, roller-skating, skateboarding, and surfing are becoming popular among teenagers as well.

ENTERTAINMENT

Although Puerto Rican teens listen to many kinds of music, most prefer tropical, rap, or rock. Teens who enjoy salsa (a popular tropical/Caribbean music and dance) are called *salseros* or *cocolos* and those who listen to rap are *raperos*, while those who like rock are known as *rockeros*. Famous salsa and rap singers such as P. Diddy, Mr. D, Mark Anthony, La India, and Gilbertito Santa Rosa are well known by teens. Rock groups such as Pearl Jam are also popular. Pop music is also part of teen culture. Youths frequently attend pop concerts in the Arts Center (Centro de Bellas Artes), hotels in San Juan or other Puerto Rican cities, and the Coliseum (Coliseo Roberto Clemente) in San Juan. Singers like Talia, Christina Aguilera, Jennifer López, Ricky Martin, Enrique Iglesias, and Luis Miguel are also popular.

Teens are allowed to dance in public. They normally dance in discos, nightclubs, or in hotel clubs located in major cities. They also attend parties at friends' houses, which are called *bailes de marquesinas* (carport dances), weddings, and other gatherings with family and friends. Although they like to dance to disco music and merengue (a typical dance originally from the Dominican Republic), they prefer to listen to salsa instead of dancing to it. Puerto Rican teens also enjoy going to the movies and the theater.

RELIGIOUS PRACTICES AND CULTURAL CEREMONIES

Religion is not seen as a specific adherence to an organized church or religious organization. Religious practices are marked by a pattern of close, intimate personal relationships that is characteristic of Spanish cultures. Thus, the individual perceives his or her religious life as a network of personal relationships with holy figures associated with Catholicism. The most popular denomination in Puerto Rico has been Catholicism since the Spanish Crown imposed this religion on the islanders during colonial times. In 1898, the Americans introduced Protestantism as a way to Americanize the island. Most Puerto Ricans are members of Pentecostal sects. When Protestants first came to the island, they agreed among themselves to avoid competition in their evangelization process. Instead, they divided the island into territories and each was assigned the responsibility of a particular Protestant denomination. As a result, almost every municipality now has a Protestant Church—either Baptist, Methodist, Lutheran, Episcopal, and so on. Jehovah's Witnesses arrived later. With the exception of Jehovah's Witnesses, most Puerto Rican teens practice traditional Christian celebrations at Christmas and Easter. Puerto Rican teens are mostly nonpracticing Catholics. They do not attend church on a regular basis, as do some teens in other parts of the world. In Puerto Rico, Catholic teens must be confirmed when they are in high school. They sometimes attend Catholic religious retreats and church-related activities. However, Protestant youths attend church regularly and are engaged in church activities more often than are Catholic kids. They are also baptized when they are teens, not when they are infants. Church or missionary work is not common among Puerto Rican teens.

Another form of religion in Puerto Rico is Spiritualism. This religion was developed in part by the religious practices of African slaves who were brought to the island and by some Spaniards who came to the island from Galicia, located in northern Spain. It is the belief of Spiritualism that people can establish contact with the spirits of dead people. This helps them to understand human problems, such as illnesses and the future. It is not the norm for teenagers to practice this kind of religion, but their parents sometimes introduce them to it.

CONCLUSION

Puerto Rican teen culture is a blend of Afro-Caribbean and American cultures. Most teens live between two worlds: the Hispanic and the American worlds. In general terms, the life of a Puerto Rican teen is active and hectic, much like in the United States. Teens are involved in social, community, and religious activities. They participate actively in politics and political activities. More and more they are joining the workforce at the age of 16 (the legal minimum working age in Puerto Rico). At the same time, they attend school and may have part-time jobs in American fast-food enterprises such as McDonald's, Burger King, Taco Bell, and Pizza Hut. Some also work as salespersons in mall stores or as cashiers in supermarkets. Like their American counterparts, Puerto Rican teens love to go shopping and to hang out at the mall, downtown, or on the square. They are addicted to electronic gaming systems such as Nintendo, Sega and GameBoy.

A high percentage of teens have been exposed to American life through cable television and trips to the United States. American television shows such as *Friends, Drew Carry, Oprah, Geraldo, The Fresh Prince of Bel Air,* and *Full House* are popular. Teens watch an average of two to four hours of television per day. However, because of the nice tropical weather of the island, most prefer to hang out with friends or go to the movies rather than stay inside watching television.

Besides teen fashion, music, language, cable television, and cinema, American culture has entered into Puerto Rican life through the transmigration process. A high percentage of Puerto Rican teens have lived, visited, or stayed with relatives in the United States, especially in cities such as Miami, Orlando, Houston, New York, Newark, and Philadelphia. This pattern of migration is reflected in the advanced globalization process of teen culture on the island. That is why in certain ways, both worlds complement each other, which makes the culture of the Puerto Rican teen unique.

RESOURCE GUIDE

Buckingham, David. *The Making of Citizens: Young People, News, and Politics.* London: Routledge, 2000.

Carrión Morales, Arturo. *Puerto Rico: A Political and Cultural History.* New York: W. W. Norton and Company, 1983.

Chang Rodríguez, Raquel. *Hispanoamérica: Su cultura y civilización.* Boston: Heinle and Heinle, 1999.

Cordaso, Francesco. *The Puerto Rican Experience: A Sociological Source Book.* Totowa, N.J.: Rowman and Littlefield, 1973.

Fitzpatrick, Joseph P. *Puerto Rican Americans.* Englewood Cliffs, N.J.: Prentice Hall, 1971.

Gallardo, José Miguel. *Proceedings of the Conference on Education of Puerto Rican Children on the Mainland.* New York: Arno Press, 1975.

Geografía e historia de América. Madrid: Ediciones SM, 2001.

Geografía e historia del mundo. Madrid: Ediciones SM, 2001.

Geografía e historia de Puerto Rico. Madrid: Ediciones SM, 2001.

Government of Puerto Rico Office. http://www.fortaleza.govpr.org/.

———. http://www.prc.org/summaries/latinapreg.htm.

Haynes, Julian. *The People of Puerto Rico: A Study in Social Anthropology.* Urbana: University of Illinois Press, 1956.

Katán Ibarra, Juan. *Perspectivas Culturales de Hispanoamérica.* Lincolnwood, Ill.: NTC, 1999.

Lewis, Oscar. *La vida: A Puerto Rican Family in the Culture of Poverty—San Juan and New York.* New York: Random House, 1966.

Maldonado Denis, Manuel. *Puerto Rico: A Socio-Historic Interpretation.* New York: Vintage Books, 1972.

Morton, J. Golding. *A Short History of Puerto Rico.* New York: New American Library, 1973.

Picó, Fernando. *Breve Historia de Puerto Rico.* Río Piedras, Puerta Rico: Ediciones Huracán, 1996.

Puerto Rican Organization. http://welcome.topuertorico.org/.

Teen Pregnancy Organization. http://www.teenpregnancy.org/usa/pr.htm.

Questionnaires were collected from 45 Puerto Rican teens representing different social classes and religions.

Nonfiction

Aliotta, Gerone J. *The Puerto Ricans. The People of North America.* New York: Chelsea House Publishers, 1991.

Pérez y González, María E. *Puerto Ricans in the United States.* Westport, Conn.: Greenwood Press, 2000.

Web Sites

http://hispaniconline.com/hh02/history_heritage.html
Hispanic Online: magazine

http://www.spanishabroad.com/puertorico/countryguide/culture.htm
Spanish Abroad: history, culture, language, food

http://welcome.topuertorico.org/
Welcome to Puerto Rico

Chapter 15

VENEZUELA

Roberto Fuertes-Manjón

INTRODUCTION

Venezuela is located in the north of South America, bordering the Caribbean Sea and the northern Atlantic Ocean. It lies between Colombia, Guayana, and Brazil. It has an area of 882,050 square kilometers and a population of approximately 24 million. The capital of the country is Caracas and Spanish is the official language.

Venezuela is divided into four distinct regions: (*a*) the Caribbean and Atlantic coastal area; (*b*) the llanos area, or central plains, used mostly for cattle feeding; (*c*) the Andean region; and (*d*) the rain forest, which borders Brazil. The climate is typically tropical, with warm temperatures and high humidity, although in the highlands it is moderate.

After achieving independence from Spain in 1811, Venezuela went through a violent and unstable period, governed by several dictators. It only became a democracy in 1959 and still is to this day. The current president is Hugo Chávez, who was an officer in the military. He had been condemned for several years for being the leader of a military coup in 1992 and was consequently accused of causing the uprising. Chávez was democratically elected in 1999 in an atmosphere dominated by intense frustration among the public.

The monetary unit is the bolivar. Some of Venezuela's natural resources are petroleum, natural gas, iron ore, bauxite, gold, and diamonds. Most of modern-day Venezuela's economy is based on the export of petroleum, which has been subject to intense market fluctuations in the past few years and, consequently, has affected the economy significantly. Oil exports cover approximately one-third of the GDP (gross domestic product) and four-fifths of export earnings. Worthy of note is the fact that multinational, and in particular American, companies, benefit most from the oil trade. Political corruption and lack of planning have not allowed oil resources to benefit the average Venezuelan.

Venezuela also exports quantities of minerals and has significant industries in food processing, textiles, steel, and motor vehicle assembly. Tourism is strong, especially on Margarita Island and the Los Roques Archipelago in the Caribbean.

A recession took place during 1981–89 and one of the consequences was a decrease in the GDP. The most recent recession occurred in 1999, but Venezuela recovered in 2000 due to an increase in international oil prices. The combination of a decrease in the GDP and an increase in inflation had a devastating effect on the economy and a direct impact on society, especially among the country's youths. One of the social components that most suffered as a consequence of this crisis was education. Educational services were significantly reduced, even more so in rural areas. At the same time, teachers' salaries were no longer competitive and many schools were forced to shut down. Hundreds of adolescents and children had to abandon school and begin working to help support their families.

The population in Venezuela is composed of a mixture of several ethnic groups, based on Spanish, African, and indigenous origins. Other important ethnic groups were the Italians, Portuguese, Arabs, and Germans, all of whom arrived in Venezuela during the European emigration during the first half of the twentieth century.

One of Venezuela's defining characteristics is its high percentage of urban population. This is due mainly to the lack of opportunities available to the rural population; consequently, people move to the cities.

There are also different social strata—the upper class, limited in number but powerful economically, with high incomes and enormous social and political influence; an insignificant and decreasing middle class; and a numerous lower class, which has increased in recent decades and directly affects youths. Venezuela's population is young. The main problems that arise among Venezuelan youths stem from political corruption, social instability, a lack of jobs, and a series of limitations and pressures that they constantly suffer from different institutions, above all from the church and the military. Although the country is mostly Catholic (96 percent), the number of Protestants has increased in recent years (*World Fact Book*, 3). Nevertheless, the Catholic Church still preserves strong political and social influence, especially on issues such as divorce, abortion, and the teaching of religion in public schools.

Even though there is no active civil war, nor any guerrilla groups in Venezuela, its proximity to Colombia (where guerrilla groups have been a problem for years) destabilizes the area. Adolescents also suffer all kinds of political pressure, living in a reality threaded with corruption and political instability; dominant factors in Venezuela during recent decades. This situation has made university and even high school students become very politically active, adopting mostly leftist positions. On the other hand, it is important to point out that rates of violence and crime are high and reflect the general atmosphere of the country. In addition, the problem of drugs, facilitated by the traffic from Colombia, is accentuated by the loss of economic power of the middle and lower classes. This has led many adolescents to work on the streets, closer to the marginalized sectors of society. Venezuela serves more as a transition area through which drugs pass than as a producer. It does produce opium in small quantities, but large amounts of cocaine and heroin, originating mainly in Colombia, pass through the country. No doubt this has directly affected the availability of drugs to adolescents.

Possibly the determining factor of Venezuela's youths and their future is the deterioration of the education system at the secondary and university level. Despite the fact that the literacy rate, which, at 91.1 percent is one of the highest in Latin America, there are problems with enrollment rates in middle and high school educational institutions, due in part to the fact that public expenditure has decreased in the past decades.

TYPICAL DAY

In general, a typical day in an adolescent's life in Venezuela depends on location. There is a marked difference between rural and city life, but usually adolescents wake up at 7:00 A.M., as most activities begin around 8:00 A.M. After getting ready and eating breakfast, they go to school or work. The education system is flexible. Some schools have classes from 8:00 A.M. to 3:00 P.M. Others begin at 8:00 A.M., have a break at 11:00, and return with afternoon classes from 2:00 P.M. until 5:00 P.M. Some offer two sessions daily: one from 8:00 A.M. to 12:00 P.M. and another from 1:00 to 5:00 P.M. In some cases (for older students) classes are offered from 7:00 P.M. to 10:00 P.M. Adolescents who do not attend classes usually do not have regular jobs either. This is due to several factors: unemployment rates among adolescents are high; they were over 14 percent in 2000

(CEPAL 2000b, 75). Many work at home, whether on a farm or elsewhere, for mere subsistence wages.

In the rural areas, adolescents tend to work on their family's farms. Others work as street vendors, selling an array of products, or they have temporary jobs. Nevertheless, adolescents generally spend a portion of their day at home, especially after dinner, when families watch television together.

In some cases students live far from their schools. These cases usually occur in rural areas where students may have to walk long distances. In cities, students can walk or take public transportation, usually a bus. There are no school buses except in a few private schools.

FAMILY LIFE

Families in Venezuela usually gather together for lunch (the main meal) and for dinner. There is usually a two-hour break for lunch and most people go home to eat and be with their families. Women typically prepare the meals, sometimes with the help of a daughter or, in the case of the upper class, a maid or cook. Much time is spent with the family and usually in the evenings they watch television together. Another family activity is visiting friends and relatives, especially on weekends.

In most cases it is the father who controls and manages the family, while the mother is in charge of the children, managing their education and their daily needs. In the middle and upper classes, decisions about a child's education are usually made by both parents. In the lower classes, such decisions are routinely made by the father. Sometimes economic difficulties force parents to make undesirable choices: for example, incorporating their children into the workforce in order to help support the family. Children in rural areas drop out of school more frequently than do city kids.

A typical day in the life of a family depends on economics as well as place of residence, i.e., in a city or in the countryside. It is also different for those living on the coast as opposed to in the interior of the country. Those on the coast tend to be more modern and receptive; the interior retains more traditional values. As a general rule, however, dialogue between parents and children is the norm.

It has become more common in the last few decades for both parents to work outside the home. In the past, the father was the main breadwinner. Women have recently joined the workforce in order to supplement the family's income. Consequently, adolescents find themselves home alone more often and, sometimes, the lack of a parental presence leads to drug use or crime. In rural areas, both parents generally work alongside their children. It is taken for granted that children will work with their parents.

Although the minimum, legal drinking age in Venezuela is 18, there is much tolerance for drinking within society. Thus adolescents many times begin to drink at a younger age. The minimum legal driving age is 16, although very few adolescents actually have cars; adolescents who have cars, when there are any, mostly belong to the upper class.

Family life is strongly influenced by income. There are enormous differences in the level of education, quality of housing, and, more specifically, future opportunities each adolescent will have. In a country where approximately 59 percent of the population lives below the poverty level, one can imagine how much this affects each family (CEPAL 2000b, 65). The social class to which one belongs is more important than ethnicity. The latter is not a determining factor because social class and racial relations are smooth and miscegenation is common.

During the last few years there have been some changes in the makeup of family life, due mainly to two factors: first, the economic recession; and second, the Americanization of society. The economic recession and lack of employment have affected family income as well as the Globalization of Venezuelan youth and of society in general, a phenomenon that has been occurring since the '60s. This Globalization determines what adolescents eat, how they dress, and even the sports they play.

TRADITIONAL AND NONTRADITIONAL FOOD DISHES

Although American fast-food chains reached Venezuela several years ago, the main staples of Venezuelan food—in which Spanish, African, and indigenous influences are notable—are a series of dishes and basic products. They include *arepas* (a cornmeal roll filled with cheese), meat, or vegetables (black beans [*caraotas*] usually eaten with rice) and bananas served in a variety of ways—fried or boiled, for instance.

On the coast Venezuelans eat fresh fish, usually fried with no seasoning, or breaded. In the countryside, especially in the llanos (plains), they eat *caraotas* with rice and bananas, as well as cheese, lots of tropical fruit, and milk.

On a daily basis food is prepared simply, using basic and traditional recipes. At Christmas special dishes are prepared; especially the *hallaca*, a type of tamale made with white corn. Although these foods can be bought at a grocery store, especially in the cities, it is more common to buy them at a market. The main problems with these types of food are that they are not always nutritionally balanced and that they lack variety. Nor are they very attractive to adolescents. The food that appeals to them is American fast food, mainly hamburgers and French fries. Consequently, food has become a divisive issue among parents and children in the last few decades.

SCHOOLING

The Venezuelan educational system in general offers a good education with flexibility in terms of scheduling and courses. There is no discrimination based on gender or race. The quality of a student's education is determined by the social class in which he or she belongs. The upper class usually send its children to private schools, many of them religious, which do not necessarily provide better teaching but do offer better facilities. Public schools have good teachers but poor facilities. Another difference between private and public schools is that private schools are often secluded, gated, and otherwise elitist. In order to enter a private or public school, family income is the defining factor, not test scores. Both types of schools are based on theoretical teaching while practical experimentation (such as labs) is less frequent. Private schools are prestigious, while public schools are not. Nevertheless, at both schools students study hard and discipline is strict.

In both public and private elementary schools, students usually wear uniforms. The high-school dress code is typically blue jeans and a blouse or a T-shirt. Females may wear skirts and dresses. Many private schools, especially religious ones, require students to wear uniforms following a European tradition. Parents are open-minded about how their children dress, although their attitude is related to their social class as well as the city where they live. Residents of small cities tend to be more formal and conservative in their clothing.

Education is obligatory beginning at age seven, and public schools are free. The cost of private schools varies anywhere from US$50 to $200 per month. The curricula at both public and private schools are similar, covering courses in the humanities and sciences. Courses include math, physics, biology, chemistry, history, geography, computers, Spanish, English as a foreign language, and literature. Private schools can be secular or religious, but in general they are Catholic. Such schools also offer religion as a course.

Historically, the education system is founded on the European system (especially French and Spanish, although there has been superficial influence from the United States in more recent decades) with similarities in the architectural layout of schools and, in some cases, similarities in pro-

High school students outside private school, Caracas, Venezuela. © M. Barlow/
TRIP.

grams that follow the U.S. model but do not have an equivalent credit
system. These similarities were implemented in the 1960s through the
'80s but are not currently in place.

One could say that the Venezuelan education system is eclectic, with a
European foundation and American contributions, a lot of lecturing, excessive homework, and an exam that students must take in order to graduate to the next grade. However, dropouts are quite numerous, due mostly
to financial difficulties stemming from one's family. Failures are also frequent. Only a small percentage of students finish high school.

Eighth grade (middle school) is when students have to decide whether
to continue on to a regular high school to major in the humanities or sciences, or whether to go to a technical school or one that focuses on
teacher education.

After middle school, students may opt to attend special programs, such
as in agriculture. There are also many good trade schools, sponsored by
the National Institute of Educational Cooperation, at which students receive free room and board. These schools are designed for those who want
to become engineers or work in technology.

Overall, teachers are well prepared although salaries are low. In order to
become a high school teacher, it is necessary to have a bachelor of arts de-

gree; to teach at an elementary school, a diploma from the Escuela Normal (Teacher Education Diploma) is required.

The worldwide educational revolution that took place in the 1960s played a major role in Venezuela, at both the high school and university levels. At the end of the 1960s Venezuela prepared for national school decentralization. In 1971 a law was passed to create 10 postsecondary, technical training institutes (*colegios universitarios*), a new structure at that time. This was done to provide technicians for the administration of the oil industry.

The main challenges that the education system faces—limiting its quality and directly affecting the shaping of youths in general—are the political and religious interference that take place on a regular basis. For example, the Pre-Military Instruction course was required as of September 2000 in the last two years of high school. A text of pre-military instruction, which had been used on an experimental basis for one year, had to be removed from the curriculum because it incited xenophobia, racism, class struggle, and anticommunism. Texts like these have been imposed upon schools by the government under direct pressure from the military. The course discussed above was also taught by the military. Its text, besides the negative aspects cited above, sent a clear and profound anti-American message to the extent that it blamed the origin of Venezuelan violence on American cinema. It was also against the influence the United States exerts on the way adolescents in Venezuela dress and eat. It demonstrated the strong influence the army wanted to have on youths.

A number of factors have contributed to the deterioration of the Venezuelan education system, to the frustration of many adolescents. These include pressure from the military, politicians, and the Catholic Church; little inversion in education; large class sizes; a lack of teaching materials and facilities for efficient teaching; and low teacher salaries. This is especially difficult if one keeps in mind the fact that the most prestigious careers, such as scientific researcher, university professor, medical doctor, engineer, and computer scientist, are not always taught with the appropriate methods. Due to the fact that political parties have considered universities as centers of power and influence and that student organizations are a source of protest, Venezuelan universities have always been highly political, even more so after the restoration of democracy in 1958.

SOCIAL LIFE

In general, social life among Venezuelan adolescents is pleasant. Young men and women are constantly together at school, although some private schools are either all male or all female. Adolescents meet not only at school, but also get together to study or to go dancing, to cafés, or to the cinema among other places. Admission to these places is not as strict as it is in the United States. Relationships grow with little interference from parents. With the exception of in remote rural areas, relationships are almost never prearranged. In the upper class one might see parents concerned about having their children marry within their social group as a way of protecting their assets. But even in cases like these, parents tend to give their children freedom to choose their mates. Premarital sex is a common practice. There are no specific programs that instruct adolescents to abstain from sex, but parents prefer that their children do so. As a mostly Catholic country, abstinence originates in church teachings and it represents a traditional value. It is not well accepted for a young woman to get pregnant and abortion is not a common practice (nor is it legal). Most teenage pregnancies end in the child's birth.

Despite the fact that there is not a rigid social structure that would prevent communication between social classes, undoubtedly members of the middle and upper classes rarely interact socially with members of the lower class and even less so with the destitute. Parents worry that their children will get mixed up in the world of crime and therefore discourage them from interacting with those lower on the social ladder. This actually reinforces an old historical tradition.

Schools in general do not organize social activities, but they do organize theater and music presentations at *ateneos*. The *ateneo* is a cultural center where teenagers meet to participate in plays or concerts. These cultural centers fill a gap that exists with schools.

RECREATION

There are many opportunities for recreation in Venezuela. In such an open and hedonist society, the search for recreation is a goal in itself.

In the area of sports, it is important to look at different contexts, such as a city versus a rural area. If an urban student does not work, he or she can practice sports, even if it is not regularly. Many schools do not have specific sports facilities. There are no organized sports. If a student lives in the rural area, he or she will not necessarily play on a regular basis because many times there are no sports facilities. On the coast, the most common activity is going to the beach to swim, surf, or fish.

Sports, however, are perhaps the main activities that bring teenagers together. There is a strong interest in baseball, a sport imported from the United States. Soccer and boxing are also popular, as are horse races on weekends.

Boating and swimming in rivers are also popular. Hunting is not a common sport, but is of interest to some people in the countryside. In the mountains, valleys, and prairies especially, sports such as hunting and fishing are common. Sports are not seasonal because the climate is uniform throughout the country all year round. For male teens, the most common sports are baseball and soccer. For female teens, they are volleyball, swimming, and gymnastics, although many sports are played by males and females alike.

Teenagers usually play sports in their neighborhoods or in city leagues. Schools do not have sports teams. Baseball and soccer players are typically sports heroes; American baseball and Brazilian soccer players serve as role models.

ENTERTAINMENT

There is not much variety in television programs for teenagers. Venezuela produces its own series, soap operas, and sitcoms. Nevertheless, it also depends on American television, especially for movies. One of the most popular meeting places is the dance club. In the past adolescents routinely danced to Venezuelan and Latin American pop music. Nowadays American music has become very popular, although teens also dance to Caribbean rhythms.

For music, teens listen to traditional and modern Venezuelan, Latin American, and Anglo (mostly American) music. They listen to all kinds of rock. Very few listen to folkloric music or try to preserve its traditions. Whatever is newest—especially if it's foreign—is the most attractive to teens.

Other forms of entertainment include attending cattle fairs, horse races, and bullfights. Bullfights in San Cristóbal (in the Andes), of Spanish origin, are famous. Rural areas are where traditions are best preserved, especially those associated with cattle and bulls. For example, in the llanos region, bullfights, called *toros coleados*, are staged regularly.

RELIGIOUS PRACTICES AND CULTURAL CEREMONIES

Some teens attend church out of habit rather than to be religious at heart; they also go to church to enjoy the festivities and not necessarily because of the religious component. No doubt Catholicism is the dominant factor at the festivals described above. Even though the number of Protestants has increased sharply in the last decades, Protestantism has not yet been incorporated into popular culture.

Venezuelan teens enjoy activities related to religious festivals or ancient pilgrimages that are specifically celebrated in Venezuela. There are carnivals in neighborhoods from elite to slum ones and religious local festivals sponsored by the city.

On the coast, the festival of Barlovento, of African origin, is observed and in the south, near the border with Brazil, indigenous festivals are celebrated.

The more traditional festivals are religious especially that of Christmas. During December and January, Las Posadas takes place to celebrate Jesus' birth. Although religious in character, this festival mixes entertainment with parties. It begins with a mass, during which a drama about specific aspects of Jesus' life is presented. At the end there is a party.

All of these festivals portray the nature of Venezuela as a mixture of different cultures: Spanish, African, and indigenous. Venezuelans have created a new culture that is capable of preserving Hispanic traditions in a practical manner, transforming and enriching them with the different ethnicities that comprise Venezuela.

These popular festivals are one of Venezuela's most appealing aspects, not only due to their rich traditions, but also for their contributions to the creation and maintenance of a musical form. Venezuelans enjoy music and each region has contributed its own characteristics and flavors. In the east, in the mining town of El Callao, they celebrate carnival with African-origin calypso and *kaico* music. In Barlovento, in the west, during Corpus Christi, there are festivals in a predominantly African area, in which the sound of drums mixes with that of a native trumpet called the *guarura*.

On the central coast, there are the Diablos Danzantes (dancing devils) in which one can observe religious syncretism clearly, as the processions mix bell music with teenagers dressed in traditional clothing and masks. In the central part of the country, they have a celebration of the Catholic Church known as Cruz de Mayo (May Cross), in which they sing religious songs mixed with secular songs. In the summer they celebrate the Fiesta de los Negros de San Antonio de Padua, in which African and European music are combined. During Christmas, besides Las Posadas, teenagers participate in Los Aguinaldos, or caroling in the *parrandas*, which are other Hispanic traditions.

Religious festivals usually have a ludic component and it is in these typical popular events that one better observes the syncretic result of Catholic customs mixed with African culture. These religious customs are not as practiced as in the Caribbean.

Despite the efforts to maintain traditional customs, one can observe concern and desire on the part of teens to participate in customs common to other Latin American countries. For example, birthdays are celebrated usually within the family circle. Venezuelans also celebrate a young woman's passage to adulthood when she turns 15 (*quinceañera*), although it is not as important as in Mexico.

Some festivals can be identified with other Latin American countries in relation to certain, pseudo-religious ceremonies associated with satanic rituals. These occur on a very small scale. Other practices, such as voodoo, are more common in the Caribbean. Sometimes they are combined with witchcraft of indigenous origin.

There are also practices that mix religion, paganism, and herbs to cure or heal and are carried out by witch doctors or herbalists. These kinds of rituals are practiced mainly by adults.

CONCLUSION

In Venezuela, there is a clear conflict between new generations and their parents, both in beliefs and in customs, which is a general tendency in most modern societies. This conflict is intensified by a somber economic and social situation that Venezuela as well as other Latin American nations share, causing teens to feel frustrated and discouraged. Specifically in Venezuela, this situation is intensified as the economy has been in decline since the '80s, to which can be added political corruption, an increase in violence, and a lack of opportunities. All of these factors generate concern for teens' futures and are reflected in major personal dissatisfaction, causing them to undervalue their country and increasing their desire to emigrate from Venezuela because the country offers no future for them.

Another consequence of this situation—which did not emerge during the '90s but did intensify during that period—is the active political involvement of educational centers, be it interference from the government or students' own political activities. Teenagers are very politically active at the university level. Their political participation begins in middle school and continues into high school, because, among other things, it is a way to advance within society. This political awareness began in the 1960s, having as its center the universities, where movements of opposition and rebellion against authoritarian regimes took place.

In general, Venezuelan teenagers are outgoing and enjoy activities outside the home. They like to have fun and love music, in a tropical environment where the goal is to enjoy oneself, in a society in which they mature emotionally at an early age. This sometimes leads to marriage at a young age; many marry before they finish university. In some cases teenagers live together before marrying. This is a consequence of the freedom given to them as well as the spontaneity and ease with which teenagers relate.

The difficulty in obtaining a university degree adds to the already existing frustration for many teenagers. One cannot forget that while teenagers in the upper classes have access to everything, the middle class has been losing opportunities on a regular basis, both in education and in work. Lower-class teens are almost excluded from society as they have very few chances to improve their future. That is why many resort to violence and drugs.

Some of the challenges Venezuelan teenagers have to face, such as unemployment, violence, drugs, and poor educational opportunities, affect the lower classes most of all. As several sociological studies in Venezuela, and in Latin America in general, have established, the weakest sector of society is the group of teenagers between 15 and 19 years. If they have dropped out of school, and especially if they are women, they are almost condemned to unemployment or underemployment. This is even more real in the lowest classes. To combat this effect, as is also the case in countries such as Chile, Argentina, Brazil, Colombia, and Peru, new projects have been initiated that follow the premise of the Young Chile program, in which they try to integrate the formative process with true integration into society. These projects seek total social immersion, which can be obtained through agreements between social centers and companies in the country. These attempts, even though useful and filled with good intentions, are not sufficient to counteract the relentless dissatisfaction that Venezuelan teenagers of all levels suffer today, intensified by the country's political uncertainty.

RESOURCE GUIDE

"Moving to Venezuela." http://www.escapeartist.com/venezuela/venezuela.htm.

"Venezuela Sommaire." http://www.unesco.org/culture/copy/copyright/venezuela/sommaire.html.

"Stock Market Articles." http://www.citycomment.co.uk/columns/columns_artikel.asp.

"An Imminent Coup in Venezuela?" http://www.athena.tbwt.com/content/article.asp.

"Venezuela Library Resources on Economic Issues." http://www.jolis.worldbankimflib.org/Pathfinders/Countries/VE/

"Venezuela's Currency in Freefall." http://www.news.bbc.co.uk/hi/english/business/.

CEPAL (Comisión Económica para América Latina e el Caribe). *Anuario estadístico de América Latina y el Caribe*. Santiago: Naciones Unidas, 2000a.

————. *Desarrollo y bienestar*. Santiago: Naciones Unidas, 2000b.

————. *Panorama social de América Latina, 1999–2000*. Santiago: Naciones Unidas, 2000c.

————. *Situación y perspectivas 2001. Estudio económico de América Latina y el Caribe 2000–2001*. Santiago: Naciones Unidas, 2001.

Dabéne, Olivier. *América Latina en el siglo XX*. Madrid: Editorial Síntesis, 1999.

Dydynski, Krzysztof. *Venezuela*. Hawthorn: Lonely Planet, 1998.

Encyclopedia.com. *Venezuela*. http://www.encyclopedia.com/articles/13391.html.

Good, Kenneth, and David Chanoff. *Into the Heart: One Man's Pursuit of Love and Knowledge among the Yanomama*. New York: Simon and Schuster, 1991.

Haggerty, Richard, and Howard Blutstein. *Venezuela: A Country Study*. Washington, D.C.: The Division, G.P.O., 1993.

La Belle, Thomas. *The New Professional in Venezuela. Secondary Education*. Los Angeles: University of California, 1973.

Murphy, Alan. *Venezuela Handbook*. Lincolnwood, Ill.: Footprint Handbooks, 1998.

Venezuela. Maspeth, N.Y.: APA Publications, 2000.

World Fact Book 2001. "Venezuela." http://www.cia.gov/cia/publications/factbook/geos/ve.html.

Nonfiction

Dinneen, Mark. *Culture and Customs of Venezuela*. Westport, Conn.: Greenwood Press, 2001.

Web Sites

General Information

http://www.laguia.com.ve/
Cantv.

http://www.auyantepui.com/
Directorio Internet Auyantepui, C.A.

http://www.eureka.web.ve/
Eureka!

http://www.exodo.com/
Exodate Corp. 2000.

http://www.arranca.com/
Melton Technologies, Inc.

http://www.au.af.mil/au/aul/bibs/Latin/LatAm2.htm
Ron Fuller.

http://www.search-beat.com/venezuela.htm
SearchBeat.

http://www.terra.com.ve/
Terra Networks Latam, S.A.

http://www.cia.gov/cia/publications/factbook/geos/ve.html
World Fact Book 2001.

Travel

http://www.gosouthamerica.about.com/cs/venezuela/
All about Venezuela.

http://www.venezuelaonline.com/indexHTML.htm
Agencia de Viajes Auyantepuy.

http://www.travel-guide.com/data/ven/ven.asp
Highbury Columbus Travel Publishing Ltd.

http://travel.state.gov/venezuela.html
U.S. Department of State, Consular Information

http://travel.yahoo.com/t/destinations/south_america/venezuela
Yahoo! Inc.

More Information

http://www.embavenez-us.org/
Embassy of Venezuela.

Pen Pal Information

http://www.parlo.com/
Parlo Inc.

http://www.geocities.com/paulina_a_m/links.html.
Penpals for You.

http://www.pen-pals.net/
Pen-Pals.net—The World's Largest Pen Pal Site.

INDEX

ABOUT THE EDITORS
AND CONTRIBUTORS

REGINA AKEL translated Joseph Conrad's novel *Heart of Darkness* for a Chilean publisher and is a grad student in English literature at the University of Warwick, United Kingdom.

GASTÓN A. ALZATE is an associate professor of Spanish, Latin American, and Women's Studies at Gustavus Adolphus College, Minnesota.

BARBARA BAILEY is a senior lecturer at the University of the West Indies and regional coordinator of the Centre for Gender and Development Studies at the Mona Campus in Kingston, Jamaica.

ROBERTO CAMPA-MADA is a grad student at Arizona State University.

MICHELLE DAVIS is a research assistant at the Center for Gender and Development Studies at the University of the West Indies in Mona, Jamaica. Her research interests include issues of youth, gender and HIV/AIDS, and gender and globalization.

ROBERTO FUERTES-MANJÓN is an associate professor of Spanish and Latin American Literature at Midwestern State University, Wichita Falls, Texas.

MANUEL GARCÍA CASTELLÓN is a professor of Spanish at the University of New Orleans.

GUSTAVO GEIROLA is an associate professor of Spanish at Whittier College, California.

MAUDE HEURTELOU is a nutritionist and a health educator in the Florida Department of Health. She has written 25 bilingual children's books and two novels that reflect her interest in Haitian sociocultural issues.

AMARILIS HIDALGO DE JESÚS is an associate professor of Spanish in the Department of Languages and Cultures at Bloomsburg University of Pennsylvania.

ROSE McEWEN is an assistant professor at the University of New York at Geneseo.

CECILIA MENJÍVAR, a sociologist, is an associate professor in the School of Justice Studies at Arizona State University.

JAVIER OCHOA works in the telecom industry and as a language consultant.

AÍDA PIERINI is a journalist and an editor of business magazines in Argentina and conducts independent research on cultural and social subjects.

JASON PRIBILSKY is a cultural anthropologist and assistant professor of Anthropology at Whitman College, Walla Walla, Washington.

ROSSANA REGUILLO CRUZ is a professor and researcher in the Department of Socio-cultural Studies at the Instituto Tecnológico y de Estudios Superiores de Occidenta, Guadalajara, Mexico.

LYDIA RODRIGUEZ is an assistant professor of Spanish at Indiana University of Pennsylvania in Indiana, Pennsylvania.

KANISHKA SEN is an assistant professor at Ohio Northern University.

LIZBETH SOUZA-FUERTES is an associate professor of Spanish, Portuguese, and Latin American Literature at Baylor University in Waco, Texas.

KRISTEN STERNBERG authors and edits texts on teen issues and global literacy. She also works in the Newspaper in Education department at *The Daytona Beach News-Journal*.

JUANA SUÁREZ is an assistant professor of Spanish at the University of North Carolina at Greensboro.

CYNTHIA MARGARITA TOMPKINS is an associate professor of Spanish at Arizona State University.